FROM TSARISM TO THE NEW EC

From Tsarism to the New Economic Policy

Continuity and Change in the Economy of the USSR

Edited by
R. W. Davies

Cornell University Press
Ithaca, New York

First published in the U.S.A. 1991 by Cornell University Press.

Library of Congress Cataloging-in-Publication Data
From Tsarism to the new economic policy: continuity and change in the
economy of the USSR/edited by Robert W. Davies.
p.   cm.
Includes bibliographical references and index.
ISBN 0–8014–2621–9 (cl.)   ISBN 0–8014–9919–4 (pb.)
1. Soviet Union—Economic policy.   I. Davies, R. W. (Robert
William), 1925–
HC335.F885   1991
338.947—dc20   90–56047
                                                          CIP

Printed in Great Britain

Contents

Part II AGRICULTURE AND THE ECONOMY

List of Illustrations and Maps

Illustrations

Maps

List of Tables

Preface

This book presents a quite detailed comparison between the tsarist economy on the eve of the revolution and the Soviet economy in the mid-1920s. Our purpose is to provide essential evidence for the reconsideration of major controversies about the two economic systems: what were the significant continuities and differences between the tsarist and the Soviet economy? Was the tsarist economy fundamentally successful and stable, and destroyed only by the disaster of the First World War? Was the Soviet mixed economy of the 1920s developing successfully, and its breakdown an arbitrary political act? Or were these societies able to achieve their economic advances only by generating profound economic or social instabilities?

The authors of the present book do not claim to have definitive answers to such questions; in any case, as will emerge, we differ sharply among ourselves about them. But in our discussions we all soon came to the firm conclusion that much of the basic knowledge necessary for understanding and comparing the two systems was lacking. Nearly all historians of twentieth-century Russia specialise on either the pre- or the post-revolutionary period; in consequence many textbooks and research publications (including my own) have tended to make sweeping comparisons based on inadequate data.

It was therefore our clear obligation in writing this book to seek to remedy this defect. Accordingly we began our work on each sector of the economy by surveying basic economic magnitudes such as production, investment and employment. This provided the background for examining the crucial continuities and differences between the two periods and the two systems. The principal focus of our interest is the process by which economic development was achieved under the two regimes.

Our book has emerged after several years of joint work. In 1985 our International Work-Group on Soviet Inter-War Economic HIstory decided to undertake this study; we were able to secure the indispensable collaboration of three specialists on pre-revolutionary history – Peter Gatrell, Paul Gregory and Maureen Perrie. In January 1987 the Fourth Conference of our Work-Group met in Birmingham to discuss the first drafts of our papers, and to plan the book. In the course of the next two years the papers were transformed into chapters for the book, and my introductory chapter surveying the results of our research was prepared and circulated. We are conscious that a great deal remains to be done even at the elementary level of quantitative comparison; and we have indicated the gaps in our knowledge in the course of the book.

Discussion Papers containing more detailed statistical data on some of the sectors are being issued. Titles available include:

R. W. Davies, 'Soviet Industrial Production, 1928–1937: the Rival Estimates';
P. Gatrell, 'Capital Investment in Russian Industry, 1908–1913';
P. Gatrell, 'Industrial Production in Russia, 1908–1913';
J. C. Shapiro, 'Who Were the NEP Unemployed?'

For further information apply to:

The Secretary,
Soviet Industrialisation Project,
Centre for Russian and East European Studies,
University of Birmingham,
Birmingham B15 2TT, UK.

Some sections of Chapters 2 and 7 have already been published in my *The Soviet Economy in Turmoil, 1929–1930* (published by Harvard University Press in the USA, and by Macmillan elsewhere, 1989).

The authors are grateful to a number of scholars who acted as discussants on the papers at the conference and provided advice and information during the preparation of the book, especially Professors Malcolm Falkus and Walter Pintner, and Drs Francesco Benvenuti, John Channon, Tatiana Kirstein, Alastair McAuley and Tibor Szamuely.

The British Economic and Social Research Council financed the projects on Soviet industrialisation of which this book is a product; the work would have been impossible without the support of the Council, which enabled the employment of Drs Wheatcroft and Ward as Research Fellows, and of the project secretary. The Ford Foundation subsidised the January 1987 conference (the grant was administered through the British National Association for Slavic, Soviet and East European Studies); and the University of Birmingham provided essential facilities.

We should also like to express our thanks to Mrs Jackie Butterley, who prepared the index, to Tim Grogan, who drew the maps, to Melanie Ilič, who undertook the exacting work of preparing the Bibliography, to Keith Povey and his associates for their editorial assistance, and above all to Mrs Betty Bennett, secretary to the Soviet Industrialisation Project, who typed most of the book and helped us to organise the conference and in other ways.

Centre for Russian and East European Studies   R. W. DAVIES
University of Birmingham

Notes on the Contributors

J. M. Cooper is Lecturer in Soviet Technology and Industry, Centre for Russian and East European Studies, University of Birmingham. Publications include *The Technological Level of Soviet Industry*, edited with Ronald Amann and R. W. Davies, *Industrial Innovation in the Soviet Union*, edited jointly with Ronald Amann, and articles on Soviet industry, science and technology, and economic history. He was formerly Editor of the journal *Economics of Planning*.

R. W. Davies is Professor of Soviet Economic Studies at the Centre for Russian and East European Studies of the University of Birmingham and was Director of the Centre from 1963–78. He is the author of *The Development of the Soviet Budgetary System, Foundations of a Planned Economy 1926–1929*, vol. 1 (with E. H. Carr), and a multi-volume history of Soviet industrialisation. The third volume of this history, *The Soviet Economy in Turmoil, 1929–1930*, was published in 1989.

M. R. Dohan is Associate Professor of Economics, Queen's College, University of New York. He is the author of many articles on the history of Soviet foreign trade and (with Edward Hewett) of *Two Studies in Soviet Terms of Trade, 1918–1970*.

Peter Gatrell is Senior Lecturer in Economic History, Department of History, University of Manchester. His Ph.D. thesis at the University of Cambridge concerned Russian industry in the first world war, and he is now completing a book on the same subject. He is the author of *The Tsarist Economy, 1850–1917*, and of many articles on Russian pre-revolutionary economic history.

Paul R. Gregory is Professor of Economics at the University of Houston, Houston, Texas. He has written many articles on Russian pre-revolutionary history and on the national income of the Russian Empire and the Soviet Union. The results of his research over many years on pre-revolutionary national income are presented in *Russian National Income, 1885–1913*.

Mark Harrison is Senior Lecturer in the Department of Economics, University of Warwick. His research interests include Chayanov and the economics of peasant agriculture and Soviet economic development and planning. He has published a book on *Soviet Planning in Peace and War, 1938–1945*, and is now writing a study of Soviet production and employment in 1941–5, and (with J. D. Barber) a social and economic history of the USSR in the second world war.

Holland Hunter is Emeritus Professor of Economics at Haverford College, near Philadelphia, Pennsylvania, where he taught economics for 41 years. He has written extensively on Soviet transportation and on modelling the performance of the Soviet economy in the period 1928–1940.

R. A. Lewis is Senior Lecturer in Economic History, University of Exeter. He obtained his Ph.D. at the Centre for Russian and East European Studies, University of Birmingham in 1975. He is the author of *Science and Industrialisation in the USSR : Industrial Research and Development, 1917–1940*, and of articles on Soviet economic history and the organisation of Soviet science and technology.

Stephan Merl is Wissenschaftlicher Mitarbeiter in the Zentrum für Kontinentale Agrar-und-Wirtschaftsforschung at the University of Giessen. He received his doctorate at the University of Hamburg. His research interests include the social and economic history of the Soviet Union and East Europe and the role of agriculture in industrialisation. He has published three books on Soviet agriculture and collectivisation in the 1920s and 1930s, and a number of articles.

Maureen Perrie is Lecturer in the Centre for Russian and East European Studies and the School of History, University of Birmingham. She is the author of *The Agrarian Policy of the Russian Socialist Revolutionary Party from its Origins through the Revolution of 1905–7* and *The Image of Ivan the Terrible in Russian Folk-Lore*.

J. C. Shapiro is Lecturer in Economics at Goldsmiths' College, London, and is preparing a book-length study of unemployment in the USSR in the 1920s. Her Ph.D. thesis, completed at the London School of Economics and Political Science, dealt with wage differentiation in British industry.

Christopher Ward is Assistant University Lecturer, Department of Slavonic Studies, University of Cambridge, and was previously ESRC Research Fellow at the Centre for Russian and East European Studies, University of Birmingham. In 1976 he completed a Ph.D. thesis at the University of Essex on Soviet textile workers in the 1920s, and his book on this subject is about to be published.

J. N. Westwood is an Honorary Research Fellow at the Centre for Russian and East European Studies, University of Birmingham, and previously held posts at Florida State University and the University of Sydney, and as an economist in a large North American railway company. He is the author of many books on the Russian railways, including *Soviet Locomotive Technology during Industrialisation, 1928–1952*, and of several general histories of Russia.

S. G. Wheatcroft is Director of the Centre for Soviet and East European Studies and Senior Lecturer in the Department of History, University of Melbourne. He is also Honorary Research Fellow of the Centre for Russian and East European Studies, University of Birmingham, where he was variously Research Associate and Research Fellow from 1973 to 1985. He is the author of many articles on Soviet agricultural and demographic history, and on the history of Soviet statistics. He is collaborating with Professor Davies on a study of Soviet agriculture, *The Years of Hunger, 1931–1933*.

1 Introduction: From Tsarism to NEP

R. W. Davies

Historians are sharply divided in their assessments of the tsarist system on the eve of the first world war and the Soviet system of the 1920s; the extent of continuity and change between the two economies and the two systems has long been a central issue in historical debate.

An influential group of Western historians argues that in the last years before the first world war both the industrial and the agricultural sectors of the economy of the Russian Empire were stable and developing satisfactorily. Others are more sceptical, and claim that the boom of 1909–13 was purely temporary; the profound contradictions within the economy meant that it was heading for another crisis.

Some, but by no means all, of the historians who take a favourable view of the trend of economic development before 1914 also hold that tsarist Russia was evolving towards a constitutional or liberal democracy; if it had not been for the accident of the outbreak of the Great War (or alternatively the unfortunate personality of tsar Nicholas II), no Bolshevik Revolution would have occurred. But many other historians, including some of the optimists about economic development, argue that the social and political structure was extremely unstable, pregnant with new revolution, and rescued from it only by the outbreak of war.

These rival assessments are extremely relevant to the history of the Soviet period. If we suppose that the tsarist regime was fundamentally stable, then there was no economic or social necessity for the transformation of the tsarist system, and the Bolshevik Revolution was a historical accident. In this case the stubborn retention of power by the Bolsheviks may in itself have been responsible for the tyrannical political and economic system which was imposed in the Stalin period. If, on the other hand, tsarism was a ramshackle and unstable structure, some kind of new economic and social system was bound to replace it.

These questions about tsarism and its economy are also relevant for those historians of the Soviet period who believe that discussions of alternatives are methodologically unsound. If we are to understand the Soviet economy of the 1920s, and why the mixed economy broke down at the end of that decade, several important questions require comparisons with pre-revolutionary developments. How far did the economy succeed in returning to or exceeding the tsarist level in the 1920s? Did the mixed economy of the 1920s suffer from the disadvantages of the tsarist economy (or rejoice in its advantages)? Was the Bolshevik government in the 1920s

1

merely using policy instruments inherited from tsarism, or did its New Economic Policy (NEP) already involve new methods of controlling the economy? Had the social and political instability of the tsarist system – if it was unstable – been eliminated by the revolution, or did it merely continue in another form?

A further intriguing question is posed by the parallel fates suffered by tsarism and NEP. Tsarism in 1909–13 was on the eve of war and revolution, and NEP Russia in the mid-1920s was on the eve of the 'great break-through' at the end of the 1920s to forced industrialisation and political repression. Was the great break-through another accident analogous to the accident which befell tsarism in 1914–7, but due this time to *Stalin's* personality or to the dangerous international isolation of the Soviet Union? Or was the NEP system, like tsarism, economically and socially unstable? If NEP was unstable, could this instability be attributed in part or whole to the same factors which were responsible for tsarist instability? Or was it almost wholly due to the new circumstances resulting from the revolution and the policies pursued by the Bolsheviks in the following decade?

There are at least three kinds of information and analysis relevant to these larger historical issues which specialists on Soviet economic development could reasonably be expected to supply.

First, how far had the national product or income of the late tsarist period been achieved or exceeded in the peak years of NEP? The issue here is not just the total quantities, but also the relation between and within the various sectors of the economy – both sectors of origin (agriculture; industry; transport; trade; etc.) and sectors by end-use (consumption; investment; defence; social services; etc.).

Secondly, what were the major continuities and changes in the institutional and administrative structure of the economy? Although the political system and the forms of legal ownership were fundamentally different from those which prevailed before the revolution, did the internal organisation of factories and farms, and their structural relations with the rest of the economy, remain largely unchanged?

Finally, the most crucial issue is the mechanism or process by which economic development was achieved under the two regimes. It is relatively easy to explain some of the major differences between sectors and subsectors in the two periods which were due to the effect of the vast upheavals of war, revolution and civil war, or to the nature of the recovery process in the different sectors. But other changes, such as the persistent decline in agricultural marketings, involve a consideration not only of the difficult and much-debated question of peasant economic behaviour but also of the impact of politics, society and ideology on the two types of economic system. This is the point at which the personal biases of historians are most evident.

These three groups of questions are arranged in ascending order of difficulty, but even the first raises considerable problems for the historian. The huge gulf between the pre- and post-revolutionary systems, and the very different primary sources used by historians in investigating them, have led to an unfortunate division of scholarly labour. Both in the Soviet Union and in the West, while many historians *teach* both the pre- and the post-revolutionary periods, it is a rare individual who carries out *research* on both periods.

The comparison even of basic statistics for the two periods raises complicated problems. In the early 1970s, Stephen Wheatcroft attempted to arrive at reliable figures for the most important single item of agricultural production, grain, before and after the revolution. He found that the data presented in both the Western and the Soviet literature were clogged with rash assumptions. In the West, economists took it for granted that the famous 'Ivantsov correction' should be applied to the tsarist official data for grain production, owing to under-reporting. Wheatcroft showed that there was far less justification for the correction than was normally assumed, and that this had seriously affected comparisons over time. In the mid-1920s the correction was applied to pre-revolutionary data, resulting in large increases in the figure for grain production. This in turn justified Gosplan's claim that a large correction should be applied to the figures for the 1920s. In the Gosplan statistics of the 1920s, the figures for both pre- and post-revolutionary grain production were too high. When in the 1960s Soviet statisticians removed the Ivantsov correction from the pre-revolutionary data they failed to make appropriate downward adjustments to the post-revolutionary data, which consequently indicate a far higher level than was justified. We are therefore confronted with various false series for grain production. In the series most popular in the West, both the pre-revolutionary and the post-revolutionary data were too high. In the current Soviet official series, the pre-revolutionary data are too low in relation to the data for the 1920s. (See Chapter 5.)

Other sectors of the economy also raise trying problems. In the 1920s, Soviet statisticians made considerable efforts to compare pre- and post-revolutionary industrial production. But by the end of the 1920s, when their work was brought to an abrupt end, their results had been published only in part, and in a garbled form. A few years ago, I made a preliminary attempt to sort out the figures, and to compare them with the estimates of Western scholars, but it is clear that an industry-by-industry study will be required if the results are to be substantially improved.[1]

The basic social statistics are in equal disarray. Data for employment across the two periods are extremely sketchy; and information about changes in occupations and in educational levels, essential if sense is to be made of post-revolutionary economic changes, has also been lacking.

When our International Work-Group on Soviet Inter-War Economic History embarked in 1985 on an attempt to seek solutions to these problems, we were fortunately able to secure the collaboration of historians specialising in the pre-revolutionary period: Peter Gatrell, Paul Gregory and Maureen Perrie played a central part in the research, and we received valuable advice from Malcolm Falkus, Walter Pintner and others. We circulated preliminary papers in advance, and then all met together in Birmingham in January 1987, at a Conference of our Work-Group, to discuss our conclusions in detail. The outcome is the present volume.

In the rest of this introduction I attempt to summarise our main conclusions; and also to indicate those matters on which our knowledge is particularly inadequate. I also present some of the main controversies about wider issues; on some of these, members of our group disagree strongly among themselves. We are conscious that in many respects this remains a preliminary study, and hope that it may lead other historians to examine these questions more thoroughly.

QUANTITATIVE COMPARISON BY SECTORS

The core of our work is our attempt to establish the agreed facts about the two periods, and to pin-point the uncertainties which remain.

The first problem was to decide on bench-mark years. We decided that it would be best to compare the years of peak performance in each period. In the case of tsarism, this was usually the last year before the war, 1913. But 1913 was a year in which the weather was exceptionally favourable to agriculture; following the usual practice, we have therefore mainly based our comparisons on average agricultural production in 1909–13 (even this figure is somewhat higher than the long-term trend, owing to the favourable weather in those years). On the other hand, the armaments industries expanded extremely rapidly between 1913 and 1916. In consequence the peak production of capital goods was achieved in 1916, and this level of production must be borne in mind when considering whether particular industries had recovered to the pre-revolutionary level during NEP. But 1916 cannot be taken as a standard bench-mark year for industry as a whole because production of consumer goods and even of mining and metallurgy declined substantially between the outbreak of war and 1916.[2]

In the NEP period, the economic or agricultural year 1926/27 is the best bench-mark for most purposes (the economic year was October 1 – September 30; the agricultural year was July 1 – June 30). It was the last year of NEP, in the sense that it was the last year in which economic relations between agriculture and industry were primarily sustained through the market: from the beginning of 1928 administrative coercion became the main instrument of the state for obtaining peasant production. Moreover, agricultural production as a whole did not increase after the agricultural year 1926/27. But there was a large variation from year to year

in the mid-1920s in the production of different types of farming, due partly
to the weather, and partly to changes in state policy. We have therefore
presented agricultural data for each of the years 1926–8, and taken an
average of the three years if there were sharp changes.

Unlike agricultural production, industrial production continued to expand rapidly in 1928. In the industrial sector 1928 was still to a considerable
extent a 'restoration' year: the increase in industrial production was partly
achieved by bringing existing industrial capital into use. We have therefore
provided industrial and related data for both 1926/27 and 1927/28 (or the
calendar year 1928).

******

There is no doubt that the economy was developing rapidly on the eve of
the first world war. According to Gregory's estimates, net national product
increased by 5.1 per cent a year between 1909 and 1913 (about 3.5 per cent
per capita).[3] The gross output of large-scale industry increased in the same
period by over 7 per cent a year, and small-scale industrial output also
increased quite rapidly (see Chapter 7). Agricultural production also rose
substantially. The high level of grain production in 1909–13 was partly due
to several years of favourable weather; but over the whole period
1895–1914 grain production grew by some 2.1–2.4 per cent a year; this was
an increase of 0.5–0.8 per cent a year per head of total population.[4] In the
case of livestock, the position is more ambiguous: Wheatcroft provisionally
concludes that livestock numbers per head of population actually declined
between 1900 and 1910, and failed to recover to their 1900 level by 1914.
Unfortunately no data about changes in the average weight of farm animals
are available for this period.[5] The economic boom in turn resulted in a
rapid increase in passengers and freight carried on the railways: in standard
units ('conventional ton-km'), the total increased by 6 per cent a year
between 1908 and 1913 (see Chapter 9).

In the aftermath of war, revolution and civil war, the economy precipi-
tately declined. Owing to the large number of additional deaths from war
and disease, the decline in the birth rate, and emigration, the population
fell to about 134 millions in 1923, as compared with 140 millions in 1914
(pre-1939 USSR territory); normally it would have increased to about 162
millions.[6] A recent Soviet attempt to analyse this population gap of some
28 millions indicates that some 10.5 – 11.5 millions died prematurely from
violence, disease and famine, 1.5–2 millions emigrated, and the remaining
14–16 million were not born due to the decline in the birth rate.[7]

The figures for the decline in industrial and agricultural production
during the civil war are far from reliable. Total industrial production is
estimated to have fallen to 30 per cent of the 1913 level by 1921. The
decline in large-scale industrial production was far greater than this: the
production of pig-iron even fell to less than 3 per cent of 1913.[8] The decline

was naturally far less precipitate for agricultural than for industrial production: during great social upheavals in peasant countries, even if the
market collapses, the peasants continue to produce their own food. But
during the civil war the decline in agricultural production was exceptionally
large. In 1921 grain production, according to one estimate, fell to 44 per
cent of 1913 (see Table 19); and livestock production to 27 per cent (see
Table 21). A severe famine occurred in the winter and spring of 1921–2. In
general, the decline in national income was far greater than in any other
belligerent country.

After 1921 the speed of economic recovery was far greater than anyone
had anticipated. According to Wheatcroft's estimates, net agricultural
production in 1926–8 (average) was about 7.5 per cent above 1909–13
(average), and about 3 per cent below 1913; as the population increased
between 1913 and 1927 by about 6.5 per cent, agricultural output per head
of population was slightly higher than in 1909–13 (average) and some 10
per cent below 1913. Within this total, there was a very sharp change in the
structure of agricultural production. In 1926–8 (average) the production of
livestock and dairy products was as much as 26 per cent above 1909–13
(average); the equivalent increase for industrial crops was 45 per cent, and
for potatoes as much as 79 per cent. But gross grain production, which was
still by far the most important item in the agricultural balance, was 5 per
cent lower, and net grain production 22 per cent lower, than in 1909–13.
(See Tables 17 and 22.)

Industrial production as a whole appears to have recovered to the
pre-war level by the economic year 1926/27, and to have exceeded it in
1928. The extent to which 1928 production exceeded that of 1913 is not yet,
however, firmly established. The data for small-scale industry are patchy;
and in the case of large-scale industry, while very detailed figures are
available, the magnitude of the price deflator which should be used to
compare data in current prices for the pre-revolutionary period and the
mid-1920s has not yet been firmly established. Peter Gatrell and I conclude
in Chapter 7 that gross industrial production in 1928 was about 20 per cent
higher than in 1913, but Paul Gregory, using a higher price deflator,
suggests that a figure of 5 per cent would be more accurate (see Chapter
12).[9] It should be noted that neither of these estimates take account of any
decline in quality of production in the 1920s which was not reflected in the
output prices.

As in the case of agriculture, the structure of industrial production had
departed considerably from the pre-revolutionary pattern in the mid-
1920s. Broadly, the capital goods industries (Group 'A' industries) had
recovered to a greater extent than the consumer goods industries (Group
'B' industries). Among the capital goods industries, the output of the
whole fuel and power group (coal, oil and electricity) considerably exceeded the pre-war level, as did civilian engineering and metal-working

production. But the iron and steel industry had not yet recovered to the pre-war level: even in 1928 the production of rolled steel was 8 per cent lower than in 1913 (see Table 37). This anomaly was made possible by the reduced output of the shipbuilding industry, and of armaments generally, and by the decline in the supply of rails to the railways. In the consumer goods industries, the food, drink and tobacco group failed to recover to the same extent as textiles and other manufactured goods. As a result of the decline in marketed agricultural production (discussed below), the food industries (and some industrial consumer goods) were held back by the lack of raw materials; this applied to small-scale artisan production as well as factory industry. Vodka production by the state, a major feature of tsarist economic and fiscal activity until prohibition was imposed in 1914, was reintroduced by the Soviet government in 1924, but it had not yet recovered to the pre-war level. In contrast, the textile industries as a whole had recovered to the 1913 level by 1927 (see Chapter 8). Important shifts had taken place since 1913 between artisan and factory production of consumer goods. Partly as a result of the development of factory production of clothing for the army during the first world war, a much higher proportion of garments and knitwear, and of leather footwear, was produced by factory industry in the mid-1920s than before the war.

In Soviet statistics the building industry does not form part of 'industry (*promyshlennost'*)', but is classified separately as 'construction (*stroitel'stvo*)' or 'net construction (*chistoe stroitel'stvo*)', and we have found it convenient to follow the Soviet practice in our own work. There is no satisfactory direct way of measuring the output of the building industry, but it evidently failed to recover to the pre-war level by 1926/27. The State Planning Commission (Gosplan) estimated building work (including agricultural and industrial building, housing, etc.) in 1926/27 at only 84 per cent of 1913 (see Chapter 7); and this order of magnitude is confirmed by rough estimates of the number of building workers (see Appendix to Chapter 2).

The recovery of agricultural and industrial production was necessarily associated with an equally dramatic and equally unexpected recovery of freight transport. By 1927, total freight carried on the railways exceeded the 1913 level by over 5 per cent (and owing to the increased average length of haul, freight measured in terms of ton-km exceeded the 1913 level by over 25 per cent) (see Chapter 9). But traffic carried on the waterways had declined substantially, so that the total freight carried by railways and waterways together did not exceed the 1913 level until 1928, when it amounted to 172.5 million tons against 164.9 millions in 1913.

We have not so far discussed internal and foreign trade. According to a Soviet estimate, by 1926 retail trade from all permanent retail outlets had reached nearly 98 per cent of the 1913 level by 1926 (see Table 39). This fits reasonably well with our information about the recovery of agriculture and industry; it should be noted, however, that no reliable comparative data are available about sales from temporary stalls and kiosks, or by hawkers and pedlars, which constituted a substantial proportion of all trade.

Foreign trade, unlike internal trade, utterly failed to recover to the pre-war level: in 1926/27 exports amounted to only 33 per cent and imports to only 38 per cent of the 1913 level (see Table 61). The decline was due to the decline in agricultural exports, particularly of grain, the most important single export: grain exports amounted to only one-quarter of the 1913 level even in the best year of NEP, and other agricultural exports fell to less than 30 per cent of 1913. While this structure of imports was imposed upon the Soviet government by the decline in agricultural marketings, the equally drastic change in the structure of imports was deliberately planned by the Soviet authorities. Imports of food and particularly of manufactured consumer goods were greatly restricted, but the import of raw materials (essential for the textile and other industries) reached 70 per cent and of machinery 75 per cent of the pre-war level by 1927/28.

The Soviet economy did not need to maintain the large favourable balance of exports over imports (the balance of trade) which had characterised the last pre-war years of the tsarist economy, because there was a drastic decline in invisible payments abroad. The pre-revolutionary national debt was abrogated after the 1917 revolution, so all interest and repayments were cancelled; and in addition Soviet citizens in the 1920s no longer had the opportunity to undertake the large tourist expenditures abroad which had been a major feature of the activities of the pre-war Russian upper classes. Nevertheless, the balance of payments was chronically in deficit in the 1920s. The pre-revolutionary excess of exports over imports had been replaced by an unfavourable balance of trade, except in the single year 1926/27 (see Table 55). A new though relatively small foreign debt was therefore gradually built up during the 1920s, amounting by the end of 1927/28 to 370 million rubles (see Table 55).

The discussion so far has considered Soviet national output in terms of sectors of origin (production sectors). We were not able to make a detailed comparison of national output by end-use, because no reliable comparison has yet been made of expenditure on consumption, administration and services in the two periods. Defence expenditure declined drastically: in current prices it amounted to some 950 million rubles in 1913 and some 700 million rubles in 1926/27 (see Table 41, including notes d and g). Soviet statements in the 1920s suggested that in real terms defence expenditure was half that of 1913; according to one Narkomfin estimate, expenditure in 1926/27 was only 40.6 per cent of 1913.[10]

Total net capital investment, on the other hand, was approximately 10 per cent below the 1913 level in 1926/27, and 10 per cent above that level in 1927/28. Major shifts had taken place within this total. Investment in housing, particularly urban housing, was much lower than in 1913; and investment in transport and communications had also declined. In contrast, investment in both the industrial and agricultural sectors was sub-stantially higher than in 1913. The reasons for this shift will be discussed later.

In Chapter 12 Paul Gregory reviews the evidence presented in the present book, and in his own book on the tsarist national income, and concludes that national income in 1928 was between 93 per cent and 107 per cent of the 1913 level. As the population had increased between 1913 and 1928, the national income per capita was 1.5 per cent lower than in 1913 even on the higher estimate for national income in 1928; on the lower estimate, it was 14 per cent lower. Gregory estimates agricultural pro-duction in 1913 on the basis of the record harvest achieved in that year. In our own estimates, Wheatcroft, Gatrell and I have given preference to the practice of replacing the harvest for 1913, in which the weather was exceptionally favourable, with the average harvest for 1909–13. This would give a total for national income in 1928 at least as high as the pre-war figure; national income per capita, however, remains distinctly below that level on Gregory's lower estimate for 1928.

In the course of writing this book Professor Gregory's results and ours came closer together.[11] In any case we have all long been in agreement that the official Soviet estimates for the mid-1920s are far too high. In 1929 Gosplan estimated that national income was 5 per cent higher than in 1913 in 1926/27 and 13 per cent higher in 1927/28.[12] The most recent official statistics state that national income in 1928 was 19 per cent higher than in 1913; the equivalent official figures for gross agricultural and gross indus-trial production are as high as 24 and 32 per cent.[13] The same sets of figures also purport to show that as early as 1926 agricultural production was already 118 per cent and industrial production 98 per cent of 1913.

Does it make much difference to our understanding of the history of the USSR in the XX Century if national income in 1928 was 19 per cent higher rather than 7 per cent lower than in 1913? This issue certainly plays a significant part in the current Soviet debates about the future of the USSR. Soviet reformers of many shades of opinion look back to the 1920s as the best period in Soviet history, and are anxious to show that the New Economic Policy was very successful. Soviet economists who express considerable scepticism about every other aspect of Soviet official statistics quote without hesitation the data in the present-day official statistical handbooks which show that NEP had brought about the complete recovery of the economy within a few years, and ignore those Soviet estimates of the 1920s which show a less successful recovery under NEP.[14] Some Soviet economists who should know better even seek to prove that the market economy was more efficient than central planning simply by contrasting the rapid growth of industrial production in 1922–8 with the slower growth in the early 1930s, failing even to mention that the 1920s were years of recovery rather than of new investment.[15]

The view that the economy had completely recovered to the 1913 level by 1926 or 1927 also played some part in the over-optimistic planning which came to prevail at the end of the 1920s. In 1927/28–1929/30 industrial production expanded much more rapidly than in the last few years before 1913. Soviet economists and planners assumed that this rapid growth was entirely due to new investment. In fact a substantial part of the growth was due to the bringing back into use of existing industrial capital, and its more intensive utilisation. The misunderstanding of the rapid industrial growth of the late 1920s led Fel'dman in his famous growth-model to predict very low capital: output ratios for the 1930s.[16]

In an international perspective, however, the differences between the alternative assessments of the extent of recovery are rather trivial. Estimates by Gregory and others show that the gap between Russia and the other great powers in national income per head of population had widened over the whole period between 1861 and 1913, but may have slightly narrowed from 1885 onwards. In 1913 agriculture was more backward than in the other major European countries, in terms of both yields per hectare and production per person engaged in farming, and the agricultural economy was far less diversified.[17] Both industrial output per head of production and labour productivity were far lower than in Britain, France, Germany or the United States; and, in spite of the rapid growth of capital goods since 1890, Russian industry was dominated by consumer goods to a far greater extent than in the industrialised countries (see Chapter 7). In 1913, national income per head of population in Russia was two-fifths of the French national income, one-third of the German, one-fifth of the British and only one-eighth of the United States.[18]

The comparative technological level of Russian industry varied considerably between industries. Industries such as iron and steel had been developed in 1880–1913 with the aid of foreign capital, and much modern plant was present. But even in these industries labour productivity was lower in 1913 than in the industrialised countries. Many other industries were extremely backward technologically. Approximately one-quarter of all industrial production was undertaken by artisans, usually employing little machinery and working in primitive conditions. Some high-technology branches of the engineering industry, particularly aircraft design and production, advanced rapidly in the last pre-war years and particularly in 1914–6. But in general Russian research and development was weak. Specialised research institutes such as those in Germany did not exist, and there was little development of R & D within industry; technology was imported rather than developed at home.

In the international perspective, the position of the industry of the USSR in 1926/27 or 1928 was less favourable than that of the Russian Empire in 1913. Gatrell and I show that the gap in production per head between the Soviet Union and the advanced industrial countries was as wide as in 1913.

Like Soviet industry, French and German industry had recovered to the pre-war level by 1926/27, and United States' production far exceeded that level (see Chapter 7). And the technological gap had widened: Cooper and Lewis show (Chapter 10) that technological advance in the West, particularly in Germany and the United States, far outstripped the limited improvements in the Soviet Union.

THE ECONOMIC STRUCTURES

Tsarism

In the Russian Empire on the eve of the first world war several different socio-economic structures were intermingled. Some 100,000 noble land-owning families – half a million people in all – owned three-fifths of the private land. Part of this private land was rented out to peasants, and by 1916 less than 10 per cent of the total sown area in the Russian Empire was directly cultivated as landowners' estates, both noble and non-noble (see Table 9). But, in spite of the decline in the economic fortunes of the nobility, on the eve of the first world war many of the very senior positions in the powerful tsarist state machine were still held by noble owners of large estates, and nobles comprised over 70 per cent of the top four classes of officials even at the end of the XIX Century.

The bulk of the industrial and commercial wealth which had multiplied in the decades after the emancipation of the serfs in 1861 was owned by non-nobles: over 200,000 industrial and merchant enterprises were owned by 'bourgeois' proprietors who, with their families, amounted to over two million persons.

The noble estates and the industrial and commercial concerns, together with the state apparatus and local government, were served by an increasing number of professional functionaries, including lawyers, engineers, army officers, doctors and teachers. The total number of persons engaged in such 'mental labour' at every level may have amounted to over a million persons; of these, a mere 130,000 were graduates of higher education establishments.

Taken together, nobles and the middle and upper bourgeois and the graduate specialists, with their families, thus comprised in 1913 a hierarchy of élites, amounting to three million or so persons out of the 140 million citizens of the Russian Empire (USSR pre-1939 territory).

In sharp contrast to the elites in their wealth, education and status, peasants comprised the vast majority of the population. Of the five-sixths of the total population which lived in the countryside in 1913, over 90 per cent were members of the twenty million peasant households, nearly all of which were engaged in cultivating individual family farms, which covered over 90 per cent of the total sown area. Most peasant households were organised into rural communes: their land was divided into strips, and in many communes was periodically redistributed. Many households also took part in economic activities outside their own farm, usually on a part-time basis: over four million peasants worked outside their village or rural district on a seasonal basis as agricultural labourers, and five million worked in building, forestry and various other non-agricultural occupations.

Most of the mass occupations apart from peasant farming formed part of what we have defined here as the industrial economy – a term which we use to embrace industry, building, railway and water transport and internal trade. Some ten million persons were engaged in the industrial economy. Of these 6.4 million were wage-workers, mainly employed in industry and on the railways. The rest were self-employed; many of these were part-time artisans, who were often engaged as peasant farmers in the summer months. (See Tables 3 and 4.)

Over the centuries, and particularly in the last half-century before the first world war, an increasing amount of total economic activity was directed towards the market. According to a Gosplan estimate, 22–25 per cent of gross agricultural production was marketed outside the rural areas in 1913 (see Table 26); and a further substantial amount, which has not been reliably measured, was sold by peasants to peasants in other rural areas. In the case of grain, 25 million tons were transported by rail or water on the eve of the first world war; this represents over one-third of gross grain production and over 40 per cent of net grain production (this excludes grain used for seed). This figure does not include the substantial amount of grain conveyed to the market by cart. The vast majority of industrial consumer goods, and some capital goods, were also sold on the market. Internal trade took place partly through large and small merchant houses, which commanded the growing wholesale trade. Some retail trade in the larger towns was handled by privately-owned larger or smaller shops or department stores; in addition, a network of consumer cooperatives was responsible for a small but growing proportion of this trade. But most retail trade was still handled by small booths and stalls in the markets, and by a large army of itinerant hawkers and pedlars.

The economic system on the eve of the first world war was thus in part a capitalist economy working for a market, and ranging from large modern factories to illiterate impoverished peasant communities. But this picture of a market economy must be modified in several important respects. First, a large part of peasant production of food, and to some extent of consumer goods, was consumed by the families which produced it, or by other families within the same village. The peasant households, and particularly the villages, were still to a considerable extent self-sufficient. Secondly, a substantial proportion of all capital goods, and some industrial consumer goods, were purchased by the state for its own use, primarily by the state railways and the defence establishments. The state as consumer, financed through the state budget, thus strongly influenced the growth of industry. Thirdly, import tariffs, though a clumsy instrument, were a deliberate device to protect state industry, and had a powerful effect. Fourthly, in a number of capital goods industries, including iron and steel, coal, oil and railway engineering, syndicates (the Russian equivalent of cartels) decided on sales quotas for their constituent firms, and fixed the wholesale prices. This was then a market economy which was managed by the state and had marked oligopolistic tendencies.

NEP

In the mid-1920s, the role of the state in the economy was substantially greater than in 1913, and the market was more closely regulated. The state sector was now much larger. In addition to the railways, which were already mainly nationalised before the revolution, nearly all large-scale industry was now owned by the state, together with the banks and most wholesale trade. Moreover, by 1926 over half of 'organised' retail trade (this excludes itinerant trade and the peasant market) was in the hands of state trading agencies or of consumer cooperatives effectively managed by the state. State industry was supposed in principle to work for the market on a self-financing basis (*khozraschet*). But, in spite of the decline in defence outlays as compared with 1913, state orders for activities financed by the budget remained an important part of capital goods' production, and were now handled centrally by a Committee of State Orders. And since the early 1920s syndicates controlling sales and wholesale prices, which existed only in certain capital goods industries before the war, had also been established in major consumer goods industries such as textiles. The state budget was also a most important instrument for controlling the economy: most investment in the capital goods industries was financed by grants or low-interest loans from the budget.

   The state had also acquired five major instruments of control over the economy which it did not possess before 1914. First, wholesale industrial prices and an increasing range of retail prices were fixed centrally by the state. Secondly, the state regulated short-term and long-term credit through a quarterly plan approved by the central authorities. Thirdly, the state endeavoured to regulate the general level of wages and the broad wage differentials between different sectors and industries, and between different kinds of skill. Fourthly, a state monopoly of foreign trade effectively imposed physical controls over all imports. Finally, an annual state plan ('control figures') endeavoured, as yet rather intermittently, to manage economic development. As part of this endeavour, by 1926 an annual capital investment plan already broadly controlled the allocation of investment between sectors and industries: the investment plan incorporated not only the investment grants from the budget, but also loans from state-owned banks, and that part of investment which was financed by enterprises or industries from their own profits.

These controls were by no means fully effective. Wage controls often failed to work. The control figures were in large part a statement of intentions rather than an operational plan. Investments which were not included in the capital investment plan were undertaken by local authorities and by consumer goods industries without central approval. But even the weakest of these controls had a significant effect on the behaviour of the economy; and import controls and credit plans were already quite effective.

In spite of the economic power of the state, NEP was still in major respects a market economy. Artisan enterprises, usually owned by individuals, worked primarily for the market, with little effective state control. Over 40 per cent of organised retail trade, and almost all peasant 'bazaar' trade, was in private hands; and before 1927 price controls in retail trade were largely ineffective. Peasant households, now numbering some twenty-five million, were primarily engaged in producing for themselves or for the market rather than for the state. Moreover, before 1928 that part of peasant production which was sold to state agencies was usually sold at prices which peasants were prepared voluntarily to accept – i.e., at near-market prices. The wage and price policies of the state were very largely attempts to manage what was still fundamentally a market economy. On the whole the state, and the different state enterprises, appeared on the market as actors, not as dictators.

PROCESSES OF INDUSTRIALISATION COMPARED

In 1913 net capital investment, according to Paul Gregory's estimates, amounted to over 11 per cent of net national product, maintaining an investment share which had been established ever since the early 1890s.[19] This was a particularly high figure for a low-income country, and was evidently an important factor in the rapid rate of growth of the economy, and particularly of the capital goods industries, from the 1890s.

The traditional explanation for the rapid rate of industrialisation, advanced by Gerschenkron and others, is that this high level of investment was to an unusually large extent financed by high direct and indirect taxes imposed on the peasant. The contributors to the present volume are in general agreement that this view requires substantial modification. Taxes were borne by the urban as well as the rural population; the urban rather than the rural population was the main consumer of those goods on which indirect taxes were imposed.

This does not mean that the peasants did not bear a heavy burden of taxation and other imposts. A. L. Vainshtein and others estimated that rents and taxes together amounted to as much as 19 per cent of net peasant income (see Table 28, including note b).

Moreover, as compared with world prices, the ratio of agricultural to industrial prices in pre-revolutionary Russia was relatively low: according to a Soviet estimate, world agricultural prices were 46 per cent above the average Russian 1913 level, and world wholesale industrial prices 39 per cent below that level.[20] There is no general agreement among historians on the extent to which this important price-difference should be regarded as a result of 'unequal' exchange due to the effect of customs tariffs on imports of industrial goods, and of other forms of 'non-economic' exploitation of the peasantry. Some economic historians argue that exchange was not unequal: the different price-ratio in Russia was entirely a normal consequence of the comparative advantage of agriculture in Russian conditions.

Direct state investment was fairly small on the eve of the first world war, amounting in 1913 to about one-seventh of all investment.[21] Nevertheless, the state budget played an important role in industrialisation. The increases in state current (non-investment) expenditure on defence, on operating the state railways, etc. in the last few years before the war were undoubtedly an important factor in stimulating the industrial boom of 1909–13. So far, however, no serious attempt has been made to quantify its effect.

The state also played an important role in encouraging foreign investment. As measured by Gregory, the net inflow of foreign investment in 1913 amounted to 578 million rubles, amounting to 25 per cent of net domestic investment (2,314 million rubles). This was an exceptionally high figure; the average net foreign investment in the five years 1909–13 was only 253 million rubles, about 12 per cent of net domestic investment (2,194 million rubles in 1909–13). Gregory's figure for net foreign investment was simply obtained as the deficit on the balance of payments (balance of trade *less* net dividends and loan repayments, etc. *less* tourist expenditure, etc. abroad). The direct data on foreign investment give a somewhat smaller total, but reveal that in 1909–14 over one-third of new investment in joint-stock capital (mainly in the banks and industry) was obtained from abroad.[22] The role of the Ministry of Finance in encouraging this investment was very considerable throughout this period.

As a result of the large inflow of foreign loans over many decades, in 1914 as much as 45 per cent of the large Russian national debt was held abroad.[23] In 1913 interest and other payments on public and corporation debt held abroad amounted to 400 million rubles, equivalent to over 25 per cent of earnings from exports. In consequence, net foreign investment did not require any net transfer of resources into the Russian economy. For many decades the sums paid abroad on account of debt had exceeded the net investment from abroad in the Russian Empire.[24]

State and foreign investment together accounted for 20–25 per cent of all investment, and may well have been the crucial determinants of the exceptionally high level of investment in the last quarter of a century before the first world war.

The direct role of the state in investment had undoubtedly declined by the eve of the first world war as compared with the 1890s.[25] But the evidence about the role of the state on the eve of the war as promoter of foreign investment and above all as consumer leads us to disagree with Gerschenkron's view that the role of state consumption and foreign investment had substantially diminished. In general we concur with Olga Crisp's view that in 1913 'there was still not only scope but actual necessity for an active role of the public sector'.[26] We have been unable, however, to make a quantitative assessment of the relative importance of the influence of the market and the state, of what she called the 'autonomous' and the 'induced' growth streams.

In the mid-1920s, in contrast to 1913, most investment outside the agricultural sector was financed and managed by the state; this was already a new mechanism for the direct planning of economic development for which there was no precedent in recent European history. And by 1928 30 per cent of all net agricultural investment in fixed capital was already being undertaken in the socialist sector (this figure includes rural housing and livestock; excluding these, the percentage of investment made in the socialist sector rose to 41 per cent).[27]

How did this rudimentary mechanism of state planning, coupled to a market economy, influence the relation between the major sectors of the economy? We have seen that it resulted in a substantial switch within total investment from housing and transport to industry and agriculture. The shift towards industry was deliberately planned by the state; but the increased investment in agriculture, which was almost entirely in the livestock sector, was an unintended consequence of the attempt to plan economic development in a market economy.

Did the existence of a large state-planned sector of the economy, together with the major social and economic changes since 1914, bring about a fundamental shift in current, as distinct from investment, resources and incomes between the major sectors? The 'scissors' (the ratio of the retail prices of manufactured goods to the prices received by the peasants for their produce) were less favourable to the peasants in the 1920s than on the eve of the first world war (see Table 29); peasants received relatively less for their products in terms of manufactured goods. On the other hand, according to Soviet estimates made in the 1920s, taxation on the peasants in the 1920s was substantially lower than taxation plus rents in 1913; and the exchange of goods between town and country was at a lower absolute level. In Chapter 6 Harrison on balance concurs with the Soviet economist

Barsov that the contribution of agriculture to industrialisation is likely to have been lower on the eve of the first five-year plan than in 1913. But on a reduced scale 'unequal exchange' between agriculture and urban large-scale industry continued.

The most important shift in the balance between the sectors in the 1920s was the reduced level of agricultural marketings. This chronic problem had its repercussions on all the other sectors of the economy, and inhibited the attempts of the state to increase the pace of industrialisation. Why did it occur, and why did state policy not succeed in remedying it? Harrison summarises the main factors involved.

First, the abolition of the more market-oriented landowners' estates probably had a negative effect on marketings. (The other major social change in the countryside was the marked decline in socio-economic differentiation among the peasantry; the evidence for this is summarised in Chapter 3. This greater equality within the peasantry is frequently given in the Soviet literature as the main reason for the decline in marketings. The extent of its influence is, however not at all clear (see Chapter 6).)

The second factor leading to a reduced level of marketings was the reduced level of taxation and the abolition of land rents. This meant that peasants who had marketed their produce before the war in order to meet these obligations now had less need to do so.

Thirdly, general deterioration in the terms of trade for agricultural produce probably discouraged peasants from marketing their output. Here Harrison is inclined to doubt James Millar's view that unfavourable terms of trade would lead peasants to sell more in order to obtain a fixed package of manufactured goods, while Merl is inclined to support Millar's position. But unambiguous empirical evidence is lacking.

In the 1920s, extra-rural sales of grain had declined particularly sharply, amounting to no more than 50 per cent of the 1913 level. The prices paid for marketed grain by the state were fixed at a relatively low level, and this led peasants to switch their production and marketings to branches of farming such as livestock, where prices were relatively high. The production of grain per head of population in the 1920s never reached the pre-war level; agriculture had shifted, partly under the influence of the price relatives, towards more intensive high-yielding activities, especially livestock farming and the production of industrial crops.

TWO SYSTEMS IN CRISIS?

Let us now return to the questions we raised at the outset. How far were the economies of late tsarism and NEP stable and capable of growth? Why did the existing social orders break down and undergo violent transformation in 1917 and again after 1927? Was this due to economic instability, or to fundamental disorders in the social or political structure – or perhaps merely to ideological choice or historical accident?

Tsarism

Economic Aspects

Many historians hold that in economic terms tsarist industrialisation was a success; a modern capitalist economy was emerging. We have already considered Gerchenkron's version of this approach, which holds that in 1909–13 the state was giving way to the market as the motive-force for industrial development, and that Russian capital and entrepreneurship were replacing foreign capital. As we have seen, the balance of the evidence indicates that the state maintained a major role in industrial development in 1909–13, owing to the growth of defence orders. McKay has shown that Russian capital and entrepreneurship was increasingly influential in a number of industries.[28] But foreign capital was dominant in the new industries such as electrical engineering, and its overall role had not diminished.

The view that the economy was prosperous and stable in 1909–13 does not, however, depend on its Gerschenkron variant. Certainly in the industrial sector the rate of growth of production and the pace of technical modernisation on the eve of the first world war were on the whole impressive. And in the agricultural sector production had been growing more rapidly than population at least since the 1880s, and by 1914 the majority of the peasants belonged to various forms of agricultural credit and marketing cooperatives. Some historians also argue that the Stolypin reform was succeeding in moving the centre of gravity in the rural economy from the village to the independent peasant proprietor, and that this had already led to even more rapid growth. Among the authors of the present volume, Paul Gregory argues that all these developments taken together show that the pattern of structural change in tsarist Russia was 'generally similar to that experienced by other countries during the first thirty years of modern economic growth', and that tsarist Russia does not appear to have had the structural characteristics of a dual economy.[29] Michael Dohan supports this general view in relation to the foreign trade sector. He argues that the import and export decisions of the economic actors were based on prices and commercial considerations, and that government policy was deliberately and successfully crafted to support a positive role for foreign trade within a market framework.

This 'optimistic' view of the pre-revolutionary economy is not supported by other historians, including several of the authors of the present volume. In relation to agriculture, no serious historian would now defend the older view that output per head of population in the Russian Empire as a whole was declining in the thirty years before the war. But the general rise in agricultural production concealed important symptoms of agricultural crisis. First, while grain production per head of population increased, the number of livestock per head declined in the Russian Empire as a whole and in each of the main agricultural regions.[30] In 1913 Russian agriculture was still primarily an agriculture which turned on grain production.

Secondly, in certain regions the crisis features of agriculture were far more general. Wheatcroft has shown that in the Central Producer Region output of grain per head on the eve of the war was somewhat lower than it had been at the turn of century, as was the number of livestock per head, and this was not compensated in this region by any substantial increase in industry and urbanisation.[31] The Central Producer Region includes the Central Black-Earth region, the long-established older centre of Russian agriculture in the last years of tsarism; it was a region of overpopulation and economic distress.

A third aspect of the pre-revolutionary agricultural economy is considered by some historians to embody growing features of crisis: the economic differentiation within the peasantry under the impact of the growth of production for the market. Lenin argued that peasant agriculture was increasingly polarised into exploitative kulaks and a rural proletariat, with the middle peasants steadily declining in importance; Lenin's analysis was supported by Soviet agrarian marxists such as Kritsman (see Chapter 3). The marxist view was challenged by Chayanov, who held that there was no general trend to greater differentiation. In Chapter 3 Stephan Merl, while acknowledging that intra-village differentiation in wealth was present before the revolution, argues that there is no evidence of increasing differentiation in the last decade before 1914, except possibly in the Central Black-Earth steppe. At our Conference and in subsequent discussion this view was questioned by Harrison and Gatrell, who argue that there was a long-term trend towards greater differentiation; they point to the steady growth of permanent agricultural wage-labourers in European Russia between 1860 and 1913, which exceeded the growth both of the population and of agricultural and national production. But no one in our Work-Group supported Lenin's claim that differentiation had led by 1913 to irreconcilable class antagonism in the village between the petty capitalist 'kulaks' on the one hand and the poor peasants and hired labourers on the other.

In Chapter 7 Gatrell and I argue that in industry as well as in agriculture the growth of production concealed serious structural problems. The development of mining, metallurgy and railway engineering with the support of the state, and the rise of the cotton textile industry, led to the establishment of large factory units based on modern technology; as Russian labour productivity was far lower than in modern Western factories, the average number of persons employed per factory was unprecedentedly high. The gathering of workers into factories in large numbers, and in poor working conditions, provided a powerful economic basis for social unrest and political radicalisation. Moreover, within most factories productivity was maintained and discipline upheld by an oppressive factory hierarchy. According to Leopold Haimson, this issue of 'human dignity' was crucial: workers complained of '*unizhenie i oskorblenie* (past or present rude and humiliating treatment on the part of foremen and managers)'.[32] Gatrell and I agree with Haimson that this was an inherent part of the pre-revolutionary industrial system.

The evidence of structural and regional deficiencies in industry and agriculture does not in itself show that the economy was in incipient crisis. Many historians, however, have plausibly claimed that the Russian economy on the eve of war must be examined in the context of capitalism as an international system.

On this question Soviet historians have developed the arguments of Lenin and other pre-revolutionary marxists.[33] Lenin described Russia as economically the most backward of the great powers, an economy in which the most modern capitalism was interwoven with a network of pre-capitalist relations. Pre-revolutionary Russia was dependent on West European capitalism for its industrialisation, but itself exploited its colonies in Central Asia. According to Lenin, Russia was at the advanced capitalist stage which he labelled 'imperialism', but this was an imperialism of a particularly backward kind, 'military-feudal imperialism'. In the Leninist analysis, this half-developed economy was bound to be shattered on the impact of war. The first world war was not an unfortunate accident but an inevitable consequence of the development of European capitalism as a world system, in which the Russian economy was bound to be involved.

Western historians such as von Laue and Geyer do not follow Lenin in believing that economic contradictions between the capitalist powers were the crucial factor in the drive to war. But, like Lenin, they hold that there was an inevitability about the first world war and Russian participation in it. According to von Laue, war did not suddenly descend upon an innocent Europe: 'violence and destruction were already in its bones', and Russia, which had inevitably been involved in 'a special effort of imitation' to meet the challenge of global power competition, was just as inevitably involved in a war which brought about revolution.[34] Geyer argues that the drive to catch up with the West led to a 'process of social and economic transformation which threatened the very existence of the system', and produced internal conflict and disorder. The irrational fears which resulted were 'projected . . . onto ancient enemies' and made Russian participation in the war inevitable.[35] Lieven, while emphasising that Russian policy was much less aggressive than Germany's, believes that it was simply impossible for Russia to accept the demotion to a second-class power which acquiescence in German actions would entail.[36] Many historians of pre-war Germany also place much of the blame for the drift to war on the destabilising policies of the Kaiser's Germany. On this view, while war was not in general inevitable, given the behaviour of Germany it could not be avoided by the Russian Empire if it was to retain its international status.

Thus in spite of their differences, these authors concur that the international power system resulted in what Lieven calls the 'ghastly inevitability' of the drift into European war. This standpoint strongly contrasts with Gerschenkron's claim that 'from the point of view of the industrial development of the country, war, revolution or the threat thereof may reasonably be seen as extraneous phenomena'.[37] From the different standpoints of Lenin, von Laue, Geyer and Lieven, both the war and the collapse of the tsarist system were a consequence of the development of European capitalism or the European political order, and the pre-war tsarist economy cannot be analysed outside this context.

Social and Political Aspects

In discussing the economy, we have been moving into wider social and political issues. Historians deeply disagree about the extent of social and political stability on the eve of the first world war. Some stress that the last decade before the war saw the narrowing of the gap between the Russian social and political order and West European civilisation. Seymour Becker presents a nobility which rationally adapted itself to new conditions, so that by 1917 'the noble estate had virtually vanished', being absorbed in the modern landowning class, the bureaucracy, the professions or in business activities.[38] Hugh Seton-Watson described a business class which included 'modern-minded industrialists, traders and bankers' and a professional class which was 'larger, more influential and less dissatisfied'.[39] On Tokmakoff's account, while the Stolypin agrarian reform had not yet achieved final success by 1914, it was leading to a more prosperous peasant agriculture; 'all that it was intended to accomplish, it steadily achieved'.[40] In the factories, according to Gerschenkron, 'the Russian labor movement of those years was slowly turning towards revisionist and trade unionist lines'; while the number of strikes had increased, they now tended to be motivated by economic rather than political demands.[41] Other historians argue that even the political system was evolving towards greater stability and a form of democracy; one German historian, for example, explained that the constitution of 1906 'transformed the Russian empire from an absolute and unlimited monarchy into a constitutional monarchy'.[42]

Every aspect of these optimistic assessments has been strongly challenged by others. According to Roberta Manning, the traditional nobility had been in crisis ever since 1861; after 1906, the dominant group was the provincial gentry, who sabotaged Stolypin's reform plans and 'contributed substantially to the crisis that eventually consumed the Old Regime'.[43]

Rieber concludes that the business classes, including the entrepreneurs, failed to form a common ideology, or a clear will and organisation; they played little role in society or politics, and were isolated from the intelligentsia, who gave them no support.[44] Haimson finds that in the large towns the mass of industrial workers were increasingly discontented and disaffected, and that the very process of the absorption of formerly alienated elements of the intelligentsia into privileged society, which others regard as contributing to social stability, left the workers increasingly under the influence of a revolutionary minority. At the same time, Haimson detects an almost equally advanced 'second process of polarization – this one between the vast bulk of privileged society and the tsarist regime'.[45] As for the peasants, according to some historians the crucial failure of the Stolypin reform was that it removed none of their grievances against landowners which had been at the centre of the vast disturbances of 1905–7. There is no agreement among historians on whether the Stolypin reform would have succeeded in modernising the structure of peasant agriculture without provoking further serious unrest. Atkinson has pointed out that in 1910–4, after a lull in 1908–9, the number of recorded peasant disturbances again greatly increased.[46] Peasant unrest was paralleled by much greater disturbances in the towns. Workers' unrest reached its climax in July 1914 with a major revolt in St Petersburg, when many thousands of workers were involved in violent clashes with the police.[47]

Whatever their disagreements about economic and social stability on the eve of the first world war, most historians nowadays reject the view that the political system was stable, or was evolving more or less smoothly. By 1914 disaffection and disillusion were widespread in privileged society. The restrictions imposed by the tsar in 1911–4 on the limited rights of the Duma took place against the background of a series of dramatic events: the mysterious murder of Stolypin in 1911; the shooting of unarmed strikers in the Lena goldfields in 1912; the trumped-up trial in 1913 of Beilis, a Jewish clerk, for the ritual murder of a Christian schoolboy; and in February 1914 the dismissal of the Prime Minister, Kokovtsev, and the appointment in his place of the aged toady Goremykin. Above all, the Russian political world was haunted on the eve of the first world war by the sinister role at Court of the debauched sectarian Rasputin, the last and most influential of the mystics or charlatans who influenced the Court.

The political atmosphere among the educated classes was summed up in November 1913 by Guchkov, former president of the Duma and leader of the moderate Octobrists: 'with every day', he told his party, 'people are losing faith in the state and in the possibility of a normal, peaceful resolution of the crisis'; the probable outcome was 'a sad, unavoidable catastrophe'.[48] But why the deepening political rupture in these years? This question brings us back to the role of accident in history. Seton-Watson argues that Russia's defeat in the war, and the preceding instability of the political system, was due to the narrow-mindedness and obstinacy of the tsar: 'first among the grave-diggers of Russia comes her last emperor'.[49] But other historians regard this as a superficial view, because the decisions by Nicholas II were taken by a man who was typical of his social stratum. For these historians the political crisis was a structural problem, due both to a deep and unbridgeable fissure between officialdom and educated society,[50] and to the stubborn resistance to change not only of the imperial family, but also of their strong supporters in the army, the bureaucracy and the Cabinet.[51] And marxists of all shades treat the political crisis on the eve of the war as the symptom of the profound conflict which had emerged with the growth of industry and commerce in the course of half a century. The outmoded superstructure of tsarist political institutions faced the new social classes born of industrialism – the industrial workers, the private capitalists and the professional groups.

NEP

The NEP system has given rise to even more vigorous controversy. As compared with what followed, the mixed economy of NEP was a relatively open society, with some degree of pluralism and free debate. Why was it abruptly replaced by the administrative-command economy and the ruthless Stalinist political dictatorship? The central issue here, as in the debates about tsarism, has been the fundamental stability or instability of the system. Was the breakdown of NEP due to its inherent defects, or to accidental causes?

Economic Aspects
The rival assessments of NEP as an economic system may conveniently be divided into three groups. First, many Western economists hold that NEP was a temporary and transitory system. It had failed to allow market forces to operate satisfactorily, even in the years of 'high NEP' (1925 and 1926), when the greatest freedom was permitted to the private sector. Many state firms occupied a monopolistic position through the power of the syndicates. Centralised state price controls resulted in the rationing of certain capital goods. The state managed investment in detail. In the present volume, Michael Dohan argues that in the case of foreign trade fundamental changes since the revolution in economic institutions, economic policy and ideology were responsible for the failure of grain exports, which were crucial to successful foreign trade. The authorities were faced with the dilemma that if they fixed procurement prices high enough to encourage production and marketing this would lead to inflation and also make exports unprofitable, but if they set prices lower than the market-clearing level goods famine and a grain marketing crisis would result. According to Dohan, the Soviet authorities were unable for political and ideological

reasons to break out of this dilemma by adopting an efficient marketing system, and therefore failed to restore exports; this in turn accelerated the shift towards the comprehensive allocation of resources by the state.

In a variant on this view, Gerschenkron argued that the Bolshevik revolution was a fundamentally reactionary event, which blocked the road to democratic capitalism in Russia. Its triumph meant that by the mid-1920s 'the conditions for the resumption of economic growth would seem to have been rather unfavourable'. This inevitably led to the shift to forced industrialisation through economic dictatorship.[52] Thus Gerschenkron believed that the objective economic conditions existed for the country to become a capitalist market economy, but the effect of the revolution was to make this impossible.

A second group of historians, among whom the late E. H. Carr is the most prominent, concurs that the economy of NEP was inherently unstable. But their standpoint is radically different. They believe that in the XX and XXI Centuries the world economy is evolving from private capitalism and a free market to forms of state planning, and that the development of the Soviet Union after the revolution exemplified this general progress. In this context Carr held that there was 'a latent incompatibility between the principles of the New Economic Policy and the principles of planning', so that the mid-1920s was a 'period of compromise, wishful thinking and evasion of the real issues'.[53] With some reservations, Carr believed that planned industrialisation required the replacement of individual peasant agriculture by large-scale socialist agriculture, and the subordination of the market to the plan.

A third group rejects both of these points of view. In the present volume, several contributors, including Cooper, Harrison, Wheatcroft and myself, argue that the economy of the mid-1920s had not reached an impasse: by 1927 it had achieved a level and type of allocation of investment which was sufficient to permit a moderate rate of expansion of both industry and agriculture. On the other hand, we do not believe that the rather unstable market relation between the state and the peasant, which was characteristic of NEP, was capable of sustaining much higher rates of industrialisation than those achieved on the eve of the first world war. Given the rate of industrialisation which the Soviet leadership imposed on the economy, the NEP system was bound to break down.[54]

Social and Political Aspects

If we assume that the breakdown of NEP was not an inevitable consequence of the economic situation as such, how far was it a result of inherent social or political instability? Opinions here are also sharply divided. Many Western historians hold that the emergence of Stalin's dictatorship was due to the retention of sole power by Lenin and the Bolsheviks, who were supported by only a small minority of the population. According to

Leonard Schapiro, 'the regime was shaped by the determination of a small, still largely unpopular, party to secure and hold power for itself and its supporters alone, in defiance of other parties and of large sections of the population'.[55]

In contrast, several monographs published since the 1960s argue that the 1920s was a period of struggle between different trends within the party, supported by different social forces and different shades of ideology. The victory of Stalin was not fore-ordained by Bolshevik victory in the revolution. Stalin's triumph was the victory of one trend within Bolshevism over the others.

Within this general framework of analysis, several different explanations are offered for the victory of the Stalin trend. Some historians argue that it was due to the accident of Stalin's personal influence. Robert Tucker presents Stalin's personality as the 'decisive trifle' that led to the breakdown of NEP. Roy Medvedev characterises the triumph of Stalin as 'an historical accident', though facilitated by conditions which favoured his usurpation of power.[56] Other historians, including Moshe Lewin, stress the complex of factors which led to the transformation of the Soviet system at the end of the 1920s: the Russian autocratic heritage; the background of the violence of world war and civil war; Bolshevik ideology and political practice; the imperatives of rapid industrialisation.[57] Stephen Cohen accepts the view that the anti-Bukharin trend was strongly supported within the party and 'enshrined the primacy of rapid industrial growth and planning over market equilibrium'. But on his assessment this did not imply the extremes of dekulakisation and over-optimistic planning which were forced through in 1929–30, or the ruthless terror; these must be attributed to Stalin's use of his personal power.[58] According to Cohen, therefore, both historical forces and Stalin's personality played a significant role in bringing about the end of NEP.

These debates, with many minor variations, have been repeated in the vigorous Soviet discussions since 1987.[59] But in both the Soviet Union and the West the study of the Soviet social and political structure of the 1920s is in its infancy, and historians have not yet assessed satisfactorily the relative importance of different influences in determining the collapse of NEP. It is to be hoped that political and social historians will undertake the kind of detailed comparison between late tsarism and NEP which we have attempted for the economy in this book.

In all these debates historians have tended to pay relatively little attention to the international position of the Soviet Union as a factor contributing to the breakdown of NEP. As we have seen, in the last years of NEP the gap in production per head between the Soviet Union and the advanced industrial countries was as wide as in 1913, and the technological gap had widened. Against this background a series of alarming international events emphasised the dangerous international isolation of the

Soviet Union in 1927, and reinforced the view of its leaders that a strong industrial economy capable of providing modern armaments was essential to survival. Historians differ about how far the apprehension of the Soviet leaders was justified by the objective international situation. I am personally convinced that the Soviet leaders were acutely aware of Soviet military weakness in face of a hostile capitalist world, and that this was an important factor in the decision to break out of the confines of NEP.

Part I
The Social Background

2 The Social Context
Maureen Perrie and R. W. Davies

As far as we can discover, no attempt has been made since the 1920s either in Western or in Soviet literature to assemble and assess the basic data on the major social changes brought about by the revolution. As this knowledge is essential background information for the economic historian, we have hazarded in this chapter a preliminary assessment of the evidence. But for both of the authors this is an 'auxiliary occupation'; we hope we may inspire others to do the job properly.

With these important qualifications, we offer some basic statistical information on major changes in the ruling elites and in the main social classes. The 'internal structure' of the peasantry is not examined here, as it is dealt with in Chapter 3; the question of unemployment is examined in much more detail in Chapter 4; relevant information also appears in Chapter 7.

RULING CLASSES AND RULING ELITES

On the Eve of Revolution

The Governing Class
In October 1917 Lenin, in a famous justification of his party's imminent seizure of power, argued that as Russia had been governed since the 1905 revolution by 130,000 landowners (*pomeshchiki*), there was no reason why 240,000 Bolsheviks should not be able to rule the country.[1] The change of ruling elites which resulted from the revolution was rather more complex than Lenin suggested.

Lenin may have obtained his figure of 130,000 *pomeshchiki* from the 1905 land census which indicated a total of 133,898 landed estates of 50 desyatinas or more (1 desyatina = 1.09 hectares or 2.70 acres).[2] This includes all private individual holdings by members of all social estates (*sosloviya*), and not just those of the nobility (*dvoryanstvo*).[3] The term '*pomeshchiki*', traditionally used to refer exclusively to landowning members of the nobility (the *pomestnoe dvoryanstvo*, or 'landed gentry'), had come to lose this narrower meaning, as large-scale landownership spread to members of other social estates in the second half of the XIX Century. The 1905 land census recorded 107,247 estates belonging to the nobility, of which just over half (58,170) were over 50 desyatinas in size.[4] The land census counted estates rather than landowners: since some landowners possessed more than one estate, the number of landed gentry families was doubtless somewhat lower than that of estates owned by the nobility.[5] The American historian Seymour Becker estimates that there were 94,500–96,500 noble landowning families in 1912, with an average of 4.5 persons per family, giving a total of about 430,000 individuals.[6]

The connection between landownership and noble status was declining in the last decades of tsarism. A comparison by Korelin, a Soviet historian, of the figures of the 1877 and 1905 land censuses, for 44 provinces of European Russia, shows a reduction in total noble landownership from 68.8 million to 47.8 million desyatinas, and a drop in the number of nobles' estates from 112,628 to 101,323, with the average size of estate falling from 613 to 473 desyatinas.[7] Noble landownership continued to decrease after the 1905 revolution: the American historian Robinson estimated a loss of 10 million desyatinas in 47 provinces of European Russia in the period of 1906–14.[8] Nevertheless, the nobility continued to dominate large land-ownership: the 1905 land census showed that although the 107,247 estates owned by the nobles represented only 14 per cent of the total of 752,881 private landholdings, they comprised 53 million out of the total of 86 million desyatinas of privately owned land.[9]

We cannot, of course, accept at face value Lenin's assumption that the ruling elite of late Imperial Russia consisted exclusively of landowners. If in the XVIII Century there had been a high correlation between noble status, large landownership and high rank in the civil service, these relationships had broken down to a significant extent by the early XX Century. Korelin's analysis of officials in the 24 classes of the Table of Ranks, based on the 1897 census data, shows that men of hereditary noble origin comprised 71.5 per cent of the top four classes, compared with 85 per cent in the mid-XVIII Century.[10] The hereditary noble status of these top officials did not, however, equate with large landownership: in 1902 only 27 per cent of top-ranking officials owned estates of over 100 desyati-nas – a proportion almost exactly half that of 1858.[11] Similar figures were provided by the Soviet historian Zaionchkovskii.[12] He noted, however, that a majority of ministers (58.8 per cent) and members of the State Council (56 per cent) were landowners in the early twentieth century.[13] The association between large landownership and political power at the same period was even more obvious in the case of provincial governors, 71 per cent of whom were *pomeshchiki*.[14]

In the armed forces, men of the noble estate continued to maintain their position, comprising more than 50 per cent of the officer corps as late as 1912, a percentage which had not significantly decreased, and may even have increased slightly, since 1897.[15] The proportion of noble landowners at the top of the armed forces, however, was even lower than in the equivalent ranks of the civil service – 17 per cent in the first four classes in 1903–4.[16]

The landed gentry was seriously attempting in the post-1905 period to adopt more modern forms of political influence, both through parties in the Duma and through the formation of extra-parliamentary pressure groups.[17] The new bourgeoisie, by contrast, although it was increasing enormously in size and wealth while the landed gentry was declining, had failed to establish itself as a significant political force within the tsarist political structure by 1914.[18] Bourgeois parties were weak and divided, and few merchants and industrialists occupied posts in the higher bureaucracy.[19]

The Bourgeoisie

The expansion of industry, trade and finance in the late XIX Century led to the growth of owners of capital whom Soviet scholars classify as the 'big' and 'middle' bourgeoisie (their 'petty' bourgeoisie, by contrast, comprises mainly peasants, artisans and small traders, who owned their means of production, but did not necessarily employ hired labour). The term 'bourgeoisie' as used here will exclude the petty bourgeoisie.

Estimation of the size of the pre-revolutionary bourgeoisie is a complex issue. The 1897 census gives a total of 281,179 members of the merchant estate, with a further 342,947 'honoured citizens' (this was a higher estate which included many senior merchants and industrialists).[20] Much industrial and commercial activity was, however, also conducted by members of the noble estate;[21] the total membership of the 'bourgeoisie', including members of their families, at the end of the XIX Century was undoubtedly significantly greater than 600,000.

The Soviet historian Laverychev attempted to estimate the size of the bourgeoisie in the late XIX Century by extrapolation from the figure of 97,000 merchant certificates issued in 1881 (5,755 certificates of the first guild, and 90,574 annual and 4,405 semi-annual certificates of the second guild). On the assumption that each certificate represented 8–10 persons (including business partners and family members), Laverychev calculated the bourgeoisie in the early 1880s to number between 800,000 and 1,000,000 persons – a figure which he then estimated to have increased to 1,500,000 by the end of the century.[22]

Laverychev's estimates seem to be based on several large and untested assumptions, but they are not entirely inconsistent with data from other sources. I. F. Gindin cited industrial tax statistics for 1912 which show 14,000 enterprises belonging to the 'big' bourgeoisie, and 199,000 belonging to the 'middle' bourgeoisie, a total of 213,000; these figures include 3,500 large industrial enterprises (employing over 200 workers); 10,000 large wholesale businesses; 22,000 medium-sized industrial enterprises (16–200 workers); and 173,000 smaller wholesale businesses and larger retail shops. Gindin did not himself suggest figures for the size of the bourgeoisie; he offered his data simply as an indicator of the number of 'gainfully occupied' members of the bourgeoisie, and as a guide to the ratio of the big to the middle, and of the industrial to the trading bourgeoisie.[23] The ratio of 1:14 for large to medium-sized enterprises in 1912 is, however, remarkably similar to Laverychev's ratio of 1:16 for first-guild to second-guild merchant certificates in 1881, suggesting a constant relationship between the size of the 'big' and the 'middle' bourgeoisie. Furthermore, if Laverychev's ratio of 8–10 persons to each merchant certificate of 1881 is held to apply also to trade and industrial enterprises in 1912, Gindin's figures of 213,000 bourgeois enterprises suggests a total membership of the bourgeoisie of about two million, including family members and partners, on the eve of the war. This is compatible with Laverychev's estimates of one million and 1.5 million in 1881 and 1900 respectively.

The 'Intelligentsia': State Officials and Specialists

In Soviet parlance, the 'intelligentsia' is defined broadly, as those whose occupation involves primarily 'mental labour'. The category therefore includes state officials, as well as other educated specialists and members of the free professions. The 1897 census gives a figure of 43,034 ranking officials in the administrative and judicial departments, and a further 46,453 office clerks, or junior officials.[24] These were state officials in the narrow sense of professional administrators; in addition, many members of professional groups such as teachers and doctors in state employment held civil-service rank. Zaionchkovskii's estimates of 384,000 ranked officials and 130–135,000 office clerks in 1903 seem to relate to civil servants in the broader sense.[25]

An estimate of the total size of the intelligentsia at the end of the XIX Century, based on the 1897 census data, has been provided by L. K. Erman. Erman gives a figure of 725,955 members of the 'civil' intelligentsia, comprising 94,000 persons working in the sphere of material production; 262,654 working in science, art, education and health provision; and 368,411 in state and economic administration; plus a further 52,471 members of the 'military intelligentsia' (mainly army officers) (see Table 1).

Erman does not attempt to provide a global estimate of the size of the intelligentsia in 1914, noting that data are not available for many categories. He does, however, provide figures for certain professional groups (Table 2), as an indicator of the rate of growth of some categories of the intelligentsia. The numbers of primary school teachers increased by at least 70 per cent between 1896 and 1911, and of doctors by 60 per cent, the average annual growth rates in both cases being higher after 1905 than before.[26]

An alternative measure of the size of the professional groups of the population is provided by the numbers of 'specialists' in terms of educational attainment. Here again, we encounter problems of definition and classification.

The 1897 census gives the following figures for the number of people who had attended higher educational establishments (*vuzy*):[27]

Establishments attended	Male	Female	Total
Universities and other	97961	6360	104321
Specialist or technical	29656	619	30275
Higher military	4181	0	4181
Total	131798	6979	138777

These census figures, as Leikina-Svirskaya has pointed out,[28] do not refer to those who have actually graduated, but to the wider category of all those members of the population who had ever attended higher educational establishments, so they include those who were still studying in 1897 as well as those who had left without graduating. Nevertheless, they constitute the best indication available of the number of people with higher education in the population at the end of the XIX Century.

Leikina-Svirskaya has attempted to count the number of actual graduates. Incomplete data record a total of about 85,000 graduates from the nine universities plus a number of other *vuzy* in the period from about 1860 to 1900.[29] The number of graduates increased markedly after 1900. In over forty years between 1859 and 1900 Russian universities produced over 60,000 graduates, but a further 40,800 graduated in the fourteen years 1900–13.[30] The growth rate of the output of the technical *vuzy* was considerably greater: these produced 11,830 graduates in 1860–1900, and a further 18,356 in 1901–17.[31] Graduates of other higher educational establishments also increased rapidly after 1900, but figures here are fragmentary: the expansion of higher courses for women was, however, particularly striking.[32] Many post-1860 graduates had of course died or retired by 1914, but Leikina-Svirskaya's figures, taken together with the census data for higher education, suggest that the official Soviet estimate of a total of 136,000 specialists with higher education still active in the economy in 1913 (1939 frontiers) may be roughly correct.[33]

The number of students in higher education was increasing in the years before 1913, but here again the figures are problematic. Official figures for 1902/3 indicate 42,884 students in 55 institutions.[34] A later official series shows an increase from 37,894 students in 41 institutions in 1905 to 73,321 students in 59 institutions in 1913.[35]

Soviet statistical handbooks of the 1930s give a figure of 124,700 students in 91 *vuzy* in 1914/15.[36] More recent Soviet sources, however, state that there were 91 *vuzy* with 127,400 students in 1914/15 on present-day Soviet territory.[37] A figure of 105 institutions in 1914 (presumably for Imperial Russian territory) is supplied by Leikina-Svirskaya, who comments, however:

Among those were incomparable quantities: famous universities and institutes – centres of Russian science – and small educational

> establishments with a specialised profile; state *vuzy* with full status,
> and private ones which did not give their graduates any rights [of entry
> into state service]; ancient ones and recently formed ones which did
> not as yet have either any history or any statistics[!].[38]

It is not clear how the Soviet statistical handbooks derive their estimates of
student numbers for 1914/15; but it is interesting that they appear to regard
these estimates relating to the 91 (or 105) institutions as the appropriate
base for comparison with student numbers in the 1920s, rather than the
lower figure supplied by the official tsarist statistical series, which presumably covered only those establishments whose degrees were officially
recognised and which enjoyed higher academic status.

During the war, the main change in the composition and size of the élite
resulted from the expansion of the officer corps. Between April 1914 and
January 1917 the number of army officers increased from 40,590 to
145,916, with 62,847 losses by January 1917, indicating that about 170,000
young men became officers during the war. Many of these new officers
were recruited from other élite social groups, but most were the products
of emergency training in the ensign schools, whose students tended to have
non-élite backgrounds, and which turned out as many as 40,000 officers in a
year.[39]

The Post-revolutionary Transformation

The Bourgeoisie
This part of the chapter should begin with a blank sub-section, to com-
memorate the disappearance of the landowning class and the big bourgeoisie during the revolution and civil war, and the final collapse of the
estate system. The estimates cited in the preceding section indicated a
pre-revolutionary membership of about half a million for the landowning
class (noble and non-noble, including families) and about 125,000 for the
'big' bourgeoisie. A large proportion of these, and a smaller proportion of
the 'middle' bourgeoisie, may well have emigrated or been killed by 1921.
It is more difficult to judge what proportion of the intelligentsia was lost in
these ways. It seems likely that many of them remained to serve the new
Soviet government.[40] We can only speculate about their motives, which
probably included a professional commitment on the part of officialdom to
serving the state *qua* state, regardless of its political complexion; a more
populist ethos, characteristic of the pre-revolutionary *zemstvo* 'third element' which viewed the role of the professions as service to the people
rather than to the state; and genuine or opportunistic conversion to
Bolshevism.

In assessing the degree of continuity between the élites of pre and
post-revolutionary Russia, it is important to bear in mind the uneven

geographical and ethnic or national distribution of certain élite characteristics in the Empire. In 1897 40 per cent of the hereditary nobility of
European Russia (though not necessarily of noble landowners) lived in the
nine western provinces, and ethnic Poles comprised 26.2 per cent of the
hereditary nobility.[41] Lithuanians and Germans were also disproportionately represented in the hereditary nobility.[42] Educational qualifications
also tended to be higher in the western provinces than in the rest of the
Empire.[43] The proportion of these elements of the old élite lost through
emigration or territorial changes after 1917 would certainly have been
high.

The new social and political structure which emerged during the 1920s
was profoundly influenced by the transformation wrought by revolution
and civil war. The revolution flattened the top and extended the sides of
the steep pre-revolutionary social pyramid. In the countryside, private
peasant farming continued, but much greater equality prevailed than
before the revolution. In trade and in small-scale industry, some private
businessmen prospered, but only 76,000 persons were recorded as employing any kind of hired labour in the whole 'non-agricultural sector' even
in 1926/27, the NEP year in which they were most numerous; and of this
total only 30,000 were classified as 'middle and large capitalists'.[44] In
Moscow, the number of factory owners declined from 1,791 in 1912 to 145
in 1926, and the number of owners of small-scale industry who were
employers of labour from 20,600 to 2,800.[45] The recorded earnings of the
top 30,000 private entrepreneurs were substantially greater than average
earnings, amounting to 7,352 rubles a year as compared with 729 rubles for
the non-agricultural population as a whole.[46] These may have been under-
estimates. But the average incomes of private entrepreneurs were certainly
lower, and their opportunities for accumulating wealth far more limited,
than those of entrepreneurs before the revolution.

Specialists and Officials

If the old tsarist estates and the new capitalist entrepreneurial classes had
almost completely evaporated, the new ruling élite – consisting largely of
senior party and state officials and economic managers – as yet existed only
in embryonic form; it was far more modest in its way of life than the
leading noble and entrepreneurial families of tsarist Russia. This was most
clearly shown by the decline in the number of domestic servants from well
over one and a half millions in 1897 to 339,000 in 1926/27.[47] Even in
Moscow, in spite of the large increase in the number of senior government
officials and professional people consequent upon the shift of the capital
from Petrograd in 1918, the number of domestic servants declined by 57
per cent between 1912 and 1926.[48]

No reliable comparison between the number of leading officials and
specialists in the mid-1920s and in 1913 has been possible; accurate data for

1913 are lacking. But such figures as are available indicate a net increase in the number of trained specialists. While some members of the professional classes emigrated in the first few years after the revolution, many more were trained. In 1914/15, there were already 124,700 undergraduate students in tsarist Russia (see p. 33 above). The number of students increased during the civil war and, although it declined in the early 1920s, remained substantially greater than before the revolution.[49] Some 90,800 students graduated in the four years 1924–7.[50] The official claim that the total number of graduates increased from 136,000 in 1913 to 233,000 in 1928 is therefore not implausible.[51] This does not, of course, indicate the comparative quality after 1914 which, in conditions of war and revolution and their aftermath, may well have declined.

Taking senior administrators, managers, and specialists together, the administrative and professional élite in the Soviet Union in the mid-1920s nevertheless, as before the revolution, constituted a tiny minority of the population. According to the returns of the 1926 census, it amounted to only about half a million persons out of a total working population of 86,200,000. This included 311,854 in 'leading posts' (senior administrators and managers of enterprises and their deputies) and 167,065 persons in specialist posts classified as 'higher technical' and 'higher'.[52] With the promotion of former workers and others, many of those employed in both 'leading' and 'specialist' posts were 'practicals' without higher education. A survey of 3,554 administrators and technical staff in higher posts at certain major factories and industrial building sites in 1929 revealed that 916, or 25.8 per cent of the total, were practicals.[53]

The influence of the social revolution on the social composition of the administration is striking. In his recent study of the tsarist and NEP administrations Rowney correctly points out that in the 1920s 'a large proportion of the total civil administrative workforce consisted of workers and peasants'.[54] In 1929 of a civil administration amounting in total to 825,000 persons, 152,000 (18.4 per cent) were of working-class and 198,000 (24.0 per cent) of peasant origin.[55]

At the highest level, personnel employed before the revolution had largely been eliminated from the administration. A comprehensive survey of 10,832 persons employed in the Central Executive Committee (TsIK) and in all-Union commissariats in October 1929 revealed that only 1,178 (10.9 per cent) were employed in state service before the revolution.[56] A careful study by Rowney concludes that 'comparisons of commissariat officeholders in the 1920s as listed in capital city directories, with those that appear in service lists (*spiski*), rank (*chin*) registers, and professional registers of 1911 through 1916 indicate virtually no holdovers from the high-rank categories in provincial administration'.[57]

Nevertheless, in the first decade after 1917, the effects of the social revolution on the social composition and political complexion of senior officials and specialists were limited in a number of respects. First, the workers' revolution had not yet brought about workers' predominance in high office. The survey of October 1929 revealed that most of those who replaced the pre-revolutionary staff were from the middle classes: only 11.9 per cent were former workers, and a further 4.5 per cent children of former workers. The percentage was somewhat greater in the very highest administrative posts, but reached 39 per cent only for the lowest groups in the hierarchy, janitors, cleaners and other ancillary personnel (*mladshii obsluzhivayushchii personal*). With the exception of the ancillary personnel, all grades were dominated by former white-collar workers, and their children.[58]

Secondly, there were very few women in administrative or specialist posts. Only 23,700 (or 7.6 per cent) of the 311,900 'leading' posts recorded in the December 1926 census were occupied by women and among the higher ranks the proportion was much lower still. In industry, the proportion of women in administrative and specialist posts was also very low: only 597 of the 37,898 leading posts (1.6 per cent) and 392 of the 16,517 higher technical posts (2.4 per cent) were occupied by women.[59]

Thirdly, while a substantial proportion of leading posts was held by party members, party membership among graduates was insignificant. The 1929 survey of administrative and technical staff in industry showed that only 5.2 per cent of those with higher education were party members.[60] In the mid-1920s the proportion would have been even lower. But as many as 10.7 per cent were classified as 'alien to us in their political complexion'.[61] In 1927/28 qualified engineers working in industry included a mere 139 party members, and only 12 of these worked in the mining industry.[62]

Finally, the obvious point should be made that the social composition of the administration does not adequately indicate the influence of the pre-revolutionary personnel. A 1929 survey of industrial staff in higher posts revealed that of 1,819 with higher education, 872 had qualified before the revolution; 124 of these were former factory owners or directors, and their influence on economic decisions must have been considerable.[63]

SOCIETY IN FLUX

The social transformation of the mass of the population in XX Century Russia is strikingly reflected in changes in educational levels and in occupational structure; in this section we set out the data which demonstrate these changes.

Mass Education

By the end of the XIX Century secondary as well as higher education was the prerogative of a small minority of the population. According to the population census of 1897, only 1,245,366, 42 per cent of them women, had attended any kind of secondary education.[64] In the early XX Century the numbers in all types of educational establishments grew rapidly. An official tsarist statistical series shown an increase from 190,829 pupils in 1,683 specialist secondary and primary schools in 1905, to 268,657 pupils in 2,477 schools in 1913.[65] The same series gives figures of 498,528 pupils in 1,738 general secondary schools, and 6,993,862 pupils in 108,254 primary schools at the beginning of 1913, a total of 7,492,390.[66]

According to the 1897 census, there were 26,569,585 literate persons in the Empire, or 21.2 per cent of the population; 29.3 per cent of males and only 13.1 per cent of females were literate.[67] The expansion of primary education after 1905 resulted in a marked increase in literacy: Rashin has estimated that the literacy of the total population increased from 21 per cent in 1897 to 30 per cent in 1913, with the level for the population aged 8 and over reaching 38–39 per cent on the eve of the war.[68] In line with patterns elsewhere, literacy in pre-revolutionary Russia was higher for males than for females, for the urban than the rural population, and for those aged 10–29 than for other age cohorts.[69] The proposed universal primary education for children aged 8–11 had not been fully introduced by 1917; a recent Western study suggests that 'there was a probability of about 70 per cent that a child growing up in the Empire in the decade before World War I should attend school for at least a year'.[70]

In the first decade after the revolution, 'secondary specialised' education – which encompassed technicians, midwives and others of similar skills – expanded very rapidly. According to the official statistics, the number of pupils in secondary specialised technical colleges (*tekhnikumy*) of various kinds, and in the *rabfaki* (the 'workers' faculties' providing adult education), increased from 48,000 in 1914/15 to as many as 236,000 in 1928.[71] In consequence, the total number of persons with secondary specialised education also rose rapidly, from 54,000 in 1913 to 288,000 in 1928.[72] The percentage of party members was much higher at this level of qualification than among graduates. In the 25 factories and sites surveyed in 1929, 17.5 per cent of the 1,487 persons with secondary specialised education were party members or candidates, and a further 3.8 per cent belonged to the Komsomol. Not surprisingly, the highest percentage of party members and candidates, 29.2 per cent, was found among the 4,062 practicals without any specialised education.[73]

At the bottom of the educational ladder, 48.9 per cent of the population were recorded as illiterate in the 1926 census, a substantial drop as compared with 1913.[74] The increase in the number of children attending school during the last decades of the tsarist period continued after 1917, with a brief break in the early 1920s. The total number of schoolchildren in attendance increased from 7,801,000 in 1914/15 (including children at church schools) to 10,727,000 in 1926/27; the number in forms 5–10 (roughly 12–17 years olds) increased from 565,000 to 1,205,000.[75] Young workers entering industrial and other occupations in the 1920s were more literate than the older generation: in 1929 13.9 per cent of all workers in census industry were illiterate, but the percentage varied from 30.9 per cent for those aged 40 and over to only 5.2 per cent for those under 23. But the educational level of factory workers, though rising, was not high; in 1929 the average worker had attended school for 3.5 years, the average worker under 23 years of age for 4.3 years. The proportion of illiterates was higher among women and among workers in those industries which involve a great deal of unskilled manual labour. Thus the percentage of illiterates was higher in the textile industries, employing a high proportion of women, and in the coal industry, than in metal-working and engineering.[76]

The Occupational Structure

Between 1860 and 1913, according to a Soviet estimate, the numbers employed in census industry, in building and on the railways increased from 1,161,000 to 5,415,000.[77] The expansion in the number of other wage-earners, including those employed in trade, and as day-labourers and porters, was equally rapid, rising from 800,000 to 4,065,000.[78] The largest single group in the latter category were the domestic and household servants, amounting to as much as 40 per cent or more of the total.

The estimation of the size of the labour-force in various sectors of the economy, in a manner that permits meaningful comparisons with the 1920s, raises many serious problems. The last and only complete pre-revolutionary population census was conducted in 1897. The 1897 census is not, however, particularly informative on the occupational structure of the Empire. The tables on occupation in the two summary volumes of census data break down the population into 65 main categories, corresponding to sectors of the economy, but do not provide any analysis of the nature of the occupation, nor the levels of responsibility, skill or education involved.[79]

1897 is not, of course, the most satisfactory base from which to compare the late tsarist period with NEP. The two decades which separated the census from the revolution were a period of rapid social and economic change, but we have reliable figures for these years only for certain categories of industrial employment, notably those covered by the Factory Inspectorate.

Comparisons of the social structure of the tsarist empire in 1913 with that of NEP in anything other than the most impressionistic fashion are therefore fraught with dangers. Such an exercise was undertaken by a Soviet statistician, B. A. Gukhman, in 1926.[80] In an Appendix (pp. 45–6 below) his estimates are discussed, and compared with other estimates, notably Rashin's for 1913 and the population census for December 1926.

From these various estimates it may be concluded that the occupational

structure of the population at the time of the 1926 census was approximately the same as in 1913. The total population had increased from 138 to
147 million (see Chapter 1). Virtually all of this increase had occurred in
the countryside, where the population had risen from 113 to 122 million
persons. Owing to the post-revolutionary division of peasant households,
the number of peasant households had increased much more rapidly than
the rural population, from some 18.7 million in 1914 to about 24 million in
the spring of 1927.[81] The number of agricultural labourers, however, had
declined sharply (see Table 3).

The population engaged in non-agricultural activities included some
members of the peasant households, and some state employees living in
the countryside, but both in 1913 and in the mid-1920s primarily lived in
the towns, permanently or seasonally.[82] The urban population at the time
of the 1926 census amounted to 26.3 million persons, as compared to an
estimated 24.8 millions in 1913. As the data in Table 3 shows, among those
engaged in non-agricultural activities, the number employed in large-scale
industry was approximately the same as in 1913, and the number employed
on the railways had substantially increased. But the number engaged in
artisan industry and construction (in terms of full-time equivalents) and in
trade had substantially declined, while the number of servicemen was only
about half the 1913 level, and the number of persons employed in various
kinds of domestic labour was less than a quarter of the pre-war level. The
number of unemployed on the other hand had more than doubled (see
Chapter 4). Little is known about the change in the total numbers engaged
in other activities, including office-work, and the education, health and
social services, owing to the lack of data for 1913; this whole topic requires
much further study.

It should be borne in mind that for some sectors of the economy the
tsarist system reached its highest levels of employment not in 1913 but
some time early in 1917. Figures for the tsarist economy during the war
period are even more problematic than those relating to peace-time, in
view of the losses of territory and movements of population involved. The
best estimate, by Mints, is that the total number employed in large-scale
industry was 2,439,000 in 1913, 2,865,000 in 1916 and 2,550,000 or
2,641,000 in 1926/27.[83] Rashin similarly estimates that employment in
large-scale industry increased during the war by about 16 per cent over
1913 levels, the highest rates of increase being achieved in coalmining (74.5
per cent) and the metal industries (69 per cent).[84] Thus large-scale industry
had not regained its 1916 and 1917 employment levels even in 1928.

THE WORKING CLASS IN TRANSITION

With the rapid recovery of industry, transport and other non-agricultural
sectors of the economy, the numbers employed in these sectors expanded

rapidly from the low level of 1920–1. Many, perhaps most, of those recruited to industry in 1922–5 had worked there before the revolution: a 1929 survey recorded that 50.7 per cent of all workers began work in industry before 1917.[85] This was in considerable part a second-generation working class, and a working class which had lost close connections with the countryside in the form of land holding.[86] But of the workers starting work in industry in 1926–7 as many as 54 per cent were previously engaged in agriculture, most of them as peasants, some as agricultural labourers.[87] And in the largely seasonal building industry, as before the revolution, workers were closely tied to the land.[88]

The industrial workers were the heroes of the October revolution and its major beneficiaries. Between 1917 and the mid-1920s their political strength greatly diminished. Many politically-active party and Komsomol members were promoted out of the ranks of the working class to official positions; and ever since 1917 the party authorities had circumscribed and destroyed any political opposition which sought to base itself on the working-class interest. The workers had effectively lost their hard-won right to strike; the penalties against strikers were already more severe than before the revolution. By the mid-1920s the Soviet working class had virtually ceased to be engaged in the stormy political activities, or exercise the political initiative, which distinguished it in 1917. But in other respects the revolution had brought a vast enhancement in the status of the industrial workers, in their rights and privileges, and in their material position relative to the peasants, the professional classes and the minor officials. At the place of work, it brought new organisations and new practices. Nearly all industrial and railway workers, and even most permanent building workers, belonged to trade unions. According to the party census, on January 1, 1927, nearly one industrial worker in ten, and at least one transport worker in thirteen, were party members or candidates, as compared with one qualified industrial engineer in 100, and one peasant in 650.[89] The proportion of party members varied widely between different industries, ranging from 13.5 per cent in the oil industry to 6.2 per cent in the textile industry; surprisingly, it tended to be smaller in the larger factories.[90] But virtually every worker must have been personally acquainted with a party member.

The trade unions and the party cells drew factory personnel closely into the political and administrative system, acting both as agents of higher authority and, to a diminishing extent, as representatives of the workers. During the industrial difficulties of 1926, they played an important role in imposing the 'regime of economy' on the workers, and some role in its subsequent relaxation.[91] But they also guarded workers against the depredations of managers, and protected them from arbitrary dismissal. As compared with pre-revolutionary times, the authority over the worker of the factory engineer and the foreman, if not of the factory manager, had considerably diminished.[92]

The enhanced status of the worker brought important material changes, including greater equality of income not only between masses and rulers but also within the industrial working class itself. The differentiation in earnings between higher-paid and lower-paid workers declined substantially between 1914 and 1928.[93] This was the result of deliberate policy. Strenuous efforts to narrow differentials between skills during the civil war gave way in the early 1920s to some increase in differentiation, but at the end of 1926 a new drive was launched for wage equalisation (*vyravnivanie*) between skilled and unskilled.[94]

War and revolution also brought wider job opportunities and less economic inequality to women workers. As in other belligerent countries, the war considerably widened the range of jobs accessible to women, and in 1914–18 female employment increased rapidly as a percentage of all workers in census industry. After declining in the first two years of NEP, it then increased steadily between 1923/24 and 1926/27, but did not recover to its wartime peak.[95] Simultaneously, the wage gap tended to narrow between industries dominated by men, such as metalworking and mining, and industries in which the percentage of women was substantial, such as textiles and food.[96] The narrowing of the gap was partly due to the introduction of equal pay for equal work, accomplished in the Soviet Union earlier than in any other country.[97] A careful study of Soviet data by an American economist shows a substantial but irregular rise in the daily wages of women relative to those of men between 1914 and 1928; in the eight industries studied the increase varied between 1.8 and 23.3 percentage points.[98] But the relative improvement in women's wages was also partly and perhaps mainly due to the fact that it was easier in conditions of NEP to raise prices and pay higher wages in the consumer industries, where most women worked.[99]

But perhaps the most important reform in working conditions for everyone employed by the state was the introduction of the eight-hour day, the call for which was emblazoned on the banners of every European socialist party.[100] The normal length of the working day declined by over 20 per cent from 9.9 hours in 1913 to 7.8 hours in 1928.[101] On the occasion of the tenth anniversary of the revolution in 1927 further legislation authorised the gradual introduction of the seven-hour day.[102]

The pleasures of increased leisure resulting from the reduced working day were moderated by the fear of being condemned to an enforced life of complete leisure through unemployment. Even on the narrow definition used in the population census of December 1926, unemployment amounted to some 9 per cent of the employed population; and numbers increased continuously throughout the 1920s (see Chapter 4). No reliable estimate of unemployment before the revolution is available: the estimate of a Soviet economist, an average of 400–500,000 in 1909–13, is certainly less than half the number of unemployed in the Soviet Union in 1928 by the same definition.

In contrast to the situation in Western Europe and the United States, the prime cause of unemployment in the USSR was not economic depression. The number of employed persons increased from 6.7 to 10.4 millions between 1924/25 and 1929, sufficient to absorb more than the natural increase in the able-bodied urban population.[103] But the growth in employment was outweighed by the continuous pressure of the migration of adult labour from country to town; according to Soviet estimates, annual net migration increased from one-third of a million to nearly one million people a year during 1923–6.[104] The reasons for the huge increase in rural–urban migration compared with the pre-revolutionary period have not yet been satisfactorily elucidated. But the growth of job opportunities, and the high prestige of the town, and of urban labour, must have played a major part.

Unemployment was a constant reproach to the authorities, an urgent reminder that the New Economic Policy was grounded in the capitalist economies of the market. It provided one of the most telling Left Opposition criticisms of official policies. The drive to support industrialisation by economy and rationalisation increased productivity and necessarily reduced employment possibilities, and sometimes resulted in an increase in unemployment. Until the very end of the 1920s it seemed to all concerned that the early stages of Soviet industrialisation might alleviate, but could not eliminate, mass unemployment.

CONCLUSIONS

XX Century Russia, both before and after the revolution, was a society in flux. The complex traditional structure of 'estates' (*sosloviya*) and 'ranks', established from the XVII Century, was disrupted in the course of the XIX Century by the rise of the market, of towns and of industry. The rise of the professions and of private industry and trade offered alternative career structures to the official ranks of the army and the civil service. By 1914 members of the nobility were to be found among factory-owners, lawyers, or even professional revolutionaries, as well as among the large land-owners. The ruling classes, and the élites associated with them, were more numerous and more complicated than at the time of the serf reform of 1861. The 1917 revolution and the civil war which followed it saw the dramatic overturn of this whole ruling structure and its replacement by a new one.

Simultaneously, at the other end of the social scale, peasants flooded into the towns, and into the factories and building sites outside the towns, to form the basis of a new industrial working class which was not recognised by the list of estates. Many workers living permanently in the towns were therefore registered as 'peasants': between 1881 and 1910 the number of 'peasants' in St Petersburg increased from 390,000 to 1,310,000, but the number of members of all other estates increased only from 408,000 to 596,000.[105] The creation of a proletariat in the marxist sense, employed in large-scale industry, building and on the railways, was accompanied by an equally rapid expansion of a vast variety of small traders, labourers, porters, domestic servants and others, catering for the economic and personal needs of the rest of the urban population. In the decade after 1917, these proletarian and non-proletarian urban masses were first greatly reduced in number under the impact of civil war and hunger in the towns, and then expanded again to approximately their pre-war size by the time of the population census of December 1926, but with a very different structure. The Bolshevik revolution was conducted in the name of and with support from proletariat. In spite of the travails and disillusionments of the post-revolutionary years, the proletariat of 1926/27 retained a higher status in NEP society, in practice as well as in theory, than in the far-off Russian Empire of 1913.

Appendix: Estimates of the Occupational Structure in 1913 and in the mid-1920s

Gukhman's estimates (see Table 3) were published in the Gosplan journal in the summer of 1926. Gukhman took as his starting point the data of the 1897 census on the occupational structure of the Empire, and updated them for 1913 on the basis of a number of more or less crudely estimated coefficients, calculated to show the effects of demographic and economic growth in the intervening years. Then, having adjusted his 1913 estimates to take into account the post-revolutionary territorial changes, he used them as a base for comparison with the occupational structure of Soviet Russia in the economic years 1922/23 to 1924/25. (His figures for the Soviet period were calculated from the 1923 urban census, the official employment statistics for hired labour, and tax data.) Table 3 shows Gukhman's figures for 1913 and 1924/25, together with data from the 1926 census. Table 4 combines Gukhman's data and the census date for hired labour with those of the official Gosplan labour statistics for 1924/25 to 1928, published in 1936.

The different series for the 1920s in Tables 3 and 4 are most compatible for large-scale industry and for transport; and least compatible for agriculture, small-scale industry and construction. Gukhman's calculations showed that employment in transportation as a whole had overtaken the 1913 level as early as the economic year 1922/23, and exceeded it by 6.4 per cent in 1924/25. Table 4 shows that wage labour in large-scale industry had reached the 1913 level by the time of the 1926 census, and exceeded it in the economic year 1926/27. (This is compatible with the incomplete but more detailed data presented in Table 33.)

The difference in the total number occupied in agriculture between Gukhman's figures for 1924/25 and the 1926 census (Table 3) is obviously not a real increase, but is due to inconsistency in the definition of the 'economically active' members of a peasant household. Gukhman himself recalculated the 1897 census figures for agricultural employment on the basis of his assumption that able-bodied members of a household aged between 15 and 55/60 were engaged in productive labour,[106] and his 1924/25 estimates were evidently based on the same criteria. The 1926 census data, however, included children between 10 and 15 years, women over 55 and men over 60.[107] If we were able to make the appropriate adjustments for the differences in the age-groups covered, the figure for 1926 would be slightly higher than Gukhman's estimate for 1924/25.

The figures for small-scale industry and construction are particularly problematic. Both before the revolution and in the 1920s, the prevalence of part-time and seasonal employment in these sectors of the economy made the calculation of labour statistics especially difficult. Gukhman's estimate is that total employment in small artisan industry in 1924/25 was 2,114,000 – 58.9 per cent of his 1913 figure of 3,590,000. But another source – a Soviet census of small-scale industry – recorded a total figure of 3½ million at the end of 1926.[108] The figure, however, included part-time artisans; it is consistent with the population census of December 1926, which recorded 1,866,000 engaged in small-scale industry as a main and 1,804,358 as a secondary occupation, a total of 3,670,000, of which 333,000 were hired workers.[109] Gukhman's estimates for 1913 appear to be derived from the 1897 census figures for main occupation, so that the figures in Table 3 evidently exclude those for whom artisan production was a secondary occupation. The best estimate of the number of persons engaged in small-scale industry in terms of full-time equivalents (i.e., including an appropriate allowance for part-time workers) is considerably lower in absolute figures than the data in Table 3: 2–2¼ millions in 1913 and 1½ millions or more in 1926/27 (see Table 35 below and Notes to the table). Thus there was evidently a real decline in employment in this sector, though probably not as great as Gukhman suggests.

In construction, the data in the 1926 census illustrate the difficulties in estimating accurately the numbers involved. The census records 364,000 engaged in construction under construction as a branch of the economy; but this figure increases to 542,000 if we include those engaged in building under the auspices of industry, the railways and other branches of the economy. But even this is only those engaged in construction as a main occupation; in addition 482,000 were recorded as engaged in construction as their first auxiliary activity, making 1,024,168 in all. This figure includes unskilled workers but excludes general labourers (*chernorabochie*).[110] Gukhman's figures for 1913 are derived by a heroic guess from the figures for main occupation in the 1897 census. It seems likely that the right comparison is therefore between Gukhman's 965,000 for 1913 and the census figure of 542,000 in December 1926.[111] But this is extremely uncertain territory.

Gukhman's 1913 figures are more consistent with the census and employment figures for the 1920s than are those of A. G. Rashin, the Soviet authority on pre-revolutionary demography and labour most frequently cited by Western historians. Table 5 compares Rashin's and Gukhman's estimates of certain major categories of hired labour in 1913. While their figures are more or less identical for agriculture, large-scale industry, rail transport, communications and domestic servants, Rashin's estimates for small-scale industry, construction and water transport are two and a half to three times as great as Gukhman's. We have already noted that these categories are amongst the most difficult to estimate: the discrepancies can largely be attributed to the fact that Rashin, unlike Gukhman, has included seasonal and part-time workers in his estimates, but without recalculating them in terms of full-time equivalents. In any event, Rashin's definitions of categories of 'hired labour' do not appear to be directly comparable to those employed by Soviet statisticians in the 1920s.

3 Socio-economic Differentiation of the peasantry
Stephan Merl

THEORIES AND EVIDENCE

This chapter has two purposes: first, to compare the level of differentiation among the peasantry in 1909–13 and the mid-1920s; and secondly, to examine the trend within each of these periods. Special emphasis is given to regional differences. After a discussion of the problem of assessing differentiation, the second section deals with differentiation by farm size, and the third section with the effect of off-farm income as a measure of differentiation.

Rival Theories

There are two strongly opposing views about differentiation in the Russian peasantry: the 'marxist' concept of class differentiation and the 'populist' or 'neo-populist' concept, which stresses the homogeneity of the peasantry. The marxist interpretation was presented by Lenin in *Development of Capitalism in Russia* (1899), an attack on the populists.[1] Using budget studies and censuses compiled by the *zemstvos* (rural local councils),[2] Lenin grouped rural households by sown area and horse and livestock numbers, to show that land and capital were not equally distributed, and that a small group of larger farms controlled the bulk of the means of production. In short, the peasantry was highly differentiated in terms of farm size and wealth. Lenin, rejecting the view of the populists, claimed that differentiation was not constrained by the *obshchina* (rural commune which periodically redistributed land according to the number of 'souls'); in reality the Russian peasantry was decomposing into classes. According to Lenin, a steadily growing number of peasant farms were deprived of their independent access to the means of production, while land and capital became concentrated in the hands of a small group of 'capitalist' farms. Following Lenin, several studies in the 1920s similarly viewed the Soviet peasantry as divided into classes (or claimed that classes were in the process of formation).[3]

In line with the populist philosophy of a special peasant tradition and culture, the 'neo-populist' Chayanov challenged this marxist interpretation.

His theory of the peasant mode of production viewed the family with its able-bodied members as the basic production unit in agriculture.[4] Chayanov's argument was based on new evidence on differentiation drawn from 'dynamic studies'.[5] These studies charted the mobility of peasant households over time by surveying *all* households in certain villages twice. The second survey was at least one and often several years after the first, and revealed that many households had changed their economic position. Many households with small sown areas increased their sown land, but the majority of those households which had large sown areas reduced it. A certain number of households in the first survey had undergone 'substantive changes' such as partition (division between family members), merger, death or emigration, and thus no longer existed as separate entities in the village.[6] These results revealed strong upward and downward mobilities when households were grouped by size of sown area, and this pattern did not fit at all into the marxist picture of progressive and permanent differentiation. Chayanov explained his findings by using the notion of 'cyclical mobility': peasant farms followed the biological cycle of birth, maturity, marriage, growth of children, ageing and death; and the movement between different stages of poverty and wealth was explained by the changing ratio during the family life cycle between the total membership of the household and the number of working members of the household (the 'consumer/worker ratio'); the younger households had more dependent 'consumers' per worker.[7] Budget studies showed that young families made up a significantly larger percentage of groups with smaller sown areas.[8]

In summary, differentiation was seen either as the polarisation of the peasantry into classes (marxist interpretation), or as a trend towards independent family farms (neo-populist interpretation).

Since the 1960s Western historians have largely agreed that there is little evidence to support the view of a full-blooded 'capitalist differentiation' in the peasantry, either in the pre-war period or during NEP, though most have accepted that a process of economic differentiation was occurring both before the first world war and in the 1920s.[9] Even Soviet historians are more cautious on this subject today.[10] The publication of Shanin's *The Awkward Class* in 1972, however, reopened the dispute.[11] Expanding on the arguments of Chayanov, Shanin identified 'centrifugal' and 'centripetal' trends in household mobility underlying the process of differentiation. The peasants' response to differentiation caused by the cumulative effects of economic advantage or disadvantage was first of all by household partition and, secondly, by redistribution of land within the commune. Shanin thus postulated multi-directional mobility in peasant households based on a special peasant mode of production, a form of mobility which thus limited class division. Shanin's book was sharply criticised by Western marxists.[12] Harrison, for example, speculated whether the continual repartitioning of farms, the most important centripetal trend in the analyses of

Chayanov and Shanin, was really 'dysfunctional' for economic growth and the accumulation of wealth.[13]

Measuring Differentiation

The basic criterion of socio-economic differentiation used in this chapter is 'wealth'. Since all three available sets of statistics (agricultural censuses, budget studies and 'dynamic studies') give data primarily related to household size, this raises the problem of whether the wealth of the household correlates with its size. Things are further complicated because available data, especially the censuses, include *all* rural households, regardless of whether or not they are engaged in agriculture. Our sources even include households merely registered in the village – even though all household members may have been away from the village for a substantial time. To examine the question of 'class differentiation' in the peasantry, therefore, information on household wealth alone is not sufficient; we also have to look at production relations among farms, but this raises further difficulties. To give one example: only a farm living on 'exploitation of others' – e.g., hiring of labour – could really be called a 'capitalist' farm in the strict marxist sense. But unfortunately the term 'capitalist farm' is often used to describe any farm producing for the market.

In analysing differentiation trends it is useful to consider at least four different possibilities:

1. A general decline in wealth (shift downward) – i.e., the number of poor households increases, and the number of wealthy households decreases
2. A general increase in wealth (shift upwards) – i.e., the number of poor households decreases, the number of wealthy households increases.

Within these two trends, two processes could occur:

3. Levelling – i.e., the share of both wealthy and poor households decreases
4. Polarisation – i.e., the share of both wealthy and poor households increases, and of middle households decreases.

Regional Differences

This chapter also considers variations in differentiation between principal agricultural zones. European Russia may be roughly divided into the fertile Black-Earth zone in the South and South-East and the less fertile (Non-Black-Earth) zone of the centre and the North-West. The Non-Black-Earth zone did not produce enough grain for local needs. The Black-Earth zone[14] produced significant grain surpluses. Average per capita holdings of arable land in the Black-Earth zone (with the exception of the Central Black-Earth region itself, which was strongly overpopulated and was an area of crisis during the whole period under consideration[15]) were at least twice the per capita holdings in the non-Black-Earth zone. In both zones, as compared with Western Europe, the land was farmed 'extensively', with lower yields. Agriculture was slightly more diversified in the Non-Black-Earth than in the Black-Earth zone, where grain was often the only crop (monoculture).[16]

DIFFERENTIATION OF RURAL HOUSEHOLDS BY FARM SIZE

The Level of Differentiation Before 1914

A comprehensive analysis of differentiation in 1909–13 is not possible because the first complete survey, covering all peasant farms, was not undertaken until 1916.[17] Before 1914 detailed agrarian censuses covered only single districts, primarily in European Russia; between 1870 and 1913 most districts were surveyed only once.[18] Differentiation between farms may be measured in terms of sown area, number of horses or livestock, use of hired labour, and ownership of agricultural machinery. Whichever criterion is used, all pre-1914 censuses show the same important pattern of differentiation: family size correlated strongly with farm size or farm wealth. Differentiation among households was therefore less if the measurement was undertaken in per capita terms rather than simply per household. The different surveys show somewhat different degrees of differentiation. Land-allotment per capita climbs only slowly from the lower to the upper strata. Differentiation was more pronounced among households as measured by 'total land per capita' (including leased land and private land), the number of horses or livestock per capita, and the amount of day-labour hired. The concentration of workers hired for at least one month and of land leased by the upper groups was even greater, and concentration was strongest for the ownership of improved agricultural machinery and the amount of purchased land per capita. For example, the upper strata had about twice as much allotted land per capita as the lower strata, but they hired about four-fifths of all agricultural labourers and owned practically all improved machinery.[19] Obviously, capital was distributed quite unequally among rural households in the pre-1914 period.

The only data allowing direct comparison with the 1920s are statistics on the number of horses or cows per household, and so our discussion focuses on these data. In 1912, 31.4 per cent of rural households in European Russia did not possess a work horse, while 6.8 per cent of rural households owned four and more (see Table 6). These figures, however, overstate the share of households without a work animal, because oxen were frequently used as work animals, especially in the South and in the Volga region. The share of households without a work animal was significantly higher in most parts of the Black-Earth zone – as many as 35 per cent of those households actually living in the village at the time of the survey – while in the Non-Black-Earth zone the share was generally less than 20 per cent.[20] This suggests that differentiation was greater in the Black-Earth zone. This conclusion is supported by data on households without a cow; as many as 30 per cent of Black-Earth households were without a cow, while only slightly more than 10 per cent of the households in the Non-Black-Earth zone were without a cow.[21] There was no significant difference in the average number of horses per household between the zones (slightly above 1 in both), even though the average number of cows per household was much higher in the Non-Black-Earth than in the Black-Earth zone.[22] Since there were fewer households without sown land than households without a work animal, especially in the Black-Earth zone,[23] many households with sown area apparently had to hire work animals and implements in order to cultivate their land.

Dependency on other peasants for cultivation was much more widespread than is indicated by the percentage of rural households without a work animal. Since the average Russian horse was quite small, similar to a pony, only in the Non-Black-Earth zone could a household cultivate its own land with one work animal. In the Black-Earth zone, with heavier soils, at least two (and, in the steppes, even four) work animals were necessary.[24] Thus in the steppes only the very small proportion of rural households owning four or more work animals could cultivate their land on their own and thus be classified as 'middle peasants' in the strict sense. Households lacking enough work animals cultivated their land mostly through a form of cooperative production, the *supryaga* (an agreement between two or more households on the common use of horses and implements). The data available for some districts show that the *supryaga* was already very important in the Black-Earth zone by 1900.[25] Around the Central Industrial region another form of hiring was spreading. Households often hired not only capital (horses and implements) but also the owner of the horses and implements, as a worker. Such peasants often cultivated land for five or more other households.[26] Apparently these households could afford to hire a worker together with his implements because the household members were engaged in profitable non-agricultural activities (see pp. 62–3 below).

Trends in Differentiation Before 1914

Was ownership of the means of production becoming more concentrated before 1914? If we look at the number of horses per household, the data show a general decline over the period 1888–91 to 1912, a trend which apparently accelerated after 1900. The percentage of horseless households increased, while the percentage number of households with 3 or more horses fell substantially (see Table 6). This shift downwards hit all household groups and was not apparently associated with increased concentration in the hands of a group of wealthy households (the average number of horses in households with four and more horses actually fell from 5.51 to 5.40 over the period 1888–91 to 1900–5).[27]

This picture of general deterioration rather than polarisation is supported by regional data. A deviating trend was to be observed only during the colonisation of the European South at the end of the XIX Century.[28] During the period 1888–91 to 1900–5, for example, the average number of horses per household fell sharply in 27 of 48 provinces (gubernii) in European Russia, and fell slightly in a further 17. Only in four provinces did the average number of horses per household rise, and in three of these – all situated in the South – a general improvement occurred, so the share of horseless households actually fell. In only four provinces did a distinct polarisation in horse ownership occur. In another 27, the decline of the share of households with four or more horses was even greater than the general shift downward.[29] After 1900, however, fewer and fewer provinces of European Russia showed a trend deviating from the general shift downwards.

As a result, households increasingly depended on one another to cultivate their land; even those with three horses had to cooperate in the *supryaga*. Even in Tavricheskaya province (in New Russia), often seen as one of the most 'capitalistic', the share of independent farms decreased.[30] This downward trend was caused by rapid increases in the rural population and continual household partitions, at a time when the total arable land, and the total number of work animals and cattle in European Russia was increasing only slowly. In European Russia the number of rural households rose from 7.9 millions in 1871 to 11.5 millions in 1905 and 13.3 millions in 1912.[31] Not surprisingly, arable land per rural household in European Russia decreased from 13.1 to 10.4 hectares between 1877 and 1905.[32] Furthermore, the number of horses and cattle in European Russia were unchanged or declined after 1905.[33]

The general shift downwards, as measured by farm size, did not seem to reduce living standards, especially when off-farm activities are taken into account (see pp. 62–3). Rather the data on per capita consumption and deposits in credit cooperatives suggested that incomes were increasing.[34] It can be argued that the rising number of horseless households reflected their more economical use, and that some households with small sown areas were better off without a horse. The number of horses per hectare was significantly higher in peasant households than on landed estates and was well above the requirement for cultivating the land in the Non-Black-

Earth zone and in the Central Black-Earth region.[35] Calculations from the 1920s suggest that if the horse was used in agriculture only and the sown area did not exceed 6 hectares[36] it was more economical to lease a horse than to feed it over the whole year. In sum, there is evidence of a general decline in capital per household as measured by the number of horses and cattle, rather than a polarisation in ownership during the pre-1914 period.

How far does evidence about the use of hired labour in agriculture modify this picture? Unfortunately, no reliable data covering the whole territory are available. Estimates of the number of agricultural workers before 1914 vary between three and five million, but all agree that there was little increase between 1900 and 1913.[37] Whatever increase there may have been was well below the increase in population. Anfimov's data suggest that the total number of seasonal agricultural labourers actually decreased between 1909 and 1913. In the southern steppes, in particular, the mechanisation of agriculture had already started to reduce the demand for hired labour before 1900.[38]

Data on the use of hired labour in rural households are available for some districts. In the Black-Earth zone, less than 0.1 per cent of rural households depended primarily on hired labourers, and the proportion of rural households which were mainly using family labour, but also employed one labourer over the entire year, was less than 1 per cent. The use of a seasonal hired worker was more widespread, and day-labourers were probably used by many rural households, especially during the harvest season.[39] A significant number of seasonal agricultural labourers were itinerant, leaving the overpopulated central districts to work in the South or South-East.[40] The proportion of landless proletarians among agricultural labourers is unknown but was probably very small; most agricultural workers did only seasonal work and were members of households with arable land.

Differentiation among rural households according to their ownership of agricultural machinery (as distinct from ploughs and other implements) was quite pronounced before 1914. Ironically, the spread of machinery (shown in Table 7) apparently reduced the demand for hired labour.

What were the pre-1914 trends? Starting from Poland and the Baltic states in the 1880s, agricultural machinery spread quickly into the southern steppes, first to estates and then to the larger peasant farms.[41] After 1900, it spread further eastward and reached Siberia after 1906. Here few estates existed, so equipment was sold mostly to peasant farmers. After 1907 agricultural machines were bought primarily by peasants. The stock of agricultural machinery and implements more than doubled between 1908 and 1913.[42]

Before 1914 the use of machinery by peasant households was limited largely to the Black-Earth zone and Siberia.[43] Ownership in 1913 was undoubtedly more unevenly distributed than for any other form of capital.

But machinery was bought by an increasing number of rural households.

A characteristic 'pre-capitalist' form of exploitation of one household by another was private money-lending. Before 1914 money-lending was clearly declining due to the rapid spread of agricultural credit cooperatives.[44]

How did the Stolypin agrarian reform of 1907 influence rural differentiation? Unfortunately we do not have sufficient data to judge its effect with certainty.[45] The reform largely failed in its aim of establishing strong peasant farms with privately owned land in place of the commune. Its principal goal was frustrated because relatively few peasants wanted to separate.[46] In 47 provinces in European Russia, the total amount of land privately owned by peasants increased from 17.04 to 27.06 million hectares between 1905 and 1915, but only a small share of this so-called 'private land' was actually held by individual peasants: 27 per cent in 1905 and 29 per cent in 1915, the rest (predominantly meadows) being held by groups of peasants or by the commune as a whole.[47]

Agrarian Revolution, Civil War and Famine, 1917–25

The revolution and nationalisation of land in 1917 ended all forms of private land ownership, whether by landlords or by peasants. What was the impact of the revolution on peasant differentiation? Perhaps the most important impact was the revival of the commune and the periodical redistribution of land. During the revolution and the early 1920s the commune even spread into regions where it was previously unknown, such as the Ukraine. Moreover, separation of private land from the commune in the form of *otrubs* (farm with only fields enclosed) was reduced. Only the *khutor* (a fully enclosed farm) survived, primarily in the western parts of the Soviet Union.[48]

How, if at all, did the agrarian revolution fulfil the peasants' eternal quest for more land? While some estates were used as a basis for collective or state farms, most expropriated land fell into the hands of local peasant communes and was distributed as 'allotment land'. (Note that there was no equalisation of land-holdings between the communes.)[49] We still do not have precise data on the effect of this redistribution.[50] The gain in land for the peasants varied greatly among the regions, and even between communes. The gain was greater if measured by the legal ownership of land (see Table 8), and was quite small if measured by arable land actually used by the peasants.

Perhaps the best way to gauge the Revolution's impact on peasant land-holding is to look at regional data. Table 9 shows estate farming in 1916; it understates the importance of the estates on the eve of the war, because during the war estates reduced their sown area, probably by 20 per cent.[51] If we include land leased from landowners and the state, peasant households in 1916 already farmed 91.8 per cent of the total land sown. Thus only in the west and the south (the Ukraine, Belorussia, the Crimea and the Central Black-Earth region) did nationalisation increase the amount of arable land in peasant use by more than 10 per cent. In most parts of European Russia, the peasants acquired only between 6 and 7 per cent additional arable land, and in the Urals and Siberia there was hardly any increase (see Table 9). If pasture land is taken into account, the impact of the revolution would appear to be somewhat greater, because peasants had somewhat more land for livestock and dairy farming. In 1927, 98.3 per cent of the land was sown by peasant farms, 1.1 per cent by state and 0.6 per cent by collective farms.[52]

Differentiation by farm size was affected not only by redistribution of land within the commune but also by more frequent partitioning of households in the case of those with larger farms. Table 10 illustrates the levelling affect of the agrarian revolution. Larger farms almost completely disappeared. The share of rural households (probably including absent households) without sown land in the RSFSR fell from 15.9 per cent in 1917 to 8.1 per cent in 1920.[53] But the data probably overstate the actual 'levelling'. The strong decline in off-farm activities (see p. 61) suggests that the decline in the number of households without sown land was a sign of impoverishment rather than levelling. Redistribution was apparently limited to land and barely touched work animals (see Table 10).

No broadly representative data is available for ownership of agricultural machinery, but information on specific localities suggests that differentiation became even more marked. In general the estate equipment was taken by larger farms, or destroyed, or used to organise state or collective farms.[54] To this extent the levelling effect of the agrarian revolution is overstated in the literature.

In summary, the agrarian revolution reduced the larger farms partly as a result of the partitioning of households and partly because of the redistribution of private land, but barely affected the trend of differentiation in ownership of animals and other capital.

The famine in the southern and south-eastern parts of Russia in 1920 and 1921, and the harvest failure in the Volga region in 1924, had a major impact on differentiation. Many surviving households lost all their work animals, so that the share of rural households without work animals dramatically increased. While the number of work horses in the USSR fell from 27.7 million in 1916 to 24.2 million by early 1921, in just one year, 1921, more than four million additional work horses perished, reducing the total to 20.0 million.[55] Districts hit by the famine often lost more than half their work horses.[56]

As a result, differentiation measured by this criterion increased and many households lost their ability to cultivate their land with their own implements. This, of course, turned out to be a temporary phenomenon, which would fade as agriculture recovered. Kritsman analysed local data for 1922 and found a high degree of 'exploitation', based on the unequal distribution of the means of production among peasant households, various forms of concealed labour hiring and land leasing (both officially forbidden until early 1925).[57] He interpreted his findings as the first stage of 'capitalist class differentiation'. While he was right to stress that the levelling tendencies of the agrarian revolution had been overstated, the situation which he found in 1922–4 was not caused by 'capitalist expropriation' of smaller households, but rather by famine and the temporary loss of off-farm income.

Differentiation in the Mid-1920s

Data on the differentiation of rural households during the mid-1920s covered the whole territory annually and hence were more comprehensive than the pre-1914 period data. Moreover, budget studies were better and samples more representative.[58] These materials suggest continuity in patterns of differentiation between the pre-1914 period and mid-NEP.

Changes in classification make it difficult to compare the level of differentiation in 1913 and in 1927. Sown area and the number of horses were no longer used as the main criteria. Instead data collected on the total value of the 'means of production' (capital) per household, a concept which included livestock, agricultural machinery, buildings other than dwelling houses, land improvements, trees and vineyards and industrial equipment, but excluded land. Using this definition, about 26 per cent of rural households in 1927 owned means of production valued at 200 rubles or less. (The value of a work-horse was about 150 rubles, and a cow about 120 rubles.[59]) These were classified as 'poor peasant' households. About 57 per cent of households had means of production valued between 200 and 800 rubles and were classified as 'middle peasants'. A further 14 per cent of the households, referred to as 'upper middle peasants' had means of production valued between 800 and 1,600 rubles. The upper stratum, defined as owning means of production valued at over 1,600 rubles, comprised 3.2 per cent of the households, and were classified as *kulaks*.[60] The pre-1914 pattern of ownership had not changed much. For example, while sown area per capita was distributed quite equally among the rural households, per capita holding of livestock, rented land and hired labour was less equally distributed, while ownership of machinery was most concentrated. Thus in 1927 about 23 per cent of all rural households rented land and 18 per cent hired labour for longer than one month, while 46 per cent of 'kulak' households leased land, and almost 50 per cent hired labour.[61] Upper middle peasants and kulaks, who made up 16.8 per cent of rural households and about 21 per cent of the rural population, controlled

44.8 per cent of the total value of the means of production, and more than 73 per cent of agricultural machinery (see Table 11).

Relative to the pre-1914 period the number of households in the upper stratum as measured by horse-ownership was distinctly lower in 1927, and overall the data for horse-ownership show a slight levelling in differentiation among rural households (see Tables 6 and 11). The percentage of households with one horse was higher in the mid-1920s, reaching above 50 per cent, while the percentage of households with two, three and four or more horses was clearly much less than in 1912 (see Table 6).

The pre-1914 differences in the regional patterns of work-horse and livestock ownership did not change in the mid-1920s, although the percentage of households without a work animal was apparently higher everywhere in 1926 than in pre-1914, and especially in the Black-Earth zone.[62] Differentiation as measured by ownership of horses and cows still remained significantly greater in the Black-Earth zone than in the Non-Black-Earth zone and Siberia (see Table 12).

Just as before 1914, many households had sown land even if they had no work animal, so they depended on other households for draft power and implements. Here information is much better for the 1920s than for the pre-1914 period. In 1926 about 50 per cent of rural households in the USSR cultivated their land independently, with their own work animals and implements. At the other extreme, about 25 per cent hired both work animals and implements.[63]

There were dramatic regional variations. In the Non-Black-Earth zone more than 80 per cent of households cultivated their land with their own implements and draft power (in the Central Industrial region somewhat less – 66 per cent). In the southern steppes, however, only about 27 per cent of households had enough implements and draft power to cultivate their own land; more than 30 per cent of households were organised into *supryagi*. Another one-third of rural households in the Black-Earth zone hired both work animals and implements to cultivate their land.[64] In 1926 this dependency on others for implements and work animals was apparently higher than in pre-1914 (especially in the Black-Earth districts hit by famine).

Did Differentiation Increase During NEP?

What was the trend during the mid-1920s? Data on work animals or cows per household suggest a general shift upwards between 1923 and 1927,[65] a shift which ended only after coercive measures against the peasantry started early in 1928.[66] The share of households without a work animal or cow was decreasing and the share of households with two or more work animals or with two or more cows was increasing (with the exception of the

Central Industrial Region[67]). Although rural population and the number of households were growing rapidly, nevertheless, in contrast to pre-1914 trends, sown area, horses and cows per household all rose during NEP (see Table 13). As noted above, the need to replace the livestock lost during the civil war and the famine was a major factor here. In terms of work animals, the recovery was far from complete in the Black-Earth zone even as late as 1927. In the Lower Volga region, for example, the 1927 stock of work animals was only slightly more than 50 per cent of the 1916 levels.[68] The number of cows per household had, however, already reached the pre-1914 level in 1927 (see Table 13). Whether or not this general shift upwards would have continued once pre-1914 stocks had been replenished is an open question.

Was there a trend during NEP towards 'class differentiation' in the strict marxist sense – i.e., were more peasants hiring labour? In 1913 some 4 million hired agricultural labourers worked on estates and peasant farms. By contrast, in 1927 there were 2.5 million agricultural labourers hired for at least one month (138,000 by state farms, 750,000 by communes or groups of peasants, and 1.6 million by individual peasants). In addition there were about 3 million day-labourers on individual farms and more than 400,000 on state farms.[69] Unfortunately, no estimates of the number of agricultural day-labourers for the pre-1914 period are available. One known difference, however, is that before 1914 most agricultural labourers were itinerant workers, while in 1926/27 only 340,000 agricultural workers worked outside their home districts, while another 200,000 worked outside their home village, but within their home district.[70] Thus the data point to a decline in the number of hired workers between 1913 and 1927. This decline was partly the result of the elimination of the estates.

The age distribution of hired labour raises the question of whether the amount of hired labour was a satisfactory criterion for measuring class differentiation in Russia. Of the 1.6 million hired labourers working in individual farms in 1927, only 51 per cent were adults, and only 24 per cent were heads of families. Almost 29 per cent were children up to 15 years old, working as nursery maids or herdsmen.[71] It should be added that even the 3.4 per cent of the rural households that hired a permanent worker in 1926 cannot easily be classified as 'capitalist' farmers. Average family size for this group was 2.76 persons while the average of all rural households was 5.07 persons. Most likely, therefore, the lack of family labour led these households to employ a permanent worker; otherwise it is hard to explain why 25 per cent of these households were headed by women (mostly widows) and why the share of the old in these households was significantly above the average.[72] Another significant group who hired workers were those working in off-farm activities, such as party members employed in the villages.[73] The share of truly capitalist farms among these households is unknown, but was probably very small. Other than the cases of necessity mentioned above, it was rare to find a 'capitalist' household using predominantly hired labour in the Soviet village.[74]

The output and stock of agricultural machinery and implements had already reached the pre-1914 levels by 1925/26 (see Table 7). Machine purchases were facilitated by government credits[75] and by 1927 5.4 million households were organised in rural credit cooperatives.[76] Machine stocks and the number of households possessing machinery increased rapidly after 1925.[77] Apparently, the pre-1914 concentration of machinery in the upper strata did not increase. In fact the differentiation of ownership probably diminished, as an increasing share of machinery was sold to cooperatives.[78] There was a relatively small number of individual farmers, especially in the Black-Earth zone, who could afford to buy a tractor or a threshing machine on their own.[79] Ironically, such purchases reduced class differentiation in the strict marxist sense: they replaced hired labour, but simultaneously increased differentiation measured by wealth or income, since poor peasants lost an additional source of off-farm income.

Hiring out agricultural equipment, which the Bolsheviks viewed as 'exploitation', seemed to be more prevalent in the second half of the 1920s than before 1914. The upper strata leased machinery to the middle strata, while the middle strata leased implements to the lower strata.[80] The hiring of equipment was quite widespread. In 1927, 58 per cent of all rural households in the Ukraine, fairly representative of the Black-Earth zone, were hiring some agricultural means of production – about 70 per cent of the lower strata and just below 50 per cent of the upper strata hired equipment from others. In all, about 20.5 per cent of all rural households in the Ukraine were leasing out equipment, including 40 per cent of households with means of production valued at more than 800 rubles, and even 14 per cent of households with means of production valued between 201 and 400 rubles.[81] Early in 1928 the Bolsheviks decided to use such leasing as one criterion of a 'kulak' household,[82] but their focus on 'exploitation' through ownership of means of production had a dubious economic basis. Such leasing was not a necessity for the upper strata, but it became a question of survival for the lower strata who could not cultivate their land without such equipment.[83]

Before 1914 the cumulative effect of economic advantage enjoyed by the upper strata was limited by the widespread partitioning of larger farms. Data from the mid-1920s suggest that each year about 3 per cent of the rural households were partitioned. Household partitioning seemed to correlate with sown area; for example in 1925/26 about 10 per cent of households with sown area of more than 11 hectares (an above-average holding) underwent partitioning.[84] In the Black-Earth zone new households generally remained in agriculture after partitioning, but in the Non-Black-Earth zone young men working in industry separated themselves (partitioned) from the parental household to avoid to sharing their wages with the family.[85] The available data do not suggest that partitioning was motivated by economic advantages inside agriculture. Dairy farming was insignificant in the Black-Earth zone and the average number of work animals after partitioning was too low for independent farming.

The Bolsheviks, believing that incomes of households correlated significantly with farm size, tried to use statistical findings on the percentage of poor peasant as well as kulak households as a basis for policy making. Unfortunately their programme of economic assistance to poor peasants failed to take into account social composition and the reasons for the poverty of this strata. In fact, most poor peasants needed credits for consumption rather than for buying a horse.[86] Some contemporary local estimates suggested that 'poor peasants' included the following sub-groups. First, about half of all poor families suffered from a shortage of able-bodied family labour; they were often households headed by a widow, invalid or elderly person, or households where the main worker was ill or absent for military service. Secondly, one-third of poor families had been hit by a natural disaster (fire, famine, death of a work animal, for example) or impoverished by partitioning. Thirdly, the remaining families were poor for unknown reasons, or described as bad farmers or even as *lodyri* (sluggards).[87]

The failure to look at the actual social composition of households was repeated when the Bolsheviks tried to implement their anti-kulak policy. When the party started to register kulaks in the villages, the arbitrariness of the criteria became evident.[88]

OFF-FARM ACTIVITIES AND MONEY INCOME
OF RURAL HOUSEHOLDS

In Russia agricultural work was seasonal. Long winters, the dominance of grain production and the relative insignificance of industrial crops and animal husbandry in most regions meant that the need for agricultural labour was concentrated around sowing and harvesting. Compared with Western Europe the per capita landholding of the pre-1914 Russian peasant was by no means small. Thus, to some extent, the poverty of the Russian peasant can be attributed to the poor use made of the available arable land and labour. The per hectare income from grain was very low compared with per hectare income from potatoes or industrial crops, yet the late XIX Century trend towards crop diversification in agriculture production came to a halt in European Russia after 1905.[89] One consequence of this was a growing problem of underemployment in agriculture. Thus the off-farm use of family labour became an important factor in differentiation by wealth and income among rural households.

Off-farm Activities of the Rural Households

Income from off-farm activities was an important factor in a household's economic well-being. Some pre-1914 data exist on the number of rural households drawing income from 'industry' (*promysly*), which was defined as all economic activity of peasants outside their own farm, including industry, trade, crafts and working on other farms in agriculture. The limited data suggest that 58 per cent of almost 19 million households within Soviet borders were engaged in *promysly* immediately before the war, including about 40 per cent of rural households in the Black-Earth zone and between 80 and 90 per cent in the Non-Black-Earth zone.[90] These off-farm activities were almost exclusively carried out by men.[91] Data on the relative importance of different off-farm activities, available only for 1900, reveal important differences in choice among the zones. In the Non-Black-Earth zone 40 per cent of able-bodied persons worked in off-farm activities at least one week a year, mostly outside agriculture. In the Black-Earth zone, however, off-farm work was less widespread and much more concentrated on working as hired labour in agriculture.[92] These regional peculiarities reflected differing regional demands for labour.

During the war off-farm activities fell dramatically, so that by 1917 only 24.8 per cent of households still had an 'industry'.[93] By the end of the civil war, off-farm activities were virtually non-existent.[94]

In the early 1920s off-farm activities quickly regained their importance. By 1925/26 about 25 per cent of all rural households again had an off-farm occupation, including about 50 per cent of households in the Non-Black-Earth zone, 20 per cent in the Black-Earth zone and 9 per cent in Siberia.[95] If we add in figures for hired work in agriculture for at least one month within the home district (to make the 1920s data more comparable to pre-1914 data), the share of households with off-farm activities in 1926 rises to about 60 per cent in the Non-Black-Earth zone, 30 per cent in the Black-Earth zone and 20 per cent in Siberia.[96] Even after this adjustment off-farm work was obviously less important in 1926 than before 1914, especially in agriculture. In the professions the number of workers in 1927/28 approached their pre-1914 levels (see Chapter 2).

Comparable data about the income earned from off-farm activities before the war and in the 1920s are not available; nor are precise data on the number of seasonal workers. Apparently off-farm activities had not reached their pre-1914 importance by 1927, mainly because the demand for seasonal labour in and outside agriculture was below the pre-1914 level.[97] There is little doubt that the problem of underemployment of the rural workforce was as severe in 1927 as before 1914.

In agriculture itself, the greater output of labour-intensive products (industrial crops and meat and dairy products – see Chapter 5) increased the labour input needed in agricultural production compared with the pre-1914 period. This affected the differentiation of rural households in the 1920s because, at least temporarily, the economic opportunities and the political climate for the development of small peasant farms were quite good. In turn, the crucial question of the size of the plot, which had led to the peasant unrest in 1905–6 and in 1917–19, had since lost some of its overall importance.

Sources of Money Income

Off-farm income greatly affected income distribution. In the Non-Black-Earth zone most rural households with less than 4.47 hectares of sown area earned at least half of their money income from off-farm activities, and only about one-third from selling agricultural products. Even for households with more than 4.47 hectares of sown area, only a small number relied primarily on money income from agriculture. As a result of off-farm income, per capita total money income was *inversely* correlated with the size of the farm in this zone, a finding quite different from that which is usually assumed.[98]

The situation was somewhat different in the Black-Earth zone. Yet even here the correlation between money income per capita, and the farm size in terms of sown area, was very weak, again due to the role of off-farm income. In the Ukraine, it was only on the larger farms, those with more than 17.6 hectares of sown area, that the per capita money income was significantly higher.[99]

Things become clearer when we realise that per capita money incomes of *all* rural strata were low compared with per capita money income in the cities. In 1925/26 the average per capita money income of a rural household was 114 rubles, compared with 291 rubles for an industrial worker. Even the richest peasant households, the 'kulaks', had an average per capita income of 246 rubles, less than the family of a worker, or even less than the family of a 'rural employee' (also classed as 'proletarian'), who had a per capita income of 270 rubles.[100] The same difference was to be observed concerning the per capita consumption of industrial consumer goods and the quality of food. The peasants consumed substantially less animal products, sugar and wheat flour, but more potatoes, vegetables and rye flour per capita.[101] 'Proletarianisation' of the peasant by working on an off-farm job could be part of a process of upward social mobility.

The so-called 'middle peasant' often had the poorest living conditions. These peasants, who were able to cultivate their land with own implements, or at least through the *supryaga*, had per capita incomes below those of the *lower* as well as the upper strata (when grouped by sown area). Lenin cited the same conditions in 1899.[102]

Data on pre-1914 money incomes are not as comprehensive, but they still point to the same regional differences.[103] The share of money income from agricultural as compared with non-agricultural activities was apparently higher in the 1920s than in pre-1914, but pre-1914 data are too limited to be conclusive on this point.

All Sources of Subsistence of Rural Households

In some cases income in kind from the peasants' own farm can be of overwhelming importance for their standard of living. Thus data on money incomes from the sale of agricultural products and from off-farm activities is not sufficient to determine the relative contribution of non-agricultural income to the 'subsistence' economy (and, hence, total real income) of rural households.

Unfortunately, pre-1914 budget data on total income including income in kind has shortcomings. For example, *gross* agricultural production is counted as 'income', regardless of whether or not it was used as a final product for sale or consumption, or as an intermediate product for feed. A second shortcoming is that processed agricultural products (e.g., butter, sugar) were counted as 'industrial products'.

Only the data for 1927 classify households by the main source of subsistence. About 64 per cent of all rural households received subsistence from agriculture in kind and their main money income from the selling of agricultural products. Many households received their basic subsistence from agriculture but earned most of their money income from handicrafts or factory work; they were on the way to becoming non-agricultural households. 8 per cent of all rural households were non-agricultural households, earning their subsistence outside agriculture, although most of them still had an additional agricultural income.[104]

Based on the size of the farm such households would be placed in the lower strata of 'poor peasants', even though many, being really non-agricultural households, had middle or even high incomes. Thus, measures of differentiation based on farm size necessarily had little correlation with the distribution of total real per capita income among rural households, and hence formed an unreliable basis for agricultural policy.

CONCLUSIONS

Farm size provides a poor indication of the economic well-being of the household (except for a slight correlation in the Black-Earth zone). The main cause for this lack of correlation is the great importance of off-farm income; this also means that classification in terms of the means of production owned by the household is also not a clear guide to differentiation in terms of economic well-being.

Any analysis of rural differentiation by wealth must also take into account the severe problem of hidden rural unemployment. In these economic conditions, a peasant taking hired work off the farm, defined as 'proletarianised' in marxist terms, was actually moving up a step in terms of income.

There were two exceptions to this general picture. First, a significant proportion of poor peasants, between 10 and 20 per cent of all rural households, were poor precisely because they lacked adequate family labour. At the other extreme, some wealthy rural households in the upper strata did well because the size of the farm allowed an efficient use of all family labour. In general, however, rural households with surplus family labour could improve their economic positions by intensifying agricultural production, thereby using more labour (and capital), by improving their agricultural techniques to increase the yields, and by engaging in more off-farm activity, gradually abandoning agricultural production if off-farm activities were more profitable. All these patterns were observed both in the pre-1914 period and in the mid-1920s. Their relative importance varied among the zones. Near industrial centres, the demand for off-farm labour was stronger, so that in the Non-Black-Earth zone differentiation by wealth and income was generally less than in the Black-Earth zone. The most pronounced differentiation was in the steppes of the Black-Earth zone, far from industry, and still committed almost entirely to grain production. There, income and wealth somewhat correlated with farm size, and differentiation may still have been growing, even though in other parts of the country it appears to have been weakening.

The data on differentiation by farm size permit us to conclude with greater confidence that the level of differentiation in terms of the size of the farms was less in 1927 than in 1913. The proportion of households without a work animal or without a cow was about the same, but the proportion of households with two and more work animals or with two or more cows was significantly smaller in the 1920s. This is true also for the average size of the farm in the upper-middle and upper strata (grouped by farm size) in 1927 when compared with pre-1914. To this extent equality within the village had increased.

There is virtually no evidence of a trend towards a 'capitalist' differentiation of the peasantry, defined in terms of the employment of labour. Practically all rural households relied exclusively or predominantly on family labour. The share of households relying predominantly on hired labour was less than 0.1 per cent in 1913 and statistically insignificant in 1927. A landless rural proletariat, engaged only in hired labour in agriculture, barely existed in the pre-1914 period and was practically non-existent in the mid-1920s.

Overall, the average size of farm was declining before 1914; no concentration of the means of production in the hands of an ever smaller number of households was evident. During the 1920s there was a general shift upwards associated with economic recovery. Although a temporary levelling after the agrarian revolution was evident, differentiation by farm size did not change significantly during the 1920s. The factors counteracting the process of differentiation were the same in the pre-1914 period as in the 1920s: redistribution of land within the village commune and, more importantly, the partitioning of larger households.

4 Unemployment
J. C. Shapiro

BEFORE 1917: WHAT DO WE KNOW?

Lenin expressed a well-researched scepticism in *The Development of Capitalism in Russia* (1899):

> it is impossible to determine even approximately the number of unemployed in an average year, because of the complete absence of anything like reliable statistical data.[1]

In spite of this warning, NEP economists must have felt the same pressures we do to estimate the level of unemployment in the later tsarist economy.

There were no series on unemployment in Imperial Russia, official or unofficial. This is certainly not unusual given the period; the situation is comparable, for example, to Britain before 1851.[2]

Nor has anyone attempted to trace the dynamics of unemployment before the revolution. The sole monograph dedicated to the subject (Kleinbort, 1925) carries an all too accurate warning that it is not a full or statistical study.[3]

The global estimate attributed to the economist Mints has become the standard:

> in the period 1900–1913 the annual average number of unemployed in all Russia was, in the winter season, not counting those first offering their labour power, about 400 to 500 thousand.[4]

Mints's calculation evidently took as its starting point five individual city censuses for three cities. The tabular presentation of these, by Kritsman, is essentially accurate; however, it oddly omits the absolute number of unemployed in St Petersburg, slightly misdates that city's 1910 census, and unnecessarily ignores Baku's vital industrial district.[5]

Table 14 presents a modified version of the Kritsman/Mints' information, extending and somewhat revising the data in accord with census records, and adding male and female sub-totals. The two censuses which far preceded the period under scrutiny – Moscow, 1902, and St Petersburg, 1900 – are disregarded.

It is not known whether Mints made his famous calculation on the back of an envelope, or attempted a more sophisticated approximation. In any event, no detail was ever published.[6]

The accuracy of the projection clearly turns on the quality and representativeness of the census findings. Other apparently independent estimates made in the 1920s turn out on closer scrutiny to be, in all likelihood, products of the same discussion in and around Narkomtrud (the People's Commissariat of Labour), based on no more information, and sometimes less, than that shown in Table 14.[7]

The critical unknown is the basis on which the censuses distinguished the unemployed. Enumerators may well have classified by regular occupation, even if the person polled was out of work at the 'critical moment' of the census. (In contrast the 1926 Census differentiated between employment status and occupation.)

Suspicion about mis-classification has led some scholars to question the validity of the data in the urban censuses. If the doubts are well-founded, Mints's estimate could require substantial upward revision.

Kruze and Kutsentov pick out the exceptional rise in St Petersburg between 1900 and 1910 in the number of workers with 'industrial occupations not precisely specified'. They argue that this group, amounting to 130,000 persons, really represented the 'half unemployed and unemployed'.[8] However, the same scale of increase is not visible in Moscow between 1902 and 1912.[9] Are Kruze and Kutsentov discerning a shift in the enumerated or the enumerators?[10]

Kruze and Kutsentov are not alone in questioning the basis of the pre-war count of the unemployed. Bradley's thorough study of pre-war Moscow led him to conclude that 'it is likely that the figures for the number of unemployed are seriously underestimated', and even 'curiously small'.[11]

Persons on relief represent another category, apart from casual labour, capable of hiding large numbers who should be classified as unemployed. Relief recipients were sizeable in number in both St Petersburg, 1910 (8,700 males, 18,700 females) and Moscow, 1912 (6,000 males, 15,300 females).[12] If a substantial number were willing and able to enter paid labour, this could add 50 per cent or more to the unemployment totals.

The three censuses in Table 14 were all taken in a period of economic expansion when unemployment might be expected to be relatively low. None of the censuses was carried out in 1909, still a year of recovery by virtually all accounts.[13] Expansion in Baku's oil industry lagged behind other branches, but by 1913 recovery and boom were well under way there too.[14]

Alternative Sources of Information

The data from the individual urban censuses are thus no more than a starting point. What further evidence is available?

Historical coverage has consisted of unsystematic compilation of lists of factory closures, cutbacks in the workforce and short-time working. As typical examples: in 1909 the Sormovo works contracted from more than 10,000 workers in January to 4,278 in August; in 1911–12 there were sharp cutbacks in Lodz cotton; in 1912 Tula samovars and agricultural machinery generally experienced conjunctural difficulties out of line with the general upswing.[15]

The direct record of employment fluctuations, from factory archives, inspectors' reports, supplemented by the periodical press, has not been systematically assembled.[16] This might add a quantum increment to our knowledge: the sheer scope of the task is evident.

Employment and Unemployment

Seasonality of work and unemployment, and the relationship between unemployment and the village, is a consistent theme in the five workers' memoirs selected by Bonnell for recent publication.[17]

Chapter 2 discusses the difficult question of estimating employment in the tsarist period;[18] an improved picture of unemployment dynamics would require an even more improved employment series.

The key unknown relationship in this period is that of the variation of employment with unemployment. During NEP they increased together, in contrast to the usual expectation in advanced capitalist countries. This was often considered paradoxical or ironical, but is a relatively common phenomenon in less developed countries today.[19]

A major difficulty in interpreting evidence made up of individual reports of redundancies, factory closures and declines in employment lies in the general confusion of the flow of new unemployed with the stock of persons without jobs at any one time. To put it most plainly, what did a worker do upon losing work? There is reasonable congruence in descriptions of economic conjunctures, and certain reports of large-scale redundancies reappear consistently. But this must be combined with an estimate of the possibilities for other work and the extent to which the unemployed remained in the towns.[20]

The 'safety valve' of the village was a safety valve for the authorities as well; reports frequently appeared of the enforced dispatch of the unemployed 'home'. Moscow *zemstvo* (local government) reports recorded a more voluntary form of return, itinerant begging. Correspondents reported an increase in begging through the boom years to 1913. In 1909 this was explicitly linked with 'the number of unemployed increasing from year to year'.[21]

Overview

In the pre-revolutionary period the scale of unemployment reported is small by NEP standards, but described in a fashion which implied a very harsh economic climate indeed. This is not inconsistent. In the complete absence of unemployment insurance and with a very underdeveloped relief network, unemployment could be, without exaggeration, a death sentence.

A definite pattern can be discerned, despite the patchwork character of the evidence. Wherever firm quantitative estimates of the *stock* of unemployed are actually presented, then the unemployment rate is not inconsistent with the urban census data, and is, at maximum, half the rate in 1926/27. As a clear example, there are a number of references to 10,000 redundancies in the Donbass coal fields in 1910. The labour force of the Donbass at the time, however, was about 200,000. Accepting the claim that the great majority of the 10,000 did stay in the area,[22] consequent unemployment would not have exceeded 5 per cent of the labour force.

Mints's estimate may thus have endured for good cause, and not only because nature abhors a vacuum. It is also possible that the more recent historians of the St Petersburg and Moscow labour markets *and* Mints, in his global estimate, are correct. This could be so if unemployment in the late tsarist period was as geographically concentrated as during NEP.[23]

The lower limit of our estimate of 1909–13 unemployment may thus be reasonably taken to be Mints's. The upper limit is certainly not greater than that offered by Markus, the Stalinist authority on such issues: 'modestly, about one million in the best years'.[24]

The difference between these upper and lower bounds is not, in fact, as depressingly wide as it may appear, particularly as the lower figure does not claim to include first-time job seekers. By all standards, historical and modern, unemployment counts are subject to substantial differences in estimate. Of all the economic magnitudes, unemployment is surely the most difficult to measure.[25]

1917–25

The impact of the first world war on unemployment, and its role in the 'impending catastrophe', finds its place in every history of the October revolution but must receive only passing mention here. Whatever the precise magnitude of unemployment in 1917,[26] like that following 1905 it does not fit the template of 'normal' unemployment.[27]

As in many belligerent countries, the war imposed many structural changes. And there is no doubt that by 1918 the threatened unemployment did come to pass.[28] The first 'solution' was the depopulation of major cities.[29] But NEP and its market relations then brought not only revival and repair to the ravaged economy.

It was evident by the summer of 1922 that the new breathing space, and the new economic structures, would bring with them unemployment on a large scale. The continuing economic recovery and employment expansion of NEP did not bring relief (nor did the policy makers expect it). It is to this, the 'ulcer of NEP', that we now turn.

UNEMPLOYMENT 1926/27

The broad features of NEP unemployment have long been known in the West. Relatively recent Soviet work makes some new use of the mass of statistical, archival and discussion material of the period. The most systematic quantitative account to date is to be found in Davies/Davies and Wheatcroft.[30] Figure 1 clearly shows the rising line of NEP unemployment, punctuated seasonally.[31]

Detailed interpretation of the fluctuations requires knowledge of the changes in regulations and operations of the labour exchanges as well as information about the state of the labour market.[32] For example, the purge of those registered on the exchanges in 1924, described in the contemporary literature, is very evident in the graph in Figure 1.

Analysis of underlying trends in new registration of unemployed and vacancies can further help to disentangle the factual and antifactual. The detailed statistics available are far in advance of their time. Labour exchange data underscore the unusual prominence of temporary work, which showed a secular increase. The ratio of permanent jobs to the total offered on the exchanges is shown in Table 15.[33] The ratio of unemployed registering to *permanent* jobs did not essentially improve. The holding of labour reserves 'external to the firm' stands out as a key pattern of the later 1920s.[34]

Alternative Estimates

To what degree do these data measure anything other than the activity of the labour exchanges? What was the relative balance between those who registered not primarily to seek work, but to obtain benefits, regularise status or preserve *stazh* (length of work service), and those who failed to register though in fact unsuccessfully seeking work?

The December 1926 population census, which recorded a *lower* figure than the exchanges, and the November 1927 census of unemployed members conducted by the trade unions, who compiled a series much *higher* than the exchanges, are invaluable points for testing the coherence of overall estimates.

Davies and Wheatcroft concluded that the November 1927 trade union census fits 'fairly well' with the labour exchange data.[35] I would be more emphatic. The trade union census fits very well with the count of unemployed trade union members registered on the exchanges, especially once they had been encouraged to register on the exchanges by the very act of that census.[36]

On January 1, 1927, the labour-exchange unemployment figure stood at 1,310,000.[37] At the critical moment of the 1926 population census a fortnight earlier (December 17), only 1,010,000 were enumerated.[38] Some

Figure 1. Unemployed registered on labour exchanges of Narkomtrud, 1921–30

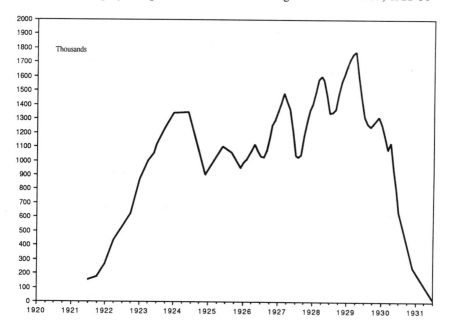

Sources: Kingsbury and Fairchild (1931), following Table VI; and *International Labour Review*, November 1926–November 1930 (given quarterly for period to December 1925, then monthly).

Soviet observers immediately took this as a sign of the number of dead souls on the labour exchanges, while the trade unions and the State Planning Commission (Gosplan) simultaneously emphasised the opposite defect of under-registration.[39]

The difference of almost precisely 300,000 may be accounted for by just two factors: first, the census failed to record a quarter of a million first-time job seekers, nearly 100,000 of them adolescents;[40] secondly, and far less importantly, an actual divergence was captured, reflecting the fortnight's difference in timing in conditions of steadily rising unemployment.[41]

In 1946 Lorimer pointed out the deficit of male adolescents in the population census.[42] Underenumeration of young people without work is, in fact, an international universal. First-time job seekers were significantly better represented among the local born, as the least geographically stable sections of this group slipped through the net. As another universal generalisation, adult females seeking work are far more prone than males to be recorded as not economically active, the more so the less trained is the enumerator.[43] And the deficit of unemployed women in the population census *is* relatively greater than that of men.

It is possible to attempt a provisional estimate of the 'true' figure which takes account of divergent discrepancies. The population census consistently shows lower results in a number of other key categories. Metal and textile workers unemployed are only half as numerous in the census as on the labour exchanges.[44] The deficit is at its extreme in Leningrad and Moscow. On the other hand, the census counted 119,000 rural unemployed, who could have had little chance to register on one of the 281 exchanges.[45] A reasonable figure for further testing is proposed here: 1.4 million unemployed on January 1, 1927. (January was neither the peak nor the trough of the economic year 1926/27; 1928 saw a further increase in unemployment.)[46]

Who Were the NEP Unemployed?

Table 16 summarises some of the population census evidence which answers the questions 'What was the unemployment rate in each occupational category?' and 'Who were the unemployed?'. (Further analysis will be found in the CREES *Discussion Paper* written to accompany this article.) We lack comparable pre-revolutionary information for the most part.

The very high proportion of women amongst the unemployed does not need to be stressed.[47] They were disproportionately but not exclusively white-collar employees (*sluzhashchie*). (Servants were counted in the latter category by the population census but this does not change the overall picture.) This represents a definite change from 1910–13, as shown in Table 14, though women actually in the labour force were already recorded then as having a somewhat higher incidence of unemployment.

The high proportion of non-manual unemployed deserves underscoring. (It is distinct from, though bound up with, female unemployment.) Some insight into this is given in studies of Soviet trade employees and suggests a structural mismatch, rather than simple deficient demand in the labour market due to the rationalisation drives carried out under NEP.[48]

Location and Migration

Our calculations show the unemployment rate varying directly with city size.[49]

In a comparison with 1913, a contraction of jobs relative to the economically active population can be observed.[50]

Labour-exchange data showed recent rural in-migrants comprising 10 to 20 per cent of the unemployed.[51] By the 1926 census count the majority of the unemployed were urban residents of fairly long standing.[52]

While many economists during NEP had identified the unemployment question with the question of agrarian over-population, there were dissenting voices, particularly from the localities. Several 1927 reports from the Ukraine emphasised that while unemployment was rising the number coming from the countryside was actually falling. Reports on Soviet trade employees also stressed the largely urban character of their heavy unemployment.[53]

New arrivals from the countryside did form a higher proportion of those taken on in industry than they did of the unemployed.[54] There is the strong suggestion here of a divided labour market, in which the long-term city dwellers shunned certain jobs, for which recruitment from the countryside was then necessary.[55]

Implications

NEP unemployment almost certainly exceeded that of the pre-war period. This was not solely because the towns were a greater magnet for settlement than before the war. Some of the root structural causes have parallels in other countries. In the Soviet Union the special complication of war, civil war and massive social upheaval resulted in uneven, but heavy, dislocation in the match of labour force to jobs. While the economy recovered a new generation – and new group of women – found entry into the active labour force difficult.

If the contrast with the pre-revolutionary period has involuntarily shown NEP in an unfavourable light, at least one strong corrective is mandatory. The existence of unemployment benefit, no matter how modest, is a critical factor demarcating the NEP period from the tsarist era. While the young Soviet state certainly did not and could not fulfil its early ambitious labour programme, the proportion of unemployed covered by benefit rose steadily through the 1920s.[56]

As the preface to the 1926 Census volume on unemployment noted, by the time of its publication in 1931 the question of mass unemployment in the Soviet Union had essentially passed into history. In the balance sheet of Stalinist industrialisation, this issue is prominent indeed on the credit side. Thus NEP unemployment must remain a spectre haunting every would-be proponent of the socialist market. Was the situation historically specific, the 'burdensome legacy' of tsarism, war, civil war, and backwardness? Or did NEP itself create or exacerbate the situation? This question has not lost its immediacy in sixty years.

CONCLUSIONS

The basic conclusions of this paper may be briefly stated, shorn of the inevitable and necessary qualifiers, conditionals, calculations, and disclaimers:

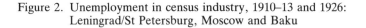

Figure 2. Unemployment in census industry, 1910–13 and 1926:
Leningrad/St Petersburg, Moscow and Baku

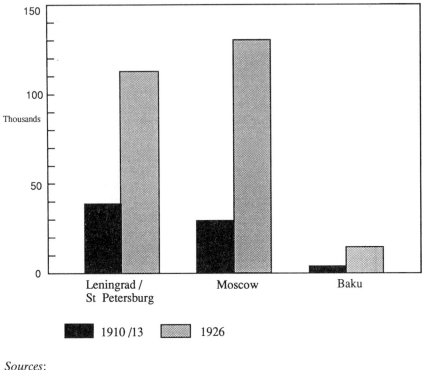

Sources:
1910–13: see sources to Table 14.
1926: *Vsesoyuznaya perepis'*, lii (1931).

1. The traditional estimate of open urban unemployment in late Imperial
   Russia, credited to L. Mints – about half a million – is based on
   evidence which may be insufficiently robust to bear its weight. But it is a
   very reasonable 'guesstimate'. In the unsystematic and variegated
   evidence of pre-1917 unemployment there is, in fact, no quantitative
   information which contradicts Mints. It is, however, premature to rule
   out higher estimates for the late tsarist period, based on scepticism
   about the enumeration categories of the censuses used in Table 14 and
   Figure 2, which are the only known raw material for Mints's estimate.

   If Mints is essentially correct, then 1926/27 unemployment was at
   least twice that of 1909–13. The comparison with 1928 is even more
   unfavourable. Figure 2 illustrates the dramatic increase in total unemployment in three cities, based on the data underlying Mints's figure.[57]

2. The rival estimates of NEP unemployment are, by historical and even

present standards, closer than is sometimes thought. Comparisons of discrepancies in the various counts produced my working estimate for unemployment on January 1, 1927, of 1.4 million, an unemployment rate of well over 10 per cent of the urban labour force.

That the ranks of the unemployed were consistently enlarged by the continuous flow from the countryside cannot be in doubt. It may be even more important that the unemployed increasingly tended to remain in the towns during workless spells. However, factors internal to the urban economy were also critical, and can easily be underplayed, especially in the period up to 1926/27.

If the unskilled expectedly suffered more in both periods, NEP is notable for its high level of non-manual unemployment and for the very high proportion which was female. Unemployment was most acute in the very largest cities: one-quarter of the unemployed were seeking work in Moscow or Leningrad. Analysis of labour-exchange records offers striking confirmation of the increasing importance of temporary work. A high flow of both new registrations and vacancies testifies to the increased casualisation of the labour market.

And what of the agenda for future research? The tsarist labour market still demands much further quantitative assessment: this is an immense undertaking. The rich vein of NEP data, on the other hand, lies near the surface, and has been far from fully worked.

Part II
Agriculture and the Economy

5 Agriculture
S. G. Wheatcroft

INTRODUCTION

Throughout this period agriculture was by far the largest sector of production and employment. It was the most basic and traditional, and at the same time the most crucial, of all economic activities. It was the supplier of nearly all foodstuffs, many raw materials and most export earnings. The fate of agriculture to a very large extent determined the fate of the country as a whole. The collapse of agricultural production in the early 1920s resulted in famine and a threat to social life. The restoration and reconstruction of agriculture was consequently of vital importance for the restoration and restructuring of the economy and of social existence. But despite its enormous importance agriculture remained the least well understood sector of the economy, and the extent and nature of agricultural recovery and reconstruction in the mid- and late 1920s are still subjects of enormous controversy.

The problem partly results from the mass of contradictory and conflicting statistical data and partly from political factors. But apart from these issues there has also been a tendency to assume that grain was the only important product, and that marketing problems were a result either of wilful concealment of available surpluses or of structural problems produced by the break up of the larger farming units, or of a combination of both. In order to assess the state and development of agriculture in this period we need a more critical and comprehensive approach which assesses the importance of all branches of agriculture and analyses the factors affecting production and utilisation of all agricultural products.

Conflicting Agricultural Production Indicators

Great care needs to be taken with the large variety of different agricultural production indices. Table 17 lists some of the most prominent series. It will be seen that the different series cover different areas (Russian Empire or pre-1939 USSR territory) and are evaluated in a variety of different prices (pre-war prices, 1926/27 prices and current prices; the present official series is merely given in 'comparable prices' and in terms of index numbers[1]). These series provide different rates of growth of production. The major difference lies in the extent of recovery between the pre-war period (1909–13 (average) or 1913) and the post-revolutionary period. The current official indices claim a 90 per cent recovery by 1924, 112 per cent by

79

1925 and 124 per cent by 1928, while earlier evaluations based on 1913 price data indicated only a 69–70 per cent recovery by 1924 and 90 per cent by 1925 – i.e., they were about 20 per cent lower.

There are far fewer evaluations of regional, sectoral or marketed agricultural production and no official current series.[2] There consequently tends to be less discussion over these aggregates, with the exception of grain marketings.

While care does need to be taken to ensure that comparable prices and territories are being used, the main source of the differences between these indicators is their different evaluation of physical products and, to a lesser extent, their product coverage.[3] These differences are a major concern of this chapter.

Loss of Statistical Credibility

To understand the loss of statistical credibility in the evaluation of agricultural reality we need to examine briefly the inter-relationship of technical and political assessments of agricultural reality: the complex disagreements between experts were transformed into political disagreements.

The problem was not so much the shortage of data but the abundance of contradictory data. The initial disagreements may be traced to the pre-revolutionary rivalry between the Central Statistical Committee (TsSK) and the local government (*zemstvo*) statisticians. They were compounded by the uncertainties of the change in statistical system during the war and revolution, and the disruption and enormous decline in production during the civil war and famine. The conflict between the aggressive nature of the procurement agents and the suspicious, defensive reaction of the peasantry lay behind the rival and contradictory assessments of the harvest and of the needs of the producers. The existence of separate groups of government statisticians in the Central Statistical Administration (TsSU), the state planning commission (Gosplan), the agricultural commissariat (Narkomzem) and other agencies increased the scope for conflict, especially when they reinforced former rivalries and different ideological and institutional outlooks.[4]

Most of the Bolshevik leaders appeared to have little understanding of the complexities of the agricultural sector, little sympathy for the peasantry, little inclination to learn more about them, and a great distrust of agricultural experts. The experience of War Communism undoubtedly persuaded many Bolshevik leaders (including Stalin) of the efficiency of strong-arm tactics in dealing with the peasants.[5] Lenin, Tsyurupa and to a lesser extent Kalinin were the only senior party and state leaders with any serious understanding of the peasantry.[6] After the deaths of Lenin in 1924 and Tsyurupa in 1927 there was no one in the Council of People's Commissars (Sovnarkom) at the USSR level with any substantial agricultural knowledge. The USSR Sovnarkom did not even include a full People's Commissar for Agriculture until Yakovlev was appointed to the newly-established post in December 1929.[7] Agriculture was politically under-represented, and economically grossly and tragically misunderstood.

Ultimately political pressure was resorted to in order to ensure that one particular series of figures, and one particular view of agricultural reality, was accepted. The political resolution of the conflict over the rival estimates of agricultural reality had enormous influence over the policy that was pursued in the late 1920s and greatly affected the future of Soviet agriculture. These later developments will not be dealt with in this volume. But we need to bear them in mind, because the picture of agricultural reality which emerged as a result of the political struggle has been frozen into the official Soviet grain statistics. The historical record has not yet been corrected, although the recent rehabilitation in the USSR of many of the leading agricultural experts of the 1920s[8] indicates that such a correction is now more likely.

PRE-FIRST WORLD WAR TRENDS AND LEVELS

Grain Production and Utilisation

Production

Grain was by far the most important product of the Russian economy before the first world war. It covered about 90 per cent of all sown area and accounted for over 35–50 per cent of all agricultural produce by value. It supplied about 70 per cent of all human calories in a direct form, but also provided over half the livestock feed stuffs by value. It supplied industry with a large volume of raw materials and provided about 40 per cent by value of all exports. The grain economy was consequently the backbone of agriculture and of the economy at large. It was of enormous economic and political significance.

There remains considerable uncertainty as to the absolute level of pre-war grain production and this is the major factor contributing to the differences in the gross agricultural production data described above. These were the subject of fierce debate before the first world war between the local government (*zemstvo*) statisticians, the statisticians in the Department of Agriculture and those in the Central Statistical Committee (TsSK) of the Ministry of Internal Affairs. The *zemstvo* and Department of Agriculture statisticians argued that large corrections were needed to the TsSK data. The result of the first agricultural census in 1916, however, failed to indicate an obvious error in pre-war grain production data.[9]

In the early 1920s both the Central Statistical Administration (TsSU) and Narkomzem were reluctant to apply large corrections to the pre-war data. When Oganovsky and Kondratiev in Narkomzem came to compile an agricultural statistical handbook in the early 1920s they included the earlier TsSK evaluations and the 1916 census results without any corrections.[10] Gosplan, however, began arguing for a 19 per cent correction to the pre-war grain data: 9 per cent for yield and a further 9 per cent for yield $(1.09 \times 1.09 = 1.19)$. TsSU reluctantly applied first a 5 per cent correction, and then in 1926 an 11 per cent correction. Subsequently Gosplan began lowering the corrections it was applying to the pre-war data. The 16 per cent correction to pre-war data in the 1925/26 control figures fell to a 12 per cent correction in the 1926/27 control figures. No pre-war figures were given in the 1927/28 and later control figures or statistical handbooks, but in the mid-1930s the pre-war correction coefficient was lowered to 3 per cent (this was presumably with the purpose of presenting a more favourable picture of Soviet agricultural performance in comparison with the pre-revolutionary years before the first world war). In more recent times (after 1960) the officially accepted figure in the Soviet Union has been reduced further and is now 5 per cent *below* the uncorrected pre-war figure!

Elsewhere[11] I have shown that there was never much justification for the large corrections of pre-war data that were forced on TsSU in the early 1920s. But we cannot obtain an accurate comparison with the 1920s simply by removing them. These pre-war figures as increased by large correction coefficients were in turn used in the calculation of the correction coefficients for the 1920s data. The pre-war data after the removal of the correction coefficients are therefore not comparable with the 1920s data, which still contain high corrections. The TsSK uncorrected data[12] are in my opinion generally the most reliable in absolute terms. But the large correction coefficients need to be added to the pre-war data for purposes of comparison with the highly corrected data for the mid-1920s. I return to this important question later when I discuss the post-war level of recovery.

There are also considerable problems in measuring the trend in grain production over time. These are a result of very large and irregular yield fluctuations, caused by variability in the weather and particularly in the incidence of drought. It is often assumed that in any five-year period the fluctuations would cancel out. While this to some extent is true, large irregularities in the spread of good and bad years make the trend highly dependent on the periodisation and technique of measurement. In the five-year period 1909–13 there was an enormous growth – 4 per cent a year – as compared with the previous five-year period 1904–8; as much as 3.5 percentage points of this are attributable to higher yields. Many observers have been tempted to ascribe this growth to the Stolypin reforms, but this assumption is very rash, in view of the very large role of the weather in this result (see Table 24).

Grain production per head of population in 1909–13 was about 0.48 tons per year in uncorrected TsSK production figures, or 0.54 tons in corrected data. Per capita production rose fairly regularly from at least the 1880s: the rise in grain production of 2 per cent a year comfortably outstripped the growth in population of 1.6 per cent a year.[13]

Utilisation

The primary and rather inelastic uses of grain are: as seed for further reproduction of grain; and as food for human consumption. Yield-to-seed ratios were reported to have risen from 3.5:1 in the first half of the XIX Century to 5.5:1 on the eve of the revolution.[14] But in the short run, barring extreme shortages of famine proportions, little change could be expected; 15–20 per cent of grain was regularly used as seed. Human consumption of grain in the rural areas, given a predominantly bread diet, was of the order of 0.2 to 0.22 tons per head per year in grain equivalents. There were slight regional variations depending on the availability and use of other foodstuffs.[15]

The secondary and more elastic uses of grain were (a) off-farm marketings: export, urban/military use, industrial use or inter-rural sales; and (b) on-farm use for livestock feed. A certain amount of grain was unavoidably wasted in transportation and storage;[16] the losses tended to increase in bumper years.

On average, urban grain food consumption norms were somewhat less than rural, about 0.2 tons per head per year. The urban population in 1914 was about 25 million with 4 million in the two major cities Petrograd and Moscow.[17] The total urban food requirement on the eve of the first world war would have been some 5 million tons, something under 8 per cent of total uncorrected grain production. In 1897, with an urban population of about 12.5 millions, urban grain food consumption would have been about 2.5 million tons or about 6 per cent of total uncorrected grain production. The urban population had been growing at a rate of nearly 3 per cent a year, which was considerably more rapid than the population at large (with a 1.6 per cent year growth) or than grain production (with a 2 per cent per year growth). But urban grain consumption norms were about 10 per cent below rural consumption norms; and the urban population was still only about one-sixth of all the population. The growth of urban consumption was therefore no great strain.

During this period there were no significant changes in the proportion of grain being used in industry or to feed the army. In 1913 industrial use (excluding milling) was some 0.4–0.8 million tons, and the army (both men and livestock) consumed about 0.8 million tons.[18]

Grain exported abroad accounted for a much larger amount, about 8 million tons in the late 1890s (18 per cent of the uncorrected harvest) and about 11 million tons in 1909–13 (about 16 per cent).[19] The amount of grain being marketed extra-rurally for export and the towns, while increasing absolutely, was apparently tending to fall (from 24 to 22 per cent of the crop); since grain production was rising considerably more rapidly than population, the amount of grain left in the countryside per head of the rural population must have been rising. This confirms Paul Gregory's findings and his criticisms of the earlier conclusions of Alexander Gerschenkron.[20]

The two series of grain-fodder balances estimated by myself in Table 18 are both more or less comparable with the above account. Series (a) uses relatively low uncorrected production data throughout; and Series (b) includes the much larger Gosplan corrected data. The main differences are in the residual items of livestock feed, stock accumulation and losses. Given the uncorrected data, the amount of grain available for livestock feed is unlikely to have been more than 13.6 million tons (20 per cent of the crop).[21] This implies rather low livestock feed norms (especially if we assume that the pre-war livestock data need correcting),[22] and partly explains the wretched state of the livestock sector in most regions.[23] As we shall see this was in marked contrast to the situation in the mid-1920s.

In terms of grain marketings, the balances in Table 18 indicate that 11 million tons was exported, 16 per cent of the uncorrected 68 million ton harvest for 1909–13 (average) and that 17 million tons, 25 per cent of the uncorrected harvest, were marketed extra-rurally. These figures should be compared with the well-known Stalin–Nemchinov indicator of 1928 which claimed that 21.3 million tons of a harvest of 81.9 million tons (i.e., 26 per cent) were marketed outside the village (*vnederevenskii*).[24] As R. W. Davies has pointed out, the figure of 21.3 million tons may in fact include a component of intra-rural sales.[25] Stalin's grain production figures appear to refer to either a slightly inflated 1913 harvest or a highly inflated 1909–1913 harvest. If we assume that it is the former, his figures are roughly comparable with the uncorrected production data that are being used here. His marketed figures are also comparable with ours, if we allow for a slightly higher level of extra-rural marketings in 1913 (1–2 million tons) and an additional 3–4 million tons for intra-rural marketings.

Extra-rural marketings of 17 million tons, 25 per cent of uncorrected data, and total marketings of 21 million tons, or 26 per cent of uncorrected data, were very large, given the relatively low level of domestic production and consumption. But, as noted above, the marketed share had probably been this high from at least the 1890s and there is no indication of any decline in overall rural per capita grain retentions.

****

The national figures conceal important differences for different regions, grains and social sectors. Since the publication of the Stalin–Nemchinov data in 1928 attention has been concentrated almost exclusively on the sectoral breakdown of grain marketings. This tends to obscure problems in the evaluation of the scale of production, and the importance of the different regions and different grains. There are also problems in assessing the reliability of the sectoral breakdown given by Stalin–Nemchinov. Below we will consider briefly the available data differentiated by region and by grain as well as by socio-economic sector of production.

The regional dimension   Russia has with good reason been conventionally divided into grain-surplus and grain-deficit regions, generally known as 'producer' regions and 'consumer' regions. Map 1 shows the location of these regions. In 1909–13 30 per cent of the population were located in the grain-deficit regions: these produced 17 per cent of the grain and imported another 6–7 per cent (4–5 million tons) from the grain-surplus regions. The grain-surplus regions, with 70 per cent of the population, produced 83 per cent of the grain and regularly exported 16 per cent abroad and another 6–7 per cent to the deficit regions.[26]

In the pre-war years there was a falling per capita production in the Northern Consumer Region (NCR) and a growth in per capita production in the Southern Producer Region (SPR) and the Eastern Producer Region (EPR). The transport balances indicate a substantial increase in grain shipments into the NCR between 1901 and 1913; this largely restored per capita grain supplies to this region (see Table 19(b)). The surpluses came primarily from the SPR; the EPR was also expanding its surpluses rapidly, but from a very low base.

The SPR experienced a substantial growth in production, primarily as a result of the extension of the sown area, and it began to exceed the Central Producer Region (CPR) as the main grain producing area. It was the SPR that provided the bulk of grain exports. Despite a slight rise in sown area in the CPR, the frequent poor harvests in this area make it difficult to identify any upward trend. Most of the surpluses from this area went to the NCR, and supplied about 80 per cent of that region's import requirements. Despite a series of poor harvests in the EPR, the upward movement in the area sown to grain resulted in a slightly upward trend both in production and in extra-regional grain transfers. Meanwhile in the NCR there was a slight decline in grain sowing, and an almost stable level of production. Given the growth of population per capita grain production was falling sharply, but this was more than compensated for by the large grain transfers into this region. The NCR achieved rising per capita grain supplies, but only at the expense of becoming increasingly dependent on external grain supplies. In 1913 it was receiving 4.3 million tons of grain

Map 1. USSR agricultural regions

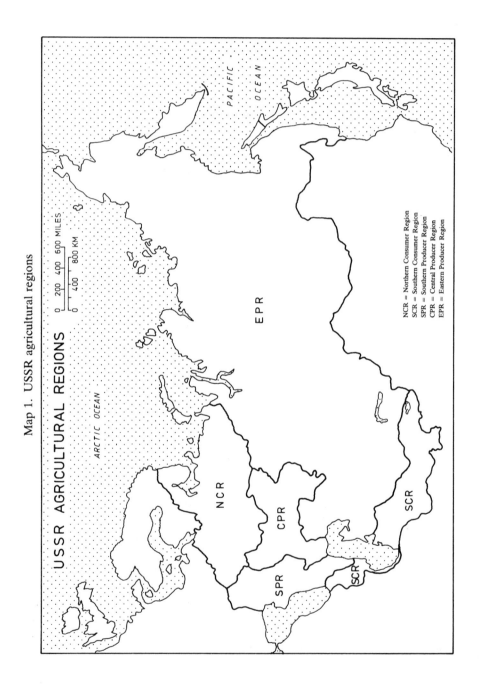

USSR AGRICULTURAL REGIONS

0   200   400   600 MILES
0   400   800 KM

ARCTIC OCEAN

PACIFIC OCEAN

NCR
SPR
CPR
SCR
SCR
EPR

NCR = Northern Consumer Region
SCR = Southern Consumer Region
SPR = Southern Producer Region
CPR = Central Producer Region
EPR = Eastern Producer Region

(about 30 per cent of its requirements), whereas in 1901 it received about 2.9 million tons (about 24 per cent of its requirements). Few comparable data are available at this time for SCR.

The different grains   Rye had always been the traditional food crop grown in the North and it was still the predominant grain, although wheat production, especially spring wheat, was increasing rapidly. This was partly the result of the expansion of sown area in the South and East and also the result of an increased emphasis on wheat as the major commodity and export grain. Amongst the non-food grains, oats fed primarily to horses was still of the greatest importance, although it was growing at a significantly lower rate than barley, the other major grain.

Socio-economic sectors   Until the 1916 census there was no reliable indication of the scale of private landowner farming, as opposed to peasant farming. The division between peasant and private land is not particularly relevant since much private land was rented out to peasants, or even bought by them. In 1916 private landowners sowed about 7.5 per cent of the total sown area, and may well have sown 10 per cent before the war.[27] Since grain yields on private estates were reported to have been about 20 to 25 per cent higher than on peasant farms[28] it is quite possible that landowner estates did account for about 12 per cent of grain production as was later claimed by Stalin and Nemchinov.

Grain marketings by landowners were undoubtedly larger than for the small-scale peasants, as indicated in the Stalin–Nemchinov figures. But it needs to be pointed out that the labour employed on landowners' estates was largely paid in money rather than in subsistence; it would consequently be wrong to assume that the high landowner marketing share can be used as a direct indicator of superiority in production. The division between 'kulaks' and other peasants given by Stalin–Nemchinov is highly dubious.

There was thus a very delicate overall balance in grain production and utilisation before the first world war. Each year the population was growing by 1.6 million, requiring an additional 0.34 million tons of grain per year for food alone, 0.4 million tons including grain for additional sowings, and 0.5 million tons per year to maintain a growing share in other forms of utilisation. The NCR was becoming increasingly dependent on the grain-surplus areas, and the CPR was finding it more and more difficult to provide for the needs of the NCR. Grain production overall was increasing fast enough to supply these needs. However, since most of the expansion was in the SPR and EPR, the regional imbalance was increasing. While it is true that the large private estates in the South West were the source of large grain marketings and exports, this was largely a consequence of the lower population densities in this area, and of the fact that the estates were employing wage labour and paying for it in money rather than grain. It was not necessarily a sign of their greater productivity, and there was no way in which the conditions prevalent in the South West could be imposed on the rest of the country, short of depopulating it.

Potatoes, Vegetables and Fruit

Inadequate attention has been paid to any of the non-grain sectors of agriculture. The various evaluations of potatoes, vegetables and fruit in Table 17 indicate that they amounted to as much as roughly a quarter of the valuation of grain. One of the reasons for the neglect of this sector is that, with the exception of most potatoes, these crops were not grown in the main village fields (*nadely*) but on the household plots (*usad'by*) and so were not included in the normal statistical accounts. Moreover, they did not enter much into international trade.[29] About 33 per cent of production (by value), however, did enter into internal commodity circulation. In the case of potatoes, 17 per cent were reported to have been sold on inter-rural markets and 15 per cent on town markets.[30] In the case of vegetables and fruit, nearly all the marketings went to the towns. The marketed produce presumably came from areas specialising in market gardening around the major towns, and especially in the NCR.

Potato production was estimated at 29.9 million tons in 1913 by Gukhman and in the early Gosplan control figures, including 9.5 million tons grown on household plots.[31] Since the 1930s the 1913 level has been reduced to 23.3 million tons, but this appears to exclude potatoes grown on household plots.[32]

The vegetable and fruit figures in these early assessments were very approximate, since they were initially based on consumption data. They are consequently not directly comparable with later data.

Because of the scarcity of data for crops other than potatoes, it is difficult to compute any overall pre-war trends or regional indicators. The growth of potato production was well ahead of population growth. Over the two periods 1895–8 and 1899–1903 potato production grew by an average annual rate of 6.9 per cent, and in the following five-year period (1899–1903 to 1904–8) by 1.5 per cent, and in the immediate pre-war five years (1904–9 to 1909–13) by 6.2 per cent per year.[33] Potato production tended to be located on peasant as distinct from landowners' land, predominantly in the Northern and Western part of the country, although it was clearly beginning to spread elsewhere.

Industrial Crops

The industrial crop sector comprised four different groups of crops: (i) the fibrous crops – cotton, flax and hemp; (ii) the oilseeds – sunflower, flax and hemp; (iii) sugar beet; and (iv) others – tea, tobacco, *makhorka* (cheap tobacco) and hops. Together their value was about 700–800 million pre-war rubles, about 15 per cent of the value of grain and considerably less than that of potatoes, vegetables and fruit. A very large share of these crops were marketed, and all of them were grown as field crops. They have therefore generally received more attention than some of the other sectors.

There has generally been far less revision of these figures than of other series. The currently accepted figures are normally comparable with the figures accepted in the 1920s.

The 1925/26 control figures claimed that roughly 84 per cent of industrial crops were marketed extra-rurally: 70 per cent of oilseeds, 84 per cent of fibres and 99 per cent of other crops (including sugar beet). Within the fibre group it should be noted that 100 per cent of cotton was marketed but only 40 per cent of hemp.[34]

About 20 per cent of all cotton supplies were imported (197,000 tons, about 43 million pre-war rubles). The main export industrial crops were flax (305,000 tons – 94 million pre-war rubles), sugar (147,000 tons – 24 million pre-war rubles) and hemp (68,000 tons – 14 million rubles). From these figures it is clear that receipts from flax exports alone covered cotton imports more than twofold.[35]

There were quite distinct regional and sectoral differentiations between the different industrial crops. Sugar beet, cotton, tea and tobacco tended to be produced on landowner estates while the other crops were grown primarily by the peasants. Cotton production was located in Central Asia, tea and tobacco production in the Transcaucasus, flax, hemp and sugar beet in the North and West, and sunflower production in the South of European Russia.

While sugar beet and potato production were growing at rates well ahead of grain production, there was a long-term decline in flax and hemp fibre production (mainly as a result of increased use of cotton), and little improvement in flax and hemp seed production. Tobacco production was growing more rapidly, and although there are no accurate figures it may be assumed that cotton and sunflower seed production were also growing rapidly.[36]

Meadow, Pasture and Rough Fodder

According to the estimates in Table 17, this sector was responsible for the production of value equal to about half the value produced by the grain sector. This is quite remarkable given the very small amount of attention that this sector normally receives. The reasons for this neglect are obvious. Relatively few statistics are gathered for this sector; it does not enter at all into international trade and only slightly into market production; most of the produce is used internally within agriculture as a raw material for the livestock sector. The evaluation of this sector involves a certain amount of double counting, but hay and fodder preparation is a very important process within agriculture. In order to understand the complexity of agricultural production, and to distinguish properly between gross production and net production, this sector must be carefully considered. In many ways it is the agricultural equivalent to the coal industry.

Various indicators for hay and rough fodder production in 1913 were calculated in the early 1920s. They are very large and range between 2,100 and 2,400 million pre-war rubles. Since the middle 1920s no further details have been published on the pre-war hay and rough fodder indicators used in more recent gross production data.

According to the 1925/26 control figures, the marketed share of hay and rough fodder production amounted to 5.8 per cent of the total; 3.5 per cent were marketed in towns and the remaining 2.3 per cent inter-rurally.[37] In international trade Russia was an important exporter of oilseed cake; 1.5 million tons of this livestock feed concentrate were exported in 1913, valued at about 80 million pre-war rubles.[38]

It is very difficult to obtain an accurate impression of long-term trends in hay and fodder availability. But there are many indications that in the Central Agricultural and Volga regions the expansion of the grain area was taking place at the expense of pasture land and fallow. This was creating severe problems.[39]

Livestock

The absolute level of livestock is known with even greater uncertainty than that of grain. After comparing the results of the first livestock census of 1916 with the standard TsSK registration data, A. E. Lossitsky, the early livestock statistics specialist in TsSU, recommended abandoning the earlier TsSK data in comparisons with the post-revolutionary period, and using instead the 1916 figures. In more recent times the veteran Soviet economist A. L. Vainshtein has gone further and suggested that since it was generally accepted that there had been a decline in livestock numbers in the first two years of the war, the 1913 livestock level ought to be considerably higher than the 1916 levels. On the basis of a comparison with regional *zemstvo* and other data Vainshtein inflated the original TsSK data by 20–89 per cent. A comparison of these figures is given in Table 21.

Both Vainshtein and Lossitsky appear to have accepted the inter-temporal comparability of the pre-war data and so their revaluations mainly affect comparisons with post-revolutionary data.

In his *Russian National Income, 1885–1913*, Paul Gregory has calculated an alternative livestock series which in my view exaggerates the growth of pre-revolutionary livestock numbers. His data indicate that horses and cattle were increasing in numbers at rates well above or very close to the population growth rates. My data indicate far lower growth rates. Gregory's growth rates are quite comparable with Prokopovich's livestock produce growth rate of 1.9 per cent a year for the 50 provinces of European Russia for 1900 to 1909–13. But Prokopovich used non-comparable data; he corrected his 1909–13 data with the results of the 1916 census, but had failed to make similar corrections to the 1900 data.[40] I therefore recommend the abandonment of Prokopovich's pre-war livestock growth indicator and its replacement by a much smaller one, probably about half this value, or 1 per cent per year.[41]

Table 17 provides an indication of the different figures that have been accepted at different times for the gross valuation of livestock produce. They differ between 2,500 and 3,000 million pre-war rubles, mostly meat and milk. These pre-war gross production figures were apparently based partly on consumption data, and therefore may not necessarily require a correction to make them comparable to make them comparable with Vainshtein's revised livestock numbers.

In terms of marketed production data published after the revolution indicate that over 50 per cent of livestock produce was marketed on the eve of the war, 45 per cent extra-rurally (to towns and for export), 7.3 per cent intra-rurally. 97 per cent of leather and hides were marketed, 65 per cent of eggs and 50 per cent of meat, but only 39 per cent of poultry and 28 per cent of milk.[42]

In foreign trade the most important livestock exports were eggs (0.25 million tons, worth about 50 million pre-war rubles), butter (77,000 tons, about 41 million pre-war rubles), breeding stock (0.061 million tons, 118 million rubles). Only 20,000 tons of meat (5.5 million rubles) were exported. The Russian Empire was a net importer of wool and leather, and of live animals for slaughter.[43]

While it is not clear how Gregory computed his livestock figures it is clear that the difference between his and the accepted series is not simply one of regional completeness. The data disaggregated regionally indicate that the small growth in livestock numbers took place in all regions with the exception of the EPR. Growth was particularly slow in the CPR, and numbers actually fell between 1905 and 1913. In the SPR, horse and pig numbers grew at a rate only slightly lower than the population growth, but cattle numbers actually fell here also.

Part of the explanation for the poor development of livestock was the over-concentration on grain production for exports. Grain exports restricted the amount of grain available for livestock feed, and the expansion of the area sown to grain was often at the expense of meadows and haylands.

No regional data are available on livestock production as distinct from livestock numbers. In the absence of reliable pre-war data on average animal weights, milk or wool yields it must be assumed that the regional livestock production will correspond to the distribution of regional livestock numbers. Marketings were, however, likely to be of far more significance in the main commercial livestock areas, the NCR and the EPR. Peasants organised into cooperatives were prominent in dairy and meat farming, which developed strongly at this time. Landowners tended to concentrate more on raising breeding stock, especially horses: the local rural authorities (the *zemstva*) also began to engage in stock breeding.

The Influence of the Weather on Production

The most significant factor affecting agricultural production in the short run, and also to some extent in the longer run (certainly in five-year periods), is the weather and, in particular, drought. It has generally been realised that the 1913 weather had been exceptionally good, but not that the whole 1909–13 period was rather exceptional. According to my drought index there was a preponderance of non-drought years in 1909–13, with the result that the average 1909–13 weather was far more favourable than normal (over + 0.3 standard deviations) (see Table 24). The other major weather factor was winter killing (i.e., the loss of winter sowings due to premature thawing followed by a sharp frost). There are no serious reports of this phenomenon for the immediate pre-war years, but reliable data are lacking.

The fact that the weather favourably influenced grain yields in 1909–13 in comparison with 1904–8 indicates that it would be rash to attempt to explain this improvement in terms of the Stolypin reforms which commenced in 1907. Most of the improvement in grain production in these five years, perhaps about 85 per cent of the increase, was due to favourable weather.

DECLINE AND RECOVERY, 1914–25

Grain Production and Utilisation

The extent of the decline in grain production is very uncertain. Contemporary estimates of the level of production were based on rough assumptions about the deviation from the pre-war 'normal' level of production; thus the uncertainty about the extent of the decline has to be added to the uncertainty about the pre-war level. Moreover, an array of different figures refers to different areas, with different correction coefficients applied to their base data.

The general trends of decline and recovery in grain production for the different series are shown in Tables 17–19. Both the TsSU and Gosplan data enable us to identify three separate sub-periods with distinctly different trends. The first four war-time years, 1914–17, were a period of fairly gentle decline in production. This was followed by four years of more precipitate decline during the civil war and foreign intervention, 1918–21; this culminated in the famine of 1921–2. This was followed by five years of recovery, 1922–6. According to contemporary evaluations, the peak 1926 harvest was still 16 per cent below the 1913 peak level and about equal to or slightly below the 1909–13 (average) harvest. Thus in terms of grain production there was at least a 13-year delay in the trend, assuming that it would recover after this. As a result of war, civil war and famine, by 1923 the population was over six million below the 1914 level. But from 1922 it rose rapidly and by 1925 it had recovered to the level of 1914; and it reached 5.5 per cent above the 1914 level by the end of 1926; consequently per capita grain production in 1926 was some 6–12 per cent below the 1909–13 level and about 20 per cent below the 1913 level.

The First World War, 1914–7
The first and immediate effect of the war was to block the exports from the 1914 and subsequent harvests. This had the effect of increasing domestic grain supplies by about 10 million tons a year until production levels fell. The removal of large numbers of adult male peasants and horses from the countryside appears to have had far less of an effect on agricultural productivity than might have been expected given the large numbers involved. For landowners' estates employing agricultural labour the effect was very significant, but for the peasant farms the level of under-utilisation of labour before 1914 enabled production to go on without major setbacks.

A more significant consequence of peasant recruitment into the army was the much larger demand for grain for the army. The size of the army grew from less than half a million in January 1914 to 5 million in January 1915, over 7 million in January 1916, and 8 million in January 1917.[44]

In terms of the total national grain balance the increase in demand for the army was largely offset by the decline in demand from the civilian population that was recruited into the army. But in terms of marketing and regional balance the disturbance was enormous. The military concentrations were located primarily in the grain-deficit or 'consumer' regions – the Western front in the NCR and SPR, and the Southern front in the SCR. In addition to the strain which the army placed on marketed grain, from 1915 very large numbers of refugees (about 6 million) came flooding into the NCR from occupied Poland.[45]

It was the disruption of normal marketing and geographical transfers that caused the initial grain supply problems rather than any shortfall in production. The state began organising grain collections for the army, but in 1916 it was forced to expand its operations to cover the urban population in the NCR. State grain collections rose sharply from 5 million tons in 1914/15 to 8.2 million tons in 1915/16. In 1916/17, the state obtained only slightly more, 8.9 million tons, despite the increase in responsibilities.[46] Since the urban population in the NCR had expanded during the war the total market requirements for the army and the Northern towns alone would have been about 9 million tons. The food grain situation was very strained, but not impossible. The problems were more the result of the transport difficulties, as can be seen from the regional production and transport data in Table 19.

There was a sharp decline in grain production in the NCR and also in the CPR, the producer region with the closest links to the NCR. Plenty of grain was available in the SPR and the EPR but from these regions it was more difficult to supply the NCR; the initial grain surpluses of these regions may well have been converted into livestock feed or vodka. From the rail transport data it would appear that shipments into the NCR were higher in 1914 and 1915 than in 1913, and that the decline began slowly in 1916.

The main change between socio-economic sectors in 1914–17 was due to the decline in the private landowner sector. In 1914–16, as a result of labour shortages, sowings probably fell by about 10 per cent. With the agrarian revolution of 1917, private land ownership was abolished and the landowners dispossessed. Most of their land was transferred to the peasantry.

Foreign Intervention, Civil War and Famine, 1918–21

The dissolution of the army after October 1917 immediately lessened the grain supply problems for the new Soviet government. A more vigorous application of the confiscation of grain stocks also temporarily eased the problem. But, with the German occupation of the Ukraine and the subsequent loss of control over other areas, grain supplies became even more strained. The Northern towns began starving and rapidly losing their populations as a result (mainly because of migration, but partly as a result of disease and famine).[47] With the subsequent outbreak of civil war, large-scale military forces were re-established. By the end of 1920 the Red Army had a strength of 3.9 million and the White Armies at their peak were estimated at just over 1 million men.[48] Very severe grain shortages in the army and the Northern cities resulted in urban famine and in extremely strict grain requisitioning policies.

No meaningful grain production figures are available for 1918 and 1919. Large parts of the grain producer regions were cut off from the grain consumer regions by military action, and the Northern cities underwent severe depopulation.

Both TsSU and Gosplan data indicate that grain production had fallen to about 54 per cent of pre-war (1909–13 average) level in 1920; this was due to a 24 per cent fall in sown area and a 29 per cent fall in yields.[49] Urgent steps were needed to get the peasants to increase their sowings. The market incentive for grain production had disappeared with the spread of the requisitioning system.

To deal with this crisis attempts were made in the autumn of 1920 to enforce sowing plans.[50] But, in February 1921, after early reports from TsSU indicated the prospect of relatively low sowings and a risk of famine, Lenin finally decided to take measures to restore the grain market with the intention of increasing peasant incentive to sow more grain.[51]

In fact the drought of the summer of 1921 made the situation considerably more desperate than initially envisaged in the spring when the changes in policy were announced. As a result of the drought, the first year of NEP was a famine year, the sown area continued to fall even in 1922, and the loss of control of the market was much more serious than earlier envisaged.

The 1921 level of state grain collections through the tax in kind (3.8 million tons) was much lower than the requisitions of 1920 (6 million tons).[52] And although there was some improvement in the situation in the NCR, conditions in the main grain producer regions greatly deteriorated. Despite the import of 0.8 million tons of grain,[53] the main producer regions faced famine. Recovery for the country as a whole was delayed to the good harvest of 1922. The relatively high yield in 1922, partly due to the improved weather, overcame the effect of the fall in sowings.

The regional breakdown is presented in Table 19. According to the contemporary TsSU evaluations in 1920, the NCR reached a low point of 55 per cent of its 1909–13 (average) grain production and then began to recover; in the main producer areas the low point was not reached until the following year 1921, and the sown area continued to fall even in 1922. In these years grain transfers to the NCR were minimal; and grain was even imported from abroad.

Recovery, 1922–6

From 1922, with good weather and a revival of market incentives, grain production began to increase despite the lower sowings of 1922. The area sown began to increase again from 1923; according to contemporary evaluations, it was still 11 per cent below pre-war levels in 1926. Thanks to the excellent weather of 1925 and 1926, the level of grain production was only just below the average pre-war levels. However, in per capita terms it was still 6–12 per cent lower.

After 1922 grain collections increased to provide supplies for the towns that began to recover their lost populations. But given the relatively low level of grain production per head of the population, it was not surprising that grain exports remained relatively low. Exports net of imports reached 0.7 million tons in 1922/23 and 2.7 million tons in 1923/24 but fell back to 0.14 million tons in 1924/25 and were still only 2.0 million tons in 1925/26.[54].

The two main producer regions, SPR and CPR, lagged in the recovery of their sown area, mainly as a result of the loss of horses and hence of draft power in the drought and famine. A comparison of the extent of the recovery of grain sown area and of horse numbers indicates a definite relationship in most areas. In 1926 the SPR, with 76 per cent of its pre-war (1916) horses, was sowing 85 per cent of its pre-war area; the CPR, with only 66 per cent of its 1916 horses, was sowing 81 per cent; and in the NCR, where horse numbers exceeded the 1916 level by 13 per cent, the grain sown area was 93 per cent of its pre-war level, but the sowings of other crops was also high. The exception was the EPR: despite having only 75 per cent of the 1916 number of horses grain sown area was already 12 per cent above the pre-war level.[55] This appears to be explained by a shift in orientation away from livestock farming in the EPR, at a time when other regions were shifting away from such great dependence on grain farming.

In NCR, with grain production in 1926 8 per cent above the pre-war level, and with transhipments of 4 million tons into the region, per capita grain supplies were higher than pre-war.

The situation in general was fairly good, as long as it was realised that the pre-war recovery was not complete (especially in per capita terms), that more draft power was needed to speed up the recovery of pre-war sown area levels, and that greater emphasis was now being given to livestock and other non-grain arable sectors. Unfortunately the government failed to appreciate these changed circumstances adequately.

Potatoes, Vegetables and Fruit

The effect of the war and subsequent distruption was to greatly increase the importance of potato and vegetable production for domestic subsistence. Potato production is reported to have grown from 29.9 million tons in 1913 to 44.8 million tons in 1925, although the scale of marketed production fell from 4.6 million tons to 2.8 million tons – i.e., from 15.5 per cent of the crop to 6.3 per cent.[56]

While the data for potato production are fairly reliable, the data for vegetables and fruit are far more doubtful. They are largely based on food consumption surveys. As a fairly rough guide it would appear that vegetable and fruit production was slightly larger in value than potato production, and its market share was more than double that of potatoes, and tended to fall less sharply.[57] The total production of potatoes, fruit and vegetables was substantially higher than before the war (see Table 17).

Industrial Crops

The decline in industrial crops production was far more precipitate than for other sectors of agriculture, but its recovery was also far more rapid. Table 20 presents an indication of these main movements for the three main groups of industrial crops. Among the fibres the decline in cotton was the most precipitate, almost as severe as the decline in sugar beet production.

These were the two crops that had earlier been produced primarily on landowner estates. Flax and hemp fibres production, both produced and used by the peasants themselves, did not fall to the same extent. And oilseed production, especially sunflowers, remained high. The growth in sunflower production was the most important factor in restoring the overall value of industrial crop production to pre-war levels.

Marketings declined sharply, from 84 per cent to 59–71 per cent. This was primarily a result of a much greater decline in the production of the more commodity-oriented industrial crops, cotton and sugar beet, and a lower decline in the more peasant-oriented crops, oilseed, flax and hemp.[58] With the decline in industrial production the import of cotton fell; even in 1925 it was only half the 1913 level. Exports of most industrial crops were very low, with the exception of oilseed exports, which exceeded the 1913 level by 1924.[59]

Meadow, Hay and Rough Fodder

This had been one of the least well understood sectors in the pre-war period and it remained even more uncertain in the immediate post-war period. Two contradictory factors affected the availability of hay in the early 1920s. The decline in overall sown area resulted in much arable reverting to rough pasture. But the great decline in livestock numbers resulted in less pasture being needed. We would consequently expect that a diminished amount of hay would be harvested, but that the livestock would be proportionally better provided with hay than before the war. Table 17 provides an indication of the value of hay and rough fodder given in contemporary calculations where it was reported to have fallen from 2,200 to 1,500 million pre-war rubles.

As regards exports, the only fodder product exported before the war was oilseed cakes; there was now a large decline in these exports, by about 75 per cent.[60]

Given the magnitude of the values concerned it is most unfortunate that the reliability of these figures is so small. Most of this value will be deducted when we consider net or marketed production, but it is nevertheless important to note that we are dealing here with a very large sector.

Livestock

As a result of the Vainshtein corrections (see p. 90 above), it appears that a slight decline in livestock numbers occurred between 1913 and 1916.[61] But whether or not this decline took place is almost irrelevant in comparison with the magnitude of the subsequent decline (see Table 21). The scale of livestock production undoubtedly reflected this decline in livestock numbers. The temporary increase in final products (leather, meat, etc.)

does not compensate even temporarily for the decline in other products if we include a component for change in stocks in our calculations. Exports were replaced by imports; extra-rural marketings were low.

In regional terms we should note the initial growth of livestock numbers in the EPR and the subsequent decline. The decline in the NCR was far less than in other areas and the recovery began in this area in 1920 and proceeded throughout the famine years. According to the TsSU data, horse and cattle numbers in 1922 recovered towards the 1916 level in the NCR whereas they were reaching a low point of 46–70 per cent of 1916 levels in all other regions. The CPR was certainly in the worst position as regards the decline in livestock.[62]

The agrarian revolution led to the loss and break up of the landowner herds which often contained the best pure-bred stock. Attempts by local authorities to preserve the pure-bred stock were seldom satisfactory.

Livestock levels began to rise again in all areas in the year after the disastrous drought of 1921. According to contemporary evaluations, by 1925 cattle numbers had almost recovered to 1916 levels and milk production exceeded the 1913 level. But the number of horses and most other livestock produce were still much lower than pre-war.[63]

By 1925 Russia had become a net importer of livestock produce. Large imports of leather, wool and live animals were in excess of net exports of butter, eggs and meat by about 8 million pre-war rubles. The major change was the decline of local production and export of leather and meat, which was a natural consequence of the attempts to build up the herds after the drought and losses of 1921–2.[64]

RECOVERY AND RESTRUCTURING, 1926–8

Grain Production and Utilisation

As I have sought to show above, grain production in the peak year of 1926 had not yet quite reached the 1909–13 (average) level and was some 16 per cent below the exceptionally high level of 1913. In the three years 1926–8 (average) production was about 6 per cent below the 1909–13 (average) level. But by the beginning of 1927 population was already 5.5 per cent higher than at the beginning of 1914, and it increased by a further 2.2 per cent in the course of 1927. Per capita output in 1926–8 was therefore some 12 per cent less than in 1909–13.

As a result of the lower level of per capita grain production than before the war, it is not at all surprising that grain marketings were significantly reduced and that little grain was available for export. But there was another major factor which contributed to the decline in marketings, and this was the change in structure of agriculture as a result of non-grain sectors becoming relatively more important. This applied to some extent to potatoes, vegetables and technical crops. But most important was the livestock sector. More grain was needed for transfer between different rural areas to feed that part of the labour force engaged in these activities. Even more important, larger amounts of grain appear to have been fed to livestock in the mid- and late 1920s in order to rebuild the herds and place livestock farming on a more secure basis than before the war. Several scholars, including Naum Jasny in the United States, and the Gosplan experts Vishnevsky and Groman, assumed that the high livestock feed norms prevailing in the 1920s, on which there is solid evidence, also operated before the war. It seems to me that the case for lower pre-war grain feed norms is much stronger (see also the evidence on the lower weight of cattle in 1913, in note 78, p. 359 below).

If I am right to assume that feed norms were higher in the 1920s, it is easy to explain the decrease in grain marketings by 7–11 million tons; see my rough estimates in Table 18. A decline in production by some 4 million tons was accompanied by an increase in population leading to a higher food consumption of some 1.5 million tons, and there was also probably an increase in livestock feed by over 6 million tons due to the use of higher feed norms.

Unfortunately this position was not appreciated by the leading Soviet political authorities. The government was far less concerned with understanding agricultural improvement than in identifying constraints on industrial development. Their main concern was the failure of grain production to support the same level of marketings and exports as before the war. With the lack of foreign credits to support capital investment in new industry, the need for foreign trade surpluses was greater than ever. Russia had exported 10 million tons a year before the war, but it was now only exporting a fraction of that amount – some 2 million tons were exported in 1925/26 and 1926/27, and only 70,000 tons (net of imports) in 1927/28.[65] In his account of the grain problem, Stalin maintained that the pre-war level of production had been restored; the main reason for the decline in marketings was the shift away from large-scale production towards more medium and small-scale producers.[66] This analysis has subsequently become widely accepted, but is profoundly misleading. The Stalin–Nemchinov data are probably fairly reliable given the convention of using the highly corrected Gosplan figures (see p. 82 above). The problem lies not in the basic data, but in the interpretation of it.

As I have sought to show, there is no mystery about the reasons for the grain shortage. The attempts of the government to control and hold down grain prices naturally increased the attractiveness of converting grain surpluses to livestock, whose value could be realised on the less restricted private market.

A comparison of sowings by the different type of grain before the revolution and in the late 1920s also indicated the shift from food to feed grains. The sharp decline in food grain sowings in 1928 was largely a result of the large winter killings by the premature thaw in the spring of 1928. A large part of the re-sowing was apparently in the form of maize.[67]

The main regional outlines of recovery of grain production and the level of regional grain transfers are shown in Table 19. The NCR had become slightly more self-sufficient than before the war; a much larger share of imports into this region now came from the SPR rather than the CPR. Grain production in the CPR was still particularly low, and the shortfall in grain transfers from this region to the NCR was partly made up by transferring grain that would normally have been exported abroad from the SPR to the NCR. The situation was also made somewhat more complicated with the extension of industrial crop production in the SCR which consequently increased the need of transfers to that area.

Potatoes, Vegetables and Fruit

The 1926 harvest of 43 million tons of potatoes was a record. Although the 1927 and 1928 harvests were slightly lower at 41.2 and 39.9 million tons they were clearly well in excess of the 29.9 million ton pre-war figure that was accepted in the early 1920s.[68] The growth by nearly 40 per cent was a result partly of an increase in sown area and partly of an increase in yield. Given the large increase in potato production it is remarkable that extra-rural marketings declined from 4.5 million tons in 1913 to 2.7–2.9 million tons between 1925/26 and 1927/28.[69] This was a decline from some 15 per cent of total production in 1913 to less than 7 per cent in the mid-1920s. Of course none of this was exported and the decline was purely reflected in a decline in urban consumption.

The data for vegetables and fruit are far more problematical as regards comparability. There appears to have been a far lower growth in overall production. There was probably some decline in fruit and vinegrowing as a result of the destruction of landowner orchards and vineyards, but this may have been offset by an increase in peasant vegetable production. But overall the level of extra-rural marketings appears to have fallen from about 33 per cent of production in 1913 to 18–20 per cent in the mid-1920s.[70] This may also have been associated with the relative decline of the more commodity-oriented orchards and vineyards in comparison with vegetable plots.

Industrial Crops

By the late 1920s there had been a quite substantial increase in the production of fibrous crops, primarily as a result of a large increase in cotton production in 1927 and 1928. By 1928 cotton production was over 40 per cent above pre-war levels. Flax production was about 25 per cent lower and hemp about 22 per cent higher.[71] Virtually all of the cotton appeared as commodity production and was processed off the farm, but a large proportion of flax and an even larger proportion of hemp was processed by the peasants themselves and used in small-scale peasant industry. According to the 1925/26 control figures the percentages of extra-rural commodity production of flax and hemp were respectively 84 per cent and 37 per cent, but by 1927/28 these proportions had fallen to 45 per cent and 19 per cent.[72] The increase in domestic cotton production enabled the scale of cotton imports to be reduced from 197,000 tons in 1913 to 145,000 tons in 1927/28, but at the same time the level of flax and hemp exports had been reduced dramatically.[73] In value terms, Russia had changed from being a net vegetable fibre exporter to a net vegetable fibre importer.

The changes in oilseed production were equally dramatic. By 1925 Soviet oilseed production already exceeded the pre-revolutionary level by 28 per cent. In the following years there was probably a slight decline, but in 1928 production was still 25 per cent above the 1913 level. However, by this time marketings and exports were much lower than the pre-war level. Whereas in 1913 about 70 per cent of oilseeds had been marketed, in 1925/26–1927/28 the proportion had fallen to 45–50 per cent,[74] and the export of oilseeds declined even more rapidly.[75]

Sugar-beet production was still about 10 per cent below the pre-war level in 1927 and 1928. Virtually all production was marketed for processing into sugar. But after the period in the early 1920s when Russia had been importing sugar, from the mid-1920s sugar exports increased, and almost reached 1913 levels of export; sugar was clearly on the path to recovery.[76]

Hay and Rough Fodder

Data on hay and rough fodder production and utilisation is certainly one of the most problematical areas and there is little reliable evidence. It does however appear to be the case that the livestock were being better fed than before the war, and that they had a higher level of concentrates in their feed. It appears that a higher proportion of grain and bran was being fed to the animals. There was a substantial decline in the export of oilseed cake as more was fed to livestock within the USSR. This partly explains the dynamic growth of the herds in these years.

Livestock

The situation varied considerably between types of livestock and the different regions. While horse numbers as late as 1928 were still well below the uncertain pre-war level (possibly 6 per cent lower), the number of cattle, pigs and sheep were already much higher. The numbers of cattle in

1928 were probably 16 per cent higher than in 1913,[77] while pig numbers were probably over 24 per cent higher. It should be noted that during these years the weight of cattle was increasing and by 1927/28 was variously estimated at 9–13 per cent above the 1913 level.[78] However, by 1928 the growth rates were beginning to slow down and in certain areas there were already signs of a livestock crisis.

The situation was in all cases much better in the northern grain consumer areas than in the southern producer regions. By 1928 the NCR even registered a substantial increase in horse numbers by 18 per cent in comparison with a decline of 9.6 per cent in the SPR, 17.7 per cent in the CPR and 6.9 per cent in the EPR. For cattle, pigs and other animals the growth in the NCR tended to outstrip that in the other areas. The EPR had begun re-establishing the livestock and dairy orientation which had been destroyed after the revolution, but developments in this direction were rudely curtailed when Stalin directed the grain collection agencies in the Urals and Siberia to seek out and collect grain stocks in these areas in the winter of 1927/28, by using 'extraordinary measures' if necessary.[79]

The Influence of the Weather

Weather conditions in the 1920s were on the whole less favourable in the 1920s than in the last pre-war five-year period, 1909–13, and in the exceptionally favourable year 1913. The estimates in Table 24 show that the deviation from trend was +0.3 in 1909–13 (annual average) and +1.8 in the wholly exceptional year 1913. In 1921–5 (annual average) the deviation from trend was almost −0.8. In the years 1926–8, which are the concern of this section, weather was 'normal', with no deviation from trend on average for the three years. The lower level of grain production in these years as compared with 1909–13 was at least to some extent a result of the favourable weather in 1909–13. Moreover, the poor harvest in 1927 as compared with the peak year 1926 was primarily due to the weather. In 1928 another important weather factor took effect: winter sowings were lost owing to premature thawing followed by a sharp frost; there are no serious reports of this phenomenon for the immediate pre-war years. These factors were not taken into account by the Soviet authorities, who hoped each year for a good harvest which would solve their problems by enabling substantial exports.

CONCLUSIONS

Current Soviet statistical handbooks claim that gross agricultural production in the USSR exceeded the pre-first world war level in 1925 by 12 per cent and that by 1928 it was 24 per cent higher than the 1913 level.

According to these figures the recovery of livestock production was slightly higher, and exceeded 1913 levels by 21 per cent in 1925 and 37 per cent in 1928, while arable production was slightly lower but still exceeded 1913 levels by 7 per cent in 1925 and by 17 per cent in 1928. My preliminary findings (given in Table 22) suggest that these figures provide a very misleading indicator of the levels of agricultural production over this period; gross agricultural production and especially arable production were much lower than current Soviet indicators suggest. In 1925, according to my estimates, arable production did not exceed the 1913 production by 7 per cent, but was as much as 13 per cent lower, approximately equal to the 1909–13 (average) level. As late as 1928 arable production was still 6 per cent lower than in 1913, or 9 per cent higher than in 1909–13 (average). Livestock production had certainly been growing more rapidly (especially if we include the growth in herds) and probably exceeded pre-war levels by 23–28 per cent in 1925. But the growth rate slowed down in 1927 and 1928 and it is possible that the 1928 levels were lower than the 1925 levels (see Table 22).

Net agricultural production, marketings (extra-rural) and especially exports were all much lower still. The major part of this poor performance was due to less grain being produced per capita than before the war, and more of it being used within the agricultural sector. The build up of the livestock herds and the development of non-grain sectors of agriculture both resulted in the higher consumption of grain within agriculture and less grain being available for marketing extra-rurally or for export.

There is no need to draw upon political and socio-economic factors to explain the low level of grain marketings in these years. Given the price incentives, the low level of grain production and the increased on-farm demand for grain the reason for the decline in marketings is in my opinion quite clear.

6 The Peasantry and Industrialisation
Mark Harrison[1]

THE HISTORICAL BACKGROUND

Tsarist Precedents

In the last quarter of the XIX Century the perspectives of tsarist Russia shifted towards an industrial future. Fierce pressures emanating from the Western European economies and Atlantic trade forced her leaders to abandon the dream of economic and military modernisation on the basis of an agrarian society of agricultural and artisan production and primary export promotion. They sought increasingly to protect the Russian economy against manufactured imports, to improve profit conditions for both domestic and foreign investors in Russian large-scale industries, and to increase government spending on public enterprise (especially railways).

Forced into industrial revolution while still uncertain of its social desirability, Russia's leaders aimed to give it a form which would conserve, as far as possible, the traditional place of the peasant in society. This form included the consolidation of peasant land entitlements allotted through the village commune under the serf Emancipation of 1861, the intended reliance of public finance upon direct taxes and rents imposed on the village on the basis of the mutual guarantee of villagers each for each other's liability, the restriction of peasant movement through the requirement of an internal passport issued by the village authorities, and the structure to be imposed upon industrial development as a result: a dual system of small-scale, non-specialised village and handicraft industries coupled with large-scale, specialised urban factory industry reliant upon a migrant, unskilled workforce recruited from the village on a seasonal contract or for a period of a few years.

Such aspirations of the tsarist government proved extremely influential in forming Western post-war historians' model of the role played by the peasantry in the industrialisation of Russia. This model was formed in the 1950s; some elements were pioneered by Theodore von Laue, but it received its most coherent and developed exposition from the pen of Alexander Gerschenkron.[2] The crucial factor in the model was the government, which maintained peasant land ties and imposed heavy taxes on the peasant economy – both direct taxes (poll taxes, land taxes and redemption dues arising from the financial clauses of the 1861 serf Emancipation) collected through the medieval institution of the peasant commune, and indirect taxes on certain necessities of peasant life (matches, kerosene and alcohol, etc.) collected at the point of expenditure. Through the state budget these revenues were ploughed back into government spending on non-agricultural development – industry, transport and social overhead capital. In the 1880s and 1890s, it was argued, the peasants paid heavily for Russia's industrial spurt, and agriculture stagnated. After the momentary instability of the turn of the century, peasant sacrifices paid off in the emergence of a more stable, consumer-led pattern of industrial development with rising productivity and incomes in both industry and agriculture.

Today little remains of the Gerschenkron model. Its dismantling began with some dissenting remarks of Kahan and continued with the more detailed research of Crisp, Gatrell, Gregory and Simms among others.[3] First, the burden of taxation on the peasantry in the 1880s and 1890s has been disputed. Direct taxes, borne mainly by peasant households, are known to have generated little revenue compared to expenditure taxes, and the rise of expenditure taxation may have reflected the spread of a consumer market as much as rising tax rates. It is true that this consumer market was spreading primarily among the urban classes, so that the peasantry was participating less than in proportion.[4] Even so, the significance of peasant taxes both in raising Imperial revenues and in lowering peasant living standards seems to have been overplayed. Peasant arrears of redemption payments may have reflected the difficulty of collecting them rather than exhaustion of the peasant ability to pay. Across the country as a whole agricultural production, productivity, yields and per capita village retentions of farm produce for peasant consumption probably rose throughout the period 1885–1913. The national picture was not reproduced in certain major regions, however – for example, in the Central Black-Earth region where yields and productivities stagnated or declined in both the grain and livestock sectors (see Chapter 5). But this regional differentiation was not a product of the fiscal policy pursued by government.

Secondly, peasant taxes were not used to pay for industrial development. Much taxation was absorbed in profit subsidies and guarantees, operating costs of government enterprise and so on, but relatively little went to finance capital spending on the economy. In most years government non-defence investment amounted to one-tenth or less of total government spending, and a similar proportion of net domestic capital formation as a whole. Peasant sacrifices paid for warfare and armaments, domestic policing and the consumption pattern of the official strata much more than for industrialisation. The supply of resources for industrial development relied for its finance mainly upon private profit and domestic savings.[5]

Soviet research has also thrown indirect light on this subject. The peasantry may have contributed resources for industrialisation although, if so, not in the way described by Gerschenkron and von Laue. When material products traded between agriculture and large-scale industry in 1913 are revalued at current world prices, it has been suggested that peasant agriculture contributed a substantial net surplus to the finance of industrial development. The main mechanism enabling this net transfer is said to have been 'unequal' market exchange between the two sectors (when Russian domestic prices are compared to the prices prevailing in the international economy, Russian industrial product prices were inflated relative to prices for foodstuffs and raw fibres). Large-scale industrial producers were able to exploit market power in the domestic economy, and this was reflected in the terms of trade facing agriculture. If this was the case, then the peasant contribution of resources for industrialisation took place through unofficial and non-budgetary channels – not the fiscal mechanisms to which Western historians had attributed so much significance.[6]

Thirdly, there is no historic link from state-led industrialisation based on peasant sacrifice in the 1880s and 1890s to a pay-off in the shape of consumer-led industrialisation after 1906. The evidence shows little difference in the pattern of state involvement in the economy before and after the turn of the century. A common thread linking the two periods was the predominant role of military and bureaucratic expenditures in the state budget; in both periods, government played a significant role in sustaining aggregate demand through expenditure on procurement from industry (especially military procurement), but little developmental role through involvement in capital formation (except for railways). It would be fair to say that in both periods national income, industrial capacity and living standards in both town and country grew regardless of government policy; industrialisation did not demand the sacrifice of peasant interests before 1900 nor present the peasant community with a return on its abstinence thereafter.

In fact, the role which Russia's leaders intended for the peasantry in industrialisation did not prove to be at all an exact forecast of its fate. By the early XX Century sections of the industrial workforce had lost their agrarian roots. Amongst the peasantry both rural small-scale industries and migrant participation in the urban industrialisation process were widespread, but the peasantry too was changing. Direct taxation of the rural population had dwindled in comparison with indirect levies on the growing mass market for consumer goods, and the collective responsibility of the village for its members' tax liabilities was ended in 1902 (in private contracts between peasants and nobles, however, collective responsibility remained an active principle). Improved communications and rising incomes meant that restrictions on movement were increasingly nominal, village-level controls on internal passports being abolished in 1906. The peasantry may have contributed to the finance of industrial growth but, if so, through unofficial, non-budgetary mechanisms such as unequal exchange between agriculture and private large-scale industry, not through taxation. New voluntary peasant associations such as supply, sales and credit cooperatives were coming into existence. Governmental perspectives were also changing. After 1904–5, tsarist officialdom was more afraid of the dangers of a revolutionary peasantry defending its traditional land aspirations than of the proletariat. In the Stolypin land reforms the regime cancelled the peasants' traditional communal obligation to the state and sought to transform communal into individual landed property.

No model of equivalent simplicity has emerged to replace the Gerschenkron model. The picture with which we are left is one of a complex and differentiated reality. The social institutions forming the channels linking the peasantry and industrial development were in fact of striking diversity. Some (e.g., coercive surplus extraction based on the peasants' joint responsibility, the exploitation of industrial market power relative to food producers, and the system of secondary employment in industry based on migrant labour) embodied an essentially conservative orientation to the peasant–industry nexus. Their conservatism lay in reinforcement of the traditional role of the peasant farm as a source of external resources for outsiders (in this case, the urban industrial economy). Other kinds of social relationship linking the peasantry to industrial development (e.g., new freedoms of movement, occupational choice and the professionalisation of work in both agriculture and non-agriculture, voluntary peasant association in cooperatives and peasant access to industrial technology) offered the possibility that industrial revolution would bring a more genuine revolution of culture, technology and property relations to the village, putting to an end the subordinacy of the village to the town and of the peasant to industry, devolving control over the surplus product of the rural economy to the rural producers themselves.

The nature of this putative more genuine revolution was, however, quite uncertain; and it was bitterly disputed. Populist observers claimed it as the foundation of a narodnik cooperative or people's economy, while to marxists it represented at best the possibility of a more competitive and perhaps more democratic style of capitalism.

War, Revolution, Recovery

How were the social relations linking the peasantry to industrial development in peace-time affected by the seven years of war, revolution and civil war (1914–21)? We can summarise change under four main headings. First, the peasantry as a whole was liberated from the rule of the landlords and the obligation to purchase or pay rent for non-allotment land. In a few weeks of 1917 a traditional mechanism of rural surplus extraction under the old regime had been destroyed with finality.

Secondly, in the course of appropriation of the landlord estates and reabsorption of Stolypin farmsteads into the old open-field system, the repartitional village commune revived and became more active and more widespread amongst the peasantry than at any time since 1861.[7] But the foundation of this revival was the political self-determination of the village, not the villagers' mutual guarantee of taxes and rents due to powerful outsiders. The self-determination of the village was facilitated by the destruction of the old, centralised political bureaucracy and by the failure of a new one to be established immediately, which led to the dispersal of authority to the localities throughout Soviet Russia.

Thirdly, the village was returned to a state of near economic self-sufficiency – not by choice but by necessity – as a result of the decline of large-scale, specialised urban industries and of urban–rural trade.[8] Coupled with this turn to rural self-sufficiency was a widespread return of urban workers and soldiers to the village; having deserted, or having been demobilised or made redundant, they returned to their native villages to seek employment, a share in family property or other relief.

Fourthly, the new regime was faced with an immediate and deep-seated food crisis affecting the urban population and military personnel. This crisis had its historical roots in the decline of industries and trade and the turn of the village in the direction of self-sufficiency in the war years; even before the emergence of the Soviet regime, the tsarist and provisional governments were forced into an interventionist food procurement policy based on price controls and requisitioning of farm grain stocks by quota, although not necessarily at below-market prices.[9] Under the Soviet regime, with further disruption and decline of the urban economy and urban–rural trade, food policy degenerated into a coercive struggle to confiscate rural food stocks based on absolute priority for government requirements over rural producer and consumer needs. At first kulaks were the target, but by 1919 the liability to participate in compulsory food deliveries had been diffused to the peasantry as a whole; in this respect the medieval principle of joint responsibility for state requirements was reintroduced.[10] Only after the transition to peace-time conditions, the advent of the New Economic Policy (NEP) in March 1921, and elimination of the consequences of the 1921–2 famine, were urban industries, trade and mutuality between town and countryside revived.

Throughout the years of civil war there was one further essential continuity with resource allocation under the *ancien régime*: the peasant resources appropriated by government agencies continued to be used for military and administrative purposes; naturally, no immediate allocation of funds to economic development was possible.

By the 1920s, the social institutions forming the channels linking the peasantry and industrial development, whether inherited directly from the past or modified and improvised by the Bolsheviks, had diversified still further. Both repressive and revolutionising mechanisms were reinforced.

Repression was reinforced by the confiscation of food surpluses and the conscription of peasant labour; while these were undertaken in war and civil war for military purposes, in 1919–20 those who advocated new coercive controls over the peasantry believed that here was a revolutionising and liberating course. With the turn to NEP in March 1921, new avenues to rural community development and cultural revolution were opened up, involving greater control by the small agrarian producers over their own products and surpluses and a more mutual relationship between the village and industry. But the social meaning of these new avenues – whether they opened out towards a new kind of socialist society based on grass-roots cooperation, or merely towards new freedoms for small capitalist enterprise – was even more fiercely disputed than before.

THE RURAL FOOD SURPLUS

In the 1920s, when Soviet decision-makers considered the role of the peasantry in industrialisation, they were concerned almost entirely with the question of the rural food surplus. To a large degree they concerned themselves only with the grain question. But grain was only a part of the rural food surplus, although a particularly important part.

Measurement

So far as is known, in the 1920s Soviet grain output did not recover to the level of its pre-war maximum, falling below the 1909–13 average even in 1926, the best harvest of the NEP period, by 3–4 per cent.[11] However, in pre-war comparison, even after taking this into account, the net surplus of grain potentially available for direction by the Soviet government into industrial development was reduced far more than the fall in output.

It is far more difficult to determine the extent of the reduction. Among the reasons for the difficulty are, first, the elusive nature and measurability of the concept of the food surplus and, secondly, the political pressures brought to bear upon it in the circumstances of the time. The source of the latter was the desire of those advocating rapid industrialisation to demonstrate the availability of a substantial food surplus (not necessarily realised at any given moment, but potentially available from village stocks). This led them to overstate yields and outputs, rural utilisation and stocks; these pressures therefore affected output estimates as well as estimates of surpluses.[12]

Such pressures were not uniformly influential in the 1920s, but were more powerful after 1925. Consequently, it is hard to compile a consistent measure of the national grain balance so as to compare successive years of NEP, or the NEP period with the pre-war years.

The most reliable element of the grain balance was that relating to non-rural utilisation. Non-rural grain utilisation declined dramatically in the 1920s compared to before the revolution. In the best year of the 1920s, 1926/27, non-rural utilisation was little more than half the pre-war record – just under 10 million tons compared to 17–20 million tons (these later estimates are slightly lower than the figures given at the time by Stalin and shown in Table 25).[13] As the consumption of grain by the urban human and livestock populations, by the army and in industry struggled up to the 1912/13 level, the squeeze was felt chiefly by exports (down to one-quarter, at best, of the pre-war). The results were a permanent shortage of foreign exchange (see Chapter 11) and a knife-edge operation for the food supply authorities. Reduced non-rural grain utilisation was attributable to two immediate factors – the failure of grain production to regain pre-war levels by a small margin and, much more significantly, the increased village retention of grain.

Reduced inter-war non-rural utilisation of grain had an important regional dimension. Stephen Wheatcroft has shown that while the Northern Consumer Region (including Moscow and Leningrad) rapidly returned to its pre-war grain deficit, the main producer regions, especially of the centre and south, failed to regain their pre-war positions as sources of a grain surplus. Compared to 1909/13 levels, the Southern Producer Region never exceeded 70 per cent of its pre-war grain surplus, and the Central Producer Region never exceeded 35 per cent. Only the Urals and Siberia showed any sign of restoring surplus production on the pre-war scale, but these constituted the least important pre-war producer region. The decline in the grain surplus of the Ukraine was especially serious, because the trend was actually worsening from 1923/24 onwards.[14]

While grain has always been reckoned a particularly strategic – even 'political' – commodity, in 1926 it accounted for only about 35 per cent of net agricultural output.[15] For all non-grain products the level of output achieved in the 1920s probably represented an improvement on the pre-war picture. By 1926/27 non-grain crop production was already about 14 per cent above the pre-war record and was still growing; livestock produce was also up on 1909–13 by some 17 per cent.[16]

For non-grain products, data on net village sales and retentions are even poorer than for grain. There appear to be two important reasons. One is the exclusive importance attached to grains at the time by agencies of both data collection and decision making. The other is the fact that the market in most non-grain products remained relatively unregulated throughout the 1920s, in comparison to the grain market where a virtual state monopoly had been achieved by the end of the decade. Available Gosplan estimates indicate clearly, however, that for non-grain products, as for grain, there was a large increase in village retentions in the 1920s by pre-war standards. For industrial crops the share of extra-rural sales fell from nearly three-quarters to a little over one-half; the share of extra-rural sales in livestock output fell from 30 per cent to 25 per cent or less (see Table 26).

As a result, in 1926 the average peasant family consumed substantially more meat per head than before the revolution, more than in proportion to the increase in livestock produce per capita; this was in addition to increased reinvestment of livestock output in increased stock herds which had also increased markedly. Per capita peasant consumption of wheat and rye flour had fallen somewhat, reflecting lower per capita yields and increased use of grain as an intermediate good in the livestock sector. Urban consumption patterns had changed in the same direction, but to an even greater extent. The excess of meat and shortfall of flour consumed by urban families by comparison with peasants had both widened (see Table 27).

What about aggregate net marketings, when all kinds of produce are added together? Adverse trends in the marketed shares of both grain and non-grain produce (adverse from the point of the view of the urban industrial economy) were offset to a small extent in the following way: non-grain output remained more actively marketed than grains, and non-grain output grew relatively rapidly, so that there was a shift in the composition of output towards more highly marketised forms of produce. But this was not enough to prevent a very substantial fall in the aggregate output share of extra-rural sales. On the positive side was rapid growth of relatively highly marketised non-grain produce; on the negative side was the sluggish behaviour of grain output, combined with the decline in the output share of sales in both grain and non-grain branches of activity. On balance, the share of agricultural output leaving the village fell from up to one-quarter in 1913 to 16–17 per cent in the mid-1920s (see Table 26).[17]

The changing ratio between grain and non-grain products was clearly not accidental. It reflected a growing diversification of both production and consumption of the rural population. The peasant household of the mid-1920s produced less grain than before the revolution, in part because it was producing more of other things. It sold less grains in proportion to output, partly because of the increased pressure of rural population relative to the harvest,[18] partly because it allocated more grains to livestock feed (resulting in more animals of higher quality). Of the increased livestock produce, a part was eaten by the peasant household as milk and meat and a part was sold. Increased non-grain produce, marketed at a lower rate than before the war, did not compensate the non-agricultural sector for the lower rate of marketing of grains out of a harvest which had barely recovered to pre-war levels.

In pre-war comparison the trend was clear: the agricultural sector was being converted away from an extensive, grain-dependent economy towards more land- and labour-intensive, high-yielding branches. In the long run this might well entail a rising share of sales in rising output. In the short run, however, it meant that peasants were seeking to command a higher share of their own grain output, and of at least some other outputs, for purposes of both consumption and reinvestment in agriculture. This had serious implications for industrialisation policy.

If we forget about pre-war comparisons, however, there was a positive side to the picture – even from the standpoint of industrialisation policy. This was that within the confines of the 1920s extra-rural food sales were rising quite rapidly, and their growth showed no sign of slowing down: as agricultural output growth decelerated the output share of extra-rural sales was tending to rise. Under 'normal' circumstances this might have given grounds for confidence, and even optimism.

Analysis

Some of these changes in the agricultural pattern, such as the relative increase in non-grain production, would doubtless have happened even without a war and revolution, and a changed set of government policies. Other changes, however, reflected contingent and historical factors peculiar to the 1920s. What these factors were, and how to weight them, remains an intractably difficult problem.

This problem is often compounded by failure to distinguish two questions which should properly be kept separate. The first question is *why food marketings were so much reduced in the 1920s as a whole, by pre-war standards*. Here three factors are frequently put forward: (1) the changed structure of agricultural organisation; (2) the dismantling of the tsarist system of direct extraction of a rural surplus; and (3) the worsened terms of trade facing peasant producers. The second question is *why food marketings became the focus of steadily rising economic tensions as the 1920s drew to a close*. Here three other factors have been proposed: (1) the disruption of urban–rural trade by the spread of a 'shortage' economy; (2) the improving terms of trade facing peasant producers; and (3) the pursuit of an incorrect relativity between prices for grain and non-grain farm produce.

Why Were Food Marketings so Much Reduced in the 1920s as a Whole, by Pre-war Standards?
First, the changed structure of agricultural organisation was identified by Stalin in April 1928 as a possible factor limiting farm sales of grain. Reporting the decline in grain sales in 1926/27 compared to 'pre-war' norms, he noted that it coincided with a major shift in the agrarian structure. Before the revolution there had existed a dualistic agricultural system of highly marketised large-scale units (kulak farms and noble estates) combined with subsistence-oriented middle and poor peasant farms. The revolutionary land settlement had replaced this dualistic structure with one dominated almost exclusively by the subsistence-oriented

middle peasantry, the role of large-scale farming being reduced to an insignificant minimum (see Table 25). In the 1920s, moreover, the average 'middle-peasant' household was both more numerous and smaller than before the Revolution. In 1913–28, the rural population had increased by 7 per cent, but the number of peasant farms had increased by almost one-fifth; budget surveys showed the decline in family size to be concentrated in the grain-surplus region, where the impact of farm fragmentation was especially serious.[19] Here Stalin identified the root of the post-revolutionary grain problem in the farm fragmentation of the revolutionary period (from this, he went on to advocate reorganisation of agriculture on large-scale socialist lines).

There were flaws in this argument. Stalin did not note that the share of sales in output had fallen *within* most farm groups (especially among kulak and middle peasant farms) as well as on average, in consequence of the changing weight of subsistence-oriented farms in agriculture as a whole. His conclusion required that smaller farms were characterised by a lower share of sales in *marginal*, not just *total* output (otherwise, redistribution of resources from larger to smaller farms would have left total sales unchanged);[20] this is possible, but unproven. Nor was Stalin justified in emphasising grain sales to the exclusion of other farm produce. In short, Stalin's perception and diagnosis were subject to great uncertainty.

Secondly, the dismantling of the tsarist system of direct extraction of a rural surplus may also have been relevant to the problem of farm sales, since an important traditional motive for peasant farmers to enter the market was to acquire cash for payment of direct taxes and rents. Results of research by a government commission at the end of the 1920s indicate that the combined incidence of direct and indirect taxation and land rents on rural incomes had fallen from 19 per cent in 1913 to no more than 10 per cent in 1926/27 (see Table 28).[21] If direct taxes paid to government are considered in isolation, then their burden on farm incomes had actually risen in pre-war comparison (from 3.1 per cent for 50 provinces of European Russia in 1912 to 4.9 per cent for the USSR in 1926/27); however, if land rent is counted as a direct levy on farm income, then in proportion to farm income direct levies as a whole had indeed fallen (from 9.5 to 4.9 per cent), and faster than indirect ones.[22]

Thirdly, the terms of trade facing food producers under NEP were unquestionably disadvantageous. According to Gosplan estimates the price 'scissors' obtaining in 1925/26–26/27 had deteriorated in pre-war comparison by up to one-third (see Table 29). The most important reason for this was not any policy of redistribution from farm incomes to government by means of indirect taxation, nor a policy of redistribution to the profits of public sector industrial enterprises through exercise of their market power to push up relative prices, but the higher unit costs of public sector industry in pre-war comparison.[23]

What was the effect of relatively disadvantageous terms of trade on farm sales? In the traditional view farm sales were discouraged, since peasants regarded manufactures as luxuries. In contrast, Millar has argued that for Soviet peasants manufactures were price-inelastic in demand; the worse the terms of trade faced by food producers, the more they had to sell in order to obtain their required list of manufactured goods.[24] Merl has sought to identify operation of this 'Millar effect' with middle peasant farms (larger farms would respond positively to relative price changes), and certainly under normal assumptions we might well expect the negative Millar effect to be more important, the poorer the farm household.[25] However, this does not help us to establish the average tendency for Soviet peasant agriculture as a whole.

On a national scale, common sense would seem to refute the Millar hypothesis: under NEP the terms of trade faced by food producers were substantially worse than before the war, yet we do not find food producers struggling to push their products onto the market in increased volume in order to make up the deficiency in their list of required manufactures. Common sense, however, may not suffice, because in comparing 1913 and the 1920s too many other important conditions are not held constant – harvests, direct levies on peasant incomes, the degree of shortage in retail markets accessible to peasant consumers, and peasant expectations about all of these things. An alternative method of resolving the issue would be to study the effects on food sales of the smaller changes in terms of trade which occurred from year to year within the NEP period. Here, other difficulties intervene.[26]

Why did Food Marketings Become the Focus of Steadily Rising Economic Tensions as the 1920s Drew to a Close?
First, the terms of trade faced by food producers improved by more than 20 per cent between 1926/27 and 1928/29 (see Table 29). The reasons for this were downward official pressure on industrial retail prices and trade markups, and rising food prices in which a dominant role was played by higher state grain collection prices in 1928/29. According to the Millar hypothesis these changes were counterproductive from the point of view of industrialisation policy because they enabled peasants to meet their requirements of manufactured goods from a smaller volume of food sales. In fact, as we have noted, the aggregate volume of food sales was still rising (in spite of difficulties confined to the grain front).

In other respects, too, the Millar hypothesis is difficult to verify. The most important problem is that, as before, so many other factors were operating to affect the urban–rural market at this time.[27] The equilibrium peasant response to changes in terms of trade is especially difficult to identify when market equilibrium was itself absent. An important consideration to bear in mind is that one may not simultaneously hold that the *adverse* (by comparison with 1913) shift in the terms of trade was responsible for reduced marketings in pre-war comparison, and that the *favourable* (by comparison with 1926/27) shift in the terms of trade was responsible for the grain crises of 1927/28–1928/29. In my view the favourable movement of the price 'scissors' in the late 1920s was an obstacle to grain marketings, not in itself, but only in so far as it reflected or contributed to other factors, for example the relativity of farm producer prices and the level of excess demand for manufactured consumer goods.

Secondly, the pursuit of an incorrect relativity between prices of grain and non-grain farm produce in 1926/27–1927/28 was almost certainly a factor inhibiting grain sales and limiting state procurements of farm produce in general – irrespective of changes in the aggregate food–non-food terms of trade. In order to cut the cost of the industrialisation programme, the procurement agencies put downward pressure on the demand price for grains. They were successful in lowering average grain prices facing producers on the market (see Table 29), but the results were counterproductive.[28] Inflationary pressures were transferred to other markets for farm produce which the procurement agencies did not control so effectively. As prices for non-grain crops and livestock products rose, farmers shifted resources out of the grain sector into these other branches, reducing grain collections, benefiting farm diversification and protecting their real incomes.

Merl has argued that the problem of relative prices for farm produce has an important regional dimension, and helps to explain failing regional surpluses not only for grains but also for other cash crops in the 1920s. In each region, state procurement agencies concentrated on trying to control the market and drive out private trade in the region's principal export produce and, having done so, to exert downward pressure on the producer price. The consequence was a general shift in marketing away from products with inter-regional importance demanded by state agencies towards products which could be absorbed locally.[29]

Thirdly, the disruption of urban–rural trade by the spread of a shortage economy from 1927 onwards appears to have been an especially important factor. Throughout the 1920s the macroeconomic burden of public sector investment programmes grew rapidly; by 1926/27 net industrial investment was perhaps 20 per cent higher than in 1913, and large-scale industrial fixed capacity was growing at more than 13 per cent per year.[30] The 1926 urban population stood at just 300,000 (1.2 per cent) in excess of the 1914 level within the same territory, but two years later the excess stood at almost 3 million (12 per cent).[31] A sustained mobilisation of resources into industrial capital formation was under way on a scale rapidly outreaching the ambitions of tsarist industrialism. The result, however, was to put the rest of the economy under growing pressure. A transition was in progress towards a shortage economy characterised by investment hunger and drive to expansion of capacity. Given government regulation of the prices and costs of public sector outputs and the government's near monopoly of the grain trade, the result was repressed inflation from 1927 onwards.[32] Food producers who sold food surpluses for cash may have found themselves unable to translate purchasing power into actual purchases of manufactures in state retail trade; thus, whether they regarded manufactures as luxuries or necessities, they may have become increasingly deterred from entering urban–rural trade.

An implication of this hypothesis is that, under conditions of shortage, an improvement in the terms of trade faced by food producers would have worsened the inflationary imbalance without improving farm sales, unless it was accompanied by a reduction in the burden of public sector investment.[33] Thus a key factor in intensifying the state of goods famine was the decision to lower industrial wholesale and retail prices early in 1927. This improvement in food producers' terms of trade can only have worsened the rural supply of manufactured goods and willingness of food producers to sell food in exchange. The state of shortage definitely constituted an incentive for villagers to switch resources into rural cottage industries in order to fill the gap in supplies, and for food producers to sell to village manufacturers rather than to urban-based collection agencies. Again, the role of these factors is hard to weigh. Small-scale private sector industries did not mushroom at the end of the 1920s under conditions of goods famine although it is true, as we have seen, that village retentions of industrial crops tended to be higher under NEP than before the revolution. In spite of intensified goods famine, overall food marketings continued to rise; however, by 1928 forced procurement (including the release of grain and meat for non-rural utilisation at the price of premature slaughter of peasant livestock) was already a factor.

In summary, the reasons for the reduced level and share in agricultural output of extra-rural sales in the mid-1920s compared with the pre-war period are known with little certainty. The increased rural population was a factor, but the urban population grew faster; meanwhile, the rural population consumed and invested more food per head than before the revolution. The abolition of large-scale farming may have enhanced the tendency towards higher village retention of food produce. The reduced burden of direct levies, especially land rents, may also have been a factor. Worsened terms of trade may have acted as a disincentive to peasant participation in urban–rural trade under NEP, but industrial profit margins did not benefit since peasant losses were swallowed up in increased industrial costs.

Other factors must be introduced to explain increasing difficulties in food procurement as the 1920s drew to a close. These difficulties did not, on the whole, have their origins in the supply side of the rural economy, but were symptoms of the trend in macroeconomic policy towards priority for industrial investment under conditions of a shortage economy. Changes in the overall terms of trade were probably unimportant; it was the progress-ive breakdown of urban–rural market equilibrium which was the decisive factor. Downward administrative pressure on the price of grain specifically weakened grain procurements after 1926. The transition to a shortage economy further weakened peasant participation in urban–rural trade from 1927 onwards. Considering its starting point, the sales performance of NEP agriculture was, under the circumstances, good.

There were no easy ways of increasing non-rural food supplies in the late 1920s. Increasing food procurement prices would lead to either open or repressed inflation. Open inflation meant explicit acceptance of cuts in real spending of either urban worker households or public investment agencies. Neither of these was an acceptable option for the political leadership of the time. Repressed inflation meant increased shortage in all regulated mar-kets, possibly leading in turn to reduced food sales by peasant households. Lowering food procurement prices might have helped food sales, not because of inelastic peasant demand for manufactures but because a cut in farm incomes would have reduced the macroeconomic inflationary imbal-ance. But, with comparatively unregulated trade in artisan manufactures and livestock produce, the degree of state monopoly required to push down the overall terms of trade faced by peasants and artisans did not exist, nor could it be created (if it could be created at all) except at the cost of further confrontation with the peasantry.

THE TRANSFER OF CAPITAL AND LABOUR

Study of food surpluses alone is not sufficient for a full evaluation of the peasant contribution to industrial development. (Credit for the first oper-ational presentation of this issue in a Soviet context is due to Preobrazh-ensky in his writing on the sources of 'primary socialist accumulation'.[34]) The main reason is that as a result of supplying food to the non-agricultural sectors peasants additionally command non-agricultural resources in ex-change. Consequently, their net resource contribution to non-agricultural development can be understood only as a balance of offsetting transfers. Moreover, the terms on which exchange takes place critically affect evalu-ation of the balance. Additionally, peasants may make an important contribution to the industrialisation process through the supply of peasant labour.

The Net Resource Balance

In the 1920s the Soviet regime devoted substantially greater budget re-sources to industrialisation than its tsarist predecessor. According to an estimate by R. W. Davies, the 1924/25 USSR state budget allocated 556 milliard current rubles (19 per cent of total expenditures) to finance of the national economy – mainly public sector industry, transport and construction – compared to 204 milliard rubles (6 per cent of total expenditures) under equivalent headings in the 1913 Imperial budget; this represented an increase in real terms of about 40 per cent.[35] In both years the greater part of government spending on the national economy probably represented current subsidies rather than capital investment; all the same, the contribution of peasant taxes to industrial growth was probably much more significant under NEP than under the tsars.

The importance of peasant transfers through the budget and other government channels for public sector industrialisation can be gauged more accurately from recently published Soviet national income accounts for 1928–30. These were based on a distinction between the 'socialist' and 'private' sectors. The socialist sector comprised large-scale industry and the bulk of construction, long-haul transport and trade; the private sector included small-scale industry, agriculture, most forestry and fishing, and some construction, trade and short-haul transport.[36] Each sector was defined to include the households dependent on it for their main source of income.

What was the balance of financial flows between these two sectors? The main results are set out in Table 30. In 1928 the private sector accounted for the bulk of unconsumed primary incomes – 3.6 milliard rubles compared to 1.6 milliards for the socialist sector. After losses, budgetary transfers (taxes and public services) and credit flows (government borrowing) were taken into account the private sector's realised accumulation was down to 1.6 milliard rubles, while socialist sector accumulation had risen to 2.9 milliards. Asset transfers from the private sector through farm collectivisation brought total realised socialist sector accumulation up to 3 milliard rubles. In other words, 'primary accumulation' accounted for about 1.3 milliard rubles, about 5 per cent of 1928 national income and nearly one-half of accumulation in the socialist sector.

This sum of 1.3 milliard rubles, however, may either overstate or understate the 1928 peasant contribution to industrialisation as such. A small part of it reflected a transfer from private to socialised agriculture; another part – unmeasured, this time – reflected a transfer from private industries to public sector accumulation in the broadest sense, including investment in military stocks, transport, construction, services and the housing stock as well as in industrial plant. What was left, after these deductions, formed the peasant contribution of resources to public sector industrialisation through government channels. At the same time, any peasant contribution to private industrial growth would remain unmeasured, leading to understatement of the overall peasant contribution.

In evaluating the overall resource contribution of the peasantry to industrialisation, official channels of taxation and government spending were no more important than other, less formal channels under both the tsarist and the Soviet regimes. These less formal channels included (a) direct resource transfers between agriculture and industry within the private sector, for example within the peasant household engaged in both farming and artisan production, and (b) resource transfers secured indirectly through 'unequal exchange' between agriculture and industry, as a result of the more concentrated structure of industrial production compared to agriculture and the greater deviation of market prices of industrial products above long run social opportunity costs of production. In order to calculate the true net resource contribution of the Soviet peasantry to industrialisation, these informal and implicit transfers must be added to those secured openly through official channels.

The pioneer in historical study of this net resource contribution has been Barsov.[37] He has estimated the resource balance between agriculture and industry in 1928 rubles for the years 1928–32, in 1913 world prices for 1928–32 and for 1913, and in marxian 'labour-adjusted' rubles for 1913, 1923/24, 1928–32 and 1937–8. From the point of view of establishing a comparison of the inter-branch balance before and after mass collectivisation and initiation of the first five year plan, these materials have been presented very fully and commented on extensively in other places.[38] Here I limit myself to brief examination of Barsov's estimates for 1928 in 1928 rubles (including comparison with alternative sources of information), and comparison of 1928 with 1913 in 1913 world prices.

Barsov originally presented his work as a balance of industry and agriculture, but close inspection suggests that this is not quite right; rural industries are neglected both as a source of manufactured products and as a destination for food and non-food farm products, so what we observe is the contribution of agriculture to urban or public sector industrial development alone. The result of the balance, when products are evaluated at the prices faced by the food producer in 1928, is an estimated net transfer of resources to agriculture from the urban industrial sector of nearly 800 million rubles. The rural food surplus was more than offset by a reverse flow of products from urban industry (see Table 31).

Wheatcroft and Davies have questioned this evaluation on the grounds that it neglects intra-rural, inter-branch flows. On the basis of the Soviet national income accounts for 1928–30, they have compiled a more strictly defined inter-branch balance. As might be expected, this shows enlarged inter-branch flows of both foodstuffs and consumer manufactures in 1928. However, by comparison with Barsov's estimate, the flow of consumer manufactures into agriculture is upvalued by far more (2.4 milliard rubles) than the supply of foodstuffs to non-agriculture (a little over 200 million rubles). As a result the net resource transfer received by agriculture in 1928 (and at 1928 prices), implied by the Wheatcroft–Davies estimate, is also much bigger – 3.0 milliard rubles instead of 800 million rubles.

This is an enormous sum, equivalent to 11 per cent of 1928 national income. How could such a transfer arise? The most important sources must have been earnings of the agricultural population from non-agricultural wage employment (mainly in the public sector) and rural secondary employment in small-scale private handicrafts and trades. This is roughly confirmed by other materials from the Soviet national accounts of 1928, suggesting an excess of consumption of the agricultural population over net agricultural output of approximately 2 milliard rubles.[39] Thus, in 1928 the farm population was very much dependent for maintenance of its living standards upon non-agricultural incomes.

In sum, examination of material product flows in 1928 prices thus suggests a big net transfer from predominantly socialised industry to predominantly private agriculture. Can this be reconciled with the picture obtained from official financial flows of an equally large net reverse flow (also in 1928 prices) from the private to the public sector? Combining these results must imply some combination of balancing resource flows from private non-agriculture to the public sector generally, and (perhaps more plausibly) from private agriculture to public sector non-industry. Neither of these resource flows would have contributed directly to industrialisation as such. In the former case, resources would at best have been transferred from private sector industries to public sector industries; in the latter, resources would have been transferred from one kind of non-industry (peasant agriculture) to another (public sector transport, construction and government services). In the latter case, however, public sector industrialisation would have been indirectly stimulated by provision of resources for complementary activities.

Barsov provides two estimates of inter-branch resource flows of the NEP period compared with before the revolution. One is given in terms of 1913 world prices and the other in terms of marxian 'labour-adjusted' rubles. Labour-adjusted rubles are conceptually rather difficult to handle, but there is now an accessible literature on them elsewhere.[40] Since the results are the same whether labour-adjusted rubles or 1913 world prices are employed, I refer only to measures based on 1913 world prices.

The reason given by Barsov for using 1913 world prices rather than 1928 domestic prices to value resources transferred between agriculture and industry is to correct the perceived undervaluation of agricultural labour-time compared to industrial labour-time when both are valued at 1928 prices and wages.[41] The chief result of correction is to upvalue agriculture's contribution to other sectors compared to the value of resources received by agriculture. Thus, for 1928 the net resource balance – an agricultural deficit of 800 million rubles when measured in 1928 domestic prices – becomes a large agricultural surplus of 1.8 milliard rubles transferred to urban non-agriculture at 1913 world prices.

But in 1913 itself, in terms of the world prices of that year, Barsov argues that agriculture yielded a much larger food surplus balanced by a somewhat lower level of supply of industrial commodities. The food surplus was 42 per cent higher than in 1928, the supply of industrial commodities 9 per cent lower. It follows that the agricultural surplus of 1913 amounted to some 3.3 milliard rubles at 1913 world prices.[42] In real terms the agricultural surplus generated in 1928 was therefore only 56 per cent of the pre-war level.

The extent of decline in the ability of urban non-agriculture to command net agricultural resources, estimated by Barsov, may certainly be called into question. As Wheatcroft and Davies have shown, the conceptual boundaries of these inter-branch flows are easily misplaced in practice. The flows themselves (especially the village supply of manufactures) are notoriously hard to measure with confidence. The sign of the net resource balance depends critically upon the standard of value employed, and this depends in turn upon difficult analytical judgements. For 1913 Barsov is reticent about his procedures and the sources which he cites do not indicate the basis of his calculations. However, some deterioration of the net agricultural resource balance of 1928 in pre-war comparison seems reasonably probable. Whatever resource contribution agriculture made to industrialisation before the revolution, it is likely to have been less on the eve of the first five year plan. This conclusion is more striking when it is remembered that in 1928 the Soviet regime had already begun its campaign of forced grain collections, although this campaign was limited to particular grain surplus regions and did not yet have a legal foundation.

What light does Barsov's work throw upon the relative importance of budgetary and non-budgetary channels of resource transfer? We have seen that Western historians have become sceptical of the importance of budgetary transfers from the peasantry for industrial accumulation in the tsarist period. The large transfer estimated by Barsov must therefore be attributed to unofficial, non-budgetary mechanisms, especially unequal exchange between agriculture and urban large-scale industry. In the 1920s budgetary transfers into public sector industrial accumulation were probably more important, while the scale of indirect transfers through unequal exchange continued on a reduced scale; these were offset in some degree, however, by unofficial direct transfers from private sector rural industries into peasant agriculture.

Industry and Peasant Labour

How did the supply of peasant labour affect industrial development in the 1920s? As a first approximation we can define three channels of influence. First was the combination of agriculture and small-scale industries within the village – often, within the peasant household. Second was the supply of peasant labour on a temporary or seasonal basis to industry and construction in more distant locations, often to an urban setting or to one in the process of new urbanisation. Third was the contribution of peasant labour to expansion of the permanent industrial workforce in large-scale industry. Each of these channels had different implications not only for the pattern of industrialisation but also for the composition and viability of the peasantry itself.

Rural artisan (*kustar'*) industries in the NEP period were substantial. Total small-scale output accounted for just less than 30 per cent of gross industrial production in 1926/27; in the second half of the 1920s small-scale output stagnated while large-scale industry grew at a rapid pace, so that by 1928/29 the share of the small-scale sector had fallen to 22 per cent at current prices.[43] But 'small-scale industry' was more broadly defined than the traditional rural artisan sector. In principle we can portray the rural artisan of the NEP period as subject to conflicting pressures of demand and competition. Economic recovery and rising rural incomes meant increased input availability and wider markets. But the rapid restoration of large-scale industry also intensified competition; the rural artisan depended in some degree on maintenance of a relatively low level of urban development and limits on regional specialisation. In 1926/27 the number of rural inhabitants engaged in small-scale industries was reckoned at just over 3 million, but this was only four-fifths of the 1913 employment level.[44] Small-scale output in 1926/27 was probably about the same as a year later, when it was evaluated at about the same level (in real terms) as in 1913 (see Chapter 7), so worker productivity in the small-scale sector had risen by up to a quarter. It is hard to evaluate the prospects for rural industrialisation at this time. The evidence of preceding sections suggests that artisan incomes tended to be used to subsidise living standards of the agricultural population and to conserve the peasant family farm, rather than for reinvestment in rural industrial development. Under the economic system of NEP the peasant-and-artisan sector therefore progressed within narrow limits, playing a necessary and irreducible part, but perhaps also a part without a great deal of room for future expansion.

In the 1920s peasants once again participated widely in industrial development through the migrant labour market. In 1928 it is estimated that 3.8 per cent (5.7 million) of the USSR population engaged in migrant labour; two-thirds of the migrant workers originated either in the industrial regions surrounding or between Moscow and Leningrad, in the Urals or in the traditional central agricultural zone of rural overpopulation.[45] To judge from data for previous years, probably more than half of these migrants were destined for non-agricultural employment. Probably the level of migrancy under NEP represented a decline on the pre-war level; the main reason for thinking this is the relative decline in sectors traditionally employing migrants such as construction, logging and domestic service.[46] In the 1920s participation in such activities on the part of the rural population was voluntary, without the element of compulsory levies to be found in the civil war period and in the 1930s.

Permanent resettlement of rural inhabitants in the urban sector proceeded rapidly in the 1920s. In the period 1923/24–1925/26 a million peasants are said to have moved to the towns. By 1928 this flow had reached a million a year, and was still rising.[47] All the same the role of the peasantry in permanent recruitment to industry in this period is easy to overstate. In the early 1920s the most important element in net recruitment to industry was former workers, unemployed or ruralised as a result of the industrial decline of the wartime and revolutionary period.[48] In the mid-1920s recruitment from the peasantry began to rise sharply, but even so most agrarian recruits had some previous experience of temporary or migrant non-agricultural wage employment in construction or other seasonal branches.[49] A typical new recruit was by no means fresh from the plough, although it would be equally wrong to portray them as skilled and disciplined cadres. As late as 1929 more than half of all industrial workers were still of worker origin, and this proportion was little different from that estimated in the mid-1920s.[50]

The influence of peasant labour upon industrial development in the 1920s was not just a quantitative one, limited to the requirement for recruiting, training, skilling and disciplining new workers. In fact, in the 1920s the peasant contribution to growth of the permanent industrial workforce was probably small, compared both to other sources of industrial growth, and to other forms of peasant participation in industrial labour – as rural artisan and migrant labour. Also important was the existence of peasant and artisan employment as a perceived alternative to wage employment in large-scale public sector industry – both in the economic sense of an alternative source of income, and also in the sense of providing an alternative model of production management and of the division of labour in society. The organisers of industrial revolution were constantly confronted with the existence of agrarian forms of production in which managerial hierarchy was absent (or replaced by a traditional hierarchy of age and gender), work-time was subordinate to natural and psychological rather than mechanical rhythms, and the object of production was immediate and visible rather than remote and impersonal.[51]

Thus, among the peasant contributions to industrial growth in the 1920s should be included not only its measured resource contribution to industrial accumulation, but also the influence of preexisting agrarian social relations taken over and reproduced within the growing industrial economy of the public sector.

CONCLUSIONS

In the Russian economy of the tsarist period, agriculture supplied important resources for industrial development. It generated a large food surplus for the urban population, the army, industry and export, including up to

20 million tons of grain annually. When agriculture's material claims on urban industry are offset against its food surplus, and when flows in both directions are valued at world prices of the time, a large net surplus (or contribution of agriculture to industrial capital formation) remains. Contrary to the received wisdom of the post-war generation of Western historians, which placed overwhelming stress on transfers through the Imperial budget, the net transfer appears to have flowed mainly through unofficial channels of 'unequal exchange'.

The NEP period saw Soviet agriculture shift to a new pattern of modernisation. In terms of the production system this meant a shift towards more intensive, high-yielding non-grain activities, with more agricultural products being consumed and reinvested within the village. In terms of social structure it involved modernisation on a small peasant basis, food producers' management decisions being relatively little influenced by relations of land rent or wage labour. The main links with the world beyond the village were product markets, taxation, the cooperative movement and migrant labour.

Under this new pattern, resources were being preempted for agricultural production and consumption of the rural population which had previously been available for non-agricultural accumulation. This had obvious and serious implications for the Soviet government's industrialisation programme. Under NEP the new regime tried to regain access to agricultural resources both through direct taxation and through the market. Official, budgetary channels of resource transfer were probably used more successfully in the NEP period than under the tsarist regime. Market channels of unequal exchange, however, were less effective. The terms of trade had shifted against the peasant producer, but the volume of urban–rural trade was so much less that in real terms the net margin of agricultural resources available for industry was much smaller than before. In any case the reason for the shift in terms of trade was higher industrial costs, not heavier indirect taxation or wider price–cost margins in industry. The net result of summing transfers through both official and unofficial channels was a substantial reduction in the peasant contribution to industrial capital formation.

The Soviet regime's struggle to regain access to agricultural resources thus failed to achieve the degree of success thought necessary to secure its industrialisation objectives. The reason for this was not agriculture's productive failure, but it did reflect agriculture's new pattern of production development. The resulting clash of the enlarged capital construction programme through which the Soviet regime sought to implement its industrial objectives with the relatively high degree of village retention of foodstuffs for both consumption and reinvestment in agriculture helps to explain the growing difficulties in management of the rural market in the later 1920s. While the drive for public sector industrial accumulation was maintained, there was no way of removing these difficulties without a confrontation with the peasantry.

Part III
Industry and the Economy

7 The Industrial Economy
Peter Gatrell and R. W. Davies

NATIONAL INCOME AND INVESTMENT

In his recent study of Russian national income by end-use, Paul Gregory concludes that NNP (net national product) increased by around 31 per cent between 1908 and 1913 (5.6 per cent a year), or by 17 per cent per capita (3.2 per cent a year). The available production series indicate that large-scale industrial production and net grain production grew more rapidly than NNP as a whole. Trade turnover roughly kept pace with NNP, but construction and livestock herds grew less rapidly.[1]

Between 1904–8 and 1909–13 total net investment increased by as much as 71 per cent, from 1,300 to just over 2,200 million rubles (in 1913 prices, Russian Empire).[2] But the annual changes in the separate items in tsarist Russia were quite erratic, especially in the case of livestock.[3]

The war almost certainly brought to a halt investment in urban housing, agricultural dwellings and farm buildings.[4] The output of agricultural tools and machines in large-scale industry declined by 50 per cent between 1913 and 1916: small-scale production cannot possibly have offset this decline.[5] Reliable data for investment in the railways are not available. The gross output of railway equipment (measured in 1913 prices) was twice as high in 1916 as it was in 1913. But by 1916 the stock of equipment was in such a state of disrepair that the increase in net investment was probably much smaller.[6]

Industrial investment during the war, and particularly investment in industrial equipment, present a more complicated picture. Contemporary sources testify to an impressive increase in investment during the war.[7] In retrospect Strumilin estimated that the stock of fixed capital in large-scale industry increased by 19 per cent, though this is probably an exaggeration; a more cautious estimate by Vorob'ev for the same period, based on the data collected for the industrial census of 1918, put the increase at 14.4 per cent.[8] The war gave a boost to the nascent Russian machine-tool industry, and supplies of equipment were also enhanced by imports.[9]

Following the precipitate decline in NNP in 1917–20, the recovery in the early 1920s was rapid. Paul Gregory's provisional conclusion, that in the calendar year 1928 national income was still some 5–10 per cent below the 1913 level,[10] may somewhat underestimate the extent of recovery; in Chapter 12, he presents a feasible range of estimates for 1928 'at best equal to 1913', and with a lower bound of 93 per cent of 1913. By 1926/27 gross agricultural production exceeded and industrial production had very ap-proximately regained the pre-war level.[11] But construction lagged. Even according to the usually optimistic estimates of Gosplan, the value of building work (*chistoe stroitel'stvo*) amounted to only 610 million rubles (in 1913 prices) in 1926/27 as compared with 730 million rubles in 1913.[12] Net capital investment (including the value of new equipment, livestock, etc. as well as building work) amounted (also in 1913 prices) to roughly 1,700 million rubles in 1926/27, as compared with 1,890 million rubles in 1913 (USSR pre-1939 frontiers). By 1927/28, net investment had probably reached 2,100 million rubles, thus exceeding the 1913 level.[13]

In spite of the lower total for capital investment as a whole, net industrial investment was already higher in 1926/27 than in 1913, amounting to at least 420 million rubles against about 350 millions in 1913 (both measured in 1913 prices).[14] This was a first fruit of planned industrialisation. Investment in Soviet industry, almost entirely based on internal sources of finance, exceeded pre-revolutionary industrial investment by both internal and foreign capital. In contrast, investment in housing sharply declined: in the case of urban housing it amounted (in 1913 prices) to only 66 million rubles in 1926/27 compared with 328 millions in 1913.[15] Net investment in transport and communications was also lower in 1926/27 than in 1913.[16] At this stage in Soviet economic development agricultural investment was squeezed to a far smaller extent. While net investment in rural dwellings and structures declined, and net investment in equipment remained approximately the same, net investment in livestock substantially increased. Total net investment in the agricultural sector was approximately 30 per cent above 1913 level.[17] In 1927/28, the pattern changed abruptly: while net investment in Group A industries and railway transport increased substantially, net investment in agriculture declined (see n. 17); this was already a 'post-NEP' pattern of investment and it will not be further considered here.

THE CHANGING SHAPE OF INDUSTRY

General

During the pre-war quinquennium, the production of large-scale industry experienced an annual rate of growth which approached that of the boom of the 1890s.[18] The value of gross output increased from about 4,300 million rubles in 1908 (in 1913 prices) to 6,100 million rubles in 1913, or by 42 per cent.[19] Growth was especially rapid in capital goods (producer goods) (Group A) industries, from the low base of 1908, which was a depressed year for producer goods as a whole.[20] By contrast, growth in Group B industries was slower but uninterrupted between 1906 and 1913.[21] Given the greater dynamism of Group A industries, their share of total output probably increased from 32 per cent in 1908 to around 40 per cent in 1913.[22]

The value of output in small-scale industry cannot be assessed with certainty, especially for the years before 1913. Gukhman concluded that gross output of small-scale industry in 1913 (pre-1939 USSR territory) amounted to just over 2,000 million rubles.[23] Two-thirds of this output was contributed by rural craftsmen, or *kustari*. Small-scale production thus accounted for almost one-quarter of total industrial production. In some branches of industry, notably foodstuffs, wood-working and clothing, the proportion was much greater.[24] The only known attempt to calculate the growth rate of small-scale industry between 1908–13 was made by Strumilin, who concluded from the tax returns that the gross output of small-scale industry grew by just under 50 per cent in current prices. This suggests that small-scale industry roughly held its position in the final years of peacetime, and shared in the pre-war boom.[25]

In Russia, as in all the belligerent countries of Europe, the first world war changed both the composition and the organisation of industrial production. The output of large-scale industry reached a peak during 1916: according to one estimate, it was 22 per cent higher (in 1913 prices) than in 1913.[26] But this conceals profound shifts in the composition of output. Whereas in 1913 nearly 70 per cent of total large-scale industrial production was reportedly destined for household consumption, by 1916 this proportion had fallen to 58 per cent. Defence requirements absorbed 25 per cent of output in 1916, compared to less than 5 per cent in 1913.[27]

According to Gukhman, the value of output generated by small-scale industry fell by almost 12 per cent between 1913 and 1916. On this basis, the share of small-scale industry in total industrial production in 1916 had probably fallen to below 20 per cent.[28] The only available estimate of the value of defence production generated by small-scale industry indicates that around 12 per cent of non-census industrial production was being devoted to the war effort in 1915–16.[29]

By 1926/27, following the precipitate decline of 1918–20 and the rapid recovery of 1921–6, the industrial economy still consisted in large part of the pre-revolutionary factories, mines, railways, shops and offices, reassembled, patched up and put to work. New industrial investment on any significant scale did not take place until the 1925 building season. The fixed capital of factories newly constructed or fundamentally reorganised between 1917 and 1926 amounted to less than 10 per cent of all fixed industrial capital.[30] The production of large-scale industry recovered extremely rapidly in the first half of the 1920s, and by 1926/27 already exceeded the 1913 level, though it had not yet reached the 1916 level. Small-scale industry also recovered rapidly. According to a Soviet estimate made in the 1920s, it had already reached the 1913 level by 1926/27;[31] on the other hand, the number engaged in small-scale industry, measured in full-time equivalents, is estimated to have fallen substantially (see Table 35). This is uncertain territory. But it seems likely that the production of industry as a whole had reached the 1913 level by 1926/27, and exceeded it by 1927/28.[32]

Largely as a result of state priority for investment in industry, the capital goods' industries as a whole regained the pre-war level of production before the consumer goods' industries. According to official Soviet statistics, in 1927 the production of Group A industries was as much as 27.5 per cent greater than in 1913: the equivalent figure for the Group B industries was only 2.2 per cent.[33] As we shall see, there were important exceptions to this general pattern.

The geography of Russian industrial production changed very little between 1913 and the mid-1920s (for the main industrial regions, see Map 2). In 1913, European Russia (excluding the Ukraine) contributed 61 per cent of total industrial production, and within European Russia production was overwhelmingly concentrated in the North West and Central Industrial regions around St Petersburg and Moscow, and in the technologically backward Urals. The Ukraine contributed 21 per cent. The Transcaucasus added a further 10 per cent with its oil production. All other regions of the country together contributed no more than 8 per cent.[34] Central Asia and Siberia, in spite of their vast reserves of raw materials, remained economically backward.

Territorial losses after the first world war deprived Russia of the industrial capacity and skills of the Baltic region and Poland. The loss of the Baltic was of particular significance, since it provided 20 per cent of engineering products in 1913 (and 44 per cent of all electrical products). The loss of Poland was less serious. Polish coal was mostly consumed locally, although iron and steel did find its way on to the Russian market. These losses were mitigated by the evacuation of equipment and inventories into the Russian interior in 1914–17: the evacuation from Riga in particular was very substantial. In all, the industrial capital equipment located in the lost territories amounted to 24 per cent of the total for the Russian Empire in 1914; at least one-quarter of this was evacuated.[35]

The post-war economy thus had to adjust to a new set of territorial boundaries. Yet, as Table 36 indicates, by the mid-1920s the industrially less developed regions of the USSR played no more prominent role in total industrial production than they had in 1913. In some cases, notably in the Urals and Siberia, they contributed less to output and employment. By 1926, as the authors of the standard Soviet textbook on historical geography state, 'not only was the old level of production restored; so, too, was the old geographical distribution of industry'.[36]

Map 2. USSR industrial regions

USSR INDUSTRIAL REGIONS

1 = West (including Belorussia)
2 = North-West
3 = North
4 = Urals
5 = Siberia
6 = Far East
7 = Central Asia
8 = Transcaucasus
9 = North Caucasus
10 = Crimea
11 = Southern Industrial region
12 = Central Black-Earth region
13 = Central Industrial Region
14 = Central Volga Region
15 = Lower Volga Region

PACIFIC OCEAN

ARCTIC OCEAN

0 200 300 600 MILES
0 400 800 KM

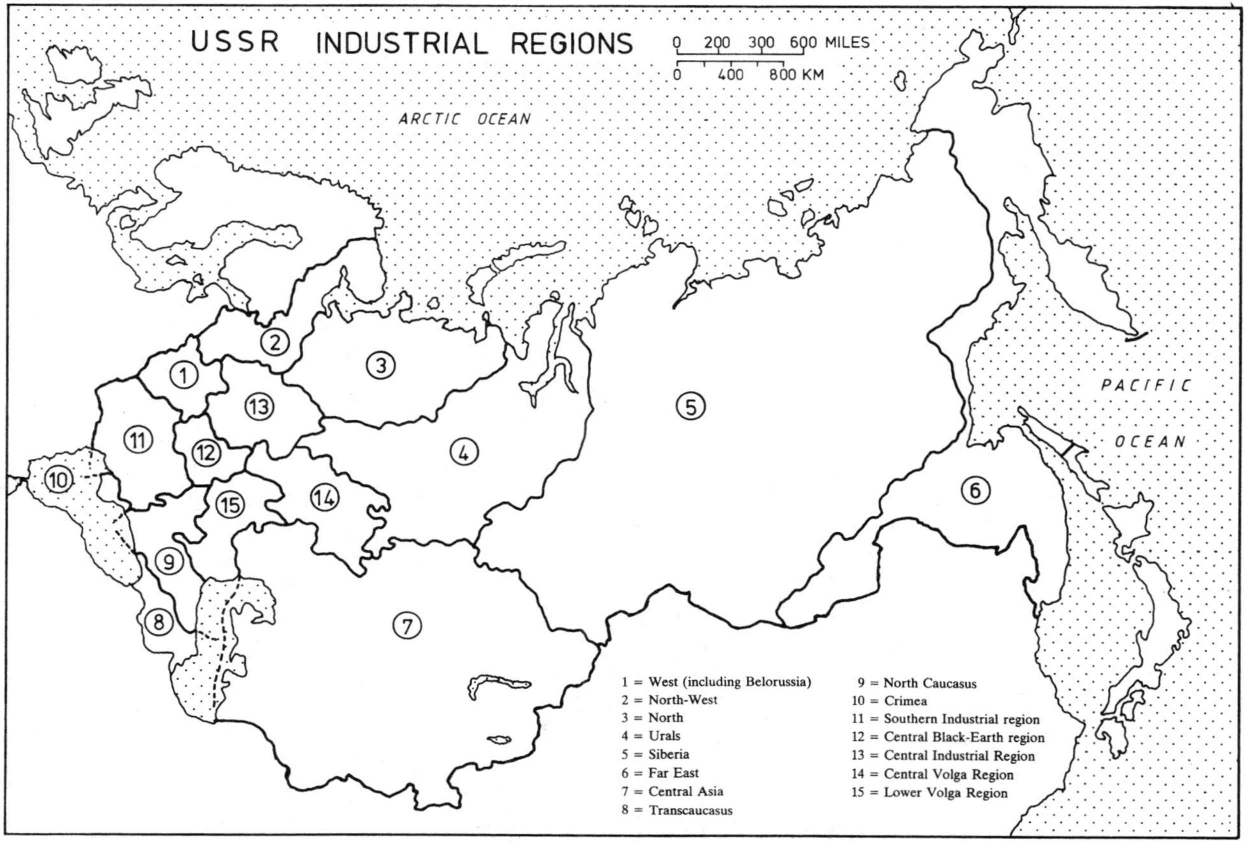

Capital Goods

Fuel and Power
The increase in coal consumption in 1908–13 by 40 per cent in physical terms and 58 per cent in value terms reflected for the most part a revival of demand from the two largest consumers, railways and the iron and steel industry.[37] The requirements of industrial consumers, especially in the North West, were met by imports of British coal. The pre-war boom in manufacturing industry increased Russian dependence on imports still further. Imports contributed 13 per cent of all domestic coal needs in 1910; in 1913 the proportion was 17 per cent.[38]

Oil output increased in value by over 80 per cent between 1908 and 1913, though the volume of crude increased by less than 6 per cent. In spite of this increase, Russian oil fields contributed no more than 20 per cent of world output in 1913, compared to 50 per cent in 1901–2. Technological change in the industry was virtually non-existent. Nor did the industry diversify to any great extent: most firms concentrated on the production of *mazut*, or black oil, which was burned as boiler fuel and which yielded higher profits than kerosene and lubricating oils.[39]

The development of electricity as a source of energy had made rapid strides in the early XX Century. The capacity of generating plant began to grow and more stations were being built year by year. Between 1905 and 1913 total consumption of electricity in tsarist Russia increased from 482 to 1,945 million KwH.[40]

The war highlighted several features of pre-revolutionary power and fuel supply. Coal was a technically unsophisticated industry in Russia, relying mainly on the physical strength and abundance of manual labour. The increase in the volume of coal output by 20 per cent between 1913 and 1916 was largely achieved by exploiting existing shafts more intensively. The war abruptly halted imports of coal. Munitions and other factories in the North West now had to rely upon supplies of coal from the South. This imposed further strain on an already over-stretched railway network. Meanwhile, industrial consumption of oil and firewood increased substantially.[41] The war also led to feverish attempts to expand the electricity supply industry. Consumption of electricity by industry alone increased by 27 per cent between 1913 and 1916. Nevertheless, investment in new capacity could not bring instant results.[42]

By 1926/27 the production of both coal and oil was greater than in 1913 (see Table 37). The oil industry was substantially modernised. The cost of extracting oil fell by over 40 per cent between 1923/24 and 1926/27, and in consequence the industry, dubbed 'the golden egg' by Kuibyshev, was able to supply substantial levies to the state budget and substantial quantities of oil for export.[43]

The production of electricity more than doubled between 1913 and

1926/27, from modest beginnings; and, with the steady development since the early 1920s of an impressive programme for the construction of power stations, including the Dnieper dam and power station (Dneprostroi), rapid future expansion was assured.

Metals

Increases in iron and steel output between 1908 and 1913 (see Table 37) rested partly on the reactivation of hitherto idle capacity, and partly on an increase in the productivity of each furnace, especially outside South Russia. The failure of the supply of pig iron to keep pace with demand was due largely to a preference on the part of producers for retaining metal within the plant, in order to process it themselves. Within the steel industry, technical change appears to have been quite satisfactory. One contemporary source noted that the output of steel per ton of pig iron increased by 7 per cent between 1908 and 1912. According to the leading western authority, 'unquestionably, southern Russia remained in the main-stream of world progress in steel making'. The war, however, interrupted that progress in Russia.[44]

In some branches of non-ferrous metals, the picture was equally bright. Copper production almost doubled between 1908 and 1913 (see Table 37), and Russia began to reduce its reliance on imports. In 1908, 22 per cent of Russia's needs were met by imports: by 1913, the figure was only 15 per cent. This situation was sharply reversed during the war, as demand expanded rapidly. There were signs that some of the best ore deposits had been exhausted by 1916. But technical advances in copper smelting had increased the quantity of copper that could be obtained.[45] In other non-ferrous and precious metals, notably gold, methods of extraction and production were much less advanced. Russia depended wholly upon foreign supplies of tin, aluminium and nickel.[46]

In 1926/27 the position in ferrous and non-ferrous metallurgy was much less favourable than in the fuel and power industries. The iron and steel industry had suffered great destruction and neglect during the civil war: production declined by 1920 to a mere 3.6 per cent of 1913.[47] No substan-tial investment was undertaken between 1914 and 1924. In spite of substan-tial expenditure on repair and restitution in the mid-1920s, in 1926/27 the production of rolled steel amounted to only 77 per cent, and of pig-iron to only 70 per cent, of 1913 (see Table 37). Railways and shipbuilding, two voracious consumers, received smaller supplies of metal than before the revolution, and this alleviated the position of the engineering industries. Even so, metal shortages were endemic.

The production of non-ferrous and precious metals also collapsed during the civil war, and also failed to recover to the pre-war level by the mid-1920s. To compensate for the deficiency of copper, imports were substantially increased.[48] The decline of gold production struck a heavy

blow at Soviet exports. In the summer of 1927, the gold industry attracted
Stalin's attention, and he appointed the prominent and successful oil
engineer Serebrovskii as its manager.[49] But many years and much human
sacrifice would be required before gold exports earned much foreign
currency for the USSR.

Engineering[50]

A great upsurge in engineering production took place during the pre-war
boom. In 1913 the gross output of machine-building amounted to about
400 million rubles (see Table 38), an increase of almost 67 per cent since
1908 (this was, however, a depressed year in the capital goods sector).
Between 1912 and 1913 alone, output may have increased by over 27 per
cent.

This feverish growth was for the most part a response to the fresh wave
of government orders, reminiscent in some respects of the stimulus given
to large-scale industry during the 1890s. Ambitious rearmament programmes, especially that of 1910 for the army and those of 1911 and 1912
for the navy, led to the construction of new shipyards and other facilities
and a subsequent big expansion in military shipbuilding. Conversion of
Russian engineering firms, such as Putilov, Nevsky and Parviainen, was
undertaken by various consortiums of Russian and European banks. and
involved the participation of major foreign companies, such as Vickers,
Schneider and John Brown.[51] Government orders for railway rolling-stock
also began to pick up again after 1911. The contemporary press was filled
with optimistic reports about the renewed flood of orders. Output of
locomotives doubled and of freight wagons almost doubled in the single
year 1913.[52]

The production of agricultural machinery probably doubled between
1908 and 1913, and amounted to 52 million rubles by 1913.[53] This industry
contributed about 13 per cent of the total value of engineering production
in 1913. The industry underwent some changes before 1913, with an
increasing emphasis on harvesters and threshing equipment. The increased
consumption of such items was not confined to landowners. A minority of
the peasants also bought more agricultural machines, helped by the credit
extended them by agents acting on behalf of International Harvester, and
by the expanding agricultural cooperatives.[54]

Some branches of the engineering industry were weak, and others
entirely absent.[55] The situation for a number of high-technology products
is reviewed in Chapter 10. In electrical equipment, production began to
make rapid strides on the eve of the war, but the industry concentrated on
the simpler items. Tsarist Russia remained dependent upon imports for its
supplies of many items. Imports accounted for 35 per cent of the market in
electrical goods, although the proportion was much higher in the case of
high-voltage plant, transformers, valves and incandescent lights.[56] Infor-

mation on shipbuilding is harder to come by; scattered evidence suggests that domestic suppliers were not able to satisfy the demand for turbines and for pumping equipment, although domestic industry could produce boilers in the necessary quantities.[57] As much as 80 per cent of steam engines, 75 per cent of textile machinery and 70 per cent of machine tools were imported; and imports may have accounted for more than half the total Russian consumption of agricultural machinery.[58]

The war transformed the metal-working and machine-building industries. New capital investment in these industries in 1914–16 was very substantial; according to Vorob'ev, their capital stock increased by as much as 33.6 per cent between January 1, 1914, and January 1, 1918.[59] Simultaneously, factories were relocated from the front to the interior of Russia. The war dramatically shifted the balance of metal-working and engineering production towards military needs. According to Soviet estimates, the proportion of engineering output destined for military consumption rose from 26 per cent in 1913 to 65 or 78 per cent in 1916.[60] Production of armaments of all kinds increased six-fold. The output of transport equipment doubled, and production of electrical equipment more than trebled: in both cases, the interests of the war effort primarily determined the final use of this output. The important war-time developments in the aircraft, vehicle, optical equipment, machine-tool and other high-technology industries are reviewed in Chapter 10.

In the mid-1920s the quantity and range of civilian engineering production considerably exceeded the pre-war level. Gross production increased from approximately 300 million rubles in 1913 to 477 million rubles in 1926/27 (see Table 7).[61] In the years of recovery Soviet industry began to produce oil-mining equipment, turbines and other types of engineering products, which had been almost entirely imported before the war.[62] The electrical industry expanded particularly rapidly, manufacturing dynamos, transformers and telephone and cable equipment as well as electric light bulbs and accumulators.[63]

New developments in the engineering industries were by no means confined to equipment for use in the capital goods' industries. The New Economic Policy anticipated that the expansion of producer goods would be supported by improved conditions for the consumer, and above all for the peasant. The production of textile machinery hitherto imported from Britain was initiated at the 'Karl Marx' factory, Leningrad.[64] In the agricultural engineering industry, which was almost entirely concerned with manufacturing horse-drawn machinery and implements for the individual peasant household, by 1926/27 production was far larger than in 1913.[65] The first Soviet tractors were produced in small numbers at several different factories in 1925.[66] The rival claims of agriculture and industry on Soviet machine-building were neatly balanced in the decision in the spring of 1927 to construct a tractor factory at Stalingrad, and a heavy-engineering factory at Sverdlovsk.

Although the mass production of tractors, lorries and other major lines of production novel for Soviet industry seemed to require the construction of new factories (though this was heatedly disputed), for the moment nearly all engineering development took place at established factories. The capacity of both civilian and military engineering works had been substantially enlarged during the feverish war-time expansion of armaments production, but by 1926/27 armaments production may not yet have regained the 1913 level.[67] Much of the war-time and some of the pre-war armaments capacity was reconverted to civilian use in the mid-1920s, the most famous case being the production of tractors in the old cannon shop of the Putilov works in Leningrad. But further unused capacity remained in both military and civilian engineering factories, and most of the facilities of the great military shipyards lay idle.[68] The number of workers in the engineering industry (including armaments) regained the 1913 level in 1925/26, but did not regain the 1916 level until the end of 1930.[69]

Chemicals

The pre-war growth of the chemicals industry gives some comfort both to those who would emphasise the growth of household consumption and to those who would stress the stimulus given by government orders. The value of gross output of chemicals (including matches) increased extremely rapidly between 1908 and 1913.[70] Two branches of the industry, rubber and explosives, proved especially dynamic. As the urban population grew, so too did the demand for rubber galoshes. Varzar noted that the factories producing galoshes, 'though small in number are very well equipped'.[71] The production of explosives was largely the responsibility of three state factories. Output of smokeless powder increased by at least 80 per cent between 1908 and 1913. Production of other explosives (especially trotyl) also increased, under the impact of rearmament expenditure from 1910 onwards.[72]

By contrast, basic chemicals (such as sulphuric acid, caustic soda and soda ash) presented a much less impressive picture. One problem was the high cost of construction and installation of modern plant. Another was the location of raw materials, far from the main manufacturing centres. It was cheaper for consumers to import soda from Germany and pyrites from Portugal and Norway, than to purchase from domestic suppliers.[73]

The chemical industry, like engineering, underwent a vast expansion for military purposes during the war. The labour force grew by about 70 per cent, at state and private explosives factories alike.[74] The technical precondition of such an expansion was the creation of new capacity in the metallurgical industry, in order to recover benzol as a by-product of the coking process. This work was led by the chemist Ipatiev, who later served the Soviet government.[75] As a result of such initiatives, the output of explosives in 1916 was ten times greater than in 1913. The quantity of dyestuffs doubled. The main branches of the industry to contract were matches and soap.[76]

The war-time expansion in the chemicals industry greatly facilitated its recovery during the 1920s. Total employment in chemicals in 1926/27 was 5 per cent higher than in 1913. One estimate of chemicals output in 1926/27 suggests that gross production was around 8 per cent above the 1913 level. Basic chemical production was apparently substantially larger than in 1913, though it was still much less than the 1916 peak. Individual branches of chemicals, notably chemical fertilisers and explosives, nevertheless gave cause for concern.[77]

Consumer Goods

Output of food, drink and tobacco increased by about 10 per cent between 1908 and 1913 (in 1913 prices);[78] the workforce increased by just under 20 per cent.[79] There was a marked increase in the output of tobacco, starch, oils and fats. Sugar refining, which accounted for one-quarter of output of this group of industries in 1913, increased less rapidly. Flour-milling in large-scale industry appears to have stagnated. Large mills enjoyed an uncertain existence, because of the irregularity of grain supply and fluctuations in demand. Small-scale production may have contributed more than 60 per cent of total output. In many areas, the village miller reigned supreme.[80]

Sugar-refining and flour-milling by large-scale industry increased rapidly during the war. According to one estimate, sugar production increased by 56 per cent in physical terms between 1913 and 1916.[81] Employment in sugar refineries increased by 16 per cent; in flour-milling, by 20 per cent. Presumably, large-scale units absorbed labour from non-census industry.[82] As the role of large-scale industry in flour production increased, standardisation of output was placed on the agenda. Before 1917, there was little uniformity in flour-milling. Kritsman reported that mills had 12 or 15 different standards of ground flour (*pomol*). He urged the introduction of a single national standard, and claimed subsequently that the resulting increase in the speed of rolling mills had doubled the daily output at large mills.[83]

During the 1920s the crucial problem for the Group B industries was the shortage of agricultural raw materials, essential for the production of food, drink and tobacco, and textiles and clothing.

The shortages were due to insufficient marketing rather than to a decline in the total production of these materials by agriculture. According to a Vesenkha study of agricultural raw materials, total production in 1926/27 was only slightly lower than in 1913. But the proportion retained by agriculture increased from 42.7 to 62.8 per cent, and in consequence the amount available for industry, and for export, declined by 37.5 per cent.

Exports, which were substantial before the revolution, were drastically reduced. Even so, total supplies available to industry declined by at least 9 per cent between 1913 and 1926/27.[84]

As a result of this decline in supplies, the production of food, drink and tobacco in 1926/27 was lower than in 1913 in census industry, and is unlikely to have increased in small-scale industry. Production statistics reflect this decline, but are confused and unreliable (see Tables 32 and 34); employment figures are more conclusive. In census industry, the number employed in food, drink and tobacco fell by 17.4 per cent, from 342,700 to 283,100[85] (see Table 33). This decline, in conjunction with the reduction in the length of the working day, indicates that the fall in production may have been substantial. In small-scale industry the total number employed in food and drink declined from 347,000 to 259,000 (full-time equivalent); the official figures for production probably exaggerate the recovery (Tables 34 and 35).

The pre-revolutionary textiles industry contributed more than 26 per cent of total production in large-scale industry in 1913. Around 28 per cent of all workers were employed in this large and heterogeneous industry, which had developed steadily and unspectacularly for decades.[86] The value of gross output of all branches of textiles increased by about 57 per cent between 1908 and 1913 (in 1913 prices), in excess of the rate of large-scale industry as a whole. This growth is confirmed by the available data on output in physical terms.[87] Not all branches of the industry were equally dynamic: for example, cotton textiles grew less rapidly than other sectors, notably mixed fabrics.

The textiles industry was predominantly an industry of large-scale units. Small-scale production was almost entirely absent in cotton and woollens. Here, large and integrated plant was the norm.[88] Small-scale industry played only a modest role in silk, flax and mixed fabrics; it was more significant in hemp and jute, where the high cost of machinery hampered the development of large-scale production.

The production of leather before 1913 was also primarily the preserve of large-scale tanneries. They were technically primitive, according to one authority; in addition, they relied heavily on imports of tanning extracts. This created serious difficulties during the war. By contrast, small-scale production predominated in the boot and shoe trades and in saddlery. The war appears not to have changed this industrial structure. Instead, the new Union of Towns and Zemstvos (Zemgor) and other agencies sought to impose some supervision over the myriad small producers.[89]

During the war production of cotton and linen textiles in physical terms increased by 10 and 30 per cent respectively, but production of woollens declined slightly.[90] The decline during the civil war was catastrophic. By 1926/27 production of textiles in physical terms was approaching the pre-war level (see Table 37). The official statistics on textiles production, which show a substantial increase in production between 1913 and 1926/27, are evidently exaggerated.[91] The development of the cotton textile industry is discussed in more detail in Ch. 8.

During the first world war and the mid-1920s, the textile industry began to enter a new stage. The factory production of lengths of cotton fabrics and woollen cloth had driven out, or partly driven out, homespun garments in the XIX Century; but the lengths were made up into garments at home or by artisans. After 1914, the garments themselves began to be produced in factories on a substantial scale for military purposes.[92] The age of mass armies pushed Russia towards the mass production of consumer goods. By 1926/27, production of garments and knitwear by large-scale industry, from small beginnings, was recorded at eight times as large as in 1913. But these two industries still employed only 41,700 workers, mainly in factories controlled by the local soviets.[93] Small-scale industry continued side by side with the new factories; the data for 1913 are uncertain, but according to one estimate artisan production of clothing, hats and knitwear actually increased between 1913 and 1926/27.[94] By 1928, over 60 per cent of woollen cloth was made into garments by census or small-scale industry, but the equivalent figure for cotton textiles was still only 17 per cent.[95] Thus, men's suits were normally made by a tailor; shirts and frocks were usually made at home. Leather footwear began to tread the same path: the proportion made by factory industry increased from 12 per cent in 1913 to 19 per cent in 1926/27. This increase was also accompanied by an increase in the production of small-scale industry.[96] But in other industries, including metal goods, the increase in factory production was accompanied by a decline in artisan production.

PRODUCTIVITY OF LABOUR

The workforce in mining and manufacturing grew by one-third between 1908 and 1913. This increase was accompanied by a modest reduction in the length of the working day, so the total number of hours worked probably increased by about 30 per cent.[97] But gross industrial production measured in 1913 prices increased by about 42 per cent, so labour productivity increased substantially.

In general, labour productivity was improved by the introduction of new machinery and by the reorganisation of industrial production. Standardisation of production hardly existed. According to one contemporary 'the parts of machines have a shape and size that is purely arbitrary, depending almost entirely on custom, tradition and factory routine'. The potential for standardisation was clearly enormous.[98]

Some minor examples can be found of successful attempts by new conglomerates to rationalise production by concentrating production of components at specialist factories. Thus, the Kolomna and Sormovo engineering firms collaborated on a range of products after 1911. The two giants in the South Russian shipbuilding industry, Naval' and Russud, began to work together in 1913 on the technical details of construction.[99] Some reorganisation also took place in cotton textiles, prompted by the need to eliminate delays and interruptions in the supply of raw materials, and to offset the increase in yarn prices after 1905.[100]

A more important factor in the growth of labour productivity was probably the speed-up that accompanied the introduction of new machinery. This was a particular characteristic of the engineering industry, where employers sought to offset the concessions they had been forced to make in 1905 by intensifying the pace of work and supervising operations more closely.[101]

In several industries, however, the absence of technical change or of plant reorganisation frustrated improvements in labour productivity. The oil industry was a striking example. Wells had to be sunk deeper after 1905, but few oil fields operated with modern rotary drills, using instead the cumbersome percussion method. Furthermore, most crude oil was extracted by means of special buckets (*zhelonki*), rather than pumps. As a result of the exhaustion of the more accessible deposits in Baku, it took on average 11 hours to extract each ton of crude in 1913, compared to 9 hours in 1903.[102]

Between 1913 and 1916 output per person in large-scale industry increased by 5 or 6 per cent.[103] The aggregate figures conceal wide variations between industries. Output per worker-day increased by as much as 32 per cent in machine-building and 27 per cent in chemicals. Three other sectors of manufacturing industry also recorded higher output per worker-day in 1916 as against 1913: metalworking, mixed fabrics and clothing. In all these five sectors, labour had been reorganised and new plant installed in order to cope with the volume of war-time demand. Mass production of a standardised product was particularly widespread in shell manufacture where productivity increased as a result of new shift systems, improved equipment (especially machine tools) and 'the elimination of teething troubles connected with the introduction of new products and the acquisition by the workforce of the necessary habits and methods'.[104] The increase in labour productivity in clothing was no less remarkable than in machine-building; the clothing industry even sustained the increase throughout 1917. Here, Zemgor played an important role: it took charge of raw materials, such as wool, and also supplied knitting frames and other equipment to newly-formed producer cooperatives.[105]

By contrast, in industries such as foodstuffs, leather, cotton textiles, woodworking and mining, labour productivity declined between 1913 and 1916. The decline was catastrophic in woodworking. These industries were hampered by the deterioration in the quality of equipment and (in the case

Figure 3. Number of workers by size of plant, 1907–27

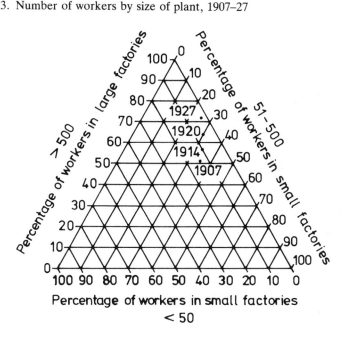

Source: see p. 369, n. 109 below.

of mining) in the quality of the labour force.[106]

In the mid-1920s, the pre-war level of production in large-scale industry was achieved by a combination of increased manpower and increased hourly productivity. The number of workers in census industry rose by about 5 per cent between 1913 and 1926/27 (see Table 33), indicating that the total number of hours worked decreased by 10–15 per cent. According to official figures, gross production increased in the same period by about 5 per cent (see Table 32). This is almost certainly an overestimate. But, even allowing for overestimation, hourly labour productivity may have increased by something like 10 per cent between 1913 and 1926/27.[107]

This substantial improvement was partly obtained by concentrating production into a smaller number of mines and factories, by standardising output, and to a lesser extent by introducing modern machinery.[108] The success of these measures distinguished industry from the railways, where reorganisation was technically more difficult, and capital repair and investment were less generously financed.

Industrial concentration after 1917 has to be set in the context of pre-revolutionary development. As is well known, Russian industry already displayed a marked degree of concentration before 1914. Figure 3 indicates the magnitude of the increase over the whole period.[109] The closer the point moves towards the apex of the triangle along the right-hand side, the higher the degree of concentration. It will readily be seen that the degree of concentration increased steadily throughout the period 1907–27. The process was not interrupted by the war; indeed, contemporary opinion that 'the war has furthered the process of industrial concentration' would appear to be validated.[110]

Both in industry and on the railways increases in labour productivity as compared with 1913 involved economic and administrative pressure on the workers. From the end of 1924 onwards, the authorities, supported half-heartedly and intermittently by the trade unions, tried to insist that labour productivity should increase more rapidly than the average wage, and sought to bring this about by systematically increasing output norms (i.e., cutting the rate for the job). The campaign was more successful in industry than on the railways, but even in industry wages outpaced productivity in two of the four years 1924/25–1927/28.[111]

INTERNAL TRADE

The increase in industrial and agricultural production between 1908 and 1913 was reflected in the performance of the tertiary sector. Total trade turnover, excluding both unlicensed trade conducted at fairs and bazaars and also transactions at state alcohol stores, amounted to 9,144 million rubles in 1913 (USSR pre-1939 territory). This represented an increase of nearly 40 per cent in the value of trade between 1908 and 1913, measured in current prices.[112]

The aggregate figures conceal differences in the experience of different kinds of trade establishment. According to Strumilin, the most rapid growth in turnover was recorded by enterprises that were required to publish their accounts (*otchetnye predpriyatiya*). This category included syndicates, the Russian equivalent of cartels, and the consumer co-operatives.[113] The number of licensed trading units grew less rapidly than estimated turnover. In numerical terms, the most important retail outlet was the small shop (*lavka*), defined as a permanent fixture that the customer might enter, as opposed to a kiosk or booth. Of the total number of licenses issued on the eve of the war, more than half were for the right to trade in a small shop.[114]

The organisation of wholesale trade changed markedly during the XIX Century. In 1800, much of it was conducted at periodic fairs, of which there were some 4,000 scattered throughout the Empire. A century later, according to official figures, the number of fairs had quadrupled, but they contributed only 7 per cent of total trade turnover, although the proportion was higher in respect of wholesale trade in the major agricultural commodities.[115] These fairs – some of them, like the one at Nizhnii Novgorod, spectacular and world-famous – gave way to other institutional arrangements in wholesale trade.[116]

By 1913, the commercial banks and larger merchant houses (*torgovye doma*) exercised a powerful leverage over internal trade. There were nearly 4,000 merchant houses registered in 1912, with a combined capital of 142 million rubles, dealing for the most part in manufactured goods and foodstuffs. Most of them originated after 1900. The majority were small businesses, but a handful played a significant role in wholesale trade in grain, sugar, fish, timber, iron, cotton, coal and oil. Firms such as Stakheev, Vtorov, Wogau and Yaroshinsky initially extended credit to selected clients, and proceeded to build new warehouses, grain elevators and other facilities. Stakheev commanded a chain of barges, tugs and railway freight wagons. Other houses bought their way into railway companies and into merchant shipping. In some cases, these concerns succeeded in establishing monopolies of purchase: for example, the Wogau house controlled virtually the entire market in soda and copper by 1913. Stakheev and Vtorov eventually established a direct interest in production (e.g., Stakheev formed the Emba Oil Co. in 1912).[117]

On the eve of the war 161 wholesale trading ventures were registered as joint-stock companies. Most of them dealt in industrial raw materials, such as minerals and metal. Among them were to be found the well-known syndicates in iron and steel (Prodameta, formed in 1902; Krovlya, 1904), coal (Produgol', 1906), oil (where Nobel and Mazut had agreed on a joint sales policy in 1905 and controlled three-quarters of oil production in 1913) and railway engineering products (Prodparovoz, 1901; Prodvagon, 1904). Shares in these companies were held exclusively by the firms that participated in the allocation of sales quotas. The main aim of such agreements was to halt the slide in prices that took place at the beginning of the century, but uncertainties about market demand led to the regular renewal of quotas, and eventually to the charge that they were responsible for a 'famine' in fuel and metal.[118] Whatever the validity of such criticism, the syndicates and merchant houses took credit for the modernisation of pre-revolutionary wholesale trade. The *torgovye doma* were responsible for improvements in the storage of commodities and in quality control. Syndicates such as Prodameta may have reduced transport costs, by assigning orders to enterprises that were close to the industrial consumer. They certainly cut the overheads of individual enterprises, which now had a unified sales organisation. The syndicates were also able to conclude more favourable contracts with their customers (for the most part merchant houses), to whom prolonged periods of credit were no longer extended.[119]

Although syndicates stipulated quotas and fixed wholesale prices, they did not intervene directly in investment decisions or in production. They covered an important but limited range of industries. Syndicates usually proved short-lived in the engineering industry before 1913, largely because of the heterogeneous nature of market demand; and they were virtually absent in consumer goods (sugar was a special case, where the state enforced quotas of output).

In retail trade the most significant developments before 1913 lay in the use of more advanced marketing practices and in the growth of consumer cooperatives. Two American firms, Singer and International Harvester, were pioneers in establishing a network of agents who were empowered to sell goods on credit to rural consumers, especially in the Urals and Siberia, areas largely untouched by retail outlets. The agents, who took a commission on sales, frequently found themselves in receipt of dealerships for a wide range of other goods. These more sophisticated marketing strategies did not come cheap. The firms had to be willing to offer credit for two years or more; inventories were maintained at a high level, given the huge area. It is doubtful whether such new marketing arrangements exceeded 2 or 3 per cent of total retail trade turnover.[120]

Consumer cooperatives were designed, as the 1897 Model Code put it, to enable their members to obtain basic goods 'at the lowest possible price or at the average market price'. They were especially popular on the periphery of the Empire, in Siberia, the Urals, the Caucasus and Ukraine, regions where the supply of goods was erratic and periodic scarcities led to sharp increases in market prices. By January 1914 there were an estimated 10,000 consumer cooperatives in existence, with a combined membership of 1.4 million. Most had been formed between 1905 and 1914.[121]

Cooperatives had a positive effect on retail trade. Their low overheads and profit margins allowed them to offer goods at low prices. They familiarised rural consumers with modern retailing practices, by undermining the custom of face-to-face haggling with a shopkeeper or itinerant merchant and by establishing the principle of a set price.[122] Although their turnover in 1913 amounted to no more than 5 per cent of the total, this should not be allowed to detract from their overall significance. The Bolshevik government acknowledged the role played by consumer cooperatives in April 1918.[123]

The first world war transformed many features of pre-revolutionary trade. Some changes, like the abolition of the state vodka monopoly, ultimately proved to be temporary.[124] Similarly, the decline in organised trade was due to wartime conditions of shortage and conscription, and would be reversed under NEP.[125] In other respects, however, the war merely confirmed trends that were already apparent before 1914. The share of fairs in trade turnover continued to decline.[126] The number of joint-stock companies engaged in trade continued to increase.[127] The power of the big merchant houses increased, as firms such as Vtorov and Stakheev moved into production as well as new spheres of wholesale trade.[128] The number of consumer cooperatives more than doubled and their membership grew five-fold, as workers struggled to obtain basic necessities at a reasonable price.[129]

The position of the syndicates during the war was more complex. Prodameta continued to control the wholesale trade in iron and steel throughout 1915, but the war weakened its role in two respects. First, many metallurgical firms marketed a smaller proportion of their output, preferring instead to produce more profitable shells themselves. In these circumstances, the syndicate was less relevant to their needs.[130] Secondly, the government established a Metals Committee in December 1915, which subsequently fixed the price of metal required for the war effort. In practice, all orders continued to be channelled through Prodameta, but at the end of 1916 the government decided to fix the quotas for individual factories. This system was streamlined during 1917, with the formation of three regional authorities, including 'Yugometa', for the southern industry. By this time the old private syndicate had virtually collapsed; but so, too, had the supply of metal.[131]

The tsarist government intervened in the market in a sluggish and selective manner, being concerned solely with laying claim to products that were destined ultimately for the front. The price of basic goods was fixed only in the case of purchases made by or on behalf of government. Civilian needs were treated as a residual, and unregulated prices continued to spiral upwards. This picture began to change only during 1917, with the declaration of state monopolies for grain, sugar, coal, leather and textiles.[132]

After the collapse of all organised trade during the Civil War, the New Economic Policy encouraged the revival of private trade. In May 1924, the XIII party congress warned against 'any measures in the sphere of private trade which would lead to curtailment of, or interference with, the general process of exchange of goods'.[133] But large-scale private trade was always regarded as incompatible with Soviet principles. Most of the pre-revolutionary private wholesale enterprises remained in state or cooperative ownership or control, and were incorporated in the new socialised network. Even in 1923/24, private wholesale trade accounted for only 18 per cent of total wholesale turnover, and by 1926/27 the proportion had declined to a mere 4.6 per cent.[134] The wholesale trade of state industry was increasingly conducted by national or regional syndicates modelled on the pre-revolutionary private syndicates. Soviet syndicates were more powerful than their predecessors, and were formed not only in the capital goods' industries but also in cotton textiles and other consumer goods' industries in which they did not exist at all before the revolution.[135]

Retail private trade, mainly carried on by individual traders, sometimes assisted by members of their families, was allowed to develop much more freely in the early stages of NEP: in 1922/23 it amounted to 75.3 per cent of all retail trade. According to the concept prevalent until 1927, private retail trade would continue insofar as the socialist sector was not strong enough to take over its activities. In the mid-1920s, this policy was occasionally departed from in practice when the police descended on a market and arrested groups of 'Nepmen' (private traders) for infringement of regulations.[136] But such cases were exceptional. With the rapid recovery of the economy, private retail trade flourished and expanded, doubling in volume between 1922/23 and 1926. But state and cooperative trade, more strongly and much more consistently supported by the authorities, expanded even more rapidly. By 1926 the share of private trade in retail turnover had declined to 40.7 per cent.[137]

The restriction of private trade in circumstances where the state was unable to build up a modern trading system in its place prevented the recovery of the retail trading network to its pre-war size. The total number of trading units (excluding trade from carts and by pedlars, which cannot be accurately estimated) amounted to 932,000 in 1912, but had reached only 644,000 by April–September 1926 (see Table 39 (b)); of these, 468,500 were privately owned. But very few private traders risked the employment of an assistant. Only 22,896 traders by main occupation were recorded in the 1926 population census as 'employers',[138] and according to labour statistics the total number of persons employed in private trade in 1926/27 amounted to only 63,900.[139] Even allowing for the under-reporting which no doubt occurred it is certain that private trading units were smaller as well as less numerous than before the revolution. State and cooperative trade was organised in somewhat larger units. But the total number of persons employed in state and cooperative trade amounted to only 451,300, for a total of 178,908 trading units, a mere 2.5 persons per unit.[140] Taking the private and socialised sectors together, according to Soviet estimates the total number of wage and salary earners employed in trade was no larger than before the revolution, and the number working in trade on their own account was substantially smaller.[141] Nevertheless, the amount of retail trade in real terms in 1926 had reached 94–98 per cent of the 1913 level (see Table 39). Whether the increase in turnover per person engaged in trade is regarded as an increase in efficiency depends on the definition of efficiency; it certainly resulted in more frequent queues.

THE INSTRUMENTS OF INDUSTRIALISATION

On the Eve of the First World War

State-led or Market-led Industrialisation?
There is no agreement among economic historians about the fundamental causes of the 1908–13 industrial boom. Some authorities, notably Alexander Gerschenkron, have argued that it was largely attributable to an increase in consumer spending, triggered off by the Stolypin agrarian reform, and was thus substantially different in character from the boom of the 1890s, which was stimulated by government expenditure. Others have stressed the continued reliance of Russian industry even in the immediate pre-war years on the role of government spending and government in-

tervention. While Gerschenkron argued that industrialisation in tsarist Russia was transformed from a state-induced process in the 1890s to a market-led process in 1908–13, other specialists regard 1890–1913 as a continuum in which the state role was decisive throughout.

Gerschenkron's hypothesis finds some support in the rapid expansion of the consumer goods' industries on the eve of the war. The gross production of the large-scale food, drink and tobacco industries increased by 10 per cent between 1908 and 1913, and the equivalent figure for the textile industries was as much as 57 per cent (measured in 1913 prices) (see pp. 137–8 above.) Small-scale industry, is also believed to have expanded repidly (see p. 129 above). These figures for the consumer industries are congruent with the expansion of retail sales in 1908–13, estimated by Gregory at between 35 and 43 per cent in 1913 prices and 38 per cent in current prices.[142]

But the increase in production was even more rapid in the case of capital goods, and the share of Group A industries in total large-scale industrial production increased (see pp. 128–9, 132–7 above).

The rapid increase of Group B industries, and the even more rapid increase of Group A industries, reflected complex changes in the pattern of consumption. The expansion of Group A industries reflected not only the growth of state demand but also the increasing demand from agriculture and from the consumer goods' industries. Between 1908 and 1913 the production of agricultural engineering, for example, approximately doubled. On the other hand, the increase in consumer demand was not solely a consequence of the autonomous expansion of the market; it was also a consequence of the increase in incomes derived from the increase in government expenditure. In 1908–13, as in the previous stages of Russian industrialisation, including the 1890s, both autonomous and state-induced expansion were present.

In our view the available evidence does not show that the role of the state in industrialisation was declining on the eve of the first world war. It is certainly true that the industrial depression at the end of the 1890s was in substantial part a result of the decline in state railway orders. But during the boom of 1908–13 state orders placed with industry again rapidly expanded. The main factor here was the huge expansion in defence expenditure, particularly expenditure on armaments. Total budgetary expenditures on defence increased by 58 per cent between 1908 and 1913; this included expenditures on munitions and shipbuilding, and 'extraordinary' expenditure on defence, which together increased from 127 to as much as 326 million rubles.[143] And after 1911 government orders for railway rolling-stock also increased rapidly.

Instruments of Industrialisation: the State Budget
In the state-led segment of the industrial boom of 1908–13 the state budget

played a crucial role, as it had in the 1890s, but it was now directed towards armaments rather than the construction of the railways. The tsarist government defined as the central purpose of its policy the need to maintain Russia's status as a great power after 1905. The government urgently sought to restore the losses to military shipping and other equipment sustained in the war against Japan in 1904–1905,[144] and hoped to stay in the arms race with the other continental powers. To this end, the Ministers of War and for the Navy framed ambitious rearmament programmes, involving the expenditure of hundreds of millions of rubles on the fleet, as well as on military fortifications, arsenals, highways, and weaponry.[145] Rearmament and its implications probably constituted the most pressing issues in industrial and fiscal policy, in sharp contrast with the situation during the 1920s.

The raising of resources to finance these programmes posed in turn a new set of problems. The tsarist budget was already over-stretched both by military demands and by the need to service the accumulated state debt (including fresh debts that had been incurred during 1904–5). The Ministry of Finance was convinced that new spending programmes must not be financed by borrowing or by printing money. The aversion to borrowing had little to do with fears of subjugation by foreign bondholders – Russia was no Egypt or Argentina – but, rather, stemmed from a straightforward belief in fiscal and monetary orthodoxy to which Russia had committed itself when she joined the Gold Standard. Russia had to strive to balance the budget as a precondition of monetary stability and the continued inflow of foreign venture capital.[146] If possible, the government hoped also to accumulate budgetary surpluses. The central problem of government economic policy was the need to reconcile the conflicting demands of tsarist imperialism with the impulse for retrenchment that emanated from the Ministry of Finance.[147]

Faced with pressure to obtain additional sources of revenue after 1905, the tsarist government proceeded to consolidate the existing fiscal system, rather than to change it in any fundamental respect. The proportion of revenue derived from direct taxation stood at 8 per cent in 1913, almost exactly what it had been in 1907.[148] Taxes on personal consumption, together with customs duties, contributed 47 per cent of total revenue in 1913, as against 49 per cent in 1907 and 45 per cent in 1900.

Taxes levied on trade and industry yielded an increase in revenue of 122 per cent in the decade before the war, compared to an overall increase in ordinary revenue of 68 per cent.[149] This increase reflected both the growth in industrial activity between 1908 and 1913 and an increase in the rate of industrial taxation imposed in 1908.[150]

The political pressures against the introduction of an income tax and increases in other direct taxes were sufficiently powerful to compel the Ministry of Finance to maintain its conventional reliance on indirect sources of revenue. The Minister of Finance Kokovtsev introduced taxes on a wider range of consumer goods and increased the rates of excise on existing goods.[151] The state monopoly of the sale of vodka had been introduced in four provinces in 1895 and extended to the entire Empire by 1902. In 1903 receipts from vodka sales comprised just over 26 per cent of total budget revenue. The picture in 1913 had changed not at all. Increased sales, together with an increase in the excise levied in 1905 and again in 1908, yielded a gross figure of 900 million rubles in 1913. The net contribution of the vodka monopoly to the state budget was a matter for some dispute. Officially, the net gain was put at 664 million rubles in 1913, that is 74 per cent of the gross figure.[152] The official figures indicate that net receipts increased faster than gross receipts in the decade preceding the outbreak of war (1903–1913): by 79 per cent and 66 per cent respectively.

Instruments of Industrialisation: Tariffs
The tsarist government also continued to exert important indirect influences on industrial development in 1908–13. Here import tariffs have pride of place. As Kahan and Crisp have pointed out, tariff policy was designed not only to stimulate industrial growth, but also, and perhaps primarily, to generate revenue.[153] The government protected both those industries that produced semi-finished goods, such as iron and steel and cotton yarn, and those producing finished goods. The level of effective protection afforded to manufacturing industry was therefore less than it might have been. Tariff policy was also criticised because fiscal necessity led the authorities to retain tariffs in full force long after the relevant industry had established itself.[154] Critics also drew attention to the specific effect of the tariff on the Russian engineering industry. The 1891 tariff (revised in 1903) had been appropriate to an industry that was then still in its infancy. By 1913, the engineering industry had made rapid strides. Yet it was given relatively little protection against imports of the more sophisticated and high-value items. Importers were encouraged by the structure of the tariff to import such items without their heavier components (engines were imported minus their fly-wheel, machines minus the base). Some machines were imported piecemeal and simply assembled in Russia, contrary to the intentions of the tariff officials and the Russian engineering industrialists.[155] Tariffs afforded a substantial measure of protection to Russian industry. But they were a crude instrument.

Instruments of Industrialisation: State Credit; the Banks
The tsarist government also influenced the level of activity in Russian industry by the negative device of refraining from state borrowing which would hamper the access of private borrowers to the money market. The shift in policy was remarkable. The total estimated value of state debt increased from 7,858 million rubles in 1900 to 11,127 million in 1908, or by

42 per cent, an increase largely attributable to the war against Japan. But between 1908 and 1914 Kokovtsev ensured that the debt increased by less than 15 per cent, to 12,745 million rubles.[156]

This restraint did not of itself have the expected effect, as Russian investors were loathe to risk their money in any kind of speculative ventures, including industrial investment. The reduction in state issues of bonds probably led investors to look for other forms of fixed-interest paper. Some funds may, as Gindin suggests, have been diverted into municipal loans or into the land banks, where higher guaranteed returns could be obtained. But the bulk of domestic savings went into deposit accounts with the major commercial banks. These in turn made them available to industrial clients.[157]

The commercial banks were instrumental also in encouraging investors to subscribe to non-guaranteed industrial securities, notably by opening special accounts ('on call'), which amounted to credit to individuals, secured by the portfolio of shares. Needless to say, the banks tended to be discriminating in the choice of industrial companies whose shares they sponsored in this way. The sums involved were substantial: on call accounts increased in value by 56 per cent in 1912–13, reaching 720 million rubles.[158]

Thus the government restraint in raising loans, coupled with the positive actions of the banks, produced the situation described in 1915 by a financial expert who was later to become a prominent adviser to the Soviet government: 'our own domestic market, even at a time of rapid industrial growth, is capable of straining its resources to satisfy the requirements of the Russian national economy'.[159] The value of domestic issues of shares, mainly for industry, increased by 51 per cent between 1908 and 1914. But foreign investment in Russian industry increased equally rapidly. On the eve of the first world war the traditional instruments of Russian industrialisation still remained of major significance.

The First World War and After

The outbreak of world war represented a quantitative rather than a qualitative break in the process of tsarist industrial development. The war magnified – in a grotesque and costly manner – the existing influence of armaments on the pre-revolutionary economy.

During the war, both the labour force and the capital equipment in defence and allied industries increased rapidly. Output of the means of destruction, which appear together with capital goods in both pre-revolutionary and post-revolutionary statistics, increased both because resources were diverted to the war effort and because labour productivity increased substantially. In some consumer goods' industries, such as clothing, the war also stimulated production. But other industries suffered from failure to obtain materials and the depletion of their labour force. The war transformed the structure of Russian industry by creating a vastly expanded armaments industry, to whose needs virtually everything was subordinated. The war created an exhausted and hungry labour force. It also saddled the new revolutionary government – if it had accepted it – with a swollen state debt.

One outstanding merit of the war-time economy from the Bolshevik point of view was that it established a plethora of regulatory agencies that could be adapted to the tasks of proletarian dictatorship. A Special Council for State Defence, established in August 1915, was responsible for assigning military orders both to the state armaments factories and to private industry. Its work was supplemented by such specialised agencies as the Metals Committee; from the autumn of 1916 the Metals Committee not merely controlled the supply of metals for defence purposes, but also fixed their prices. The tsarist government also established the tradition of controlling (or rather attempting to control) food supplies from the countryside to the towns and the army. From November 1915 the Special Council for Food Supply endeavoured to set maximum food prices; and in 1916 the government moved towards closer control over grain, unsuccessfully attempting to introduce a grain levy towards the end of the year. In March 1917, the new Provisional Government established a full grain monopoly.[160]

These instruments for management of industry and agriculture were adapted and strengthened by the Soviet government during the Civil War. The commissariat responsible for managing industry, Vesenkha (the Supreme Council of National Economy), established at the end of 1917, was based on the war-time planning agencies of the tsarist and provisional governments. In 1921, the New Economic Policy led to the temporary disbandment of the government grain supply agencies and to a decline in the role of central government over industry. But Vesenkha continued, and was supplemented by a new planning agency Gosplan (the State Planning Commission), established in the spring of 1921.

The Mid-1920s

During the years of economic recovery after 1921 the Soviet authorities maintained and, where it was absent, established an imperfect but on the whole effective machinery for planning the economy – or at any rate for its central management. The major instruments by which the tsarist government had controlled or influenced the economy – the state budget, and the protection of Russian industry with the aid of customs tariffs – were wielded effectively by the Soviet state. But they were supplemented in the now much larger state-owned sector of the economy by controls over finance, prices and wages. The 'scissors' crisis of 1923 impelled the party to authorise the use of a combination of fiscal, credit and price policies to restore the delicate balance between industry and the peasantry.[161] During the next four years, until the balance was finally upset at the end of 1927, the central aim of Soviet economic policy was to manipulate the scissors between agricultural and industrial prices so as to place an upper bound on the exploitation of the peasants by the state while at the same time directing resources into state industry.

Financial Controls

In manipulating the financial controls, the Soviet government, following the successful currency reform of 1924, for a couple of years sought almost as vigorously as any capitalist government to maintain the stability of the currency, or even to enhance its value. This required a balanced budget. To this end the principal pre-revolutionary revenues were restored (see Table 40). The most notable of these was the revenue from the state vodka monopoly, which had disappeared during the first world war when the tsarist government introduced prohibition. State vodka sales did not return to the pre-war level. But the restoration of the notorious 'tax on drunkenness' as the most important single source of revenue was a dramatic instance of the victory of economic expediency over social principle.[162] Excises were also imposed on textiles and other industrial consumer goods, which did not bear tax before the revolution. Other new sources of revenue included a personal income tax, directed at recovering some of the profits of private traders and other 'Nepmen', and an agricultural tax (a direct tax on peasant incomes). The system of mass loans from the population also began to be introduced in the mid-1920s. But the most striking change in the post-revolutionary budget was the large increase in various kinds of taxes and other imposts levied on the income and profits of state industrial and trading enterprises.

The relations between the state budget and state industry were confused and complicated. From 1922 onwards, the principal state industries acquired monopolistic or oligopolistic powers through the formation of national or regional syndicates (see p. 145 above). During the 'scissors' crisis of 1923, the central state authorities introduced price controls so as to close the scissors by reducing the prices charged by the syndicates. Price controls were quite effective in relation to capital goods. But pressure from the continuous increase in the purchasing power of the population on the retail market for consumer goods tended to push up their prices in spite of the controls. In any case, unlike consumer goods, most capital goods were sold to other state enterprises, and ultimately paid for by the state budget, and this provided a powerful argument for keeping their prices particularly low. Both prices and profits therefore tended to be much higher for consumer goods than for capital goods. The cotton textile industry was the most prominent example of a consumer goods' industry which financed its own investment, and also provided a substantial proportion of its profits to the state budget and the banks for general use. In contrast, investment in the capital goods' industries, including electric power, was provided almost entirely by the state budget and the various state banks.

The state budget did not simply act in relation to the economy as a mechanism for transferring profits from high-profit to low-profit sectors. As compared with 1913, budget expenditure on defence had been drastically reduced, and the large pre-revolutionary expenditure on interest and repayment of state loans had vanished from the budget with the abrogation of the national debt.[163] In place of these items, expenditure on the national economy greatly increased (see Table 41). Industry was the principal recipient of the additional allocations. According to a Vesenkha report, net allocations from budget and banks to Vesenkha-planned industry, after deducting taxes and other payments made to the budget and the banks by industry, amounted to 193 million rubles in 1925/26 and 309 million rubles in 1926/27.[164]

Physical Controls

While the crucial means of implementing state policies in the mid-1920s was the provision of finance, financial measures were increasingly supplemented by physical controls. The quite detailed import controls were the most effective of all the physical controls wielded by the authorities during NEP. And throughout NEP the Red Army and Navy, the railways and other organisations financed from the state budget directly negotiated their industrial requirements with Vesenkha through the Committee of State Orders.[165] Arrangements for the central allocation of iron and steel, and fuel, supplemented by elaborate detailed negotiations between syndicates, trusts and factories, were also firmly in place by 1926.[166]

The stage which Soviet planning had reached by 1926/27 may be illustrated by the important case of capital investment. Capital investment was already largely financed by central government; but it was for the most part undertaken without central government intervention once the financial provisions had been settled. Orders for capital equipment were normally placed direct between trust and trust; no effective syndicate for engineering products was in operation. A committee on engineering, responsible for distributing orders to engineering factories, was not established until the spring of 1927,[167] and the struggle to establish effective methods of planning capital equipment continued into the 1930s.

The construction of buildings, as distinct from the provision of capital equipment, was nominally controlled by a Building Commission of the Council of Labour and Defence, and in industry by the Vesenkha Building Committee and Permanent Conference on Building, supported by the very active central committee of the building workers' trade union.[168] All these committees had different chairmen; they did not act in concert; and their influence was small. The majesty of the apparatus of control reflected the impotence of the authorities. The building industry in fact remained at the primitive technical level prevalent before the revolution. It was 'most backward and disorganised', the chairman of its trade union declared;[169] on another occasion he complained, with pardonable hyperbole, that *'our methods of work are still the same as they were in the Stone Age'.*[170] Building materials were produced in numerous small factories, usually controlled by the local soviets.[171] As we have seen (p. 41 above), building labour was still largely seasonal, recruited afresh on the market in every building season. The establishment of the State Institute for Projects of Metal Works (Gipromez) in February 1926 was a significant initial step towards central management of the future shape of industry.[172] But the procedures and practice of physical planning were still crude and unsystematic. Much remained to be done.

THE COMPARATIVE PERSPECTIVE

In spite of the progress made between 1908 and 1927, the Russian and Soviet economy continued to lag far behind the great industrial powers. The immensity of the gap to be bridged, in terms of both production and technology, was highlighted by the first world war. The gap was described frankly and more or less accurately in numerous contemporary Soviet publications and pronouncements. Soviet industry, like tsarist industry in 1913, continued to be dominated by the Group B industries to a greater extent than in the major industrial countries.[173] The first five-year plan, trenchantly complaining about the 'burdensome inheritance' from tsarism, pointed out that the return to the pre-war level 'reproduced the main disproportions' of the tsarist industry; the high share of the textile and food industries in total production was combined with 'very weak development of machine building and electrical engineering, a relatively small percentage of iron and steel and the almost complete absence of the chemical industry'.[174]

The comparative statistics for output per head of population, which were frequently cited, showed that in the Soviet Union the production of consumer goods was lower, and of capital goods much lower, than in any of the other great powers. Even the amount of paper consumed per head of population in 1926/27, in this land abundant in forests and hungry for knowledge, had reached only 14 per cent of German and a mere 6 per cent of United States' consumption.[175] Soviet national income as a whole in 1927 was estimated to have been no higher than the national income of the United States half a century earlier in 1880, even though the population of the USSR was substantially larger.[176]

The gap between the Soviet Union and the industrialised countries was dramatically indicated by the minute quantities of mechanical energy and mechanical motive-power used in the Soviet economy. The total consumption of energy per head of population, including human and animal muscle-power as well as the mechanical energy provided by coal and other fuels, reached only 41 per cent of the equivalent figure in the case of Germany and a mere 13 per cent in the case of the United States. The difference was almost entirely due to the small amount of mechanical energy available in the Soviet Union, which obtained two-thirds of its energy imports from human beings and animals, lagging behind such semi-industrialised countries as Italy and Japan, and ahead only of the Asiatic countries.[177] 'The Soviet producer', Gosplan commented when it presented these estimates in the summer of 1927, 'is worse equipped for the struggle with nature as a result of this burdensome inheritance than the producers of other countries'.[178]

Soviet dependence on human and animal power, while in large part a function of the technical backwardness of agriculture, extended to the whole of the economy with the exception of the most modern segment of factory industry. A circumstantial comparison between bricklaying in Germany and the Soviet Union by a German bricklayer working in the USSR plausibly argued that the much lower Soviet productivity resulted partly from the lower skill of the Soviet bricklayer, who did all the fetching and carrying himself rather than being supported by unskilled labour, and partly from the quality of the tools used.[179] The quality of Soviet small tools was a very frequent matter of complaint, and affected workers in every sector of the economy.[180]

In factory industry itself, the gap in terms of mechanical power was not so forbidding. The total mechanical power available in Soviet industry, owing to its relatively small size, was naturally much smaller than in the industrial countries, amounting according to Soviet estimates to 3.3 million horsepower as compared with 15.8 millions in the United Kingdom and 52.5 millions in the United States.[181] But such industries as iron and steel and cotton textiles, and important sections of the engineering industry used relatively modern equipment and modern production methods, as they had in 1913. Horse-power available per worker in factory industry was estimated at 1.4 in the Soviet Union as against 2 in the United Kingdom, 2.1 in Germany and 4.3 in the United States.[182] But Soviet workers were less skilled than workers in the major industrial countries, and Soviet industry was poorly provided with technical staff.[183]

As a result of the smaller amount of mechanical power available per worker, together with the lower level of skills, labour productivity (output per person employed) was lower in the Soviet Union than elsewhere. A Soviet estimate indicated that the average industrial worker in 1926/27 produced only one-half as much as a British worker and a mere one-seventh as much as a United States' worker.[184] The variation between industries was considerable. Output measured in tons per worker in 1928/29 varied from 14.9 per cent of the United States' level in the sugar industry and 17.2 per cent in iron and steel to 28.6 per cent for cotton textiles and as much as 84.0 per cent for crude oil.[185]

In France, Germany and the Soviet Union industrial production approximately recovered to the pre-war level by 1926/27. The Soviet achievement was impressive: the decline in production, and the damage and destruction of industrial plant, had been far greater than in the other belligerent countries. But production in the United States and other industrial countries which had suffered no war damage far exceeded the pre-war level. In consequence, the Soviet share in world industrial output had declined.[186] The comparative Soviet position varied greatly between different industries. In several established Soviet industries, such as coal and textiles, production had not fallen much further behind the rest of the world. But even in established industries such as iron and oil the lag had considerably increased.[187] The Soviet Union, largely cut off from world technology between 1917 and 1923, and unable to undertake substantial new investment, had made little progress. Gosplan pointed out that in the USSR 'the electric power and oil industries, in spite of high rates of growth, are still lagging considerably behind international progress in terms both of their level and the absolute increase in their output, while in other industries (e.g., chemicals, motor vehicles) the position is definitely unfavourable'.[188] A young power engineer drew attention even more dramatically to the nature of the technological race with capitalist industry:

> We must naturally take as our models the achievements of the West and America, we must catch up and overtake them. But there is no kind of static state over there in the creation of these models. We can observe the uniquely stormy dynamics of the process over there.[189]

The position was particularly alarming in the new high-technology industries. The survey in Chapter 10 below shows a widening gap with the industrialised countries, in terms of both quantities produced and the technologies used, in the tractor, vehicle, optical equipment and bearings industries, and in machine tools.

While the production gap between Soviet and Western industry in the mid-1920s was as wide as in 1913, and the technological gap yawned even wider, the rate of growth of Soviet industry was already higher and more consistent than in the capitalist countries. The Gosplan control figures noted with satisfaction that the plan to increase industrial production by 13 per cent in 1926/27 'has no parallel in the development of the US'.[190] A year later, after this plan had been exceeded, Gosplan remarked in the control figures for 1927/28 that *'periodical crises'* were 'inevitable companions of capitalist development', and contrasted the 'sharp breaks and zig-zags' in the growth-curves of capitalist countries with the 'unbroken advance' which had already characterised Soviet economic growth for several years.[191] This achievement was undeniable. But could this rapid rate of growth be maintained within the framework of NEP once recovery was complete?

CONCLUSIONS

A comparison of the industrial economy in 1913 and 1926/27 must not lose sight of the broader features of society and the political system. The scope for economic development was profoundly altered by war, revolution and civil war. Some of the consequences of these events were favourable to economic development, but others tended to inhibit economic development.

The tsarist state had been committed to the pursuit of international prestige and power and correspondingly devoted resources to that end. The ambitions of tsarism culminated in the first world war. By contrast, the Bolshevik government had no such immediate pretensions. The decline in military expenditure substantially reduced a major item of the pre-revolutionary budget and released industrial capacity. The abrogation of the tsarist debt, much of it incurred in order to support the diplomatic pretensions of the regime, removed an incubus from the state budget and the balance of payments.

The policy of the Bolshevik government strongly supported industrial expansion. A combination of financial and price controls, together with some physical controls, enabled the direction of resources towards industrialisation. Imports were directed towards the needs of industry, and particularly the needs of industrial investment, to a much greater extent than in 1913. The tsarist government, by contrast, exercised largely an indirect influence on industrial activity before 1914, much as it had done during the 1890s. Decisions about investment, production and marketing were largely entrusted to private businessmen, although the concentration and cartelisation of industry ensured that the number of such decision-makers was strictly limited. When the tsarist government did impose direct controls, it did so simply in order to mobilise resources for war.

The social revolution also transformed the conditions of industrial production. The recovery of production took place against the background of a shorter working day, which workers had gained as a result of the 1917 Revolution. As a result, the growth in output after 1920 was achieved by an increase in numbers employed, together with some increase in the hourly productivity of labour. On the railways, pre-war levels of operation were attained only by a substantial expansion in employment.

Another consequence of the social upheaval was the decline in agricultural marketings (though not in production) as compared with 1908–13.

This was due partly to the elimination of private estates and the greater equality among peasant households, and partly to the growth of the rural population; but it was also a result of price policies unfavourable to the countryside and favourable to industry (the 'scissors'). The shortage of agricultural raw materials hindered the recovery of the consumer goods industries, and some of the retained raw materials were used by peasants for domestic production. The lack of agricultural products for export was the main cause of the drastic decline in foreign trade.

The revolution also changed many features of internal trade. During the late tsarist period, wholesale trade had been increasingly controlled by private syndicates and merchant houses; after 1917, these were nationalised, and by the mid-1920s the state syndicates covered a wider range of industries, and were more powerful, than the pre-revolutionary private syndicates. In the years before 1914, private retail trade became more organised and widespread; after the revolution, owing to the limitations on private trade, both the number of retail trading outlets and the number of persons engaged in retail trade were considerably smaller than before the revolution.

In 1926/27 production in large-scale industry already surpassed the pre-war level. In certain basic industries which had given cause for concern before 1914 (notably coal and oil) the prospects for growth during the mid-1920s were encouraging. In others, especially ferrous and non-ferrous metallurgy, the situation was much less promising. In engineering, there were now signs that the product mix had become more diverse and less dependent on military products. Soviet industry began to manufacture engineering products of some sophistication that were imported hitherto. The consumer goods industries in the mid-1920s, in contrast to the position on the eve of the first world war, were hampered by a shortage of raw materials.

Although construction (building work) and total capital investment had not recovered to the 1913 level, investment in industry had increased substantially, at the expense of investment in dwellings and in transport. But in 1926/27 industry still primarily relied on the pre-revolutionary capital stock. Industrial equipment and buildings had suffered more than a decade of neglect, and were often urgently in need of replacement rather than overhaul. The recovery in industrial production on this basis also meant that the pre-war geographical distribution of industry was reproduced. The dispersal of industrial capacity remained a task for the future.

In spite of the rapid recovery of Soviet industry by 1926/27, the gap in production between the USSR and the advanced capitalist nations was as wide as in 1913. The technological gap was wider still. Moreover, the growth of industry had failed to check the scourge of mass urban unemployment, a far more prevalent affliction under NEP than before the revolution.

In short, while the revolution of 1917 had wrought many significant changes in the economic and social structure, major features of the Soviet economy in 1926/27 were recognisably those of the pre-revolutionary period. Above all, peasant agricultural production was overwhelmingly preponderant, with consequences for every aspect of the economy. But within five years a vast social and economic transformation had taken place, which eradicated much of this pre-revolutionary legacy.

8 The Textile Industries
Christopher Ward

ON THE EVE

On the eve of war and revolution the Russian Empire was one of the great textile centres of the world, fourth after Britain, America and Germany.[1] During the XIX Century the prime factors influencing location were proximity to markets and the availability of cheap labour. Consequently growth was not confined to the original artisanal centre around Ivanovo-Voznesensk, but fanned out into the poor-soil regions of North-European Russia. By the late 1850s Vladimir *guberniya* (province) had lost its lead to the regions surrounding Moscow and St Petersburg. With the Emancipation of the serfs in 1861, the next decade gave a boost to industrialisation in general and promoted the spread of the factory system in textiles to other provinces;[2] by the third quarter of the century the inheritance that was to pass to socialism was taking final shape; concentration of ownership now went hand in hand with the concentration of production in large units.[3]

Textile manufacture relied heavily on mass demand, so in Russia growth and development were sensitive to fluctuations in the peasant economy. In the first decade of the XX Century the tendency to monopoly capitalism received further impetus from the consumer boom occasioned by the end of the redemption payments paid by the peasants subsequent to emancipation; but only in the last three full years of peace is there much evidence of market diversification through rising urban sales.[4] In 1913 cotton was far and away the biggest sector of the industry (measured in terms of gross output), followed by linen, wool and silk (see Tables 42 and 43). By 1913 over 90 per cent of all factory-based cotton machinery was situated in the Central Industrial Region and in the Western and North Western parts of the Empire. Post-emanicipation developments, however, had once again altered the balance between regions. As St Petersburg diversified into metals and engineering, textiles – although still expanding – declined in importance; increasingly, the capital's mills worked up specialist lines and high-quality cloths. In Moscow guberniya large factories sprouted to the east and south-east of the city, particularly as domestic weaving gave way to the power loom. Ivanovo-Voznesensk grew up as a mono-industrial town; 148 of the district's 190 enterprises, employing 145,000 out of 150,000 workers, were textile mills.[5]

Although the Russian industrial revolution swept away domestic and artisanal spinning, there is evidence that small-scale manufacture, much of it cottage based, was still flourishing in the first years of the XX Century.[6]

Until the Emancipation most weavers worked on the putting-out system, thereafter the balance shifted in favour of mechanised production.[7] In subsequent decades the Lancashire loom steadily encroached on this last stronghold of the artisan,[8] but there is little doubt that handloom weaving continued to be important down to the first world war. Geographically, domestic weaving was centred on the Moscow/Ivanovo-Voznesensk axis; village artisans around Bogorodsk were still working up yarn from the Morozov mills in 1914.[9] One modern Western historian traces a rapid decline in domestic textile working of all kinds in the last decades of the XIX Century.[10] Nevertheless, there was still a substantial – if unevenly distributed – handloom weaving presence in the Ivanovo-Voznesensk district at the turn of the century.[11] Although some attempts have been made to quantify the importance of small-scale industry in Russia,[12] the exact extent of domestic textile working will remain obscure until regional studies are undertaken.

COLLAPSE AND RECOVERY

Cut off from fuel and raw materials and heavily reliant on long-distance transport, textile mills quickly fell victim to the temporary agrarianisation of the Russian economy after 1917. According to one Soviet source, cotton textile output dropped to 40 per cent of the 1913 level in 1918, 7 per cent the following year and 5 per cent by 1920.[13] The Central Committee of the Textile Workers' Union thought that only 7 per cent of cotton spindles and 11 per cent of looms were operating in spring 1919, and the Union's monthly journal recorded only 19 functioning mills with under 300,000 working spindles in summer 1920,[14] compared with nearly 8.5 million in 1911.[15] Decline continued until the autumn of 1921. In June 1921 99 per cent of all spindles stood idle,[16] and to all intents and purposes economic activity ceased entirely during the following four weeks; in August cotton mills spun just half-a-million lb of thread.[17] Some other factories were able to keep going a bit longer because they used local peat fields for fuel.[18] But all experienced the equality of poverty. The only difference was in the timing of the collapse: for the Moscow district the low point came in spring and early summer 1921, for Petrograd late 1919 to early 1920, and for Ivanovo and Vladimir summer 1920.[19]

Subsequent recovery was spectacular. 90 per cent of all equipment functioning in big mills in 1913 was back on stream by 1926/27.[20] By 1927 cotton and linen had exceeded 1913 output levels (see Table 42) and all branches – excepting silk – employed something like the number of workers present before the war (see Table 43).

Recovery in the different localities was a complicated and varied process. Some mills which closed during the civil war did not reopen until the late 1920s, or were stripped of their machinery and aborbed into neighbouring enterprises.[21] Others, like the Karabanovskii combine or the Leningrad factories formerly owned by the Anglo–Russian Cotton Company, approached their pre-war output well before 1925.[22] Nevertheless, the plethora of factors influencing the timing of closure and re-opening had no general effect at all on structure and location. Although some resources were invested in engineering plants making textile machinery, foreign purchases continued to be made from traditional suppliers like Platt Brothers of Oldham.[23] Moreover, no new mills were built before 1927; the first new mill, Krasnaya Talka, built in 1927, was simply an addition to the Ivanovo-Voznesensk agglomeration.[24]

Thus during NEP the Bolsheviks administered their inheritance wherever they happened to find it. But the importance of light industry to the alliance with the peasantry meant that wherever there were textile mills, their relative significance increased in comparison with pre-war times.

Leningrad provides the best illustration of this trend. We have already noted the relative decline of textiles there after 1850; by 1912 textile output by value was about half that of metals and the number of metalworkers three times greater than the number of mill hands.[25] Sixteen years later textiles accounted for over one-quarter of all output and was the biggest single industry. Metals now took second place, contributing 18 per cent or so by value to the city's economy.[26] In terms of employment the trend is more striking still. This shift was probably due to the decline in arms production. During the civil war Petrograd was, of course, far worse hit by agrarianisation than any other major town we know about, but even in 1921 the number of metalworkers stood at 26.6 per cent of the 1913 figure, while for textiles the proportion was 8.8 per cent. Four years later metal enterprises employed 60.3 per cent of their pre-war numbers, but textiles as many as 98.9 per cent.[27]

For the Central Industrial Region the picture is much more straightforward. The mono-industrial structure of Vladimir and Ivanovo guberniyas meant that virtually all recovery by mid-decade was based on textiles.[28] Vladimir had about half its pre-war equipment back on stream by the end of 1922, next year Ivanovo produced roughly one-quarter of all Soviet yarn;[29] and by 1927/28 both had surpassed their 1913 output levels.[30] But they were overshadowed by the Moscow region. Moscow guberniya alone accounted for 40 per cent of the entire Soviet output of cotton by value in 1926/27.[31] Within the province 47 per cent of all industrial output by value in 1923/24 was cotton textiles, and the percentage rose to 50 during the following economic year.[32] Textiles were not the primary industry in the city itself, where large numbers were employed in chemicals, metals, printing and transport, but in the suburbs – and particularly in the rural hinterland – cotton mills dominated the industrial landscape.[33]

While the regime could derive much satisfaction from gross output figures, accounts in the main trade journals and newspapers[34] clearly show that scarcely a week passed without some criticism of the inability of the industry to produce good quality yarn and cloth. Much of this may be illusory, a by-product of successive productivity drives – all somewhat hysterical in tone – rather than a true reflection of the situation in the factories. Nevertheless the sheer weight of evidence strongly indicates that quality was poor in comparison with the immediate pre-war years. This was almost certainly occasioned by three factors: the progressive ageing of the machine stock; the sharp reduction in the import of good quality foreign fibre; and the declining power of the foreman subsequent to the liberalisation of the factory regime after 1917. 'Bad spinning' in Leningrad's Ravenstvo mill, for instance, resulted in a one ruble fine before the revolution but now, complained someone in 1927, the only penalty was a sharp word from the overlooker 'forgotten within a minute'.[35]

We have already noted that domestic working played a subsidiary part in weaving during the first years of the XX Century. Rather patchy evidence suggests that artisan endeavour continued to be important throughout the early 1920s. In general domestic workers were massed in the poor-soil regions of the Russian countryside and concentrated around industrial centres. These nests (*gnezda*) of artisans were sometimes integrated into the production chain of a particular industry and additionally provided a reserve of skilled or semi-skilled labour in times of expansion.[36] This was clearly so in the textile industry. Trusts in both Ivanovo and Moscow guberniyas recognised a duty to spin counts suitable for handloom weavers. The fact that in 1926 over 38,000 handlooms in the Moscow district were idle because large mills could not or would not produce the right yarns, and that artisans were thus occasionally supplied with imported thread, is a further indication of the strength of domestic weaving.[37] Nevertheless, however important domestic weaving may have been to the household economy of some peasants, it remains the case that some 97 per cent of cotton fabrics were woven in large factories in 1928.[38]

ORGANISATION

The pattern of management and control established in the industry after 1921 was in many ways new; its organisational antecedents, however, are to be found in the strategies adopted by the Bolsheviks' political opponents in 1917 and developments occurring during and before the first world war.

In 1903 48 enterprises were merged to form the giant Nevskii hosiery complex in St Petersburg, a project financed by the Anglo–Russian Cotton Company. Ten years later the Danilovskii, Konshin and Gyubner factories, controlling between them half of all cotton printing in Moscow, were combined.[39] Cartelisation projects like these provided the organisational basis for tackling the problems of war-time production, when difficulties occasioned by the evacuation of factories from the western borderlands were compounded by the impact of conscription on the labour force, the disruption of foreign trade, and changes in the product range required by the military.[40] At least nine special committees of the Ministry of Trade and Industry were formed between September 1915 and December 1916 to control prices, allocate raw materials, dictate output levels to the combines, and finally to fix harvest prices inside the Empire.[41]

Out of this grew Tsentrotkan', a committee set up by the owners and the Provisional government in the summer of 1917 to try to impose order on a chaotic supply situation. It was taken over by the Moscow soviet in December 1917 and used as a registration body for nationalisation. Renamed Tsentrotekstil' the following March, membership was expanded to include workers, engineers and other interested organisations. As economic collapse accelerated Tsentrotekstil' assumed sole responsibility for all textile production, and in December 1918 created Natsional'tkan' – a sub-department – to deal with its original business, the administration of nationalised enterprises. By the end of 1919 almost all mills had been taken into public ownership, but so vast was the industry that a single chief administration (*glavk*) answerable to Vesenkha, the commissariat responsible for industry, never emerged. Instead the industry was divided into forty sub-departments; Glavtekstil' acted less as a directing agency and more like a coordinating committee between the sub-departments and Vesenkha.[42] By 1920 there was precious little production for these bureaucracies to administer. Consequently, as the sinews of the national economy atrophied, authority shifted to the localities. Regional or mill-based shock committees, proletarian and communist in composition, arose to pick over the carcass of what was left of the industry. In an attempt to keep production going, warehouses and fuel dumps were scavenged and output concentrated in a few selected mills. Evidence of their activities is scarce, but in the Ivanovo-Voznesensk region at least twenty two such committees were busy at various times between September 1920 and March 1922.[43]

The principles underlying the organisational forms which emerged after the X party congress in March 1921 were those considered expedient for effecting the alliance with the peasantry and enforcing economic accounting (*khozraschet*), the key NEP slogans for light industry. Directors were responsible for matters of internal production, but power was shared with factory committees and the enterprise party secretary, a source of some conflict.[44] A 1924 Statute made it plain that directors should look to the trust in which factories were now grouped, and not to the consumer, and that their functions were administrative rather than entrepreneurial. Wage regulation, for instance, was increasingly a matter decided between trade unions and various state agencies.[45]

Trustification – the regional grouping of the factories in one industry – was given legal expression in two decrees issued by Vesenkha and the

Council for Labour and Defence (STO) in August 1921.[46] These, together
with several other orders promulgated during the following autumn and
winter, advanced the proposition of a limited form of *laissez-faire* and
confirmed administrative devolution, but in ways far removed from the
freebooting activities of shock committees. Trusts were given the right to
manage their own material and financial resources, were enjoined to buy
and sell on the open market and to keep profit and loss accounts.[47] The
April 1923 decree on trusts systematised many of these points while
simultaneously reducing local competence; henceforth STO price guide-
lines became increasingly binding.[48] Four years later, in summer 1927, the
Statute on Trusts tackled once more the uncertain relationship between
centre and periphery: trust functions were limited to technical supervision
while Vesenkha – recently reorganised – fixed prices and handed down
production targets. Confusingly, the glavki which had been a feature of the
civil war again began to play an active role, though so powerful was the
Textile Syndicate (VTS, discussed below), that it managed to get rid of a
resurrected Glavtekstil' in December 1927.[49]

Trustification proceeded very rapidly in textiles. The industry accounted
for nine of the original twenty-three trusts registered with Vesenkha in
December 1921,[50] and by the following autumn there were 52 textile trusts
encompassing 484 mills and employing over 250,000 workers. The biggest
were in the cotton sector – a Vesenkha exhibition staged in October 1922
attracted displays from 18 cotton trusts which between them employed just
over 200,000 workers and office personnel.[51] Subsequently trusts grew as
more factories were reactivated, but it is clear that the largest mills were
put to work first and many smaller ones combined (see Table 43). In the
early NEP years recovery was accompanied by frequent reorganisations.
Only in mid-decade did trust structure take on some definite shape;
thereafter changes seem to have been made much more slowly. Three
trusts – the First, Second and Third – were designated as of 'All-Union
significance' and placed directly under the control of Vesenkha. All others
were regionally based, and their administration shared between Moscow
and the localities.[52] In Ivanovo guberniya, for example, Ivanovo-
Voznesensk State Textile Trust was run by Vesenkha, Ivtekstil' – centred
on the provincial capital – by the RSFSR, and Ivanovo-Voznesensk Guberniya Trust by the local council for national economy.[53]

While trusts resembled the defunct regional unions of the civil war years,
VTS was something like the Provisional Government's Tsentrotkan'. It
held a key position in the national economy because it became the main
channel of supply to the peasantry,[54] and it lasted just as long as NEP.
Founded out of the ruins of Glavtekstil' and abolished late in 1929 VTS
was, in effect, a joint-stock company functioning under state auspices.[55]
Although the initial reason for its creation was to prevent excessive price
cutting among competing trusts,[56] the Syndicate's objectives soon fanned

out to include the coordination of storage, procurement, and finance. State orders were distributed through it and foreign purchases organised by it. Simultaneously VTS gradually assumed the role of wholesale agent. By 1926 more than two-thirds of all textile output passed through its hands, and a year earlier Ivanovo-Voznesensk State Textile Trust had agreed to dispose of its entire production this way.[57] In February 1927 all stores were placed under Syndicate control, all sales administered by the Syndicate and all advance orders channelled through the Syndicate. Next year all consumer cooperatives were obliged to give the Syndicate six months' advance notice of their requirements for cloth. After 1927 VTS also began to take on planning functions.[58]

As with the Provisional government's textile committee Tsentrotkan', trustification was intended to order and control the market, but it also created several new problems. Mills grouped together under the NEP variant of socialism had not always evolved together under the tsarist variant of capitalism. As NEP unfolded, the fixed assets and product range of a given trust sometimes bore little relationship to the tasks imposed on that trust; in spite of the regime's wishes, the market forces favoured those mills best fitted to serve consumers' needs.[59] Beyond this the party constantly cut across evolving lines of communication and control. Although, in 1922, the XI party congress insisted that local party organs should not meddle with economic administration, the next congress in 1923 partially reversed the devolutionary tendencies previously obtaining and restated the party's right to interfere in decision-making. The drift towards recentralisation and line-over-staff policy-making was clear by 1925 when the Organisational Bureau of the party, and not the competent specialist bodies, decreed the administrative structure of the industry, and it became more evident still throughout the following two years when the same Politburo sub-committee led the campaign for lower prices and rationalisation.[60]

CONCLUSIONS

Textiles were a major industry in pre-revolutionary Russia. They continued to be a very important sector of the early Soviet economy, particularly because of the special conditions obtaining under NEP. These special conditions ensured that recovery was very rapid after 1921, in spite of the fact that virtually all production had ceased during the late civil war period. There were no changes in the location of the industry, but the Soviet regime began to concentrate production in the larger mills, and introduced new organisational forms, notably trusts and the All-Union Textile Syndicate. Cotton remained far and away the largest of the textile industries, and the largest of all Soviet industries.

Part IV
Other Sectors

9 The Railways

J. N. Westwood, with the assistance of Holland Hunter, and incorporating contributions by P. J. Ambler, A. Heywood and F. M. Page

RUSSIAN IMPERIAL RAILWAYS ON THE EVE OF THE WAR

There were about 71,000km of public railway route at the end of 1913 in the Russian Empire (excluding Finland). About one-third of the mileage was privately owned. However, the private companies were subject to as much regulation, though not so much interference, as the state companies. The Ministry of Ways of Communication (MPS), headed by a professional railwayman turned minister, supervised railway operation, while the Ministry of Finance had its hand in tariffs and financial matters and, together with the Ministry of War, had an influential voice in the approval of schemes for new lines. Of the 13,000km of new route under construction in 1913, two-thirds was being built by private companies.

In the following pages, physical units are the preferred measure of resources devoted to railway transport, but it is worth remarking that Vainshtein's ruble figures[1] suggest that the accumulation of railway assets was accelerating on the eve of the war, the net annual increment averaging, for the Empire, 121 million rubles in 1908–13 and as much as 152 million in 1913.

Traffic Levels

Briefly, railway freight traffic in 1913 amounted to 158 million tons, of which 26 million were loaded in areas later detached from Russia, leaving 132 million as the figure of originated freight in 1913 from areas within the inter-war frontiers. This was the third year of a rapid growth which followed the near stagnation of the years immediately following the Russo–Japanese War. The annual percentage increases were 1909 7, 1910 5.4, 1911 11.1, 1912 11.1, 1913 10.5.[2]

Ton-kilometres, which by measuring both weight and distance of shipments provide a more complete picture of the work actually performed, showed a similar pattern. Their longer-term trend can be seen from the following milliard ton-km figures: 1883 10, 1893 16, 1903 37, 1908 53, 1913 77.[3]

169

Passenger-kilometres developed equally fast, from 4 milliards in 1883, 6 in 1893, 15 in 1903, and 20 in 1908, to 29 milliards in 1913.[4]

From Table 4 it will be seen that in 1913 almost half the freight traffic was attributable to three commodity groups: coal, cereals and timber. Hard coal tonnage amounted to 22 per cent of the whole by 1913, compared to 17 per cent in 1899. The virtual tripling of coal tonnage over those fourteen years was largely attributable to the aggressively expanding market for the Donets coal produced in the southern Ukraine. Much of the cereals traffic was destined for the export ports, with the Black Sea continuing to predominate over the Baltic ports, helped by the expansion of the grain areas of the North Caucasus that had been achieved by the privately-owned Vladikavkaz Railway. However, the export trade was only part of the cereals traffic: the movement of food from production to consuming regions remained vital. Of other traffics, oil was interesting because the railways were losing their share of this to pipelines and shipping.

If only the lines in Europe are taken into consideration, traffic density (intensity of use of running track) was higher than in Germany. The most intense use was in and around the Donets Basin, with some sections carrying more than 7 million ton-km per km. The route from the Polish industrial region south-eastwards into the Ukraine, and the approaches to the ports of Odessa, Riga and St Petersburg had lesser, but substantial, densities (over 3 million ton-km/km), and similar densities were beginning to appear on lines carrying Donets coal to the centre.

Adequate or Inadequate?

Readers of *Doctor Zhivago* and *August 1914* may recall the railway journey in each book. These were journeys that were pleasurable and traditional experiences, implying a transport process that was unhurried but sure. Yet in the decade separating the war against Japan from the war against Germany the members of the state Duma, whenever they debated the railways, left an impression of a transport service that was ramshackle, inefficient, profiteering, and generally burdensome. Soviet commentators have tended to take the critical view. Sidorov, for example, in his study of the railways in the first world war,[5] represents the orthodox view, and backs his analysis with a useful foundation of statistics. His first criticism is that, despite an obvious economic and strategic requirement, new railway construction was insufficient. There was a particular need to improve transits between the Ukrainian (Donets) and Polish mining areas and the industrial areas, and to the Baltic ports. Industrialists, among others, demanded the construction of new lines as well as the reconstruction of existing routes. The growth of rail traffic after 1910 had left the growth in mileage far behind.

Moreover, continues Sidorov, quoting contemporary critics, the growth of freight traffic not only outpaced railway construction, but also the provision of rolling stock. There was a shortfall in 1913 of 2,000 freight locomotives and 80,000 goods wagons (there were 19,835 locomotives and 485,600 goods wagons in 1913 – increases respectively of 2.6 and 12 per cent over 1908). About a quarter of the locomotives were over 40 years old, he claims, using his evidence rather too freely. Meanwhile, the locomotive works in the last pre-war years were working at only 20–30 per cent of capacity, and the wagon works at about one-third.

Sidorov ascribes these evils to a penny-pinching quest for profits on the part of both state and private railways. This is an interpretation which deserves, perhaps, more than a polite cough. After all, the railways' operating ratio (operating expenses as percentage of operating revenues) was so low, averaging 60 per cent in 1912 and 1913, that it is hard to dispute that the railways could have done more for their clients and still turned in a healthy profit. Nevertheless, an alternative view of the same evidence is possible, and this view does not depend on the circumstance that all the state and some of the private railways' profits were destined for the state budget.

Quality of Service

First, it is worth remarking that the policy of restricting investment at a time of traffic growth has also been the salient feature of Soviet transport policy and has resulted, by and large, in a railway system which carries heavy traffic for a minimum investment. In principle, this seems a good idea until such time as the service deteriorates to a level which brings extra social or transport costs that exceed the realised economies. The argument of the critics of the tsarist railway service is that it did indeed deteriorate, and that this is proved by complaints about freight awaiting shipment which accumulated at stations. This was particularly evident in the autumn, when grain shipments and fuel-stocking coincided. Critical politicians had a fine time telling of the huge grain dumps they had seen at stations.

But it is debatable how far a railway system should go in ensuring that for every shipment there is an empty vehicle waiting. This has always been a sensitive issue; the Vladikavkaz Railway tried to smooth demand for tank wagons by charging more at peaks, and all it got for this exercise in efficiency was moral indignation on the part of its clients. Writing about the 1930s, Hunter has shown[6] that even freight backlogs amounting to half as much as the freight actually shipped could be cleared within months if only railway output could be raised by a few per cent (which was usually possible in the spring). The point is that the existence of delayed freight awaiting shipment is not necessarily a demonstration of neglect, but is just as likely to indicate a railway administration desperately anxious to score high utilisation rates for its rolling stock.

There can be little doubt that, insofar as they enjoyed a monopoly situation, the railways made use of that advantage. However, they were not necessarily in pursuit of the highest possible profits. The government also had other goals in mind; thus it used its powers of intervention to impose tariff adjustments. Its decisions were not immune to the influence of pressure groups. Sometimes the government itself imposed concessionary tariffs, especially in support of the export trade. At other times large industries or syndicates successfully pressed for concessions. The Donets coal companies managed to obtain freight rates that may have been only one-tenth the average cost of moving coal, which gave them no small advantage in their struggle to extend their market to Moscow and the Urals. But in any case the power of the railways was limited because they were in fact not a total transport monopoly. While in 1913 (within the USSR pre-1939 frontiers) the railways produced 65.7 milliard ton-km, the inland waterways produced 28.5 milliards.[7] The waterways were largely limited to bulk freight, to the warm season, and to the not always advantageously-placed rivers; nevertheless, they sensibly diluted the railway monopoly.

Finally, whatever deterioration there might have been in freight service, there can be little doubt that passenger services were improving markedly over this period. This is an assertion which is hard to prove statistically, but eye-witness accounts seem to support it, as do the railway passenger timetables, and the figures for the acquisition of new vehicles – in 1909, unusually, new passenger cars outnumbered new freight cars.

Railway-building Policy

As regards railway construction, a close look at the lines actually started reinforces the similarity between the 1909–13 period and that of the five-year plans. Indeed, it would perhaps not be fanciful to regard the period between 1914 and 1927 as an interregnum breaking an essential continuity of policies. In the last few years before 1914 there was an emphasis on short lines for relieving bottlenecks or for gaining access to raw materials, and where new routes were in course of creation it was normally a matter of linking existing lines to form a continuous route. Thus a new outlet for Donets coal was in course of creation through Kharkov. Similarly, a new route from Moscow eastwards to Kazan' was being put together. There was just a handful of completely new long lines under way; these included the economically insignificant but costly Amur Railway, more useful lines in the Urals, and the Tyumen'–Omsk line in Siberia. In the south, the enterprising Vladikavkaz Railway was extending its empire in the North Caucasus. The criticism that mileage completed fell far short of traffic growth is as invalid for the last tsarist decade as it is for the Stalin years.

Before such a criticism can be taken seriously, it must distinguish between lines built for transit and lines built for access – the former ease bottlenecks while the latter make them worse. In the case of the last tsarist years the relief of bottlenecks was a constant theme. In 1911, for example, the Donets Railway laid twelve short sections of track, mainly about 6km each in length; some of these were for access, but they were mainly to relieve bottlenecks. By 1913 the length of line under construction was increasing, although far short of the heady days of the late XIX Century. Almost 13,000km were under way at the end of 1913, contributing to the spurt of openings that would take place during the war. All in all, the rate of construction seems to represent a sensible compromise between the demands of development and economy of resources. A much more valid criticism would be directed at the failure to address the pressing problem of local transport, but that is another story.

Train and Track Renewal

How far rolling stock provision was inadequate would ideally be measured by the delays suffered by freight. This is impossible, so other clues must be followed. Before doing this it might be realistic to dismiss the accusation that failure to order enough stock left the railway supply industry high and dry. It is the function of a railway to link markets, not to provide them, and there was neither an explicit nor an implicit duty to support the vehicle and locomotive manufacturers. It was unfortunate that in a mere three years at the turn of the century four new locomotive builders had set themselves up, just in time to see the railway boom recede. While several of the works successfully converted to other production when railway orders dried up, the Nikolaev shipyards actually turned to locomotive production in 1910. There were simply too many locomotive builders, and this imbalance was not corrected until Soviet times.

Were there enough locomotives? Sidorov and others answer negatively, and point to the 'failure' of the railways in the war as demonstration. But perhaps the issue is not as clear-cut as that. The figures themselves are worth elucidating. The 2.6 per cent increase of locomotive stock between 1908 and 1913 is a net increase, after the withdrawal of locomotives which would have been the oldest and weakest. Subtracting, presumably, locomotives built for non-common-carrier railways, Sidorov calculates new locomotives as 535 in 1913, somewhat less in 1911 and 1912, but around 500 units in 1909 and 1910. These locomotives were, by 1913, bigger, with the two freight designs around 1½ and 2½ times more powerful than their predecessors. According to Page and Nurminen, about 1,800 older and weaker locomotives were withdrawn in 1910–14.[8]

With goods wagons, on the other hand, technical improvement was hardly a factor in the immediate pre-war years. It was only in 1914 that a 20-ton van was introduced to replace the prevailing 16- to 18-ton designs. Thus the statement that wagon stock rose only by 12 per cent from 1908 to 1913 is an accurate assessment of the extra capacity provided (except that scrapped wagons must have included some small old vehicles), and this had to cope with a traffic increase of around 30 per cent. In 1912 and 1913 there was a sharp increase in deliveries of freight wagons, which according to one source amounted to 9,700 in 1913 (plus 1,065 passenger vehicles).[9] Meantime, wagon utilisation was rising quite rapidly; ton-km per *available* wagon rose by more than 14 per cent 1911–13, while ton-km per *working* wagon increased by less than 9 per cent over those years,[10] which suggests that vehicles also spent less time idling. In other words, and as might be expected, the 'shortage' of goods wagons was a reflection of their better utilisation. Again, critics seem to be barking up the wrong tree. If they had directed their criticism to technical rather than statistical matters they would have been on firmer ground. Here the pre-revolutionary railways were in several respects distinctly antiquated. It was eccentric, to say the least, for the Russian railways, with coal as much as one-fifth of total freight, to have less than 3 per cent of their wagon stock in the form of open wagons. Vans made up two-thirds of the stock, and coal was carried largely in roofed vehicles or on low-capacity flat wagons. Again, by 1913 a solution of the coupling problem was overdue, but this was left to Soviet times. Railways which attempted to use American-size locomotives soon discovered that the economies of high horsepower were dissipated in a trail of broken couplings.

A third major input into the railways, together with locomotives and wagons, is the rails themselves. Rail deliveries clearly indicate an increase in investment in track renewal in the pre-war years. These amounted to about 20 million poods annually in 1909 and 1910, or 325,000 tons. 1911 saw a 25 per cent increase, and then in 1912 562,000 tons were received, dropping to 509,000 in 1913.[11] Assuming an average weight of rail of 33kg/metre, 1,000 tons is sufficient to lay or re-lay 15km of single track. If the average annual delivery of rails in 1910–13 was 450,000 tons, and the average length of new line built was 1,320km, then, on average, after the needs of railway construction, 362,000 tons were available each year for re-laying, or 5,430km. Since it was the custom to re-lay secondary track with used heavy rail from the principal lines, and since rail might be expected to last 5–7 years on the very heavy traffic sections and 7–20 years elsewhere, it would seem that provision of replacement rails was not only adequate in those four years but was sufficient to build up stocks (or, perhaps, to make up backlogs of deferred maintenance). In short, the provision of rail in these final pre-war years was probably more than adequate.

Labour Productivity

Typically, a railway system that is under-equipped makes up for the deficiency by employing more workers. Hence labour productivity falls as traffic growth outpaces investment. Because of the complex interrelationships within the railway economy this is not an infallible observation, but it is general enough to be worth pursuing.

There are certain difficulties to be circumvented in calculating labour productivity on the Russian railways. Strumilin's figures[12] differ from other versions, but they are consistent enough to provide a guide over the last imperial decade.

One characteristic of these years is immediately apparent, the tendency of the railways to inflate or deflate their labour force over short periods. Such changes have little to do with traffic development and, because of the slowness with which under-equipment manifests itself, are equally unlikely to be related to investment. In 1899–1901, according to Strumilin's figures, the workforce increased by a not easily explicable 26 per cent at a time when 'conventional' ton-km rose by 3 per cent and mileage by 14 per cent. The workforce continued to rise steadily until, in 1905–6, there came another jump: a 10 per cent increase to deal with traffic growth of 8 per cent and mileage expansion of 4 per cent. In 1908 a peak was reached at 844,000 workers, and then there was a bumpy decline down to 1913.

Table 45 converts Strumilin's figures for 1908–13 to percentage changes, and shows that in those years productivity rose as much as 39 per cent. It is true that if passenger-km were removed from the calculation the productivity gain would be slightly less (1913 would then be 135 per cent of 1908) but, even so, the picture presented by Table 45 is hardly one of a railway substituting labour for capital; unless, of course, the labour force was being worked increasingly and excessively harder.

Accident Rates

One sign of railways and railway workers being driven too hard is a rising accident rate. Here a defender of the tsarist railway system is on unsure ground, for there are copious figures available and they do not tell a happy story. Strumilin[13] gives four separate figures, for total killed and injured and railwaymen killed and injured, and relates them to mileage, number of workers, and traffic expressed in train-km. Total casualties has the virtue of including passengers who come to grief, but it also embraces the Anna Karenina syndrome and the sales record of the state liquor monopoly. Such factors are not absent from the figures for railwaymen, of course, but are probably less influential there, so the discussion will be confined to the latter. Here Strumilin presents tables which show that although there were good years and bad years the accident rates climbed remorselessly upward. Casualties among railwaymen amounted in 1897 to 21.1 per million train-km, 119.6 per 1,000km of route and 11.15 per 10,000 workers, and rose to 39.6, 260.7, and 21.78 respectively in 1913. In 1913 they totalled 17,712, of which 904 were deaths (*total* deaths on the railways in that year were 3,531). There was an especially high rate of increase in 1912 and 1913, and also in 1894–96.

However, Strumilin's figures, and his analysis of them, are not invulnerable. First, figures for injuries, which of course are reported injuries, are notoriously imperfect at most times and places. The letter, and equally important the spirit, of health and safety regulations are very influential, and are factors which can vary over a period. Corpses are counted more precisely, so it is perhaps safer to compare the death rate rather than the casualty rate. The main objection to this is that changing first aid and medical services can reduce the ratio of deaths to casualties; but although railway medical services were improving, over ten years this does not seem to be a very weighty factor. Secondly, while Strumilin was right to compare casualties with traffic, his choice as traffic denominator of train-km may have produced an over-gloomy result. On most railways of that time it was in shunting and in the depots that casualties seemed particularly high, and train-km as a denominator rather minimises this factor. A somewhat more suitable denominator would be combined ton-km and passenger-km, although this, too, may not fully reflect the tendency for casualties to occur less during open-line movements than at handling points. Table 46 rearranges Strumilin's data in the right-hand column; neither column presents a pretty picture, but the revised version shows a quite different trend. A careful, if not mischievous, selection of base periods could show that the death rate, and hence accident rate, far from deteriorating as Strumilin suggests, was actually improving. To this should be added the claim in a Soviet newspaper that 1913 was notable in that there were no major disasters to passenger trains.[14] It is also worth noting that the German Empire railways had a death-rate not widely different (an annual average, 1907–10, of 7.1 railwaymen deaths per milliard conventional ton-km), and that the (admittedly larger) US railroads in 1913 registered 3,715 employee deaths compared to the 904 of the Russian railways.

All in all, the 1913 picture is not of a railway system in decline. In later jargon the railways might even have been described as dynamic. On the other hand, it could be argued that the hesitation in traffic growth of 1913 presaged a downturn in which flocks of chickens would come home to roost.

THE IMPERIAL RAILWAYS AT WAR

And indeed flocks of chickens did come home to roost in 1914–17. But commentators seem over-ready to treat these as railway chickens. To paraphrase perhaps a majority of historians, what happened in these war years is that Russia engaged in a war and ended with a defeat, the 'failure' of the railways contributing to this result.

The course of the war, so far as the railways are concerned, is well-known and uncontroversial; contemporary memoirs and studies like those of the Carnegie Foundation tell the same story. The demands of mobilisation (which after all had been the deciding factor in persuading Nicholas I to allow railways to rear their unwelcome head in his Empire) were more than met, insofar as the railway transport plan was fulfilled ahead of time. Then came disturbances to the normal traffic flows. To replace British and Polish coal, Donets coal was sent even further and in new directions. The port of Vladivostok and hence the Trans-Siberian line became vital. The Archangel line, whose capacity might be described as little more than one puff and a whistle, was optimistically expected to carry a heavy traffic of British coal as well as munitions. Up to summer 1915 the railways seemed to be coping quite well with most problems, as well as supplying the fronts, but then came the defeats in Poland. The evacuation of Poland, coming on top of everything else, was accomplished quite well, but the dislocation it caused was never fully overcome. The railway administration seems to have functioned well in the war, but it was crippled by the decision to place the Western railways under military control. The latter administered about a third of the network and seemed unable to compromise its military preoccupations by adopting sound railway operating practices. The most wounding manifestation of this was the accumulation of badly-needed goods wagons in the military zones. Meanwhile, although railway operating workers were excused military service, workshop personnel had been called up. To this was added a metal shortage. The percentage of rolling stock in bad order grew. Measures to improve railway operation were adopted. Railway construction was accelerated; over 8,000km was completed in 1915–17, with over 13,000km under construction in 1917. Powerful locomotives and high-capacity goods wagons were ordered from the USA to cope with the flow of imports through Vladivostok. From summer 1916 a deterioration set in. But collapse was not inevitable. The basic figures for railway stock indicate a grave but not catastrophic situation: the number of serviceable locomotives dropped from 16,400 to 15,700, and the number of goods wagons awaiting repair rose from 24,000 to 46,000 (about 10 per cent of the total) between summer 1916 and summer 1917.[15] So far as supplies for the front are concerned, it might be argued, on the basis of plausibility rather than statistics, that difficulties of production and allocation were far more important than difficulties of transport. To ascribe the defeat of the Russian armies to transport difficulties smells of the 'stab in the back' explanation which defeated armies find so comforting.

Reliable traffic figures for 1914–17 are not available, and the difficulty of reconciling the several versions of these figures will be seen from n. 16.[16]

The figures point to a slight decrease of freight traffic in 1914, and then to a substantial increase well above the 1913 level in 1915 and, most likely, in 1916 as well, accompanied by an exceptionally sharp increase in passenger traffic. In these circumstances, it must surely be wrong to describe the railways as inadequately prepared. They had capacity in reserve in 1913, despite the economies of the preceding years. What they were not prepared for was an extraordinary war. They were not prepared for the loss of Baltic and Black Sea shipping routes. They were not prepared (and why should they have been?) for the evacuation of Poland. They were not prepared to have one-third of their mileage controlled by military officers who had learned nothing from the American Civil War but thought they had learned everything from the Russo–Japanese War. In the circumstances, it could be argued that it was not the railways which failed the Empire, but the Empire which failed the railways.

REVOLUTION TO RESTORATION

When the revolution occurred the railways were still functioning, and could be recognised as a transport system which, though hard-pressed and beginning to show signs that maintenance had been too long deferred, still operated in a regular and foreseeable kind of way. Timetabled trains might well be late, but they still ran. The three years of civil war changed all that. The battle lines were so fluid that, at some time or other, most lines were fought over, some more than others. Recruitment of the able-bodied, flight or harassment of managers, and unavailability of components, meant that before long the railways functioned on a hand-to-mouth day-to-day basis, steadily losing the capacity to handle even the diminished traffic of the time. Recovery after the civil war was slow at first; in 1921–2 there was a crippling fuel crisis, which became a railway crisis, and it was only in 1924–5 that some semblance of a recovery could be recognised.

In the end, it seems, quite a high proportion of managers and officials continued to serve. The MPS had become the NKPS (People's Commissariat of Ways of Communication), but time-honoured practices and routines survived. The political head of the NKPS tended now to be a senior party personality rather than a proven railway administrator; this change was not reversed until the 1940s. No doubt the administrators hankered for the good old days, when the trains ran to time and made a profit; it is not surprising that 1913 continued to be a yardstick in railway as well as in party circles.

The railways met with far less competition from the waterways, whose prospects had been shattered by seven years of war. Even in 1928, the waterways were carrying only a little more than half their 1913 freight, even though post-war territorial losses had diminished their worthwhile route mileage hardly at all. Like the railways, the waterways were fought along during the civil war, and their craft were vital and targetted instruments of war. Their decline was far more perceptible than that of the railways, and in the 1920s waterway traffic, because of its slowness and the inherent need for regularity and planning (if only to avoid craft being iced up hundreds of miles from destination), was handicapped at a time when chaos, improvisation, and rapid change were successively and sometimes simultaneously the prevailing climates. Railways were far more flexible, and in the 1920s it was flexibility which counted.

The waterway situation was as follows. The length of actually exploited waterway dropped from 72,000km in 1913 to 51,300 in 1924, and then rose to 71,600km in 1928.[17] Freight tonnage was 32.7 million tons in 1913 (inter-war frontiers), and reached a mere 18.3 million in 1928.[18] Expenditure on the waterway infrastructure (in comparable prices) was 58 million rubles in 1913, declined to 14 million in 1923/24 and rose to 35 million in 1926/27.[19] Apart from some wooden barges, no river craft were built in the 1920s until the Sormovo works succeeded in giving birth to a tug in 1926/27. Thus capacity continued to decline during NEP. Total horsepower in service fell by one-third between 1922 and 1928, and barge capacity by 39 per cent.[20]

Highway transport was usually a complement rather than a competitor for rail transport. Its development over these years is hard to quantify because it was administered by several authorities and because the question of when is a road not a road was answered differently by successive generations of statisticians who, for example, never seemed able to decide whether a camel track or cow path should or should not rate as an unsurfaced road. It is safer to confine analysis to first-class highways (*shosse*), which totalled about 18,000km in 1913 (of which two-thirds were under the MPS and most of the remainder under the local government *zemstva*). Expressed in current prices per existing kilometre, expenditure by the MPS on first-class road repair rose from 450 in 1913 to 580 rubles in 1914, and by the *zemstva* from 350 to 391 rubles. In the 1920s, in current prices, such expenditure was 50 rubles in 1922/23, 250 in 1924/25, and 490 rubles in 1926/27.[21] Because prices had greatly increased, the decline compared to 1913 was considerable. As for vehicles, greatest reliance was placed on survivors of the 25,000 automobiles imported during the War; in mid-1919 13,488 automobiles of all types were serviceable. Imports recommenced in 1921, and in 1922–7 there were 5,275 new vehicles (of which 4,500 were imported) but this was not enough to compensate for write-offs.[22]

For the railways, the reduced territory meant a traffic loss. There was also a trackage loss, but this was almost exactly compensated by the mileage of new line built since 1913. So far as operating statistics are concerned, the reduced territory on balance probably slightly enhanced the apparent efficiencies as presented by statistical data. Losses of territory in the west had meant the disappearance of intensively-used routes in Poland, but against this a high mileage of lines whose significance was primarily military had also been lost. Finland had not been a heavy-traffic area, while the creation of the Baltic states of Estonia, Latvia and Lithuania meant the loss of much low-traffic line, including whole networks of 2ft 6in gauge trackage. Lines built since 1913 had for the most part been short routes to speed traffic flows, or access lines to produce more traffic. An exception was the long Murmansk Railway, which briefly acquired importance in 1916–17 but was now moribund; the NKPS wanted to close it, but was thwarted by local opposition. The recently-completed Amur Railway had a similar statistical effect when it returned to the NKPS. But these, and a few other lines of doubtful economic benefit, were more than balanced by the loss of low-traffic territories. Table 47 shows the overall effect.

Changes in traffic flows, occasioned both by territorial shifts and by new economic policies, were a source of great difficulty, especially in the early post-war years, but should not be exaggerated. On the face of it, and without any good statistical data, it would seem that the disruption of traffic flows was no worse, relatively speaking, than that suffered by the Austrian railways, and was certainly less than that experienced by the German railways after 1945. All the same, it is correctly emphasised as one of the long-term disabilities imposed by the events of 1914–19. Table 48 gives figures for pre-war and post-war traffic, divided into commodity groups, and it is not hard to see, or visualise, that there were few traffics which in one way or another were not affected. For the most part, railways can take such changes in their stride, but not when their main traffics are radically redistributed. The two most important traffics of the Russian railways were coal and grain, and both were seriously affected. Donets coal before 1913 had been expanding its markets, but with the loss of Polish and British coal this commercial process became a necessary economic change. The railways in 1913 were only just coping with the Donets coal flow, and the expansion of its consuming region created a heavy burden, as can be seen from the lengthening of its average haul. With grain, the change was not quite so marked, but was serious enough. The most dramatic change was the reduction of exports, leaving the Black Sea ports with over-capacity; a new railway route linking Kherson with the grain areas had only just been put together, Novorossiisk had excellent grain-handling facilities that were little used henceforth, Odessa attracted significantly less traffic. On the other hand, in the 1920s the reduction of marketed grain offered relief to the railways in terms of operating bottlenecks, although not in terms of glowing operating statistics.

Some inkling of the sad physical state of Soviet railways in the early 1920s can be gathered from contemporary photographs. Worn rails, rotten sleepers, lines of deteriorating locomotives awaiting a spare part or capital repair, decrepit goods wagons, broken passenger cars, and temporary repairs to bridges all represented a backlog that had to be overcome before pre-war standards of service could be restored.

SOVIET RAILWAYS IN THE MID-1920s

The state of the railways in 1927, and in the course of the preceding decade, are described quite accurately in the existing literature. The changes, the crises, and the advances were on so grand a scale that any inaccuracies in the data are insignificant. The statistical vessel is, as a matter of fact, unseaworthy, mainly because in the difficult years of revolution and civil war records were not properly kept and, in particular, too much worthless data was sent in from the periphery to the centre. Strumilin, in his essay, has heroically attempted with some success to produce figures for certain aspects, in which methodological imperfections are carefully ironed out, but the shortcomings of the primary data mean that his figures are an improvement rather than a perfecting. Fortunately, by the mid-1920s the statistical service of the NKPS had attained its 1913 level (perhaps it was the first NKPS department to do so), although some doubt surrounds the competence of the railway section of the Central Statistical Administration.

Traffic Levels

Tables 48 and 49 give a fairly complete picture. Economic disruption, and later the changes of industrial location which the government was beginning to favour, naturally led to an increase in the average length of haul. A consequence of this longer haul was that freight ton-km reached the 1913 level earlier than did the tonnage of freight despatched (1925/26 as against 1926/27). Similarly, because of the rapid growth of commuter traffic, passenger-journeys reached the 1913 total three years before passenger-kilometres (1924/25 against 1928/29). These examples, using the statistical headings which are the basis for so many others, illustrate that choosing a year in which it might be said that 1913 levels were regained can be a matter for debate. Perhaps 1926, in which freight and passenger kilo-metres, taken together, exceeded for the first time those of 1913, is the most defensible choice. For the record, and not for any intrinsic signifi-cance, operating revenues covered operating costs for the first time since the war in 1922/23, and continued to do so.

With the waterways *hors de combat*, and what little competition there had been between separate railways in 1913 now a thing of the past, the railways were much more of a monopoly. On the other hand, government control of their activities had not diminished in its scope and was more thrusting. In such conditions the attainment of a net profit in 1924/25 says little about efficiency. Although on paper the NKPS Tariff Committee dominated in questions of rate-fixing, the fact that this committee included representatives from several other commissariats meant that it would not only strive for railway profitability, but also for the general economic restoration of industry and agriculture, and for the success of state, as opposed to private, industry and trade. In 1924, for example, a third of the traffic was moving at less than cost; coal, just as in 1913, was monstrously favoured, moving at about half its real cost.[23] Efforts were also made to favour particular areas (typically by reducing long-distance rates for certain commodities) and even, sometimes, for certain enterprises. Meanwhile, as the enthusiasm for NEP cooled, rates for private freight were heavily surcharged, especially after 1926.

Capital Investment: Track and Structures

As regards the investment effort, Strumilin's ruble figures can hardly be improved upon, but nevertheless, unfortunately, have to be appreciated as pretty arrangements of digits rather than as a useful guide to the capital value of the railway system; they are, perhaps, useful as confirmation of conventional wisdom. For the later 1920s the figures are somewhat more meaningful. One source gives gross investment in the railways, at current prices, as 220 million rubles in 1924/25, almost doubling to 430 million in 1925/26, then increasing to 715 million in 1926/27 and to 731 in the 1928 calendar year.[24] These represented 18–20 per cent of the total invested in the whole economy in those respective years. A preliminary comparison of net investment in transport and communications in 1913 and the 1920s indicates that the pre-war level of investment had not been reached in 1926–7, but may possibly have been exceeded in 1927/28 (see Chapter 7). But, in general, enumeration of physical units is probably a better guide to the investment effort; a ton of rail is always a ton of rail, but rubles are heterogeneous. The data for the production of locomotives and goods wagons, and the supply of rails, indicate that the 1913 level of investment had not been reached by 1927–8, except possibly in the case of locomotives.

The first of such physical units is easily dealt with. This is route mileage, which according to the post-second world war statistical handbooks rose from 70,300km at the end of 1917 to 76,900 at the end of 1927 (a figure, incidentally, which would remain static for the next couple of years). Wisely enough, new trackage had been kept to a minimum in the 1920s; there were problems enough, especially with rail supply, to justify the priority given to restoring existing lines. The addition to mileage between 1921 and 1927 of 5,100km has to be compared with the 12,000km officially under construction in 1921.

Restoration was achieved at different speeds for different categories of the railways' plant. This was inevitable, since track and infrastructure, apart from being indispensable, had suffered proportionately more. The track was in an abysmal state, not so much from war damage (which always turns out to be less than it looks at first sight) as from years of neglect. For reasons explained earlier, it seems likely that track standards were quite high in 1913, with adequate reserves of rail in hand. With both war demand and accelerated railway construction demanding steel, it is safe to assume that rail stocks were run down during the war, with re-railing and re-sleepering falling behind normal requirements. During the civil war, by all accounts, this steady decline became a catastrophic plunge. It must have been the combination of worn rails and rotten sleepers which proved so dire, because rail which is not properly supported takes heavy punishment. In 1922 it was calculated that within two years all sleepers would be over-age.[25] That is, about 152 million sleepers needed replacing by mid-1925. In fact, in the three years 1922–5, only about 50 million were replaced.[26] Given the likelihood that most of the new sleepers were of untreated softwood, with a life of only three years, this was not a rate of progress which would catch up the backlog. The rate hardly improved in the following years, moreover, with annual replacements of around 19 million.

Soviet industry seems to have supplied an increasing tonnage of rails, starting from a very low base of 45,500 tons in 1922/23, growing in succeeding years to 59,100, 109,000, 189,700, 224,600 and, in 1927/28, 278,000.[27] Even the 1927/28 figure was far behind 1913, and was approximately at the 1909 level (which was 325,000 tons for the whole Empire). Taking the four years 1922/23–1925/26, assuming an average rail weight of 33 kg/m, and an allocation of enough rail to lay an average of 500km of new line each year, there would have been enough rail available to re-lay about 500km annually. With a total mileage of 73,000km, and an assumed 10 per cent of the mileage carrying heavy traffic and requiring rail replacement every five–seven years, with the replaced rail handed down to less busy lines, it is clear that the rail deliveries were not even enough to stabilise the situation, let alone reduce the backlog. Given this situation, it is not surprising that the track problem would bedevil Soviet railways for three decades or more.

With bridges, the destruction of the civil war had been more or less repaired by 1925. In fact, since so many of the destroyed bridges had been due for replacement in any case, the bridge situation was probably better than in 1913 in the areas over which the wars had been fought. But for the network as a whole, about one-tenth of existing bridges needed replacement simply to accommodate the heavier locomotives that were increasingly desirable.

Locomotives

Table 51 surveys the locomotive situation. There was no shortage of locomotives in the mid- or even late 1920s. Indeed, it is possible to argue that there was no shortage at the beginning of the 1920s either, with the delivery of hundreds of German- and Swedish-built freight engines. Admittedly, at some times and places, there was a shortage of available locomotives, simply because too many were out of order, but that is something else. In fact, there was a difference of opinion in the early 1920s between advocates of locomotive building and those who claimed that it would be better to get the 'sick' locomotives back into service. Any discussion of this controversy is hampered because it is difficult to know how many locomotives really were 'sick' at any given time. It is not certain what the adjective meant. A new locomotive, otherwise in good order, but awaiting delivery of a spare part, presumably occupies the same weight in the figures as a superannuated wreck awaiting its official write-off. Strumilin tried to find his way through this jungle by adopting the convention that 'sick' locomotives were those whose driving wheel tyres had worn out, which is a sensible way of proceeding but does not produce figures that are accurate enough to support a discussion. All that can safely be said is that locomotive stock was adequate for two reasons: a limited number of locomotives had been acquired which were considerably more powerful than those they were replacing, and the repair of 'sick' locomotives tended to put back into service the most useful designs while relegating to the scrapheap the old and obsolete. So locomotive power, in terms of horsepower available, usually stayed ahead of traffic growth even though, in terms of locomotive units produced, the 1913 level was not surpassed until 1928/29.

Freight and Passenger Vehicles

According to Strumilin,[28] the number of goods wagons available depends on whose figures are believed, the Central Statistical Administration's or the NKPS's; for October 1923 the two figures were as wide apart as 367,000 and 433,000. At about that time the vehicle stock was at its most depressed since the civil war, with about one-third of its strength awaiting repair. Unlike with locomotives, new construction was far behind requirements. Yakobi's Gosplan compilation[29] suggests zero output for 1924/25, then in the following year 299, plus another 203 built in railway workshops. But the following year saw a grand effort, with 4,482 wagonworks' deliveries and another 4,060 from railway shops. In 1927/28 things really got going, according to Yakobi, with 9,550 produced by industry and the railways phasing themselves out with 1,537. Another source[30] gives 7,900 new goods wagons and 387 new passenger vehicles for 1928. By 1928 there was a stock of 472,000 freight and 23,000 passenger vehicles, to be compared with the 1913 Empire figures of about 475,000 and 31,000.[31] (This, incidentally, is one of several indications that long-distance passenger services were lagging behind in the railway recovery.) Different sources give different figures, but all point to a lower production of vehicles, and especially of passenger vehicles, than in 1913.

By 1927/28 only 7.2 per cent of the goods wagon stock was unserviceable, which was as good as, and probably better than, the 1913 percentage. However, just as in 1913, there was a misguided concentration on the conventional 2-axle van. The 1927/28 output by industry did not include a single open wagon suitable for minerals. Admittedly, there was a contingent of 4-axle vans, a taste of things to come, but apart from nearly 2,000 flat-cars and a handful of tanks all production was of the traditional type. True, the van, like its American cousin the boxcar, was a versatile vehicle able to carry almost anything, but it was inefficient both in terms of loading effort and in utilisation of its cubic capacity. Its ubiquity is hard to explain; conservatism and inertia seem the most likely explanation, but perhaps it all had something to do with the Russian Soul. On the credit side, though, and partly attributable to those new 4-axle vehicles, the average capacity of cars had risen from 15.2 tons in 1913 to 17.6 tons in 1928. Little progress had been made with couplings, and not much more with brakes; in 1928 only 3 per cent of the goods wagons were equipped for automatic braking, and some, probably most, of these did not have the brakes but only the air-pipe which allowed them to be included in automatically-braked trains. Still, in both respects the small advance was an improvement over 1913 and put the Soviet railways on the same level, abysmal though it was, of the British companies.

Operating Standards

By 1928 most of the usual efficiency indices had at least regained the 1913 level, or even exceeded it. The percentage of moving goods wagons having loads was almost exactly the same (72 per cent), while the daily mileage travelled by goods wagons had lengthened from 72 to 85 km. Due largely to longer hauls, the turnaround time of wagons was inferior to the 1913 level. The average commercial (yard to yard) speed of freight trains at 14.1 km-h in 1928 was slightly higher than 1913 (13.6 km-h). However, technical speeds (which subtract the time spent on water-stops, etc.) were inferior (21.1 km-h versus 22.0 km-h). Freight locomotives were averaging 137 km per day in 1928, considerably better than the 119 km of 1913. Moreover, they were hauling trains that were significantly heavier (420 against 302 net tons). Passenger trains made similar progress; the average long-distance train as early as 1922/23 was probably as big as the 1913 train, although during the rest of NEP this figure (fluctuating around 36–37 axles) hardly changed. In terms of which year represented a return to 1913 levels, it is possible to point to 1925 for average commercial speed, 1925 (probably) for daily locomotive mileage, and 1923 for average freight train weight.[32]

Labour Productivity

Railway labour productivity during NEP received a good deal of attention from Strumilin.[33] He is not confident of the precision of the primary data, mentioning two differing figures for the workforce in May 1920 of 1.27 million and 1.5 million, but has no doubt that either figure is far more than the railways needed for the traffic level of that time; experts, he said, felt that 682,000 was the optimum number. As in the years before 1913, the number of workers employed seems to fluctuate quite widely, and not always in tune with traffic or mileage. In 1913 (USSR pre-1939 frontiers) 691,000 workers (of whom 116,000 were temporary) were producing 132,000 conventional ton-km per head, in 1921/22 838,000 produced 30,000, and by 1926/27, after ups and downs, a workforce of 1,004,000 (of whom 121,000 were temporary) achieved 103,000 ton-km per head. However, taking an unrefined view of the working force and the combined passenger and freight traffic, it is possible to say that, broadly speaking, productivity remained behind traffic growth but nevertheless moved upwards with it when the latter was expressed in ton-km/km (that is, in intensity of traffic).

It seems almost self-evident that part of the extra labour, compared to 1913, was required because the poor state of track and rolling stock demanded disproportionate maintenance efforts. Other factors, like the increased use of wood fuel, would have had a similar effect. Also, the reduced working hours, regular holidays, and 42-hour rest periods which were introduced by the Provisional government and its successors were reckoned to add 30 per cent to total labour requirements.[34] Another source states that the average nominal railwayman's working day was 9.9 hours in 1913 and 7.7 hours in 1925.[35] But these factors hardly explain the expansion of the labour force from 1923 onwards, and such expansion should not have paralleled the growth of traffic, as it did, by and large. The labour situation on the railways during NEP requires thorough study, but in the meantime it is legitimate to doubt the two widespread assumptions that labour was used as a substitute for unavailable capital, and that the increasing traffic was made possible by an increasing labour force. There could be some truth in these assertions up to about 1924, but the proposition seems doubtful thereafter.

Questions of morale are usually difficult to measure, but were probably more important than is realised. Absenteeism is one indicator, and it is interesting that absence without cause declined from 3.1 days per worker per year in 1922/23 to 1.5 days in the following year. (Track workers showed a more pronounced improvement, from 24.1 days in 1921/22, 6.1 in 1922/23, to 2.2 days in 1923/24.)[36] As Table 50 shows, the accident rate was quite alarming. Although improving year by year, in 1927/28 it was still double the 1913 rate.

So although the broad lines of what happened to Soviet railways in the 1920s seem uncontroversial, there remains a lot of explaining to be done. In the meantime, more care than is habitually exercised should be devoted to avoiding false cause-and-effect interpretations. In particular, there is no really convincing evidence that railway transport shortcomings, after 1922, were a drag on the economy. Efficiency indices for the most part depended on the existence of enough traffic to put the railways into a position where their advantages as bulk movers could be exploited. It was all too easy to blame the railways for undermining the economy when in reality it was the reverse that was happening.

CONCLUSIONS

A distinction has to be made between railway operation and railway policy. The former, in both tsarist and Soviet times, was the function of the Ministry, whereas the latter was the affair of the government, which took the advice of several ministries, of which the Ministry of Ways of Communication was only one.

This chapter is based mainly on statistical sources, and perhaps too little attention has been paid to the other kinds of written record: memoirs, reminiscences, the day-to-day concerns of the railway press, and the records of government and party discussions. The impression conveyed by such sources would have been of a Railway Ministry which, in both 1913 and in 1927, felt quite pleased with itself. In both those years the railways could look back on a period of upsurge, following difficult years.

The government, however, had changed both in its nature and its preoccupations. In 1913 the government's first railway priority was military, its second financial, and its third imperial economic and political development. By 1927 this order of priorities had changed. The Commissariat of War was less influential, partly because of the changed international and military situation, partly because new railway construction was confined to lines which had already received military approval in tsarist times. The first priority of the Soviet government was to avoid a transport crisis, the second was to have a railway system which would actively support economic development, the third was to achieve these two aims with a minimum of resource allocation.

On technical matters, the tsarist government took the advice of railwaymen (more accurately, of railwaymen who chaired commissions and committees but who may not always have had the agreement of their professional colleagues). In the 1920s, the government was still willing to take the advice of senior railway professionals (who, of course, had spent their formative years imbibing the traditions of the imperial railway service), but the professionals differed more openly among themselves, so that the government could not always be sure what they were recommending.[37]

In 1913, so far as can be judged from the statistical evidence, the moral and physical state of the railways was not at all as poor as pre-revolutionary critics and Soviet commentators suggested. Admittedly, it could be plausibly argued that the railways by 1913 were making enough profit to justify improving their service at the expense of certain efficiency indices (notably by accepting lower rolling stock utilisation indices in order to make better provision for peak demands). But, perhaps as a result of the new-found profitability, investment both in plant renewal and in new lines was substantial and, as the outbreak of war showed, the railways did in fact have a certain reserve capacity on which they could call. In view of what happened in the 1930s, it might be argued that railway operators were too traditional in their approach, and that radical new methods would have enabled a better service to be provided at no extra cost, but this was true of all railways and, moreover – as indeed the 1930s showed – rapid change could bring its own costs.

The terrible years of 1914–21 brought the railways to a situation in which they were barely functioning at all. The damage to the track in these years of neglect would take decades to repair. Nevertheless, by the mid-1920s most indices of performance were near the 1913 level, and thereafter they improved. But the performance of the labour force was plainly inferior to that of 1913, and there were major material deficiencies; the government was able and willing to allocate enough resources to enable the railways to surpass the 1913 performance, but not to surpass the 1913 standards of physical well-being. In the late 1920s, railway administrators were well aware that, without faster renovation, the railways would sooner or later reach a critical point. But the prevailing attitude in the transport commissariat was unambitious optimism: the feeling seems to have been that there would be a slow improvement. The demands on the railways would grow steadily but only slowly, so that there would still be time for railway capacity to catch up.

But it did not happen like that. Both in 1913 and 1927 the railways were facing in a direction that they were not destined to travel. On balance, they were better prepared for the first world war than they were for the first five-year plan.

10 Research and Technology
J. M. Cooper and R. A. Lewis

INTRODUCTION

Economic development in the XX Century has taken place against a background of increasingly close links between science, technology and economic life. Industrial performance, in particular, can be seen as a reflection of the degree of integration between the research laboratory, the design engineer and the factory floor. Thus, the tsarist legacy in science and technology and the developments during the first decade of Soviet power were of key importance to the industrialisation programme which began with the first five year plan.

This chapter reviews and contrasts the commitment of the Russian Empire and the USSR to science and technology, first, by examining the inputs into scientific research and development (R & D) in the two periods in terms of funds, manpower and the development of facilities, and secondly by assessing the 'output' of the R&D system – the level of science and technology. The level of scientific research is assessed through a simple quantitative analysis of the relative performance of Russian and Soviet scientists; to assess the level of technology, we have undertaken brief case-studies of high-technology branches of the engineering industry. These were at the forefront of contemporary technology, and also posed acute problems of production organisation, materials quality and human skills.

This chapter is a preliminary survey; much research remains to be done, particularly on the pre-revolutionary period.

THE PRE-REVOLUTIONARY SCENE

The Scientific Research Effort

Both Soviet and Western writers have concluded that science and technology in the Russian Empire were underdeveloped and underfunded.[1] The organisation of science and technology was particularly backward: growing numbers of specialised research institutes were established in countries such as Germany, but the tsarist government showed little inclination, in spite of the lobbying of some leading scientists, to foster a network of state research institutes. The leading state-funded scientific organisation, the Imperial Academy of Sciences, was more a scientists' club than a research organisation. On the basis of optimistic assumptions, we estimate that central budgetary expenditure on science was 6.3 million rubles in 1912, 9.6 million in 1913 and 9.7 million in 1914.[2] These sums comprised less than 0.3 per cent of total budget expenditure.

The Ministry of Education was the largest disburser of funds for science. Its expenditure, which included the funding of the Imperial Academy of Sciences, comprised some 40 per cent of the total in each of these three years. The Chief Administration of Land Use (*Zemleustroistvo*) spent almost as much as the Ministry of Education on a variety of establishments, farms and stations engaged in scientific and experimental work.

The government did not provide any substantial support for indigenous industrial technology. The Ministry of Trade and Industry gave a small amount of money to support technical societies and technical museums.[3] Its mining department funded the Geological Committee which can be considered a science-related activity.[4] Support for industrial research was also provided through the Ministry of War: the sum of just under 500,000 rubles was allocated to the organisation of a central scientific and technical laboratory, which after the revolution became an independent institute under the Supreme Council of National Economy (Vesenkha). At the same time the domination of Russian industry by foreign capital meant that there was little funding of R&D activities by industry and little development of R&D organisations within industrial enterprises. Technology was imported rather than developed at home.

The Russian Empire also relied heavily on imported engineering skills. Bailes suggests that in 1897 the engineering profession in Russia was more dominated by foreigners than any other.[5] The engineers like the scientists campaigned for change and for government recognition of the importance of engineering training and of the need to foster pioneering ideas. In the early years of the XX Century the supply of domestically trained engineers somewhat improved; Bailes considers that by 1914 Russia was producing 'most of its graduate technologists'.[6] Foreign companies were replacing foreign nationals with local personnel. There is considerable variation in the numbers cited for those in the engineering profession. The 1897 census records a figure of 4,010 graduate engineers, and on this basis a Soviet source has calculated that there were 7,880 in 1913.[7] But the Soviet historian Leikina-Svirskaya, after a careful investigation, concluded that by the end of the XIX Century 'the number of engineers of various specialities amounted to nearly 12,500'.[8] In a later study she estimated that 11,800 technical specialists had graduated by 1900, and a further 18,356 in 1900–17, but adds that these are 'incomplete data'.[9] The nine major technical societies had a membership of 6,520 in 1914.[10] These data can be compared with estimates for the number of graduate engineers in France and Germany in 1914 of 42,850 and 65,202 respectively;[11] in 1910, there were an estimated 77,000 engineers in the United States.[12] While, from the beginning of the century in particular, laboratory facilities were being established in the universities, polytechnics and technical institutes, they tended to be more for teaching than for research. The higher education sector, in its turn, failed to provide the necessary conditions for large-scale scientific research.

Scientists were therefore largely thrown onto their own resources. They worked in laboratories in their homes, and established societies to foster research. Nevertheless, a scientific profession had emerged and was growing in size by the first world war. Soviet statistical sources cite a figure of some 10,000 for the total number of scientists (*nauchnye rabotniki*) – including the humanities – in 1913 (see Table 52).

The professional scientists' desire to drag Russian scientific organisation into the XX Century was given a boost by the outbreak of the war. The breaking of the industrial and commercial links with Germany cut off Russia from the source of many important industrial products and the major source of its imported technology. In the effort to solve the resulting problems scientists received a more sympathetic hearing. Funds were made available for research and those scientists who had lobbied for funding to study Russia's natural resources saw some of their ideas come to fruition with the formation within the Academy of Sciences of the Commission for the Study of the Natural Resources of Russia (KEPS). However, these war-time developments were only a small step along the road to a comprehensive science policy.

Scientific and Technological Performance

Science

In spite of the enormous handicaps, individual Russian scientists, such as Chebyshev, Lebedev, and Mendeleev, had made a significant impact on world scientific development, particularly in chemistry and mathematics. To estimate the contribution of the Russian scientific profession as a whole on the eve of the first world war, an analysis was made of five German scientific journals, *Annalen der Physik, Berichte der Deutschen chemischen Gesellschaft, Matematische Annalen, Zeitschrift für analytische Chemie, Zeitschrift für anorganische und allgemeine Chemie*, and *Zeitschrift für Elektrochemie und angewandte physikalische Chemie*. In the years 1911–13 about 5 per cent of the articles published in these periodicals originated in the Russian Empire.[13]

High-technology Engineering

The overall picture of tsarist Russia which emerges from the existing literature is of an economy which was importing technology rather than developing it at home. Examples of indigenous technical developments are the exception rather than the rule. Much detailed work needs to be done on the technological level of tsarist industry; here we have undertaken an initial review of some branches of engineering which were at the forefront of technical change. (See Table 54.)

Aircraft The origin of the Russian aircraft industry dates from 1910 when a number of individual enthusiasts built 15 aeroplanes. Factory production effectively started in the following year. In the period 1910–13 there were three enterprises building aircraft on a regular basis. The largest producer was the Moscow 'Duks' works of Yu. A. Meller, previously known for its manufacture of bicycles and motorcycles. Most of its products were copies of French designs, including Farman and Nieuport models; some were built on a licence basis. The second largest producer was the St Petersburg S. S. Shchetinin factory, founded in 1909. French models were built, but also some of original design. The Russko–Baltic wagon factory (RBVZ), known for its automobile production (see p. 194 below), began building aircraft in 1910, first in Riga and from 1912 at its new aviation division in St Petersburg. Under the design leadership of I. I. Sikorskii, this factory made the greatest contribution to Russian aviation technology. Sikorskii was responsible for the world's first four-engined plane, the 'Russkii Vityaz'' built in 1913, leading to the creation of the famous 'Ilya Muromets' later in the same year. Built in many variants during the war at the Petrograd factory, including a bomber version, this aircraft was a remarkable achievement of the young Russian industry. Before the war many planes were also built on a one-off basis by small workshops and individual engineers. Total output in 1913 was 280 aeroplanes, of which 206 were made by the three main enterprises.[14] Not surprisingly, the early Russian aircraft industry experienced many problems of supply of appropriate materials, equipment and skills.

During the war the aircraft industry expanded substantially. Output grew to 1,870 in 1916 and 1,897 in 1917.[15] The largest producer was the 'Duks' works, with a peak output of 543 units in 1917, followed by the Shchetinin factory. The Russko–Baltic works built the 'Ilya Muromets', but not in large numbers. New producers entered the field in 1914, including the Odessa 'Anatra' factory, the Moscow 'Moska' works, the Slyusarenko factory in Petrograd (transferred from Riga), and the V. A. Lebedev works, also in Petrograd. By 1917 there were eleven plane building factories employing a total of 7,385 workers. As before the war, most of the planes built were of foreign design, in particular French. Some domestic models also entered production: the 'Ilya Muromets' was followed by the M-5 and M-9 flying boats of D. P. Grigorovich, built at the Shchetinin works.

In view of the weakness of the motor industry in general it is hardly surprising that the building of aero-engines was poorly developed. The earliest producer was the Riga 'Motor' factory, which began to make engines in 1911, including original models designed by the factory's director, F. C. Kalep. In 1912 the French company 'Gnome-Rhône' opened a small works in Moscow and began assembling engines, initially from imported parts. At the outbreak of war these were the sole producers and together employed only 250 workers. In 1915 the 'Motor' works moved to Moscow and expanded its activities, and new capacity for engine building was created at the Petrograd works of the Russko–Baltic company. In addition, the French 'Salmson' company built a works in Moscow. In the following year a few engines were made also by the 'P. Il'in' carriage and vehicle works in Moscow and by the new 'Dyuflon i Konstantinovich' ('Deka') factory at Aleksandrovsk (Zaporozh'e) in the Ukraine. In 1917 there were five serious aero-engine factories employing almost 1,900 workers.[16] The engines built were almost all of foreign design – French, German (Mercedes) and British (Sunbeam). The scale of output in 1916 is variously reported as 578 engines[17] or 1,300; the latter figure may include engines assembled from imported parts.[18] To an even greater extent than for plane building, aero-engine production suffered from inadequate availability of high-quality steels and non-ferrous alloys.

By the end of the period in addition to the above-mentioned factories there were two enterprises making propellers. In 1917 the specialised aircraft industry consisted of 16 enterprises employing more than 11,000 workers and employees.[19] There were also new factories under construction, including two plane building works in Yaroslavl' for the Shchetinin and Lebedev companies, and another owned by the latter in Taganrog. The Lebedev company also had a plant in Penza which was just beginning to make propellers. In Moscow the first specialised aircraft instrument works, 'Aviapribor', was being built, while the Podolsk 'Singer' factory was organising the manufacture of aircraft magnetos. The industry was thus expanding at a quite rapid pace. However, the tsarist achievement must be seen in perspective. Most of the aircraft and engines were of foreign design, with a substantial involvement of foreign technical expertise. By international standards the scale of output was still modest. While Russia built 1,900 planes in 1917, and a far smaller number of engines, in 1918 France produced more than 23,000 planes and 44,000 engines.[20]

Motor vehicles 'Russia entered the first world war completely lacking an automobile industry', claims one Soviet historian writing in the mid-1960s.[21] In fact, as more recent Soviet works have acknowledged, there was vehicle production in Russia from as early as 1896, and more than 1,000 vehicles were built from then until 1915.[22] This total is very similar to the number built during the first decade after 1917. The very first car, the 1½ hp 'Yakovlev i Freze', of original design, was built in 1896 at a small factory in St Petersburg. From 1900 P. A. Freze built the French 'De Dion Bouton', at first using imported components, later with domestically-made parts, except for the engine. Other early producers were bicycle manufacturers. The largest Russian bicycle works, the 'Rossiya' factory in Riga, built a number of cars between 1899 and 1902 (the 'Rossiya–Leitner'), while the Moscow 'Duks' works built some 100 'Duksmobil' cars between 1904 and 1906 on the basis of an 'Oldsmobile' licence. A number of one-off models were built by individual engineers and some coach-builders made car bodies for imported chassis. Aided by low duties, imports of vehicles grew steadily, rising from 40 in 1901 to 563 in 1907.

In the immediate pre-war period there were three firms building motor vehicles on a regular basis. Between 1906 and 1909 the most important was the 'Lessner' works of St Petersburg. In 1905 it built a batch of vehicles for the postal service, and during the next four years produced cars of four models and a number of commercial vehicles. The scale of production was small – several dozen were made over five years – prices were high and orders difficult to obtain. More significant was the Russko–Baltic wagon building works of Riga founded in 1874 and one of the most advanced engineering factories of tsarist Russia. Under the leadership of a Belgian engineer, car production was organised in 1907 and the first 'Russo-Balt', based on a Belgian design, appeared two years later. The vehicle shop of the works was well-equipped for an output of up to 250 cars per year and employed progressive production methods, including elements of interchangeable parts manufacture. At first some components were imported; later full domestic production was achieved. The cars were of modern design and acquired a good reputation for reliability. A third producer was the small 'Puzyrev' works in St Petersburg, which built some 40 cars of original design between 1911 and 1914, when the factory was damaged by fire. Before the war a number of other firms built vehicles on a small scale, including the 'Nobel' diesel engine works of St Petersburg and the 'P. Il'in' coach-building works in Moscow.

There is no doubt that domestic producers faced many problems. The small scale of production led to high costs, making it difficult to compete with imports. Furthermore, high-quality steels and some technically complex components were in short supply and were expensive to import because of high customs duties. The annual imports of vehicles greatly exceeded domestic production: in 1911 2,717 vehicles were imported, rising to a peak of 5,416 in 1913 and 4,590 in 1914.[23] By the war domestically built vehicles accounted for less than 10 per cent of the total stock. As noted above, between 1896 and 1915 approximately 1,000 motor vehicles were built in Russia, but in 1913 alone 45,000 were built in France, 34,000 in Britain and 20,000 in Germany.[24]

The war gave rise to developments of great significance for the future Soviet motor industry. In 1915 the Russko–Baltic works was evacuated from Riga and its equipment transferred to the company's other plants in Petrograd, Tver' and Fili (near Moscow), where a new factory was under construction. The production of vehicles virtually ceased. Recognising the urgent need for motor transport for the war effort, the Main Military-Technical Administration in early 1916 concluded contracts for the construction of six new vehicle factories with an aggregate capacity of 7,500 units per year. The new works were in Moscow (Kuznetsov and Rya-bushinskii 'AMO'), Fili ('Russko–Baltic'), Rybinsk ('Russkii Reno'), Yaroslavl' ('V. A. Lebedev'), Rostov-on-Don ('Aksai') and Mytishchi ('Bekos').[25] Of these, only the Russko–Baltic and 'Russkii Reno' companies had previous experience of automobile production. The Mytishchi works was to be a government-owned enterprise; the remainder, private. By October 1917 these new enterprises were at various stages of completion in terms of construction and the installation of equipment. The best advanced was the Moscow 'AMO' works, where preparations were in hand for building the Italian 1½ ton 'Fiat-15' truck. Parts were purchased from Italy permitting 'AMO' to assemble 432 trucks in 1917, 779 in 1918 and 108 in 1919.[26] The Yaroslavl' works was incomplete, but also assembled some Fiat and Crossley trucks from imported parts. These war-time factories provided the foundation for the Soviet motor industry. During the war a number of enterprises, including the Izhora and Putilov works, built armoured cars on the basis of 'Russo-Balt' and imported chassis. Russia also pioneered the building of semi-tracked vehicles according to an invention of A. Kergess and some examples were built by the Putilov factory.

Tractors   Were tractors built in Russia before the Revolution? The impression given by almost all Soviet works is that they were not and that tractor building was entirely an achievement of the Soviet regime. However, there is evidence that the activity was under way before the war: according to one Soviet source 'several tens' of wheeled tractors were built in 1913.[27] The model was the 'Russkii traktor' designed by the inventor Yu. V. Mamin and built at a factory in Balakovo in the Saratov region.[28] Before the war a number of machine-building factories were preparing to build tractors, including the Rostov 'Aksai' company, and factories in Khar'kov, Kolomna, Bryansk, and Kikchas in the Ukraine. Almost all intended to make foreign models using imported engines and other components.[29] The war probably aborted all these projects.

Bicycles and motorcycles   It is easy to overlook the fact that in the late XIX and early XX Century the manufacture of bicycles was a relatively advanced activity from the point of view of production technology. It required very high precision work and promoted the development of specialised machine tools.[30] Large-scale bicycle production was organised quite early in Russia, the leading firm being Aleksandr Leitner in Riga. His 'Rossiya' works founded in 1880 produced up to 15,000 bicycles a year.

Another producer, but with a smaller scale of output, was the Moscow 'Duks' factory founded in 1884.[31] Total output in 1912 was 11,228 units, of which 4,907 were manufactured in the territory of the future USSR.[32] The fate of bicycle building during the war is not known.

The two principal pre-1917 bicycle factories also built motor cycles on a modest scale. The first Russian motor cycle, the 'Rossiya', was built in 1901 at the Riga Leitner works. In the immediate pre-war period there was only one producer, the Moscow 'Duks' factory, building a 2½ hp model. Its output rose from 72 units in 1910 to 133 in 1912.[33]

Optical equipment The first enterprises for the production of optical equipment appeared in Vilnius and Warsaw in the late XIX Century, but proved to be short-lived, unable to withstand foreign competition. Longer lasting was a branch of the German 'Zeiss' company in Riga, engaged in the assembly of optical instruments from imported parts.[34] The Russian optical industry really dates from 1905 when an optical workshop was created at the Obukhov works in St Petersburg to meet the needs of the navy. Foreign specialists and workers were employed. In 1907 the shop began to assemble binoculars and in the period up to the war it made gun sights and other optical instruments on a small-scale batch production basis.[35] This small workshop provided valuable experience for Russian technical specialists in the field of optics, some of whom played a prominent role in the Soviet period (e.g., A. L. Gershun and S. I. Frieberg). All ciné equipment was imported, usually from the French Pathé company. Before 1917 there was no organised production of cameras, although some individual enthusiasts created their own equipment. There was also no domestic production of optical glass during the pre-war period. In general, Russia was heavily dependent on imports for all types of optical equipment. It has been estimated that some 500,000 cameras and 1,500 ciné projectors had been imported by 1917.[36]

The war led to some important new developments. In 1914 in Petrograd the 'Russian company for optical and mechanical production' was founded, with majority ownership in the hands of Schneider–Creusot. A new factory was rapidly built for the production of optical equipment and of detonators for shells. Cut off from the principal supplier of optical glass, Russian optical specialists tried to master the secrets of optical glass smelting, but without success. In the end they managed to persuade the Birmingham Chance company to sell the technology for 600,000 gold rubles. The production of optical glass was organised at the Petrograd porcelain works.[37]

Sewing machines Like bicycle manufacture, the mass production of domestic sewing machines helped to promote progressive production methods, in particular precision machining and the manufacture of interchangeable parts. In pre-revolutionary Russia this was a monopoly of the

Singer factory established at Podolsk at the turn of the century.[38] This works had limited independence. All design work was undertaken abroad by the parent company, many parts were imported and the equipment was supplied from abroad. Less than half the total number of parts of the two basic models built before the war were made at Podolsk.[39] Nevertheless, for tsarist Russia this was an unusually well-equipped engineering works with modern methods of production. According to an American visitor in 1910, the Russian workers at Podolsk had 'developed remarkable accuracy and speed. The men are working to the same gauges as the men in the Singer shops at Elizabethport, New Jersey. While not up to the speed of the Elizabethport men, the difference is so slight as to excite the admiration of an American'.[40] By 1914 the works employed more than 5,000 workers.[41] Soviet sources give a 1913 output of 271,000 units, but this appears to understate the pre-war achievement.[42] According to contemporary statistics, the output of sewing machines reached 311,363 units in 1911 and 460,257 units in 1912.[43] During the war the output of sewing machines fell sharply as the factory switched to production for the front.

Timepieces The mass production of timepieces was not strongly developed in tsarist Russia. Simple wall clocks of the 'grandfather' type were made by a few workshops using primitive equipment and hand labour. At only one works, the Moscow factory of B. Reinin, was there an attempt to organise mechanised production. Before the revolution a number of foreign firms established clock assembly shops in Moscow and St Petersburg. This development was prompted by government tariff policy, which imposed high customs duties on finished timepieces, but lower duties on unassembled parts.[44] The only exception to this general picture was the clock and watch industry of Warsaw. Here there was small-scale production of silver watches, in addition to the making of alarm and wall clocks. In 1912 the Warsaw output amounted to 412,500 units.[45] It has been estimated that total 1913 production in Russia, including assembled clocks, reached 700,000 units.[46]

Bearings[47] The manufacture of bearings is a high-precision activity essential for the production of a wide range of engineering products, in particular motor vehicles, aircraft and machine tools. Small-scale production of primitive bearings began in Russia at a small factory in Moscow in 1898. A major obstacle was the lack of suitable special steel. This Moscow factory remained the sole producer during the pre-war period: most needs were met by imports. In 1914 the Swedish SKF company founded a trading house to supply bearings to Russian industry and in 1916 SKF purchased the Moscow works and began its reconstruction.

Machine tools[48] A vital key to development in all the branches we have discussed is the availability of machine tools which are able to manufacture parts with precision and on a large scale. The pre-war Russian engineering industry was heavily dependent on imported metal-working machine tools. Of the entire machine-tool stock in 1913 domestically built machines probably represented little more than one-quarter of the total. Machine-tool building began in the 1870s. Early producers included the Moscow 'Bromley' factory and the 'Lessner' and 'Nobel' works in St Petersburg. In the 1890s there were attempts to establish specialised machine-tool production, but these ended in failure. It was really from 1908 that the industry began to develop. Output increased from 1.5 million rubles in 1910 to 2.8 million in 1912, and 3.3 million in 1913. In unit terms some 1,800 machines were built in 1913 (1,490 within pre-1940 Soviet boundaries). The most advanced machine tools were built at factories in Warsaw and Latvia; together these locations accounted for almost 60 per cent of total output in value terms in 1912.[49] The largest producer was the Warsaw 'Herlach and Pulst' factory; a well-equipped works, it began machine-tool building in 1908 and by 1913 employed 750 workers. Second in importance was the Riga 'Felzer' works, which built machine tools from 1896. In Moscow the 'Bromley' factory was the principal producer and in St Petersburg the 'Phoenix' works. The latter began machine-tool building in the 1890s and before the war came under the financial control of the British Greenwood and Batley company. In general the technical level of machine-tool building was low. The government's tariff policy protected the making of heavy, simple machines and made difficult the establishment of profitable domestic production of more complex, precision types. Government ordering of machine tools for railway workshops and the military created a secure market, but did not promote technical progress.

The requirements of war-time production created a substantial demand for machine tools, but with the exception of the 'Bromley' works, the main pre-war producers contributed little to the war effort. The 'Herlach and Pulst' factory was evacuated to Khar'kov but not restored. The 'Felzer' factory was transferred from Riga to Nizhnii-Novgorod in 1915, but virtually ceased machine-tool building. The 'Phoenix' works cut back machine-tool building and concentrated on munitions. Only the 'Bromley' factory expanded its machine-tool building. There was some government action to increase domestic production and the new market situation led to a sharp rise in machine-tool prices, making their manufacture more profitable. New producers appeared, some establishing relatively large-scale manufacture. These included the Tula arms factory, the Podolsk 'Singer' works, and a number of locomotive and wagon works. The output of machine tools increased, although the precise magnitude of the expansion is uncertain. According to one source, 1917 output was 43 per cent higher than 1913, giving a volume of output of almost 5 million rubles. The 1916 output could well have been even higher. There is some dispute about the qualitative achievement. According to Grinevetskii, machine-tool building before 1914 was 'one of the weakest and most backward sectors of Russian machine building', but during the war it 'grew extraordinarily, not only quantitatively, but also with respect to quality'. Many factories 'undertook production of a normalised or mass type: Tula, "Shtolle" (Moscow), technical schools, the "Zemgor" combines, Kramatorsk, Sormovo and the Bryansk factories built extremely intricate and complex machine tools and made better products than the majority of Scandinavian and other wartime exporters'.[50] This assessment is disputed by Soviet writers who stress that the machines were generally simple, operational types for munitions production by low-skilled operators. However, it has been acknowledged that the war-time manufacture of machine tools was a 'good school of large-batch production'.[51] The majority of the war-time machine-tool builders abandoned the activity after the Revolution.

NEP

The Scientific Research Effort

The revolution of October 1917 brought to power a government which saw modern science and technology as a key progressive force. The response of some scientists to the Bolshevik takeover was emigration. These included I. I. Sikorskii, the aircraft designer, who was to find fame and fortune in the United States. Most were distrustful rather than actively hostile to the new regime. The vast majority would appear to have stayed; some, such as the energy specialists Kirsh and Grinevetskii, only to die as a result of the hard living conditions of the civil war years. Bailes gives a figure of approximately 15,000 engineers with higher education in the country in October 1918.[52] A survey in the early 1920s points to a figure of some 14,000.[53] In the intervening years technical higher education provided few graduates, so there were not many new recruits to the profession. In Bailes's words 'the old technical intelligentsia emerged from the revolution and civil war with losses, but largely intact'.[54]

Those scientists who had been leading the struggle for specialised research laboratories and institutes now found encouragement even in the difficult times of the civil war. Many became involved in the creation of independent research organisations. For example, in 1923 there were some 15 R&D establishments under Vesenkha.[55] By the mid-1920s the basic structure of an R&D system had been firmly established and many of the most famous Soviet research institutes had been created.

This was the case in some of the engineering branches with which we are concerned. The leading Soviet institute for aviation research, the Central Aero-Hydrodynamic Institute (TsAGI), was created at the end of 1918 on the initiative of Professor N. E. Zhukovskii.[56] In 1925 a Central Design

Bureau was established at the former 'Duks' works GAZ No. 1. Shortly afterwards a reorganisation resulted in the establishment of design teams attached to GAZ No. 5 under N. N. Polikarpov and for the development of flying boats at the Leningrad 'Krasnyi Letchik' works under D. P. Grigorovich.[57] In the automobile industry a Scientific Automobile Laboratory (NAL) was created in 1918; three years later it was transformed into the Scientific Automotor Institute (NAMI) under N. R. Brilling.[58] In addition to work on cars and lorries, this institute was involved in R&D for the tractor industry and on aero-engines. In 1918, the leadership of D. S. Rozhdestvenskii was instrumental in the foundation of the State Optical Institute (GOI) on the basis of work which had been undertaken within the auspices of KEPS towards the establishment of domestic production of microscopes and other optical apparatus.[59]

The available data for the research effort of the Russian Empire and the USSR provide clear support for the picture which we have just outlined. There are no firm statistics for the number of research establishments in the mid-1920s; at the beginning of 1929, according to Soviet data, their numbers were many times greater than they had been in 1913. In the economic year 1926/27 the government allocated over 50 million rubles to various scientific organisations, as against our generous 1913 total of 9.6 million. In real terms this represented an increase of perhaps 150 per cent.[60] However, the picture presented by these figures needs to be modified in various ways. First, the foundation of numerous research establishments need not signify an equivalent increase in research activity, but simply its more formal organisation. Indeed, many of the newly-founded independent organisations were not entirely new creations but based on work which was already being done in various laboratories. We have noted that GOI was formed on the basis of work being done under KEPS; other institutes, too, developed out of the war-time activities of this organisation.[61] TsAGI was based on the work of Zhukovskii's research group at the Moscow Higher Technical School.[62] However, in all these cases the scale of activity was much increased. Secondly, our financial data does not provide a measure of the total funds being spent on science. Both in 1913 and in the mid-1920s some funds were flowing to research establishments through other channels than directly from the state budget. A large part of this was indirect funding of industrial R&D by enterprises and other industrial organisations on a contract basis.[63] In 1913, however, funding from outside the state budget was doubtless a larger part of the total funding than in these later years. Consequently the increase in total funding between our two periods was not as large as the increase in budgetary allocations.

The development of a network of industrial research establishments was one factor responsible for a different pattern of distribution of state funding in comparison with the pre-war years. Towards the end of NEP these organisations were absorbing upwards of one-quarter of budgetary expenditure on science. By 1927/28 the resources going to them were in real terms equivalent to the total budget expenditure in science in 1913.

After the revolution the Academy of Sciences passed out of the control of the commissariat for education; it will be discussed separately below. When we compare the spending of the commissariats of education of the various Soviet republics in the mid-1920s with the figure for the Ministry of Education in 1913 which is obtained by excluding the expenditure on the Academy, we find that by 1927/28 the sum had increased by about 80 per cent in real terms.[64] Many new research organisations which were independent of the existing higher educational establishments had been established under the commissariats of education. Higher education had also expanded; the number of universities and other *vuzy* had grown and the number of lecturing staff in the mid-1920s was three times as high as in 1913. However, the number of students had also increased and the general effect of the formation of independent research organisations by commissariats of education was to siphon off research from all but the most prestigious universities and polytechnics.

The years immediately after the revolution saw the initial steps towards the transformation of the Academy of Sciences into a great R&D organisation in response to pressure from certain sections within the Academy and from the new government. New scientific establishments were set up; the number of research personnel under the Academy had reportedly more than trebled by the mid-1920s. The period also saw the start of what was later to become a network of republican and branch academies; the Ukrainian Academy of Sciences was established as early as 1919.[65] However, the Academy's relationship with the Bolshevik government was somewhat strained.[66] Many people saw it as reflecting all that was bad about science under the tsarist regime and various proposals were made for its abolition or replacement. This ambivalence towards the Academy is undoubtedly reflected in the fact that the budgets for the years 1925/26 to 1927/28 envisaged little more than level funding;[67] in spite of the organisational developments within the Academy and a greatly increased staff, real expenditure was probably not substantially above the pre-war level.

If the categories of expenditure in the 1913 budget and the budgets of the mid-1920s are comparable, then state expenditure on research also increased much less rapidly in real terms in the agricultural sector than in the education sector. Indeed in 1925/26 it may even have been no higher in real terms. However, expenditure by the commissariats of agriculture grew substantially in 1926/27 and 1927/28 and handsomely exceeded the pre-war level in the latter year.

A growing number of R&D organisations and increasing resources meant more jobs. The prospects of a career in science thus opened up for more young people and also for a wider cross-section of society, female as well as male. In 1927, there were perhaps twice as many scientific workers as in 1913 (see Table 52).

Scientific and Technological Performance

Science

The NEP years are generally considered to have been a period of increased scientific activity. Western authors who discuss Soviet science tend to see them in a similar way to their colleagues writing on the cultural field, namely as years of excitement and progress.[68] Our analysis of Soviet contributions in our sample of German scientific periodicals supports a picture of greatly increased activity in comparison with the tsarist period (see Table 53). Between 1926 and 1928 more than twice as many articles originating in the USSR appeared than had been published in 1911–13 by Russian scientists who were working in centres which were subsequently to become part of the Soviet Union.[69] The proportion of the total number of articles which this work comprised had also doubled. Only in the case of *Annalen der Physik* does the evidence point in the opposite direction and this can be explained by the appearance of a new journal *Zeitschrift für Physik* at the start of the 1920s to which Soviet scientists were frequent contributors.[70]

High-technology Engineering (Table 54)

Aircraft After the October Revolution aircraft production fell sharply; only 255 planes were built in 1918, and a mere 44 in 1922, with only 8 engines.[71] The industry began to revive from the end of 1922 when STO approved a three-year development plan. Production in 1923/24 exceeded 200 planes, but only 13 of these were combat planes for the air force.[72] In the following year, 1924/25, the air force received 264 planes, although these were almost all reconnaisance aircraft.[73] Between 1922 and the end of 1924 some 700 planes were imported. By 1927/28 output had reached 575 units, including 495 combat planes;[74] the peak war-time level of output in unit terms was not attained until after the end of the first five year plan.

In the period to 1927 four enterprises accounted for the bulk of aircraft production: the former 'Duks' works in Moscow (GAZ No. 1), the Leningrad 'Krasnyi Letchik' (GAZ No. 3) based on the former Russko–Baltic factory, the Moscow 'Aviarabotnik' (previous identity not known), and the Moscow 'Samolet' (GAZ No. 5) based on the former 'Moska' works.[75] Most of the batch-built aircraft were of foreign design and there was a strong emphasis on relatively simple training and reconnaisance types, including the U-1 (based on the Avro-541) and the R-1 (based on a De Havilland design). The latter, of dated design, accounted for more than half of total output. In an attempt to strengthen technological capability the German Junkers firm took over on a concessionary basis the Fili motor vehicle factory built by the Russko–Baltic company during the war. This agreement was operational from the beginning of 1923 to March 1927, when it was terminated by the Soviet side. Meanwhile, the domestic design capability began to strengthen with the appearance of original models, some of which entered regular production. Notable was the work of A. N. Tupolev at TsAGI on the creation of all-metal designs. The first all-metal plane, the ANT-2, appeared in 1924, followed by the ANT-3 (R-3) reconnaissance plane and the ANT-4 bomber in 1925. The latter was the world's first all-metal, twin-engined, heavy monoplane bomber. Advanced for its day, it entered batch production in modified form as the TB-1 in 1929.

The development of aero-engines was less successful; here the general weakness of the engineering and metallurgical industries made itself felt with particular force.[76] Until 1927 almost all the engines built were of foreign design and relatively low power; the inadequate level of engine-building hindered the development of the aircraft industry as a whole. The principal factories were the former 'Gnome-Rhône' works in Moscow, now known as the 'Ikar' GAZ No. 2, the former 'Motor' factory in Moscow, which became GAZ No. 4, and the former 'Deka' works in Zaporozh'e. From 1924 GAZ No. 4 was enlarged when it merged with the former 'Salmson' factory. In 1927 the 'Ikar' and 'Motor' factories were merged to create Zavod No. 24 (the 'Frunze' factory). In the early 1920s aero-engine manufacture was also organised at the 'Bol'shevik' factory in Leningrad (the former Obukhov works). Two research centres were created: an aero-engine department led by B. S. Stechkin at TsAGI and a similar department at the vehicle engine research institute, NAMI (N. R. Brilling and A. A. Mikulin). The most successful product of the period was the 'M-5', based on the 400 hp 'Liberty-12' engine dating from the end of the war. This was built at the 'Ikar' factory from 1924 and became the basic engine for planes built for both the air force and the civil air fleet. Its production technology was more complex than anything previously experienced, and problems of manufacture and materials led to a much shorter service life than was typical for foreign-built engines of the time. The first engine with elements of original Soviet design to enter batch production on any scale was the highly successful air-cooled 100 hp 'M-11' designed by A. D. Shvetsov; it was produced from the mid-1920s to 1959. There are no data on the scale of output of aero-engines in the 1920s. It is clear that imports played a major role: of the total number of engines installed in the entire stock of planes of the air force in 1928 70 per cent were imported. However, despite the problem of engines, the aircraft industry must be considered one of the successes of Soviet industrial development in the decade to 1927.

Motor vehicles The vehicle factories were nationalised in 1918. Until the
end of the civil war their main activity was the repair of the existing vehicle
stock, although there was also some assembly of new trucks from imported
parts. The formation of NAMI played an important role in consolidating
the research and design forces of the motor industry. In March 1921 seven
enterprises were united to form a Central State Administration of Automobile Factories (TsUGAZ), charged with developing the large-scale
production of motor vehicles and the creation of new, Soviet models. In
addition, some vehicle factories were controlled by the 'Prombron'' corporation (*ob"edinenie*), including the former Fili 'Russko–Balt' factory,
now known as the 1st *broneavtomobil'nyi zavod* (1–i BTAZ). It was this
works which in 1922 built the first Soviet light car, the 'Prombron', an
improved version of the 'Russo–Balt'. Five were built at Fili before the
factory transferred to the aviation industry, and a further 20 were made by the
Moscow 2nd BTAZ works between 1923 and 1926. The Fili works was not
the only one to leave the motor industry in the early 1920s. The Rybinsk
'Russkii Reno' works switched to aero-engine building, the Rostov 'Aksai'
to agricultural machine building and the Mytishchi 'Bekos' factory to
another activity, not identified. By 1925 there were only three vehicle
factories of any real importance: the 1st State Automobile Factory,
'AMO', the 4th State Factory (the former 'Il'in' works in Moscow, now
known as 'Spartak'), and the 1st State Auto-repair Factory in Yaroslavl'
(the former 'Lebedev' works). This provides evidence that vehicle building
was still not regarded as a matter of the highest priority.

Until 1924 the 'AMO' factory was engaged in the repair of 'White'
lorries and as an increasing share of the parts were made by the factory
itself they became known as 'White-AMOs'. In 1924 work began on
building new lorries, the model chosen being the same, 1916-model,
'Fiat-15' previously assembled by the factory, although over time a number
of design changes were introduced. The first 'AMO-F15' appeared in
November 1924 and from then on the scale of production greatly expanded: in 1925 113 were built, in 1926 342, in 1927 407 and in 1928 692.[77]
In 1925 the Yaroslavl' factory built its first lorry, the 3 ton Ya-3, with a
design similar to that of the 'AMO' model and using the 'AMO' engine.
Later heavier versions were made and supplied with imported engines –
the Ya-4 with a 70 hp Mercedes engine and the Ya-5 with the American 93
hp Hercules. The scale of production at Yaroslavl' was extremely small in
the period before 1928.

Having consolidated research and design resources, NAMI began working on the development of a new Soviet light car, the NAMI-1. The basic
design scheme was borrowed from the Czech 'Tatra-12', but it is claimed
that it was completely reworked to give an original model.[78] The first
example was built by the Spartak factory in the summer of 1927 and
small-scale production was then organised: more than 500 were made

before its removal from production in 1931. This was a definite achievement of the young Soviet motor industry, although the NAMI-1 was not an entirely successful design. During the first five-year plan the Spartak works became an affiliate of 'AMO'. Another achievement is also worth noting: in 1927 the first Soviet armoured car, the 'BA-27', was built on the basis of the AMO-F-15 chassis.

In 1927 total Soviet vehicle production amounted to a modest 478 units. This compares with a 1926 output of 54,500 in Germany, 200,000 in both France and Britain, and 7,500 in Czechoslovakia.[79] It was not until the first five-year plan that the Soviet motor industry underwent vigorous development.

Tractors After the October Revolution the first tractors were built in 1919 by the Petrograd Obukhov ('Bol'shevik') works and preparations were underway for the organisation of tractor production at the Mamin and Kolomna factories.[80] In 1919–20 'Bol'shevik' built some 25 75 hp 'Holt' caterpillar tractors, but most of these went to the army rather than agriculture.[81] Soviet agriculture was then beginning to gain experience of tractor use. In October 1920 it was estimated that there were 1,500–2,000 tractors in the country, of which only 600 were in working order.[82] By this time the prospects for the wide-scale use of tractors in agriculture had been transformed by the appearance in 1917 of the light, small, universal Fordson model in the United States, which quickly entered mass production. Before 1917 tractors had generally been heavy and slow, with oil engines, and had been built in small quantities at a high unit cost.

The real development of tractor building in the USSR dates from 1923. In April STO approved a plan prepared by Gosplan according to which output was to increase from 694 units in 1923/24 to 3,400 units in 1925/26. Production was to be organised at existing factories, predominantly on a small-batch basis. While initially foreign models were to be made, work was also to proceed on the creation of original designs.[83] In the period 1923–6 tractor production was organised at several machine-building enterprises. At the 'Vozrozhdenie' factory in the Saratov region Mamin pursued his efforts to create a viable original design. The 12 hp 'Karlik' was built in 1924, followed by the 16 hp 'Gnom'. These were low-powered machines and not very successful: only 10 tractors were built between 1924 and the end of 1926.[84] Continuity with the past was also a feature of work at a factory in Kikchas, where before the war an original design for a wheeled tractor had been created. By the early 1920s the 'Zaporozhets' was in production, but in 1923 manufacture was transferred to the 'Krasnyi Progress' factory in Bol'shoi Tokmak. In 1924/25 159 'Zaporozhets' were built, and in 1925/26 282, but work ceased in 1927.[85] The Kolomna works also built tractors, at first the 'Mogul' and then an original design, the 'Kolomenets'. Between 1923 and 1926, when it ceased tractor building, 203 were built. In 1925 the Bryansk works also built the 'Kolomenets', making 25 units. Another producer was the Leningrad 'Bol'shevik' works, which made caterpillar tractors, mainly of the 'Holt' type. It is likely that many of the 75 tractors it built between 1924 and 1927 went to the military.

By the end of 1927 there were effectively only two tractor enterprises, the Khar'kov locomotive factory, making caterpillar tractors, and the Leningrad 'Krasnyi Putilovets' building the 20 hp Fordson. The former organised a tractor shop in 1923, part of the equipment coming from the Warsaw machine-tool factory of 'Herlach and Pulst', evacuated to Khar'kov during the war. From 1924 it built the 50 hp 'Kommunar', used mainly by the army. Production remained on a modest scale throughout the period, rising from 43 units in 1924/25 to 103 in 1926/27.[86] At the Leningrad factory the first Fordson copy was built in 1924. Here the larger scale of production permitted the use of more modern production methods, with elements of conveyor assembly and interchangeable parts manufacture. Production grew from 73 tractors in 1924/25 to 404 in 1925/26, 623 in 1926/27 and 1,115 in 1927/28.[87] The factory was visited by a delegation from the American Ford company in April 1926. It reported that 'the machine tools often seemed to be modern, the layout logical, but production lagged in an atmosphere of dirt, workers' committees, laziness, and poor supervision'.[88] Total Soviet tractor production in 1926/27 amounted to only 918 units. Imports were substantial; the Ford company was the principal supplier. In 1925 Ford exports to the Soviet Union peaked at 10,515 units between 1922 and the end of 1926 Ford supplied a total of 19,755 tractors.[89]

By the end of 1927 the Soviet Union had succeeded in establishing an embryonic tractor industry, but the scale of production was quite inadequate to meet the country's needs. The tractors built were of dated design, often of low quality and of very high unit cost. However, by this time the decision had been taken to build a new, specialised factory at Stalingrad with a capacity (later raised) of 10,000 tractors a year.

Bicycles and motorcycles   In the Soviet period bicycle production first was organised at a factory in Khar'kov, which made 2,200 units in 1924.[90] In 1925/26 output reached 4,263 units, rising to 7,495 in 1926/27.[91] By international standards this was a very small scale of production, Britain, for example, manufactured 725,000 in 1928. True mass production was not organised until the end of the first five-year plan period when the Moscow and Penza bicycle factories entered service.

Motor cycle building was not resumed during the first decade following the Revolution. The first Soviet prototype, the 'Izh-1' of the Izhevsk machine-building works, did not appear until 1929, and batch production of motor cycles was not organised until the second five-year plan.[92]

Optical equipment   Soon after the revolution the new optical-mechanical factory in Petrograd (known as GOZ, later GOMZ) began to work on the creation of ciné equipment, at first making a batch of Pathé projectors and then, in the second half of 1918, a projector of original design, the 'Rus'.[93] GOI, which had been founded in the same year, played a major role in consolidating the young optical industry. In 1923 the Petrograd factory of optical glass (later LENZOS) resumed production using the Chance process, but great difficulties were encountered in making defect-free glass. In the process of overcoming these problems a new smelting process was devised and put into operation in the summer of 1926. It is claimed that the import of optical glass ceased in 1927.[94] At the beginning of 1925 GOZ and a number of small optical workshops were united to form a trust of the optical-mechanical industry, TOMP, under the control of Vesenkha. At GOZ the production of ciné projectors expanded and new original models were created, including the 'GOZ' mobile unit and the 'TOMP-4' stationary model.[95] In 1925 a repair workshop in Odessa began making Pathé-type ciné projectors.[96] Total Soviet production of ciné projectors in 1927/28 reached 3,115 units, which must be considered a creditable achievement.[97] However, the production of cameras had still not been mastered. In 1925 there was an attempt to create a camera at GOZ, but only a prototype was made. Three years later the factory created the 'Fotokor' plate-type camera, but batch production did not begin until 1930. Batch production of binoculars began at GOZ in 1927. The scale of output was extremely modest: only 125 were made in 1928/29.[98]

Sewing machines   In the case of sewing machines, the new regime inherited in the Singer works a factory very well-equipped for precision mass production,[99] but was faced with the task of making domestically the items previously imported. This import substitution was achieved by the beginning of the first five-year plan.[100] In general, the Podolsk mechanical factory, as it became known, appears to have served as a valuable school of experience of modern, precision, production methods. The output of sewing machines increased steadily from 52,400 units in 1924/25 to 275,300 units in 1927/28.[101] The pre-war peak was almost attained in 1928/29, when output reached 425,241 units.[102] The Podolsk factory remains today the principal producer of domestic sewing machines.

Timepieces   After the Revolution, production resumed in 1922 when the Moscow 'Aviapribor' factory began to make simple, cheap, wall clocks and alarm clocks assembled from imported parts. In 1924 capacity expanded when the 'Nov'' (former Reinin) works was merged with 'Aviapribor'.[103] Production reached 500,000 units in 1925/26, rising to 950,000 units in 1928.[104] In December 1927 STO decided to build a new factory for the production of 1 million pocket watches and other timepieces per year. In the event, the equipment of two American factories was purchased to create in 1930 the 1st and 2nd Moscow timepiece factories, making pocket watches and alarm clocks respectively. Wrist watches were not produced until the late 1930s.

Bearings (see n. 47)   During the civil war production of bearings ceased, but in 1921 negotiations began for the conclusion of a concession agreement with SKF. This eventually became operational in the spring of 1923. The Swedish company took over its old factory and resumed the making of ball and roller bearings. Production rose from 4,000 units in 1923 to 25,000 in 1925, 56,000 in 1926 and 76,000 in 1927. By the end of 1928 SKF employed 700 workers and 20 Swedish technical specialists at the bearings factory and a foundry in Moscow. This scale of production was extremely small and quite inadequate to meet the rapidly growing needs of Soviet industry. It was not until 1929 that Vesenkha decided to build a large new works (GPZ-1) with a capacity initially set in May 1929 at 11.3 million units per year. The SKF concession was terminated in 1931 and the old Moscow factory became GPZ-2. Soviet writers acknowledge that the SKF concession made a useful contribution to the development of the engineering industry.

Machine tools   During the civil war machine-tool building virtually ceased. Two of the first enterprises to resume production were the former 'Felzer' works, now at Nizhnii-Novgorod and renamed 'Dvigatel' Revolyutsii', and the Moscow 'Bromley' factory, renamed 'Krasnyi Proletarii' in 1922. The 'Phoenix' works was moth-balled until 1925, when it resumed as the 'Sverdlov' machine-tool factory. Given the spare capacity in the engineering industry and the stocks of equipment imported during the war but not installed, it is not surprising that machine-tool building was given little official attention during the early years of NEP. It was not until the end of 1925 that the revival gathered pace. In March 1926 a Section of Machine-Tool Building was created under the Convention of Syndicates of the Metal Industry. It had limited powers, but helped to raise awareness of the importance of machine tools and initiated a process of rationalisation. At this time the number of producers was beginning to rise, but each factory built a wide range of different models, usually of dated design, making it difficult to employ modern production methods. The models built were mainly copies of foreign designs dating from before the 1920s. New enterprises included the Odessa 'Lenin' factory, the 'TsK Mashinostroeniya' in Samara, and the 'Samotochka' works in Moscow. Only the latter had previous experience; it built machine tools during the war as the 'Yu. Shtolle' factory. There was also some machine-tool building at enterprises of the armaments industry, including the Tula and Izhevsk plants.

In 1925/26 1,122 units of metal working equipment were produced, rising to 1,873 in 1926/27. It is doubtful whether the peak pre-revolution output was attained even in 1927/28. According to one source, 1927/28 output in terms of pre-war rubles amounted to 4.8 million rubles.[105] The claim by Rozenfel'd and Klimenko that treble the pre-war output was produced in 1926/27 is simply not credible.[106] In 1927/28 domestic production met only 19 per cent of total sales, the same proportion as in 1912. It was not until 1929 that a specialised trust, 'Stankotrest', was created and machine-tool building began to receive high priority.

CONCLUSIONS

1. In the case of the development of scientific research, the 'standard story' of both Western and Soviet literature has been to contrast the neglect of the tsarist period with the immediate steps taken to foster science under the Soviet government. The evidence which we have surveyed here suggests that the standard story generally stands up to scrutiny and that, in the case of R&D, the NEP years were not years of recovery but years of expansion.

2. However, it is also clear that there are considerable gaps in our knowledge which prevent a full comparison of the R&D effort in the two periods. In particular, we have at present little information on the size of the R&D activities of Tsarist industry, both before and during the first world war. Some writers in discussing particular fields make some reference to the extent of industrial scientific activity.[107] Our survey of scientific periodicals turned up three publications submitted from Russian industrial organisations: two were by the chief chemist at the Putilov plant; the other, on cellulose, originated in the Prokhorov Trekhgornaya textile mill in Moscow.[108] The standard story considers that such bits and pieces of information are a good reflection of a general lack of activity. This conclusion has not been based on solid detailed research into the activities of pre-revolutionary industrial companies and enterprises. However, our review of high-technology engineering points to a heavy reliance on foreign expertise, although the domestic Russian capability should not be understated, especially in the aircraft industry.

3. There does not appear to have been a vast brain drain of Russian engineers after the revolution. On the other hand, virtually all foreign engineers probably departed.

4. In the engineering branches which we have considered the results of a comparison of 1916 with 1927 are not in general very impressive in terms of either output or technological level, especially if account is taken of developments in the West during the first post-revolutionary decade. The best performance was achieved in the aircraft industry. Here there does appear to have been a clearly recognised priority and a coherent development strategy. But the same cannot really be said of

the motor and tractor industries, and certainly not of machine-tool building. In the case of the less important precision items, the pace of development was modest, although there were worthwhile achievements, including import substitution in the manufacture of sewing machines and the mastery of the production of optical glass. However, it is surprising that Soviet industry was unable to make cameras, motorcycles and most types of modern machine tools ten years after the revolution. It is difficult to avoid the conclusion that in the advanced technology sectors of the engineering industry the country fell even further behind the West during the first decade of Soviet power than it had been in the immediate pre-revolutionary period.

5. This brief review indicates the vital importance of developments in Russia during the first world war and the inadequacy of comparisons restricted to the pre-war years. Consumer-related activities suffered during the war, but the aircraft, motor, machine-tool, bearings and optical industries underwent further technological development and expanded their production capacities. The Soviet aircraft and motor industries were founded on the new facilities created during the war and, in general, war-time production provided valuable experience of precision, large-scale manufacture.

6. During the 1920s Soviet comparisons with the pre-revolutionary achievement were usually based on output data referring to the pre-war years, and the principal source of statistics appears to have been the Ministry of Trade and Industry's compilation *Fabrichnozavodskaya promyshlennost' evropeiskoi Rossii*. But more recent Soviet works based on archival research present higher estimates of the output of some high technology products, in particular aircraft and motor vehicles (see p. 193 above and n. 14 below). It would not be surprising if this also applied to other items. The output statistics used in the 1920s were gathered by the Ministry directly from the producer enterprises as part of a review of customs duties. It would be understandable if firms in new, high-technology sectors understated their volumes of production in order to retain or increase tariff protection from imports. This question requires additional research.

7. During the 1920s the scarcity of appropriate skills resulting from the loss of foreign expertise was clearly a major problem hindering the development of advanced sectors of the engineering industry. In this context the creation of central research institutes – TsAGI, NAMI and GOI – must be considered a farsighted policy. It is interesting that in the case of the machine-tool industry, which lagged particularly severely during the period, an equivalent institute was not created until 1931. The bearings industry was exceptional in maintaining foreign expertise through a concessions agreement.

8. The Bolsheviks came to power as a party committed to the radical

transformation of backward Russia. During the 1920s advanced technology, and the machine in particular, were acclaimed as the principal instrument for modernisation. In view of this commitment, the formidable obstacles notwithstanding, it is surprising how cautious and incoherent was the practical development of the high-technology engineering industries during the first ten years of the new regime. Meanwhile, in the capitalist world these industries experienced rapid technological change and underwent substantial expansion in terms of output. The gulf between the vision and the practical achievement, and the widening gap between the latter and the reality in the West, help to explain why a policy of rapid industrialisation gained increasing support from the mid-1920s.

11 Foreign Trade
M. R. Dohan

After examining the important role of the foreign sector in the pre-1914 economy, we trace its destruction during the first world war, the revolution and civil war and then describe the unsuccessful foreign struggle to restore trade during NEP.[1] As NEP proceeded, it became clear that the role and conduct of foreign trade would differ radically from its pre-1914 model.

The many quantitative comparisons of foreign trade in the pre-1914 Russian economy and in the Soviet economy in the 1920s presented here point to dramatic changes, yet stand mute as to the underlying reasons for the failure of the foreign sector during the NEP. Three questions are considered in this chapter. First, what was the relationship between the foreign sector and the domestic economy and how did they change over the period? Secondly, were the foreign trade crisis and associated economic disequilibria in 1927/28 the result of policy mistakes that could have been corrected? Or, thirdly, had the transition from tsarism to Soviet NEP caused fundamental changes in the economic, political and social structures which were to prevent both the recovery of foreign trade to pre-1914 levels and, in turn, the resumption of industrialisation within the institutional framework of the NEP?[2]

RUSSIAN FOREIGN TRADE AND ECONOMIC GROWTH, 1900–13

Overview

The pre-1914 Russian economy was still predominantly agricultural yet it had a large and rapidly growing industrial sector.[3] Exports were largely derived from the agricultural base; imports met the rapidly expanding needs of the industrial sector and the growing middle class. In the period 1900–13 Russian exports and imports grew at about 6 per cent per year; imports increased rather steadily, but exports, closely tied to the grain harvest, grew only in fits and starts (see Table 55). These growth rates were somewhat more rapid than national income, and considerably more rapid than agricultural output. Russia's principal trading partner was Germany, followed by England and France, but by 1913 her principal source of foreign capital had shifted from Germany to France. An effective if somewhat ad hoc combination of tariff, monetary and economic policies nursed exports, curbed imports, attracted foreign loans and direct investment, balanced the foreign account and subsidised investment in industry.[4]

The Russian balance of trade was usually favourable in the two decades before 1914. During 1909–13 exports averaged 1,500 and imports 1,133 million rubles; the trade surplus, while quite volatile, averaged 367 million rubles or about 25 per cent of exports (see Table 55).[5] Interest payments on foreign debt, and remission of profits together averaged about 345 million rubles per year during 1909–13. These payments, together with tourism and other 'invisible' items, caused a deficit on 'current account' which was offset by a combination of long-term borrowing from abroad by the government and of foreign private investment.[6] After a devaluation in 1895 and careful manoeuvring by Witte on international financial markets, gold convertibility of the ruble was finally achieved in 1897,[7] which led to increased foreign capital inflow into the Russian economy.[8] Import demand continued to be curtailed by high protective tariffs and by directly subsidising domestic producers of some imports. This suggests that despite the 1895 devaluation, the pre-1914 gold ruble was overvalued. These high import tariffs, especially those levied on consumer goods and fibres, also provided a major source of government revenue for tsarist fiscal policy.[9]

During the pre-1914 decade foreign capital continued to flow into Russia to finance investment in industry, mining, railways, and other infrastructure as well as for loans to the government. It is difficult to assess, however, the actual contribution of foreign capital in providing additional real resources to the economy in general. Based on the structure of the balance of payments during the period, foreign capital was probably less important than has been generally assumed, so that domestic investment, estimated to be about 11 per cent of NNP in 1913, had to be based on domestic saving.[10] There is no doubt, however, that the foreign sector taken as a whole (exports, imports, tariff revenues, capital flows and capital investment) was an important mechanism in converting domestic resources into investment in the tsarist economy.

Tsarist Exports and Economic Growth

Russian economic growth during 1900–13 could not be categorised as 'export-led'. On the contrary, the tsarist ministers were continually looking for ways to stimulate exports.[11] In retrospect, the growth of Russian exports in the pre-1914 period appears to have depended on a precariously balanced system of peasant taxes and debt repayments, fiscal policies and government measures, such as favourable railway tariffs and even export subsidies, deliberately crafted to support the marketing and export of grain and other agricultural products via a private market mechanism.

The composition of Russian exports during 1909–1913 shown in Table 56 reveals the reliance of exports on agriculture. Including furs, fish and sugar, 76 per cent of exports in 1909–13 originated in the agricultural sector.[12] Grain (including oilseed and oil cake) made up nearly 50 per cent, flax 5.7, butter 4.2, eggs 5.1, and sugar 2.7 per cent of total exports. Most of the remaining non-agricultural exports were derived from her natural resources and included timber (9.6 per cent), oil (2.5), and mining (1.6 per cent).

It has been estimated that the ratio of exports to GNP in 1913 was only 8 to 10 per cent.[13] The export–output ratio for grain and related products was only 12 per cent. Export–output ratios were much higher for many products, however, and in 1913 amounted to 68 per cent for flax, 55 for butter, 34 for eggs, 58 for timber, 96 for manganese ore, 49 for asbestos ore, but only 11 per cent for oil.[14]

Russian exports basically depended on the exportable surplus of a relatively poor agricultural sector so that the ratio of marketing to output (*tovarnost'*) became a critical determinant in the growth of agricultural exports. In the pre-1914 period a disproportionately large share of marketed output came from estates and larger farms, which suggests that unequal distribution of land ownership and differentiation of income was a key social institution in the market supply of agricultural goods and hence to exports (see Chapters 3 and 6).

Growing export demand played an important role in the development of the market production for certain goods, such as flax, butter and eggs, and even barley and wheat, and large portions of marketed output were exported in the pre-1914 decade.[15] During this period, however, agricultural output grew more rapidly than exports and was increasingly produced for the growing domestic markets.[16] Grain output in particular (with the exception of barley) failed to keep pace with growing domestic demand so that the growth rate of exportable grain surpluses slowed. Thus, even though grain exports grew during this period, the share of grain exports as a fraction of grain output (*eksportnost'*) declined.[17] As a result, relatively small fluctuations in the harvest caused disproportionately large fluctuations in grain exports and, in turn, caused major balance of payments problems.[18]

Foreign capital played a relatively small role in producing exports, although often foreign merchants worked within Russia buying agricultural goods, such as flax, butter, eggs, and sugar.[19] Some non-agricultural exports – e.g. manganese ore, asbestos, oil, platinum and timber – were produced partly or largely by foreign companies.[20]

Russian exports of flax, furs, platinum and manganese ore held major shares of the world market, so that world prices for these products were sensitive to the volume of Russian exports. Such products, however, comprised only 8 per cent of total exports during 1909–13. The Russian oil industry, once the world's largest exporter of oil, had stagnated after the 1905 revolution and played a minor role in world markets by 1913.

Relatively little capital, domestic or foreign, was invested in producing exclusively for exports and the role of 'export' industries in the economy as a whole was equally small.[21] The output of most major Russian industries, such as metals, metal-working and textiles, was used almost entirely in domestic markets, and, in turn, most domestic and foreign capital was invested in sectors for producing output used domestically or in the infrastructure (especially railways and housing). Despite the view of Soviet economists such as Lyashchenko,[22] pre-1914 Russian industrial-isation cannot be fitted into either an 'export-enclave' or an 'export-led' model.[23] On the contrary, exporters of grain, animal products, and timber and most other products had to compete directly with growing domestic consumption in the decade before the first world war.

Import Dependence and Import Substitution

Russian imports during 1909–13 were dominated by industrial materials and fuels (42 per cent), foodstuffs (20) including large amounts of herring and tea, and manufactured consumers' goods (22); equipment constituted only about 15 per cent of imports (see Table 58).

The composition of Russian imports evolved continuously over the three decades prior to 1913 as domestic production replaced or supplemented imports of one good after another. This process of import substitution was particularly dramatic for cotton fibre, copper, steel, cloth and many types of machinery. Russia even became a net exporter of some products formerly imported including cotton cloth, sugar, oil, and linen cloth.[24] This process of import substitution and export promotion was actively fostered by the government through tariff protection, government orders, location of railways and the railway rate structure, and export premiums.[25]

The import-dependence, as measured by import-consumption ratios, varied from good to good in 1909–13 and reflected not only resource endowments and economies of scale but also the relative scarcity of skilled craftsmen, designers and managers. Like most industrial economies, Russia depended entirely on imports for so-called 'non-competing' goods: rubber, jute, copra, tea, coffee, tin, nickel and aluminium in 1909–13. More importantly, Russian industry and especially the rapidly growing consumer goods industries relied heavily on imports for cotton fibre (45 per cent of total supply), wool fibre (33 per cent), leather, dyes, tanning materials, paper (60 per cent), zinc (59 per cent), lead (97 per cent), ferro-alloys, and to a lesser extent, coal, copper (20 per cent) and several chemicals.[26] On the other hand, by 1913 domestic industry supplied all or most of the domestic demand for iron and steel, many basic industrial chemicals, sugar and most manufactured consumer products.

Thus, even though 42 per cent of imports were consumer goods, they accounted for only a small portion of total consumer spending. Most manufactured consumer products and foodstuffs consumed by urban workers and peasants were produced domestically. Only tea and herrings, which made up 7 per cent of total imports in 1909–13, figured at all in the budgets of the general population. The remaining consumer goods imports in 1909–13, viewed as 'luxury goods' by Soviet writers, added diversity and quality to the consumer goods purchased primarily by the middle and upper urban classes. Even here, import substitution took place as the markets grew and the technology became better known (sewing machines).[27]

The Russian pattern of import dependence on machinery was very distinct. The large Russian machine-building industry, protected by tariffs and supported by government orders, supplied about one-half of the machinery installed in 1913, including a large part of the growing demand for agricultural, railroad and electrical equipment and a substantial portion of the textile and metal-working equipment.[28] These were often the simpler types, mass-produced with well-established technologies.

Russia basically relied on imports for recently developed products such as aeroplanes, tractors, cars and radios, for equipment to invest in the metallurgical, chemical and other new technologies developed in Western Europe and the United States, and for technologically complex equipment not yet demanded in large quantities such as large generators, printing equipment and precision tools.[29]

This distinctive pre-1914 Russian pattern of machinery production, however, did not reflect technological stagnation and backwardness. Rather it was an efficient use of Russia's resource endowment of the time and, in part, reflected normal economies of scale and expected lags in technology transfer. In the case of pre-1913 Russia, however, it also reflected a scarcity of skilled personnel, designers and entrepreneurs relative to other factors of production, a scarcity accentuated by the increased tempo of industrialisation in the period 1890–1913. The abundance of unskilled labour, capital and natural resources relative to skilled personnel gave Russia a comparative advantage in the mass-production of fairly standardised products, such as ploughs, small motors and simple lathes, and a comparative disadvantage in producing large generators, chemical equipment and other specialised products which were design- and management-intensive relative to the quantity produced.

To compensate for this scarcity, Russia imported both the scarce labour skills directly and the technologically complex machinery that embodied those skills. The scarce labour skills were supplied from abroad through the foreign ownership of industrial, mining and trading firms (e.g., Singer and International Harvester) and the widespread hiring of foreign engineers and managers by both Russian and foreign owners.[30] The pattern of machinery supply in the pre-1913 economy strongly economised on scarce skilled personnel by relying on domestic production for mass-produced and simple machinery and on imports for the technologically more complex machinery.[31] This pattern was reenforced by a tariff system that was biased in favour of high value-to-weight equipment and discouraged imports of simple and labour-intensive equipment.[32] As a result, the Russian machine-building industry developed quite rapidly in the pre-1914 period, adopting new technologies and producing new products as markets expanded, and often with the help of foreign capital and engineers (see Chapter 7).

Dependence of Russian industry on imports for materials and advanced machinery in 1909–13 was quite substantial, but, as Holzman noted, it was continuously evolving and resembled more the demands of a rapidly growing industrial economy requiring raw materials, diversified consumer goods and technologically advanced equipment rather than a backward, stagnant, agrarian economy.[33] Dependence on imports was merely the other side of the process of converting agricultural and natural resource surpluses into industrial materials and investment goods through foreign trade.

In sum, the foreign sector played important and multiple roles in the industrialisation process by supplying materials and machinery, technical personnel and managers, new technology and capital and by efficiently converting agricultural goods into industrial materials, machinery and consumer goods – roles that were all encouraged to varying degrees by government policy within a market framework. This was the 'model of growth and trade' that the new Soviet regime inherited.

THE FIRST WORLD WAR, THE REVOLUTION AND WAR COMMUNISM

Relative to other sectors of the economy, Russian foreign trade was devastated during 1914–20. The entire infrastructure of tsarist foreign trade including skilled personnel, trade treaties, tariff and trade policies, exchange rates, financial institutions, and a functioning market system, was swept away. The restoration of foreign trade, therefore, depended not only on the physical production of exports and the distribution of imports, but also on rebuilding this foreign trade infrastructure.

The First World War

During the first world war, the state gradually took control of foreign trade to assure the supply of materials to the war effort. Increasing amounts of armaments and materials for the war industry were imported, so initially imports fell only slightly. Exports, however, collapsed after 1914, as export territories were lost, output diverted to war production, ports blockaded, and transportation disrupted. Russia, moreover, was at war with its major trading partner, Germany. Trade treaties were denounced, German traders expelled, businesses confiscated. This struck particularly hard at export sectors, such as flax, where German firms played a major role.

The balance of trade shifted from a surplus of 146 million rubles in 1913 to a deficit of 1,873 million rubles in 1916 and Russian foreign debt rose to 13,800 million rubles, almost double the foreign debt in 1913.

Revolution and Civil War

The revolution, civil war and war communism completed the destruction of the commercial and financial networks and institutions that had supported foreign commerce. The remaining foreign personnel fled, the merchant middle class was dispersed, and private banks and private enterprises (including foreign-owned enterprises) were nationalised.

Tsarist debts were repudiated in January 1918. Foreign trade was regarded as one of the 'commanding heights' of the economy, and a state monopoly of foreign trade was proclaimed in April 1918 in order to gain control over export receipts and imports. In reaction to the Soviet signing of the Brest-Litovsk Treaty with Germany, however, the Supreme Allied Council established a *de facto* economic blockade. Russian foreign trade slowed to a virtual standstill by the end of 1918.

Repudiation of the tsarist debt, establishment of the state monopoly of foreign trade, and nationalisation of foreign enterprises, while often defended in ideological terms, were in fact largely pragmatic responses to economic and political crises.[34] For example, after the collapse of exports, the Soviet regime was not able to service the huge tsarist debt (debt service was approximately 345 million rubles per year during 1909–13 and was much higher by 1918 due to the war debt).

Regardless of the reasons, these Soviet actions, clothed in revolutionary rhetoric, seemed to confirm the worst fears of the capitalist nations, so that the indirect economic and political impact of these actions was devastating. The Allies responded by supporting anti-Soviet forces in the civil war. The 1918 Allied embargo on Soviet trade was tightened in July 1919 and Russian assets abroad were seized.[35] As a result, foreign trade ceased and many industries exhausted their supply of raw materials or fell into disrepair for the lack of spare parts,[36] and the flow of foreign technology and modern equipment into Russia halted. The mechanism of industrialisation and modernisation of tsarist Russia had been shattered. Overcoming the economic, military and technological vulnerability inherent in an economy dependent on foreign trade was to become a major pillar in Soviet economic policy.

RECOVERY

In order to understand the momentous changes in foreign trade by 1927/28, it is important to look at the year-by-year difficulties encountered by the Soviet authorities as they attempted to restore foreign trade between 1921 and 1925/26. For these persistent difficulties gradually led to an abandonment of the initial policies and premises for restoring foreign trade in NEP. The data for foreign trade, volume and price indices and related matters are relatively complete for this period and are presented in Tables 56–61.[37] Comparisons of Soviet foreign trade during NEP with tsarist Russia are not adjusted for territorial losses; this is not too inaccurate for total trade volume because the pre-1913 inter-regional trade of tsarist Russia with the separated areas would be measured as 'foreign trade' in any adjustment; it is less accurate for individual goods (see Appendix Note).

The Initial NEP Model of Foreign Trade

Once NEP was launched, early efforts to rebuild Soviet foreign trade drew heavily on the pre-1914 model as did many other aspects of Soviet economic policy. Domestic and foreign trade were to be stimulated and guided by market forces and prices, exports were to be 'commercially profitable', trade surpluses would be earned and the ruble would be reestablished on international money exchanges.[38] Foreign investment and technology were to be attracted by offering 'concessions' for investment by foreign capital.[39] The early plans to restore exports, shown in Table 60, relied heavily on the pre-1914 experience with its dependency on agriculture and especially grain. Imports, with one important exception, were dictated by the import dependencies inherited from the tsarist economy.

The administration of foreign trade, as one of the 'commanding heights' of the economy, however, differed greatly from the tsarist model which had relied on indirect controls and the market mechanism. Due to the initial shortages of foreign reserves and to domestic inflation, foreign trade was, and had to be, tightly controlled. The monopoly of foreign trade restricted the right to import and export to a limited number of firms and agencies specialising in foreign trade including *gostorg*, cooperatives and mixed domestic-foreign companies. These agencies were intended to operate under the close supervision of Narkomvneshtorg (People's Commissariat of Foreign Trade) according to foreign trade plans drawn up to meet specific policy objectives (see Table 60). In practice, control over these agencies was incomplete and foreign trade agencies often worked at cross purposes with one another and with agencies supplying goods to the domestic markets. As a consequence, the foreign trade apparatus went through numerous reorganisations during NEP to strengthen control and to increase coordination with domestic market needs; these culminated in the 1925 merger of Narkomvneshtorg into Narkomtorg (People's Commissariat of Trade), the commissariat responsible for internal trade.

Initial Measures to Restore Foreign Trade

Intensive efforts were made to rebuild the foreign trade infrastructure in the early 1920s under the leadership of Leonid Krasin.[40] The Allied blockade was lifted in July 1920 and a number of trade and other treaties were signed (in particular with Germany and then Great Britain) between 1920 and 1924. The USSR succeeded in establishing Soviet trade personnel abroad in a variety of institutions from official trade delegations to Soviet-owned stock companies and cooperatives; these in part replaced the private domestic and foreign firms so prominent in pre-1914 trade.[41] Anti-Soviet trade sanctions almost disappeared by 1924 and Soviet exports, which consisted mainly of raw materials and other bulk commodities, found fairly easy access into old markets. As Lenin had predicted, few capitalist nations hesitated to trade with the Bolsheviks. Germany, Britain and other countries even began to grant short-term trade credits.

Poor Recovery of Foreign Trade

The recovery of foreign trade lagged far behind the rest of the economy, as the following figures show (1913 price weights, data approximate):[42]

	Agricultural output	Industrial output	Exports	Imports
1913	100.0	100.0	100.0	100.0
1920	–	14.6	0.1	2.1
1921/22	50.6	21.6	4.1	19.7
1922/23	70.3	32.3	8.8	10.8
1923/24	73.8	44.6	24.5	17.0
1924/25	73.9	72.0	24.4	30.7

In 1921/22 exports were negligible, but food, raw materials and railroad equipment were imported and paid for by depleting the inherited gold stock from 1,292 million rubles to less than 300 million rubles by January 1, 1923 (see Table 55). In 1922/23 foreign trade was more carefully planned and controlled. Imports were sharply trimmed; export increased and a modest trade surplus was achieved for trade across European borders (see Table 60). But trade remained low relative to 1913 levels and lagged far behind the rest of the economy.

In 1923/24 an ambitious foreign trade plan was 'successfully fulfilled' (see Table 60). Export volume almost tripled and imports increased nearly 70 per cent. Exports were 'commercially profitable'.[43] The large trade surplus of 94 million rubles resulted in the only balance of payments surplus during the entire period; this permitted the import of gold, silver and coinage to support Sokolnikov's controversial monetary policy and the 1924 currency reform which brought about temporary currency stability and limited convertibility of the ruble.[44] Foreign reserves, the cornerstone of these policies, rose to 445–540 million rubles by October 1, 1924, the highest point during the NEP (see Table 55). Foreign reserves, it was argued, were crucial both to internal monetary reform and for reestablishing the convertibility of the ruble.

The sudden surge in exports was due to the astonishing increase in grain exports, just two years after a severe famine, and seemed to hold out the promise of restoring Soviet exports along tsarist lines. This initial success in exporting grain had a major influence on foreign trade planning, particularly in drawing up the over-optimistic 'First Perspective Plan for Foreign Trade 1923/24–1927/28', prepared in Gosplan in late 1924, and the ambitious annual foreign trade plans for 1924/25 and 25/26 (see Table 60).[45]

In 1923/24 70 per cent of imports consisted of raw materials, mostly for light industry, the output of which was limited by insufficient raw materials rather than capacity or demand. Despite the stated policy of 'limited goods intervention' to hold down domestic prices, few consumer goods were actually imported. With spare capacity still available in most industries, little machinery was imported. Even with this rapid growth foreign trade lagged far behind industry and agriculture.

In 1924/25 foreign trade suffered a major setback due to the poor harvest. Export revenue rose a modest 7 per cent and actually fell in volume. Grain exports ceased between October 1924 and June 1925. Expenditures on imports, however, were increased by 64 per cent to combat the growing 'goods famine'. More raw materials were supplied to light industry and, for the first time, modest quantities of goods were imported for a 'goods intervention' in the countryside in time for the harvest.[46] In addition, in the spring of 1925, emergency grain imports, amounting to 15 per cent of total imports, were made in order to slow the rapid inflation of bread prices in cities and grain deficit areas.[47] The USSR was a net grain importer in 1924/25! The resulting trade deficit of 165 million rubles, huge relative to foreign reserves and export revenues, was covered partly by German credits and partly by reexporting gold imported the previous year as part of the currency reform (see Table 55).[48]

The year 1925/26 promised to be an excellent year for foreign trade, but ended in crisis. With the prospect of an outstanding harvest, planners initially projected a 115 per cent increase in exports, a 40 per cent increase in imports and a trade surplus of 190 million rubles (see Table 60). Output, investment and internal trade plans incorporated these import quotas and were in the process of being implemented.[49] But in early autumn 1925 a rapid inflation in grain procurement prices coupled with other problems forced a sudden and sharp reduction in grain exports and hence in the entire export plan. This in turn forced a reduction in the import plan and in the output and investment plans dependent on these imports. This downward revision, undertaken by the Politburo itself, was completed only after the XIV party congress in December 1925. The export plan was cut 35 per cent, imports by 32 per cent and the trade surplus set at only 35 million rubles.[50] Output plans for both light and heavy industry were reduced, together with investment and capital repair plans.[51] Even with these reduced plans, the supply of some industrial materials ran out and by September 1926 several 'above-quota import plans' were approved to prevent industries from shutting down for the summer due to the lack of raw materials.[52] The scenario of cutting back industrial output plans because of raw material shortages recurred frequently over the next few years.

Overall, exports grew by only 21 per cent in 1925/26; the original grain export plan was only 40 per cent fulfilled and the value of some major agricultural and timber exports actually fell (see Table 56). Imports, while much less than originally planned, actually grew 5 per cent. As a result, the trade surplus of 35 million rubles projected in the revised plan turned into a trade deficit of 80 million rubles (see Table 55). The prospects of restoring foreign trade in the NEP seemed much more gloomy than two years previously.

Abandonment of the NEP Model of Foreign Trade

In 1926/27 planners abandoned their use of pre-1914 marketing and export ratios and drew up a conservative foreign trade plan (see Table 60), based on a moderately good harvest and the need to supply raw materials to industry.[53] Implementation of the plan was strictly supervised. Exports rose 17 per cent to 779 million rubles on the basis of modest grain exports and better prices. Imports in particular were tightly controlled. The policy of importing consumer goods for the 'goods intervention' was ended, and raw materials and machinery imports were increased sharply.[54] Wool, cotton and hides alone accounted for 31 per cent of total imports in 1926/27; nevertheless, the material shortages persisted. Overall, imports were reduced 5 per cent to 714 million rubles and a 66 million ruble trade surplus was achieved. Despite 'successful plan fulfilment', foreign trade still lagged far behind the other sectors (see Tables 60 and 61) and was increasingly unable to meet the accelerating demands of industrialisation for materials and machinery.

Events in the autumn of 1927 could only reinforce that pessimism. The 1927 grain harvest had been poor and the worsening procurement crisis threatened grain exports which had been the basis for export expansion in the previous two years. The problem was compounded by sharp price increases for imported raw materials (especially cotton), and in September 1927 it appeared that the USSR's real import capacity might collapse.[55] The 1927/28 export plan, however, was kept close to 1926/27 levels, but imports were to be increased because of the machinery purchased with German credits and the price increases for raw materials. For the third year in a row, shortages of (imported) raw materials were projected as limiting the growth of light industry in 1927/28. This contributed to the goods famine, which in turn was believed to be partly responsible for reducing grain marketing and grain exports. And, coming full circle, the lack of exports limited the imports of raw materials. Many Soviet planners believed that the economy was at an impasse.[56] As Zalkind concluded:

> The basic cause for these deficits [of goods] consists in a scarcity of raw materials for these fields. The increase in the price of foreign raw materials, and also the impossibility of increasing the allotment [of foreign exchange] for the purchase of foreign raw materials do not give the possibility to develop to the necessary degree those fields of light industry working on imported raw materials: cotton cloth, wool, leather.[57]

The grain marketing problem turned out to be worse than anticipated and grain exports completely collapsed. Nevertheless, total exports in 1927/28 were basically unchanged from the previous year. To cope with this export crisis, the government made a major shift in export policy and non-grain exports were 'forced' regardless of commercial profitability and in spite of growing domestic shortages.[58]

Despite the problems with exports, imports rose by 33 per cent to 946 million rubles. Import prices were higher, imports of raw materials for industry were greater than planned, machinery imports were increased, financed largely by German credits, and in the July–September quarter of 1928, grain was imported on an emergency basis. (For the second time in four years, the USSR had become a net grain importer in terms of value, see Tables 56 and 58.)[59] As predicted, shortages of materials, both domestic and imported, again curtailed the growth of light industry, and slowed the newly undertaken expansion of heavy industry.[60] [61]

The resulting foreign trade deficit was 168 million rubles and the deficit in the balance of payments was estimated to be as much as 247 million rubles (see Table 55). About 155 million rubles of gold and platinum had to be exported and the foreign exchange reserves were reduced to about 330 million rubles, their lowest point since 1923 (Table 55). The balance was financed by short-term credits, and Soviet foreign debt rose to 370 million rubles.

In 1927/28 foreign trade was clearly one of the weakest sectors in the economy (see Table 61). By 1927/28 exports had reached only about 32 per cent and imports about 47 per cent of 1913 levels measured in 1913 prices.[62] In contrast to its role in the tsarist period, the continual problems in the foreign trade sector had hindered the recovery of the NEP and now threatened to stall further industrialisation of the USSR by limiting imports of machinery and materials.

What had changed?

A COMPARATIVE SUMMARY: 1913 VERSUS 1926/27 AND 1927/28

In 1926/27 and 1927/28 the role of the foreign sector in the growth of the economy differed greatly from the pre-1914 tsarist model.

Similarities

There were some continuities. The tsarist distribution of trade between countries reemerged; Germany quickly regained its preeminent position with Britain in second place.. Traditional tsarist exports continued under NEP, though the composition had shifted sharply away from grain toward oil, timber and furs. The composition of imports resembled the pre-1914 pattern simply because the industrial structure inherited from the tsarist period needed the same materials. (The major pre-war imports of manufactured consumer goods and foodstuffs, however, had been virtually eliminated due to the shortage of foreign exchange earnings.) The pre-1914 policy of import substitution was also accelerated, especially for cotton fibre, dyes, tea, paper, ferro-alloys, machinery, and even non-ferrous metals. Although export and import prices were higher, the overall commodity terms of trade were more or less the same as in 1913, except that export prices of furs were much higher, and oil much lower, while the import prices of cotton was much higher. Perhaps the most important continuity, at least until the mid-1920s, was the perception by many Soviet officials that the tsarist experience with foreign trade was still highly relevant to Soviet planning and policy.

By 1927/28, however, the tsarist model of conducting foreign trade on the basis of a modified market mechanism by and large had been abandoned. Why?

Failure of the Export Mechanism

The export structure had changed markedly between 1913 and 1927/28. Grain exports were negligible, crop exports in general were much less important and oil and sugar, furs and cotton cloth had become relatively more important (see Table 56). These changes in the export structure were mostly due to relative changes in volume and not to shifts in relative price structures (with the exception of furs) (see Tables 57 and 61).[63] The most important factor in the decline in exports was the inability to obtain sufficient 'exportable surpluses' of grain and other agricultural products. The failure of grain exports to recover during NEP was devastating. Grain exports, which accounted for almost 50 per cent of tsarist exports, reached only 25 per cent of 1913 levels in 1926/27 and 5 per cent in 1927/28. Other agricultural exports also failed to recover and reached only 25 per cent of 1913 levels in 1926/27 and 29 per cent in 1927/28. Even these modest levels were achieved only by forcing exports in the face of growing domestic shortages. The direct causes of this export failure were the lower marketing–output ratios (*tovarnost'*) in the 1920s and the greater domestic demand for exportable products, such as eggs, butter, flax, timber and grain, due to rising urban wages, higher rural incomes, and increased investment. As a result, overall export–output ratios (*exportnost'*) were far below the pre-1914 levels. Gross grain exports were 15 per cent of output in 1909–13 (average), 3 per cent in 1926/27 and less than 1 per cent in 1927/28. The equivalent figures for flax products were 68 per cent in 1913 and 18 per cent in 1927/28, and for manufactured butter about 55 per cent of all marketing in 1913 and only 16 per cent in 1927/28.[64]

The causes for the decline in agricultural marketing and in grain marketing in particular are complex and still not completely clear (see Chapters 5 and 6). Some were permanently rooted in the revolution and Bolshevik ideology. The estates and large farms which had figured prominently in pre-war agricultural marketing had been eliminated and the Bolshevik leaders had basic antipathy toward the relying on markets and the restoration of peasant capitalism in the countryside. Other causes for the diminished marketings, such as the flawed price and fiscal policies, could have been remedied.

For example, attempts to purchase sufficient products from the peasants for export often contributed to inflationary pressures in agriculture (as in the autumn of 1925) or distorted agricultural prices (such as the increased prices of animal products relative to grain in the autumn of 1927). As a prominent Soviet economist wrote at the time:

> success in the livestock groups has turned out to be not entirely favourable for stimulating the sale of grain products, thanks to a significantly increased break [in prices] between the livestock group and grains. The producer preferred to sell animal products before grain products and he sold them in such quantities, which, because of the total receipts, gave him the possibility to retain part of the grain for himself.[65]

Whatever the reasons for diminished export–output ratios, NEP agriculture clearly could not serve as the basis for restoring foreign trade and

industrialisation along the tsarist lines without resolving the related problems of agricultural marketing and the rural goods famine. By 1927 it was
stated that the 'future growth of exports requires a complete reconstruction
of the export fields of the economy', including the abandonment of the
pre-1914 reliance on grain exports.[66] Industrial exports, less dependent on
the harvest, were stressed.[67]

The major so-called 'industrial' exports of the tsarist period – timber, oil,
sugar, ores and cotton cloth – had become more important and together
equalled 31 per cent of exports in 1926/27. Further export growth, however, was not hopeful. Except for oil and furs, the traditional 'industrial
exports' had also failed to regain 1913 levels by 1927/28 (see Tables 57 and
61). Timber exports reached only 40 per cent of 1913 levels because lagging
output failed to keep up with the rapid rise in domestic demand from
higher rural incomes and growing industrial investment.[68] Manganese ore,
mined mostly under a concession agreement by Harriman, faced limited
foreign demand and increased competition on foreign markets.[69] Sugar
was basically an agricultural product and suffered its attendant problems.
Cotton cloth required agricultural inputs or imported fibre and was already
in short supply domestically.[70]

Fur exports were the unexpected success story of the NEP and equalled
15 per cent of all exports in 1927/28 because both export quantities and
prices were much higher than in 1913. Further growth of fur exports,
however, was limited by the supply. Only oil held out the promise of
expanded exports as output greatly outstripped domestic demand. Oil
exports in 1927/28 amounted to 14 per cent of all exports and the volume
exceeded 1913 exports by 150 per cent as the investment in the oil industry
in the early and mid-1920s yielded increased output which was marketed
aggressively abroad.

By 1927/28 attempts to increase exports of some products had required
some price cutting to regain traditional market shares, but basically, export
markets were not a significant barrier to expanding Soviet exports (with the
noted exception of manganese ore, perhaps oil, and several minor exports). In general, the supply of exports remained the fundamental problem for the NEP economy, and planners had few grounds for predicting
any rapid solution of this problem. Even in the midst of the grain marketing crisis of 1927/28, desperate Soviet planners felt compelled to base the
expansion of exports for the first five-year plan on the resumption of
large-scale grain exports.[71]

Import Shortages

The allocation of import capacity was the subject of continual debate
during NEP. After two years of limited 'goods intervention', imports of

consumer goods were abruptly ended as being a less effective use of foreign exchange than importing raw materials directly for light industry.[72] Imports of most foodstuffs and manufactured consumer goods, which had made up almost 20 and 22 per cent of imports respectively in the pre-1914 period were cut back and by 1927/28, this 'industrialisation (*industrializatsiya*)' of imports was almost total. Imports of food in 1927/28, even with the emergency grain imports, were about 12 per cent of all imports, and only 19 per cent of 1913 levels, while manufactured consumer goods were reduced to only 3 per cent of imports and equalled just 10 per cent of 1913 levels (see Tables 58, 59 and 61).

Machinery imports climbed steadily after 1925 and equalled 27 per cent of imports in 1927/28 in contrast to 15 per cent in 1913. Since total imports were lower, the volume of machinery imports was still 20–40 per cent less than in 1913 and imports supplied 30–40 per cent of machinery installed in industry (including the electric power industry). The distinctive pre-1914 pattern of dependency on machinery imports reemerged and, as before the war, agricultural and railway equipment was supplied mostly from domestic production. Machinery imports were usually financed by credits, so that, in the short run, increased imports of some types of machinery did not compete directly with other imports.[73]

The pre-1914 dependence of industry on imported materials quickly reemerged during NEP, and imports grew throughout the NEP, increased sharply in 1926/27 and were not cut back significantly in 1927/28 despite the export crisis. In 1927/28 imports of cotton fibre wool and hides were still about 20–40 per cent below 1913 levels. Imported cotton fibre, some 16–20 per cent of imports, supplied 45 per cent of total cotton fibre requirements in 1926/27 and 41 per cent in 1927/28. Wool fibre, about 7 per cent of imports, supplied 51 per cent of marketed supply in 1926/27 and 47 per cent in 1927/28. Nevertheless, shortages of imported industrial materials plagued light industry throughout NEP, and toward the end of the period even affected the metal-working industries. Imports of some non-ferrous metals actually exceeded the 1913 levels as early as 1926/27, but shortages, particularly of copper, were noted both in 1926/27 and 1927/28. The growing conflict between consumption and increased investment was starkly reflected in the foreign trade sector, where scarce import capacity had to be allocated either to raw materials for the consumer goods industries or to metals and other materials for the metal-working and other capital goods industries.

Shortages of (imported) raw materials, not equipment capacity or labour, restricted the growth of the consumer goods and eventually the machine-building industries. The policy of import substitution, therefore, received even higher priority in the 1920s than before the war and the pre-1914 expansion of cotton, copper, lead and zinc production resumed.[74]

The most successful example during the NEP was the paper industry; by 1926/27 output exceeded 1913 levels and paper imports were actually reduced.

Trade Deficits and Foreign Debt

In place of the regular large trade surpluses of the pre-1914 decade, the USSR had small favourable trade balances in only three years, 1922/23, 1923/24 and 1926/27, and these were offset by much larger trade deficits in 1921/22, 1924/25, 1925/26 and 1927/28. The cumulative trade deficit for 1923/24 – 1927/28 was about 260 million rubles.[75] Even though the USSR was no longer burdened with the heavy costs of servicing the pre-1914 foreign debt and investment, or with tourist expenditures abroad, net 'invisibles' expenditures abroad were still significant.[76] This payments deficit was financed partly by exporting precious metals, some from domestic production, but mostly through short-term credits. Foreign exchange reserves had been depleted from 1,292 million rubles in 1913 to just 300 million rubles on January 1, 1923; they rose briefly to about 450 million rubles in the mid-1920s, and then fell back to about 313–330 million rubles by the end of 1928 (see Table 55). To finance the balance, Soviet foreign debt increased from 78 million rubles in 1923/24 to 370 million rubles on January 1, 1929 (see Table 55).[77]

The long-term international capital markets remained inaccessible during the NEP, and, despite a policy of concessions, direct foreign investment did not return. This is not surprising in light of the repudiation of the tsarist debt, recent nationalisation and the overt hostility of some if not all Bolsheviks to 'capitalism' and especially 'international capitalism'.[78] But by 1927/28 the USSR had succeeded in obtaining substantial short- and intermediate-term foreign credits, especially from Germany and England, especially for importing machinery. These short-term debts, however, made an immediate claim on Soviet export revenues and created pressure to renew the credits under costly terms with the same trading partner, so that by the end of 1928 this newly acquired debt was already becoming burdensome.

The Tsarist Versus the Soviet Model

By 1927/28 exports were no longer based on commercial profitability and open market purchases, tariffs played no significant role in either limiting imports or providing revenue, and the Soviet attempt to restore the convertibility of the ruble on foreign exchanges had been abandoned.

The ruble, probably overvalued in 1913, became even more overvalued relative to other currencies during 1925–7 (see Table 61). Soviet agricultural wholesale prices rose from 138 (1913=100) in 1923/24 to 169 in 1925/26, industrial wholesale prices were 210 in 1923/24, dropped to 177 in 1924/25, but rose again to about 200 in 1925–7. In 1927/28 an index of market prices would have been even higher in the absence of price controls (see below). German wholesale prices, on the other hand, remained around 133–140 throughout this period. Prices of Soviet exports fell from 170 in 1924/25 to 144 in 1926/27, while import prices declined even more. This rise in domestic relative to foreign prices had two effects. First, in July 1926 the USSR completely abandoned a rather abortive attempt to reestablish the convertibility of the ruble on foreign exchanges. Secondly, after 1925 the export of timber and many agricultural products became increasingly unprofitable from the viewpoint of the Soviet export agencies.[79]

Price Policy and Export Profitability
At the beginning of NEP most Soviet planners believed that world prices – converted at the official exchange rate – should set the upper limit to domestic prices, particularly in the case of imported and exported products bought by state agencies.[80] When falling world prices and rising domestic agricultural prices made many exports unprofitable in terms of the official exchange rate in 1925/26, Soviet exports were continued. Soviet trade officials, however, were concerned about losses on exports and tried to reduce the official purchase prices for butter, eggs and flax in 1926 because of the decline in foreign prices.[81] This concern, together with fear of renewed inflation and support for the classical concept of the gold standard, put considerable pressure on Soviet officials to hold down prices in general and agricultural prices in particular in the mid-1920s.[82]

During this period Soviet agricultural procurement price policy was in temporary disarray; state prices offered to the peasants were lowered, then raised, as officials were caught between trying to reduce prices to restrain inflation and maintain export profitability on one hand and encourage sowing and marketing by raising procurement prices on the other. Sowing and marketing were apparently quite sensitive to relative prices between grain and other agricultural products.[83] The idea of export profitability lingered on; as late as mid-1927 Soviet officials noted favourably that lower domestic prices and higher foreign prices had restored commercial profitability to grain exports.[84]

Perhaps the most important economic policy change after 1926 was that, in an attempt to control inflation, the government increasingly tried to set procurement prices and official retail prices at lower than the market clearing levels. This policy not only aggravated the goods famine for specific goods, but also increased the general disequilibria in consumer markets at the macro-level (repressed inflation) by leaving more currency in the hands of the populace. It also caused major distortions in the relative price structure at the micro-level and, as seen above, mismanagement of relative prices in late 1927 contributed to the grain marketing crisis of 1927/28.

By late 1927 the retail and wholesale price structures had been frozen at below market-clearing prices. Stable prices, even if only nominal prices, had become a symbol of political success, and the role of prices in resource allocation diminished rapidly as the government allowed the dichotomy between private traders' prices (market-clearing prices) and the official state and cooperative prices to grow. Confronted with growing excess demand for all products, the government failed to respond with indirect fiscal measures such as higher taxes or higher official wholesale prices. Instead it restricted and eventually eliminated the private trader and continued the policy of setting both low procurement purchase prices (of grain) and the retail prices of consumer goods. In the case of grain, deliveries fell and in the case of consumer goods, the shelves were emptied even more quickly. This misguided price policy was a fundamental error and reflected a lack of understanding of the functioning of a market system.

By 1927/28 the concept of commercial profitability of exports had been abandoned; exports of most products were forced by allocating export quotas among domestic firms and trade agencies which were supposed to fulfil these plans regardless of the relationship between domestic and foreign prices, and in spite of great excess demand at home. Under tsarism marketing by peasants and exports by producers and traders were private responses to market prices and profit incentives carefully crafted by state policy; increasingly in 1927/28 the Soviet government relied on a rather crude mechanism of state procurement of output by state agencies at a fixed set of prices and allocated to internal use and exports by government decisions. The essence of the market mechanism had been abandoned.

Tariffs and the Conduct of Foreign Trade

In the tsarist model, goods were imported by numerous independent domestic and foreign firms operating within a market system with a high tariff structure. As noted above, import tariffs performed three crucial functions in tsarist industrialisation policy: protection of individual industries, raising tax revenue from the populace and managing the overall demand for imports.

From the very beginning, the NEP apparatus for the conduct of foreign trade – namely the monopoly of foreign trade with its system of administrative allocation and licensing – was fundamentally different from either the tsarist market mechanism or the NEP internal market mechanism. Trade was conducted only by a few firms which operated under an import–export plan, import permits and tight currency controls; this system effectively protected domestic industry and restricted imports (but not the demand for imports). This, combined with the prevailing ideological view that import tariffs were regressive and added unnecessarily to costs, acted together to keep import tariffs relatively low during most of NEP. The policy of low import tariffs, however, meant foregoing two major macroeconomic benefits of the tsarist tariff policy – raising tax revenues and reducing internal demand for imports. Higher tariffs would have helped to reduce excess aggregate demand in the mid-1920s and to force domestic firms to recognise the high real cost of imports. In 1927 tariffs were finally raised sharply on numerous imports to try to reduce the requests for imports from domestic firms and to transfer import profits to the government.[85] But new tariff policy was too little and ineffective. Although Soviet prices had increased relative to world prices, making the Soviet ruble greatly overvalued, the new 1927 tariff policy failed for a more profound reason. Namely, by 1927/28 the NEP market system, with its reliance on prices, market incentives, and economic management through fiscal and monetary policies, was being abandoned. Producers were pressured to meet output targets rather than to cover costs, and the demand for materials and goods was rising rapidly due to the increased levels of investment and to the inflationary wage and fiscal policies adopted by the Soviet leadership towards the end of 1927. As a result, the price mechanism was rapidly losing its ability to ration and allocate goods. In such circumstances, higher tariffs could do little to restrain the growing demand for imported raw materials and consumer goods.

Weakened Mechanism for Technology Transfer
While the first world war accelerated some technology transfer into Russia, the subsequent events of 1917–20 had completely destroyed the traditional mechanisms for transferring technology. Even after trade resumed, machinery imports were insignificant until 1925. Thus, in a period when Western industrial economies were rapidly expanding the output of new products such as tractors, vehicles, electrical equipment and chemicals, the Soviet economy was still struggling to restore the production of a pre-1914 product mix using for the most part pre-1914 technology and an ageing stock of equipment.[86] As a result, the pre-1914 technology gap between Russia and the West widened dramatically between 1913 and 1924 and created a new urgency to modernise the Soviet economy.

During 1923–5 the Soviet government increased its efforts to attract foreign firms to invest in the USSR through the controversial policy of 'concessions'. It failed, however, to attract any significant foreign investment, in part because of the basic ideological mismatch of foreign capital with Bolshevik ideology and policies.[87] By 1927/28 the concessions policy had begun to evolve into the distinctly Soviet mechanism of transferring technology through the direct purchase of technical assistance including foreign designs and foreign-built factories, the direct hiring of foreign engineers and technicians, and the import of modern equipment both for production use and as a prototype to be copied for domestic production. The tsarist mechanism for the transfer of technology (but not capital) had been partly replaced and the efficient pattern of machinery imports restored.

CONCLUSIONS

By 1927/28 the role of the foreign sector in the national economy had diminished greatly in comparison to the pre-1914 economy. The years 1926/27 and 1927/28 are often cited as years when Soviet domestic output reached 1913 levels of the tsarist economy. This was certainly not true for foreign trade. The material shortages, grain marketing crisis, the lack of exportable surpluses and the goods famine in the countryside all pointed to fundamental disequilibria in the NEP economy of 1927/28.

The Soviet attempt to restore the functioning of the foreign sector, a fundamental part of pre-1914 economy, had failed and only a few elements of the tsarist model remained. The tsarist policy of import substitution was accelerated. Foreign technicians and technology had been reintroduced into the economy. The pre-1914 patterns of raw material and machinery imports and of agricultural, timber and oil exports reemerged (with the notable exception of grain exports and consumer good imports). Trade was resumed with traditional partners, Germany and England.

For the most part, however, the essential components of the tsarist model had been discarded. The market export mechanism, once guided by prices and commercial profitability, gave way to administrative forcing of exports. Grain exports, once the mainstay of tsarist export policy, were negligible in 1927/28, and agricultural exports were still far below pre-1914 levels. Tariff policy failed to control the demand for imports and contributed little to state revenues and fiscal policy. Repeated import shortages hindered the growth of industrial output. The balance of payments ran frequent deficits, gold reserves fell, and short-term debt began to accumulate. Conventional monetary policy was abandoned and the ruble became completely inconvertible. Concessions failed to attract direct foreign investment, and long-term capital markets remained closed to the Soviets. In sum, the once intimate relationship between the world economy and the Russian economy had ended.

The failure to restore the foreign sector of the economy, however, was not by intent or neglect, but rather resulted from both a series of domestic policy errors and, more importantly, from fundamental changes in the economic institutions, economic policy and political ideology, particularly those that affected agriculture and marketing and, in turn, exports. The problems in the export sectors cascaded over into the rest of the foreign sector and the economy as a whole, and hastened abandonment not only of the tsarist model of foreign trade but of the entire NEP experiment. The fundamental mechanism of the tsarist foreign sector, and hence, of Russian industrial growth, could not be put back together.

Appendix Note: Loss of Territory and Foreign Trade

The area of Latvia, Estonia, Lithuania, the 'Polish Provinces', and Bessarabia comprised only 2.3 per cent of land and 15 per cent of population, but contained a substantial industrial base (see Chapter 7).

These separated territories produced substantial agricultural output including barley (13.5 per cent of total output), rye (8.5), flax (19), eggs (14) and butter (22 per cent). The actual impact of this territorial loss on Soviet agricultural exports may have been larger, however, because these areas had become increasingly oriented toward export markets (particularly for flax, butter, eggs, barley and corn).

Soviet economists estimated that due to the loss of territories exports should be reduced by 11.1 per cent for 1909–13 and 14.5 per cent in 1913. Imports should be reduced by 26.7 per cent – much more than the adjustment for exports – due to large imports of coal, cotton, wool, dyes, rubber, etc. into the Polish and other Baltic industrial centres (see Troyanovskii *et al.* (eds), 1926, pp. 219–47; A. Mikoyan in Belen'skii *et al.*, 1928, pp. 17–18).

These estimates overstate the aggregate adjustment for territorial loss because the Soviet estimates considered only trade of the separated territories with foreign countries and did not consider the large inter-regional trade of the separated territories with the rest of Russia. *Ceteris paribus*, this inter-regional trade would become international trade with the new boundaries. As I indicated in earlier research, it is not clear that the overall volume of pre-1913 trade of the territory destined to become the USSR was significantly different than that of tsarist Russia; the separated regions were net importers of grain from the rest of Russia and exporters of manufactured products to the rest of Russia. The composition of trade of the new USSR would have been different, however, with more grain exports, less flax, butter and eggs and fewer imports of coal, cotton, etc. and greater imports of manufactured goods. This problem of inter-regional trade deserves further study and makes pre-1913 and NEP per capita comparisons of foreign trade tenuous. Unless otherwise stated, comparisons of tsarist foreign trade with NEP foreign trade are not adjusted for territorial change.

Similarly, when comparing per capita supply of various manufactured and agricultural products, such as cloth, allowances should be made for the 'export' of manufactured goods from the separated provinces to the rest of Russia. Omission understates 1913 per capita consumption in the USSR territory and hence would overstate the recovery of the per capita consumption of these goods during NEP (see Dohan, 1969, pp. 157–9).

Part V
The National Income

12 National Income
Paul R. Gregory

Comparisons of the Soviet economy of the late 1920s with the Russian economy on the eve of revolution shed light on the relative starting point of Soviet forced industrialisation and on structural and institutional differences between the late Russian and early Soviet economies. This chapter poses a simple question and explains why an exact answer is hard to obtain. The question is: How much more or less national output (national income) did the Soviet economy produce in 1928 than in 1913? The ratio of 1928 national income to that of 1913 is the broadest measure of the economic recovery of the NEP economy from revolution and civil war.

Earlier chapters in this book have focused attention on the separate branches of the economy which collectively supply the answer to this question. National income is the sum of the net outputs of the individual branches. The chapters on the individual branches – agriculture, industry, and transportation – volunteered judgements on the output of that branch during NEP relative to the pre-revolutionary period. This chapter takes a look at the whole. The two years chosen for comparing national income are 1928, the end of NEP (or alternatively the initial year of the five-year plan era) and 1913, the peak year of the tsarist period.

This chapter does not claim to provide a conclusive answer to the level of 1928 national income relative to 1913. Rather, it seeks to define a feasible range. It can only provide a range for a number of reasons. First, we are dealing with historical data from a remote time period. Secondly, the break in economic and political institutions caused by the revolution means that we are dealing with data gathered by different statistical agencies with different methods, interests, and goals. Thirdly, national income estimates, even under the best of circumstances, have unknown but possibly substantial margins of error. For these reasons, it would be foolhardy to expect to pinpoint with great accuracy the starting point of Soviet industrialisation. It may well be that any attempt to determine relative 1928: 1913 Russian national income is doomed from the start because margins of error swamp any 'true' differential. Speaking in favour of the effort to narrow the range of uncertainty is the fact that the 1920s was a period of fertile data collection both by government agencies and research institutes in the Soviet Union. Competent statisticians worked in the statistical apparatus, and many carried over experience from the tsarist period. Moreover, economists outside the Soviet Union have worked extensively with both the pre-revolutionary data and the 1920s data to provide independent estimates relevant to this study.

Determining the starting point of Soviet industrialisation is important for a number of reasons. If the Soviet industrialisation drive began well prior to recovery to pre-war levels, some of the rapid growth of the 1930s should be attributed to the higher rates of growth associated with the recovery process. Ultimately, the starting point of Soviet industrialisation is more important in evaluating the successes or failures of the early five-year plan era than in assessing long-term Soviet economic performance. Since 1928 we have observed more than a half century of Soviet economic growth. Whether the Soviet Union began its industrialisation drive slightly above or below pre-war levels would not change any long-term assessment of Soviet growth. Perhaps the main reason for interest in the relative starting point is that the monumental decisions of the late 1920s in favour of forced industrialisation and collectivisation were based to some extent on contemporary assessments of the NEP recovery.

THE OFFICIAL SOVIET ESTIMATES

This chapter uses the various estimates of Russian and Soviet national income to evaluate relative 1928: 1913 national income. The 'official' Soviet series linking 1913 national income to the 1920s serves as our reference point. Is the picture of recovery presented by the official Soviet series an accurate depiction of reality? The 1920s was a period of eventful statistical activity in the Soviet Union. Soviet statisticians set up an apparatus for gathering national economic statistics. They did innovative work on national economic balances, and they began work on the first national economic plans. This statistical work included national income comparisons with the pre-revolutionary period. Gosplan statisticians linked major components of national income such as agricultural, industrial and transportation output to pre-revolutionary levels, and they also experimented with calculating national income by social categories of income earners.

It was during the late 1920s that the 'official' Soviet estimates of Soviet 1928 national income relative to 1913 national income were prepared for Gosplan by Strumilin, Nikitskii, and Kats. The definitive statement of this estimate appears in the control figures for 1928/29 which were published in 1929.[1] The Gosplan calculation uses the marxist material product concept which omits many services and uses Prokopovich's calculation as its starting point for estimating 1913 national income.[2] Although Gosplan described its national income figures as only crude estimates at the time, the figures from 1929 continue to be cited without amendment by Soviet statistical handbooks to the present day.

The Gosplan estimate declares that the economic recovery from revolution and civil war was complete by the mid-1920s and that the five-year plans began from a national income well above the pre-revolutionary peak in 1913. *The official figures place 1928 Soviet national income 19 per cent above 1913 and per capita income 9 per cent above 1913.* According to the official figures, the Soviet economy regained the pre-war national income level by 1926 and pre-war per capita income by 1927. This represents a remarkable recovery because official Soviet statistics place 1920 national income at 40 per cent of the 1913 level.[3]

Subsequent research has focused on the main finding of the official Soviet estimates of relative 1928: 1913 national income; namely, that the recovery of national income to the pre-revolutionary peak was completed by 1926. Research on this matter has taken place almost entirely outside the Soviet Union. Once the Soviet authorities settled on the 'official' Gosplan figures, research on this subject ceased in the Soviet Union for all practical purposes.

POTENTIAL ERRORS IN THE OFFICIAL SOVIET ESTIMATES

The official series calculated the ratio of 1928 to 1913 national income by converting 1928 national income into constant prices of 1913 and then dividing by 1913 national income. Table 62 shows how Gosplan arrived at its result. The first row of Table 62 gives the Gosplan estimates of 1913 and 1928 national income in current prices. They are 14.5 milliard rubles for 1913 and 27.2 milliard rubles for 1928. In current prices, 1928 national income was 1.88 times 1913 national income. The second row gives the Gosplan estimates in constant 1913 prices. The 1913 figure is, of course, 14.5 milliard rubles and the 1928 figure in 1913 prices is 17.2 milliard rubles. The ratio of the 1928 figure in current to constant prices (27.2/17.2 = 1.58) is the implicit price deflator used by Gosplan to convert 1928 national income into the prices of 1913. This 1.58 deflator will play a prominent role in subsequent discussions. Gosplan's finding that 1928 national income was 119 per cent of 1913 can be arrived at either by taking the ratio of 1928 national income in constant 1913 prices to 1913 national income (17.2/14.5 = 1.19) or by taking the ratio of 1928 to 1913 national income in current prices (1.88) and dividing by the price deflator (1.58). Table 62 shows that errors in the official estimates can enter in three ways:

1. The 1913 figure can be wrong
2. The 1928 figure (in prevailing 1928 prices) can be wrong
3. The deflator used to convert 1928 national income into 1913 prices can be wrong.

Controversy Over Current Price Estimates

S. N. Prokopovich was a pioneer in studying the national income of tsarist

Russia. In fact, his estimate of the national income of the 50 European Russian provinces in 1913 (published in 1918) served as the basis for Gosplan's own calculation of 1913 national income.[4] In 1931, as an emigrant, Prokopovich published in England the first critical assessment of the official Gosplan figures. Prokopovich's main criticism was that Gosplan had overstated the degree of recovery by not adjusting for the considerable deterioration of product quality between 1913 and the 1920s. Prokopovich argued that this quality deterioration would not be reflected in the official industrial output statistics (these multiply the number of shoes in 1913 and 1928, for example, by the price of shoes in 1913 without adjusting for quality change). On the basis of scattered industry studies, Prokopovich concluded that product quality in industry in 1928 was some 20 per cent below that of 1913. A 20 per cent downward adjustment of industrial output yields a 5.5 per cent reduction in 1928 national income to 25.7 milliard rubles (Table 63, row 2). If one applies Gosplan's own implicit price deflator (1.58) to the Prokopovich figure, 1928 national income in 1913 prices (16.2 billion) drops to 112 per cent of 1913 from Gosplan's 119 per cent.

A second critic of the official series, M. E. Falkus, argues that Gosplan slightly underestimated 1913 Russian national income (for pre-1939 USSR territory).[5] Falkus finds that the original Prokopovich estimate for 1913 contained a number of figures that were averages for 1909–13 rather than 1913 figures. Although Gosplan apparently corrected for some of this averaging in its 1929 calculations, Falkus concludes that 1913 national income was 15.0 milliard, or 3.5 per cent above the Gosplan figure. Falkus's adjustment places 1928 national income at 115 per cent of 1913 versus the Gosplan 119 per cent (Table 63, row 3).

If one accepts both the Prokopovich and Falkus adjustments, 1928 national income would have been 108 per cent of 1913 versus Gosplan's 119 (Table 62, row 4). The two adjustments combined yield a 1928 national income 8 per cent above the pre-war peak and a per capita figure about equal to the pre-war peak. The basic Gosplan conclusion remains intact: the recovery of both national income and per capita income was complete by 1928.

Both Prokopovich and Falkus use the Gosplan estimates for 1913 and 1928 as their starting point.[6] In retrospect, one would imagine that it would have been very difficult for Gosplan economists to come up with conceptually comparable 1913 and 1928 national income figures in current prices. Property rights had charged; new ways of gathering statistics were being employed; and new types of market relations had developed. It would thus come as no surprise if Gosplan had missed the mark by a wide margin. For this reason, it is important to have estimates of 1913 and 1928 national income in current prices that are independent of the official Gosplan figures.

An unplanned by-product of my study of Russian national income was a calculation of relative 1928: 1913 national income.[7] Although my primary interest was Russian economic growth from 1885 to 1913, it appeared that it would be relatively easy to link 1913 and 1928 national income. I had deliberately patterned the pre-revolutionary accounts after Abram Bergson's study of Soviet national income beginning with the benchmark year 1928.[8] Both studies employed Western concepts of national income by the 'end-use' categories of consumption, investment, and government expenditure. Because of these common procedures, I anticipated that the 1913 and 1928 national income figures in current prices would be conceptually comparable. Whether this is indeed the case will be discussed below.

Table 64 compares the official Gosplan estimates of 1913 and 1928 national income in current prices (both in their original form and adjusted to conform to Western national income concepts) with Bergson's and mine. This comparison yields the rather startling conclusion that they are in remarkable agreement. The ruble figures are fairly close. The Gosplan ratios of 1928 to 1913 national income in current prices range from 1.88 to 1.87, while the Bergson–Gregory ratios range from 1.77 to 1.83 depending upon whether factor costs or market prices are used. Using the Gosplan implicit price deflator on the Bergson–Gregory figures yields a 1928: 1913 ratio of national income in constant 1913 prices of from 112 per cent to 116 per cent versus the Gosplan estimate of 119 per cent. The substitution of the Gregory–Bergson figures does not alter the basic Gosplan conclusion of a completed recovery prior to 1928. By the standards of historical statistics, the differences between these figures are not very significant.

Tables 62–4 show that the various estimates of 1913 and 1928 national income in current prices are in basic agreement. The adjustments called for by the alternate estimates are relatively minor, especially in view of the wide error ranges in historical statistics.

Controversy Over the Price Deflator

The agreement among the current-price estimates still does not rule out substantial errors in the official Gosplan estimates. If Gosplan used an incorrect price deflator, the official estimates could still be flawed. In fact, the most substantial controversy surrounding the official Gosplan estimates centres on the measurement of price inflation between 1913 and 1928.

The noted Soviet authority on national income, A. L. Vainshtein, argues in his 1969 monograph on Soviet national income that Gosplan grossly overstated 1928 national income (in 1913 prices) by understating the amount of price inflation between 1913 and 1928.[9] As shown in Table 62, Gosplan converted 1928 national income into 1913 prices using an implicit deflator of 1.58. As an authority on the history of Soviet prices,[10] Vainshtein felt that this deflator was much too low because the various price indices compiled during the 1920s by different organisations (including Gosplan) generally found much higher price increases. Vainshtein believed (on the basis of evidence presented in Table 66) that prices roughly doubled between 1913 and 1928. This leads to a striking conclusion: *if Gosplan had used a doubling of prices instead of a 58 per cent price increase, Gosplan would have calculated 1928 national income at 94 per cent of 1913 (instead of 119 per cent) and per capita income at 86 per cent of 1913 (instead of 109 per cent)*. This result is shown in Table 65, row 1. Because of this apparent deflation error, Vainshtein recommended a recalculation of the historical series.

Vainshtein's conclusion that Gosplan's 1929 calculation grossly over-stated the NEP recovery finds additional support in a study by Gosplan published in 1927. The national income figures cited in Gosplan's 1926/27 control figures show that 1926/27 planned national income and per capita income were respectively 20 and 25 per cent below 1913.[11] If one applies Gosplan's growth indices in its 1929 publication to these 1926/27 figures, 1928 national income would have been 92 per cent and per capita national income 83 per cent of 1913 (Table 65, row 2). These figures concur with Vainshtein's conclusion that the recovery was far from complete in 1928. Vainshtein and the control figures for 1926/27 agree closely that the major source of distortion in the official Gosplan figures is the understatement of the degree of price inflation between 1913 and 1928.

Vainshtein's criticism focuses attention on the key importance of price indices. Table 66 summarises the various price indices published during the 1920s. Gosplan, the Central Statistical Administration, the Kon''yunk-turnyi Institute, and the Supreme Council for the National Economy (Vesenkha) compiled price indices at the factory, wholesale and retail levels. By the late 1920s, the pattern of pricing had become quite complex, a fact that greatly complicates comparisons of 1928/1913 price levels. First, goods were changing hands in different markets at different prices. In the retail trade network, there were substantial differences among state, cooperative, and private market prices, with the highest prices being charged in private markets. Goods also sold for different prices in agricul-tural markets with state procurement agencies purchasing agricultural goods at lower prices than private dealers. The published retail price indices deal with multiple prices by averaging prices in the three types of markets according to market shares. The Central Statistical Adminis-tration 1928 retail price index, for example, stood at 177 (1913 = 100) for state trade, at 187 for cooperative trade, and at 272 for private trade, with a weighted index of 214 – implying an approximate 37 per cent share for private trade.

The growing administrative allocation of industrial goods in the late 1920s raises a second pricing problem. Prices received by factories were becoming increasingly arbitrary as were wholesale prices. By the late

1920s, the gaps between factory transfer prices, wholesale prices, and retail prices were rising. Producer prices were 62 per cent above 1913 in 1928; wholesale prices were 85 per cent above 1913; and retail prices (even including the artificially low prices in state outlets) were more than double 1913. These figures show that market linkages between producer, wholesale and retail prices had been disrupted by 1928 and that factory transfer prices of state-owned enterprises, especially, had increasingly come to serve an accounting function rather than an allocative function.

Vainshtein concluded that retail prices should be the standard for deflation.[12] Wholesale and factory transfer price indices captured trends in artificial accounting prices. The two published retail price indices showed prices at least doubling between 1913 and 1928, and this is the rationale for Vainshtein's choice of an implicit price deflator of 2.0.

The appropriate method of deflating 1928 national income is not to divide by one single price index, but rather to deflate each subcategory by an appropriate price index. As Table 66 shows, one has a broad range of choice of price indices relating 1913 to 1928. In my own research, I constructed two national income deflators to determine whether Gosplan arrived at the 'low' price deflator criticised by Vainshtein by systematically using the lowest available price deflators in each case.[13] For the 'best' deflator (Table 66), I selected from the published price indices the one that appeared to be most appropriate for the sub-category. For retail trade, for example, I used the Central Statistical Administration weighted index of retail prices in state, cooperative, and private markets. For farm consumption in kind, I used the Central Statistical Administration weighted index of retail agricultural prices. To calculate the 'lowest' deflator, I used the lowest published price deflators that I could find for each sub-category. For retail trade, for example, I used the index of retail prices in state stores only. If my 'low' national income price deflator duplicates the implicit deflator (1.58) used by Gosplan in its 1929 publication, then Vainshtein's mystery of the low deflator is resolved.

My experiment yielded the following results: The 'best' implicit price deflator turned out to be 1.96 (slightly below Vainshtein's suggested 2.0), and the 'lowest' deflator was 1.71 (about 8 per cent above the Gosplan implicit deflator). If we apply the 1.96 deflator for Gosplan's own figures, 1928 national income would be 93 per cent of 1913 national income and per capita income would be 85 per cent of 1913. If we apply the 'low' 1.72 deflator, 1928 national income would be 109 per cent of 1913, and per capita income would equal 1913. *It thus appears that the deliberate choice of the lowest possible price deflators explains why Gosplan found such a rapid recovery in its 1929 study. When more reasonable price deflators are used, one finds that the recovery was still not complete in 1928.*

Any results based upon the lowest price deflators are implausible because they, in effect, assume that all 1928 transactions took place in state-controlled markets. If one accepts the official current-price figures as accurate, then one must conclude that the recovery of national income was not yet complete in 1928 and that per capita income was still more than 10 per cent below the pre-war peak. If one accepts the lower alternate estimates in current prices cited in Tables 63 and 64, then one must conclude that 1928 national income was more than 10 per cent and per capita income 15 per cent below 1913.

More Criticism of the Current Price Estimates

The evidence presented in Tables 62–4 showed basic agreement among the competing estimates of national income in current prices (within a normal margin of error for historical statistics). The fact that the various estimates agree does not conclusively establish their credibility because they share the same basic statistical raw materials and they draw upon each other in a number of cases. R. W. Davies and S. G. Wheatcroft raise important questions about the conceptual comparability of the 1913 and 1928 figures in current prices.[14] In comparing individual real expenditure categories in 1913 and 1928, Davies and Wheatcroft are perplexed by the steep drop in real consumption of farm income in kind indicated by my figures (1928 = 57 per cent of 1913). Davies and Wheatcroft suggest that this result is caused by the failure to net out of retained farm income agricultural shipments to local villages from the 1913 figure. If Bergson's 1928 estimate nets out such shipments (and includes them properly in retail sales), my 1913 figure is too high and understates the NEP recovery.

The proper calculation of consumption of farm income in kind is incredibly complex for both conceptual and data reasons. For Russia in 1913, retained farm consumption is a major expenditure category accounting for almost one-third of net national product.[15] Dikhtyar finds that, although 82 per cent of the Russian population was rural in 1913, the volume of retail trade in rural areas accounted for only 28 per cent of total retail trade.[16] These figures suggest that most rural agricultural marketings do *not* show up in 1913 retail trade figures. As Davies and Wheatcroft point out, I estimated agricultural marketings in a way that would not capture deliveries by road to local markets. By understating total deliveries, the retained farm consumption (net output minus deliveries) would be overstated. This overstatement would be necessary, however, if the retail trade figures fail to capture transactions in local rural markets. As this discussion shows, it is crucial to know the extent retail trade captures transactions in rural markets, but this information remains beyond our grasp.

Retained farm income is inherently difficult to calculate for reasons noted above. It would be foolhardy to argue that my figures for 1913 are accurate or conceptually the same as Bergson's. Because of the difficulty of sorting out retail sales and retained farm income, it may be more reasonable to rely on total personal consumption rather than to compare individual components. Table 67 shows that total personal consumption in 1928 was 85 per cent of 1913 using market prices. It shows that retail sales in 1928 and 1913 were equal, providing some support for my suggestion that less rural sales found their way into retail sales in 1913 than in 1928. The decline to 85 per cent of 1913 of personal consumption appears more probable than the drop in retained farm consumption to 57 per cent appears in isolation. It may indeed be the case that the total consumption figures are more comparable than the individual components of consumption.

Let us consider the maximum amount by which the recovery rate could be raised by a different treatment of retained farm consumption. If one assumes that farm consumption in kind in 1928 was equal to 1913 while making no offsetting reductions in retail sales, 1928 national income would have been about 4 per cent greater than 1913 and per capita income would have been about 5 per cent below 1913 (using the 1.95 price deflator). I believe that such an adjustment well overstates the recovery because much off-farm consumption in kind fails to enter the retail trade figures in 1913.

The above discussion established that Gosplan used an unreasonably low price deflator to convert 1928 national income into 1913 prices and shows that there is basic agreement concerning the estimates of national income in current prices. If this were the end of the story, one could conclude that the official figures grossly overstate the recovery. Instead of being 19 per cent above 1913 as claimed by Gosplan, 1928 national income would have been 5 to 12 per cent below 1913. The story does not end here because we cannot be confident that the 1913 and 1928 current-price national income estimates (despite their basic agreement among themselves) are conceptually comparable. It is extremely difficult to calculate farm income in kind in a comparable manner for both 1913 and 1928. Yet if one set of estimates in current prices must be changed, then basically all estimates (including the official ones) must be changed.

Physical Production Series

We can draw on one additional source of information to shed light on the issue of the NEP recovery. Rather than estimating 1913 and 1928 national income in current prices and then applying a price deflator to 1928, we could alternately aggregate physical production series. Relatively little work has been devoted thus far to aggregating physical production series into a national income series. The following discussion presents only some preliminary evidence.

Other chapters in this volume have discussed the sector output indices. The most reliable physical output series are for agriculture and transportation because these sectors produce homogeneous products that can be tracked in physical terms over time. Yet even when products are homogeneous, such as in agriculture, great ingenuity and detective work are required to obtain reliable aggregated production series. Let us consider the various branch indices. In Wheatcroft's study of agricultural output (chapter 5 in the present volume), 1928 net agricultural output is given as 98 per cent of 1913. Westwood finds that the output of the transportation sector had recovered to 1913 levels by 1928 (see Chapter 9). Gatrell and Davies argue that construction in 1928 was 15 per cent below its 1913 peak and conclude that employment in trade in 1928 was probably less than in 1913, although the real volume of trade was about the same (see Chapter 7). Agriculture, transportation, construction, and trade, which accounted for 70 per cent of 1913 national income, had either just barely recovered their pre-war peak or were still slightly below that peak in 1928.

Large-scale and small-scale industry accounted for another 20 per cent of 1913 national income. Nutter, in a massive research effort, compiled an index of industrial production from available physical production series and concluded that 1928 industrial output was essentially the same as 1913.[17] It is difficult to gauge the reliability of the Nutter series because of the sparse data on small-scale industry in both 1913 and 1928 and because of the difficulty of dealing with heterogeneous products such as machinery. In this regard, we must recall Prokopovich's conclusion that there was a significant deterioration in the quality of industrial production between 1913 and 1928, which would not be captured by Nutter's physical production series. If one accepts Prokopovich's suggestion that a quality-deterioration adjustment is required, Nutter's series would show a decline in industrial output between 1913 and 1928.

If one adds Nutter's finding of a barely completed recovery of industrial output by 1928 to the other production series, *one must conclude from the available physical production series (that account for some 90 per cent of 1913 national income) that 1928 national income must have been approximately equal to 1913. There is no supporting evidence of a 1928 output level 19 per cent above 1913 as claimed by the official Gosplan figures. If one applies a quality-deterioration adjustment to industry, then 1928 national income would have still been slightly below 1913 and per capita income would have been less than 90 per cent of 1913.*

The alternate approach to estimating industrial production is to deflate the value of industrial output in 1928 into the prices of 1913 and then compare this figure with 1913 industrial output. Wheatcroft, Davies and Cooper conclude (after making some minor adjustments in the official data) that gross industrial production in 1928 was about 20 per cent higher than in 1913.[18] Upon reviewing this and other studies of Soviet industrial output statistics,[19] I find that students of 1928: 1913 industrial production indices must grapple with the very same problems and puzzles as the student of national income. It appears just as difficult to determine comparable 1913 and 1928 figures in current prices and then to find appropriate price deflators. For both 1913 and 1928, it is difficult to determine the value of output of small-scale (non-census) industries. For large-scale (census) industries, the value of output can be determined with greater precision, but it again appears that Soviet authorities used an unrealistically low price deflator (1.65) to convert 1928 industrial output into 1913 prices.[20] If we apply a more reasonable price deflator to Soviet industrial output (the 1.86 from Table 66), then one would have to conclude that 1928 industrial output was about 5 per cent above 1913. This result is close to the physical output series of Nutter.

These remarks confirm that a considerable sorting out still needs to be undertaken both for national income and for industrial production. The choice of price deflators, in both cases, appears to determine the outcome. This necessary 'sorting out' constitutes a heavy research agenda for the profession, which may require many years of work.

THE FEASIBLE RANGE

This chapter has reviewed the existing estimates of relative 1928: 1913 national income. It raises as many questions as it answers, but we are in a position to define a feasible range within which the 'true' figure falls. It is my conclusion that the official Soviet estimates showing 1928 national income at 19 per cent and per capita income at 9 per cent above 1913 can be dismissed as gross overstatements of the NEP recovery. They are based upon a 'low' implicit deflator that is not supported by contemporary price indices. The evidence points to a national income deflator of between 1.9 and 2.0. With basic agreement among the different estimates of 1913 and 1928 national income in current prices, a price deflator of this magnitude would yield a 1928 national income at best equal to 1913 and probably below 1913. The lower bound would be a 1928 national income 93 per cent of 1913, and this lower bound is supported not only by my study of national income but by Vainshtein and an earlier Gosplan calculation. In any case, 1928 per capita income would have been at least 10 per cent below 1913. The only way to reproduce the official Gosplan result (with a more reasonable deflator) would be to raise the estimate of 1928 national income in current prices substantially relative to 1913. If one current-price estimate is raised, then they basically all must be raised because of their internal agreement. The available physical production series point to a 1928 national income about equal to that of 1913. The physical production series support the proposition that, at best, 1928 national income was equal to that of 1913 with a substantial per capita gap still to be recovered.

Tables*

Table 1. The intelligentsia at the end of the XIX Century: Erman's estimates
(Russian Empire)

Sphere of employment				Number
Military				52471
Material production[a]				94000
Science, art, education, health				262654
State and economic administration				368441
State service			151345	
Central government		99549		
Ranked officials[b]	53096			
Office clerks	46453			
Local government		51796		
Private employment by				
capitalists and landowners			204623	
Private legal practice			12473	
Sub-totals	99549	151345	368441	
Total				777566

Source: Erman (1963), 162–7 (based on the 1897 Census).

Notes: [a] The figure of 94,000 for material production comprises 61,027 persons in occupations (such as engineers and technologists) which clearly involved primarily mental labour; plus a further 33,000 in categories (such as 'mechanics, technicians and machinists') where occupations involving physical and mental labour were not distinguished.
Erman estimated that about a quarter of the latter group was involved primarily in mental labour.
[b] Erman's figure of 53,096 ranked officials includes, in addition to the 42,034 in the administrative and judicial departments, 6,612 ranked officials in the surveying department, 390 diplomats and 4,070 courtiers: see *Obshchii svod*, ii (1905), 256. According to Zaionchkovskii, however, the court category in the census included occupations which were not equivalent to those of ranked civil servants: Zaionchkovskii (1978), 18.

* NB: metric tons are used throughout this volume.

Table 2. The intelligentsia, 1896–1911: Erman's estimates (Russian Empire)

	1896	1906	1911
Teachers[a]	91736	113118	153360
Medical workers		49798	63281
Doctors	13770	17096	21747
Fel'dshers[b]	30959	21670	27173
Midwives	9778	11032	14361
Postal-telegraph clerks	40931[c]	31809	39713

Source: Erman (1963), 169.

Notes: [a] 1896 figures are for all categories of teachers; 1906 and 1911, for primary school teachers only.
      [b] Figures for 1896 include apprentice pharmacists.
      [c] 1896 figures include postmen.

Table 3. Estimates of the occupational structure of the gainfully-occupied
population 1913–26 (USSR pre-1939 territory; thousands)

Branches of the economy and occupations	Gukhman's estimates		Census
			December
	1913	1924/25	1926
I. Agriculture			
1. Householders and family	52500	57100	70533*
2. Hired workers	3000	1500	1202
Total I	55500	58600	71735*
II. Industry			
1. Large-scale industry	2817	2110	2792
(a) Employers	41	1	2
(b) Hired workers	2776	2109	2790
2. Small artisan	3590	2114	1866*
(a) Householders and family	2730	1730	1565*
(b) Hired workers	860	384	301*
Total II	6407	4224	4658*
III. Construction			
(a) Householders and family	460	190	216*
(b) Hired workers	505	280	148*
Total III	965	470	364*
IV. Transport			
1. Railway	705	896	890
2. Water	135	103	
			403[a]
3. Local	315	230	
Total IV	1155	1229	1293[a]
V. Communications	72	90	—[a]
VI. Trade			
(a) Householders and family	1190	326	478
(b) Hired labour	510	490	678
Total VI	1700	816	1156
VII. Rentiers	820	54	—[a]
VIII. Army	1200	600	631
IX. Other	4661	3741	6383
Total	72480	69824	86220

Sources: 1913 and 1924/25: Gukhman (1926), 263.
    1926: *Vsesoyuznaya perepis'*, xxxiv (1930), 2.

Notes: [a] Figures for transport are divided into 'railway' and 'other'. No separate
    figures are provided for 'communications' or 'rentiers'.
    *Figures are *not* comparable with Gukhman's, see text, pp. 45–6.

Table 4. Employed persons in certain branches of the economy, 1913–28
(USSR pre-1939 territory; thousands)

Branch of the economy	1913	1924/25 (A)	1924/25 (B)	1925/26	1926 census	1926/27	1928
Agriculture	3000	1500	1797[a]	2008[a]	1202	2078[a]	2037[a] (1676)
Large-scale industry	2776	2109	2109	2678	2790	2839	3096
Small-scale industry	860	384	390	427	301	423	408
Construction	505[b]	280	287	426	148[b]	549	723
Transport	1555	1229	1058	1240	1293	1302	1270
Rail	705	896	806	962	890	1006	971
Water	135	103	86	99	}403	111	104
Other	315	230	166	179		185	195
Communications	72	90	82	94	—	95	95
Trade	510	490	374	471	678	515	532

Sources: 1913, 1924/25 (A) and 1926: see Table 3, figures for 'hired labour'.
1924/25 (B), 1925/26, 1926/27 and 1928: *Trud v SSSR* (1936), 10–11
(annual averages).

Notes: [a] Figures for agricultural employment in the *Trud v SSSR* series include
forestry and fishing. The figure in brackets for 1928 is for agriculture
only.
[b] Comparison unreliable.

Table 5. Estimates of hired labour in certain branches of the economy, 1913
(Russian Empire; thousands)

Branch of the economy	Gukhman estimate	Rashin estimate
Agriculture	4420	4500
Large-scale industry	3335	3350
Small-scale industry	1075	3000
Construction	615	1500
Rail transport	815	816
Water transport	160	500
Communications	92	91
Servants	1620	1550

Sources: Gukhman (1926), 251.
    Rashin (1958), 171.

Table 6. Rural households by horse ownership, 1888–1925

Working horses per household	Percentage of households				
	1888–91[a]	1900–5[a]	1912[a]	1922[b]	1925[b]
None	27.3	28.5	31.4	35.3	34.1
1	28.6	30.2	32.1	50.6	51.0
2	22.1	22.6	22.2	10.7	11.2
3	10.6	9.5	7.5	2.1	2.3
4 and more	11.4	9.2	6.8	1.3	1.4
Total	100.0	100.0	100.0	100.0	100.0

Sources: 1888–91 and 1900–5: Anfimov (1980), 152–3.
1912: Shanin (1972), 48.
1922 and 1925: Smirnov (1927), 36.

Notes: [a] Pre-war: refers to 48 provinces of European Russia.
[b] 1922 and 1925: RSFSR (without Kazakhstan) and Ukraine.

The table gives only a rough estimate of the trend. The data are not completely comparable because the territory covered changed.

Table 7.   Supply of agricultural machinery and implements, 1901–1926/27
(million rubles at prices of pre-war price-lists)

Total value of agricultural machinery sold		*Total value of agricultural machinery sold*	
1901	30.3	1914	94.9
1905	39.7	1916	12.6
1909	78.3	1923/24	20.6
1910	86.1	1924/25	71.9
1911	108.2	1925/26	117.8
1912	116.2	1926/27	123.3
1913	109.2		

Sources: 1901–1916: Anfimov (1962), 63.
          1923/24–1926/27: *Sotsialisticheskoe khozyaistvo*, no. 1, 1929, 18.

Note: Includes all imported and domestically produced agricultural machinery
          and implements.

Tables

Table 8. Distribution of agricultural land (without forests), 1917–27
(million hectares)

	1917	1927
Peasants	240.4	314.7
Privately owned[a]	} 105.7	–
State[b]		36.1
Church	2.6	–
Cities, institutions	7.0	4.9
Total	355.7	355.7

Source: Danilov in *Leninskii Dekret* (1979), 296.

Notes: The total agricultural land (including fields, meadows, pastures, garden plots) is given in *Statisticheskii spravochnik 1928* (1929), pp. 84–5, as 284.2 million hectares.
[a] Apparently including land owned privately by peasants.
[b] Public domain, Imperial estate.

Table 9. Share of the estates in sown area, number of horses and number of cows, by regions, 1916 (pre-1939 USSR territory)

Territory	Percentage of sown land	Percentage of number of horses	Percentage of number of cows
USSR	8.2	4.0	2.8
Territory of the USSR by republics			
RSFSR	5.3	2.7	2.2
Ukraine	18.5	10.7	6.5
Belorussia	10.1	5.8	5.9
Turkmenistan	0	0	0
Uzbekistan	3.2	0	0
Trans-Caucasus	5.3	4.8	2.8
Territory of the RSFSR by selected regions			
Crimean ASSR	25.3	13.5	11.1
Central Black-Earth	11.1	6.8	4.3
West	6.5	3.8	5.4
Central Industrial	6.5	4.8	3.7
Mid-Volga	7.3	4.6	3.2
Lower-Volga	6.8	3.8	2.7
North-Caucasus	5.7	7.3	5.3
Urals	0.7	0.9	0.7
North	0.6	0.4	0.3
Siberia	0	0	0

Sources: Percentage of sown land: Calculated from data in *Osnovnye elementy* (1930), 23–41.
Percentage of horses and cows: Calculated from data in *Osnovnye elementy* (1930), 90–107.

Table 10.   Distribution of horses and sown area between households, 1917–20 (per cent of rural households)

Households by sown area (hectares)	1917	1920	Households by number of working animals	1927	1920
Without sown area	10.6	4.7	none	29.0	27.6
0.1–2.17	30.4	47.9	1	49.2	63.6
2.18–4.35	30.1	31.6	2	17.0	7.9
4.36–10.89	25.2	15.3	3	3.4	0.7
more than 10.90	3.7	0.5	4 and more	1.4	0.2
Total	100.0	100.0		100.0	100.0

Source: Khryashcheva (1926), 82.

Note: These data are for 22 provinces of the RSFSR, mainly in the Black-Earth zone.

Table 11. Distribution of means of production by size of farm, 1900–5 and 1927 (per cent)

Strata by number of working horses per household (horses)	1900–5		Strata measured by value of means of production per household (rubles)	1927			
	Per cent of rural households	Per cent of total horses		Per cent of rural households	Per cent of total means of production	Per cent of total horses	Per cent of agricultural machines by value
Lenin's proposed grouping							
none or 1	58.7	19.7	0–400	52.4	20.6	30.8	4.0
2	22.6	29.4	401–800	30.8	34.6	38.1	22.7
3 and more	18.7	50.9	above 800	16.8	44.8	31.1	73.3
Total	100.0	100.0	Total	100.0	100.0	100.0	100.0
Usual grouping in the 1920s							
none	28.5	–	0–200	26.1	4.9	6.5	0.5
1–3	62.3	67.6	201–1600	70.7	79.0	86.0	68.7
4 and more	9.2	32.4	above 1600	3.2	16.1	7.5	30.8
Total	100.0	100.0	Total	100.0	100.0	100.0	100.0

Sources: 1900–5: calculated from data in Anfimov (1980), 152–3.
1927: calculated from data in Danilov (1957), 406; Danilov (1979(a)), 39.

Notes: Pre-war: 48 provinces of European Russia:
1927: territory of the USSR.

Table 12. Rural households without work animals, cows or sown area, by regions, 1926 (per cent)

Region of RSFSR or Republic	Number of households surveyed	Percentage of households		
		Without work animals	*Without cows*	*Without sown area*
Siberia	34 804	13.3	9.1	9.0
Non-Black-Earth zone				
North-East	27 886	32.4	8.5	2.9
North-West	47 522	25.1	9.4	6.8
West	25 579	10.2	8.0	0.9
Central Industrial	91 857	36.1	15.4	5.1
Vyatsk	14 810	29.6	12.6	6.5
Urals	29 962	22.3	10.3	5.9
Belorussia	10 563	13.1	4.4	1.5
Black-Earth zone				
Ukraine	62 913	38.6	31.2	3.7
Central Black-Earth	52 448	36.5	27.1	1.1
Middle-Volga	40 292	37.1	24.5	3.6
Lower-Volga	48 777	37.0	25.5	6.6
North-Caucasus	52 664	43.6	31.5	11.3

Source: Itogi desyatiletiya [?1928], 136–41.

Table 13. Rural households, 1916–27 (USSR pre-1939 territory)

	1916	1923	1925	1927	1927	
					1916=100	1923=100
Population[a]						
— (millions)	119.16	117.11	121.79	127.58	107.1	108.9
Households						
— (millions)	21.01	22.83	23.96	25.02	119.1	109.1
Average number of members per household	5.67	5.13	5.13	5.10	89.9	99.4
Average sown area per household (in hectares)	4.26	3.14	3.49	3.80	89.2	121.0
Average number of work horses per household	1.27	0.78	0.83	0.90	70.9	115.4
Average number of cows per household	1.20	0.99	1.12	1.14	95.0	115.2

Sources: Population and households: *Osnovnye elementy* (1930), 2–3.
Members per household: Calculated by the author.
Sown area per household: Calculated from data in *Osnovnye elementy* (1930), 23.
Work horses and cows per household: Calculated from data in *Osnovnye elementy* (1930), 90–1.

Notes: Sown area, horses and cows in peasant farms by data not corrected for undercounting.
Corrected data are about 3–5 per cent higher for work horses and cows and about 20–30 per cent for sown area.
[a] Including absentees.

Table 14.   Unemployment in three urban censuses, 1910–13 (thousands)

		Unemployed (thousands)			As per cent of labour force		
		Male	Female	Total	Male	Female	Total
St Petersburg	1910	25.4	13.0	38.4	4.3	4.8	4.5
Moscow	1912	19.7	9.7	29.4	4.0	4.4	4.1
Baku[a]	1913			3.7			3.4[b]

Sources: Kritsman, 'Bezrabotitsa v dorevolyutsionnoi Rossii i v SSSR', in *Bol'shaya sovetskaya entsiklopediya*, v (1930), col. 214.
Petrograd po perepisi naseleniya 15 dekabrya 1910 g. (Petrograd, [?1915]).
Moscow: appendix to Bradley (1985), 362–75, with slight adjustments.
Baku: 'Perepis' naseleniya Baku, 22 oktabrya 1913 goda', in *Rabochee dvizhenie v Azerbaidzhane v gody novogo revolyutsionnogo pod"ema*, i (1967).

Notes: [a] For Baku the industrial district has been included here. The unemployment rate there was reported to be about half that in the rest of the urban area.
[b] Calculated as a per cent of the labour force including servants, but, for Baku, not white-collar employees. Other cities include the latter.

Table 15. Temporary and permanent vacancies and unemployed registration, 281 labour exchanges, 1926–9

	1926/27 1st half	1926/27 2nd half	1927/28 1st half	1927/28 2nd half	1928/29 1st half
Ratio of all places offered to new registrations (per cent)	64.0	129.5	94.5	150.9	128.4
Ratio of permanent jobs offered to total offered (per cent)	22.2	21.6	21.5	17.9	17.3
Industrial	39.5	29.4	35.7	27.2	24.5
Intellectual	22.4	19.6	20.4	28.2	16.7
Transport	71.7	29.9	15.9	9.9	4.4
Building	10.9	18.1	10.0	13.5	8.2
Unskilled	24.1	21.1	17.7	16.5	18.3
Other	59.2	18.6	33.1	6.9	16.6
Ratio of permanent jobs offered to new registrations (per cent)	14.2	28.0	20.3	27.1	22.2
Industrial	22.4	35.0	33.9	35.3	25.7
Intellectual	15.2	21.4	21.3	48.1	34.3
Transport	140.7	56.8	30.7	29.1	15.8
Building	7.0	26.8	8.0	21.7	9.4
Unskilled	12.3	25.3	13.9	20.2	17.5
Other	77.6	42.5	64.1	20.2	31.3

Source: *Voprosy truda v tsifrakh* (1930), 48–9 and *Voprosy truda*, 1927–1928.

Table 16. Urban unemployment rates by sex and occupation, 1926 census

| | Unemployed as per cent of category[b] | | |
	Male	Female	Both sexes
Manual workers	9.5	11.8	10.0
Factory workers	7.0	9.4	7.7
White-collar employees[a]	8.8	15.0	11.3
Servants	16.7	5.8	5.9
All other	8.8	18.1	11.9
Professions	1.7	4.5	2.5
Owners with hired labour	0.6	0.2	0.6
Owners with only family or artel'	0.6	0.7	0.6
Lone self-employed	1.1	1.1	1.1
Family members helping	0.2	0.1	0.1
All of above groups	6.7	9.8	7.7
Of these, Agriculture	2.0	1.3	1.7
Factory industry	6.9	10.1	7.7
Artisan industry	4.2	6.5	4.7
Building	11.4	32.6	12.3
Rail transport	4.9	15.2	6.0
Other transport	8.2	19.7	9.1
Trade and credit	8.4	13.5	9.7
Establishments	9.0	17.8	12.6
Other	12.1	8.1	9.8
Workers and employees only	9.2	13.0	10.6
Other self-supporting, occupation not indicated, or without occupation	1.2	0.9	1.0
Military	0.8	3.2	0.8

Table 16. *continued*

	Per cent distribution of unemployed by occupational category:		
	Male	*Female*	*Both sexes*
Total	100.0	100.0	100.0
Manual workers	51.3	26.2	40.8
Factory workers	19.3	13.8	17.0
White-collar employees[a]	34.7	53.9	42.8
Servants	0.1	5.2	2.2
All other	34.6	48.7	40.5
Professions	0.2	0.2	0.2
Owners with hired labour	0.1	0.0	0.1
Owners with only family or artel'	0.7	0.2	0.4
Lone self-employed	1.8	0.7	1.3
Family members helping	0.2	0.1	0.2
All of above groups	88.9	81.4	85.7
Of these, Agriculture	3.8	2.3	3.2
Factory industry	23.6	17.6	21.0
Artisan industry	6.6	4.0	5.5
Building	4.9	0.8	3.2
Rail transport	5.8	2.9	4.9
Other transport	5.3	1.5	3.7
Trade and credit	12.8	8.9	11.1
Establishments	16.1	30.9	22.3
Other	10.1	12.4	11.0
Other self-supporting, occupation not indicated, or without occupation	1.7	1.5	1.6
Military	0.9	0.0	0.5
First-time job seekers	8.5	17.2	12.1

Source: *Vsesoyuznaya perepis' naseleniya 1926 g.*, **xxxiv** (1930), 118–19, and 160.

Notes: [a] *Sluzhashchie* can generally be translated as white-collar workers or employees. Note, however, that in the 1926 census servants were included in this category, because of a desire to include them in the marxist category 'unproductive labour'.
  [b] Calculated as: unemployed/(employed + unemployed) in given category.

Table 17.   Gross agricultural production

	Grain	Potatoes and vegetables	Industrial crops	Hay and fodder	Livestock	Total
(a) *Pre-first world war (Russian Empire)*						
(i) Net/gross Prokopovich: 50 provinces of European Russia (million rubles at 1896–1900 prices)						
1896–1900 (average)	1458	415	196	50	832	2951
1909–13 (average)	2024	526	289	103	1053	3995
Average annual growth (per cent)	2.6	1.8	3.0	5.7	1.8	2.4
(ii) Goldsmith : average annual growth (per cent)						
50 provinces	2.5	2.5	1.6		1.8	2.2
72 provinces	2.8	2.8	1.1		1.8	2.5
(iii) Gukhman (million rubles at 1913 prices)						
1913	5033	1626	835	2501	2927	12922
(b) *USSR pre-1939 territory (million pre-war rubles)*						
(i) Gosplan : Gukhman						
1913	4385	1124	732	2107	2472	10822
1922/23	2663	1328	288	1865	1746	7890
(ii) Gosplan : 1925/26 control figures						
1913	4450	1275	641	2434	3033	11833
1924/25	2379	1259	437	1608	2424	8107
(iii) Gosplan : 1926/27 control figures						
1913	(4094)	(1011)	(707)	(2240)	(3077)	(11129)
1923/24	(2530)	975	406	1517	2411	7838
1924/25	(2307)	1077	461	1490	2653	7988
1925/26	3308	1226	715	1878	2874	10001
(iv) Gosplan : 1927/28 control figures						
1924/25	2750	3136[a]	515	– [b]	2848	9249
1925/26	3642	3630[a]	705	– [b]	3173	11150
1926/27	3779	3830[a]	646	– [b]	3325	11580
(c) *USSR pre-1939 territory (million 1926/27 rubles)*						
(i) Gosplan : 1927/28 control figures						
1926/27	3736	6494[a]	810	– [b]	5577	16617
(ii) Gosplan : 1928/29 control figures						
1925/26	3743	2144	875	3257	4862	14880
1926/27	4019	2112	757	3171	5106	15689
1927/28	3739	1983	902	3720	5169	15513
(iii) TsSU : 1929						
1925	4302	2075	890	3568	5057	15893
1926	4533	2213	769	3977	5371	16863
1927	4289	2199	915	4043	5425	16871
1928	4271	2253	967	4078	5622	17190
(iv) Gosplan : 1929/30 control figures						
1925/26	3608	2181	888	3704	4962	15342
1926/27	3881	2319	766	4145	5377	16485
1927/28	3592	2265	911	3985	5521	16273
1928/29	3551	2502	965	4200	5351	16568

Table 17. *continued*

	Grain	Potatoes and vegetables	Industrial crops	Hay and fodder	Total arable	Livestock	Total
(v) Gosplan : 1931 Plan							
1928						5688[c]/5832	14569[c]/14714
1929						6174[c]/5409	14739[c]/13974
(vi) Gosplan : (1939)							
1913	3841					4579	12507
1929	3348	2258	876	2577	9059	5686	14745
(vii) SIPS (1983) : low estimate							
1909–13							
(average)	3930					4326	12050
1913	4566	1201	519	2120	8406	4486	12891
1924	2543					4239	
1925	3584	1621	655	1911	7771	4735	12506
1926	3815	1621	536	2113	8085	5079	13164
1927	3584	1538	674	2233	8029	5181	13210
1928	3641	1709	741	2320	8411	5181	13648
1929	3584	1701	696	2214	8195	4480	12675
(viii) SIPS (1983) : high estimate							
1909–13							
(average)	4618					4326	12786
1913	5358	1201	519	2175	9253	4486	13738
1924	2971					4239	
1925	4191	1621	655	1953	8420	4735	13155
1926	4427	1621	536	2156	8740	5079	13819
1927	4144	1538	674	2272	8628	5181	13809
1928	4237	1709	741	2362	9049	5181	14286
1929	4144	1701	696	2253	8794	4480	13274
(d) *Post-second world war (pre-1939 USSR territory) (1913 = 100)*							
(i) Recent official Soviet (1960)							
1913					100	100	100
1917					81	100	88
1920					64	72	67
1921					55	67	60
1922					75	73	75
1923					84	88	86
1924					82	104	90
1925					107	121	112
1926					114	127	118
1927					113	134	121
1928					117	137	124
(ii) Johnson and Kahan (1959–63) (1913 = 100)							
1913					100	100	100
1928					118	115	116

(*continued on page 268*)

Table 17. *continued*

	Grain	Potatoes and vegetables	Industrial crops	Hay and fodder	Total arable	Livestock	Total
(iii) SIPS (1983) (1913 = 100)							
1913	100	100	100	100	100	100	100
1923	60	120	58	68			
1924	56	118	64	66			
1925	78	128	109	87	91	128	97
1926	84	143	103	92	94	134	102
1927	78	142	130	91	93	133	101
1928	80	151	142	94	98	125	102

Sources:
(a) (i) Prokopovich (1918), 33, 41, 44. 'Net/gross' as used here means that grain production excludes seed but includes grain used as livestock feed.
(a) (ii) Goldsmith (1961), 448, 450.
(a) (iii) Gukhman (1925), 130–5.
(b) (i) Gukhman (1925), 130–5.
(b) (ii) *Kontrol'nye tsifry . . . na 1925–1926* (1925), 46–7, 62–3, 72–3.
(b) (iii) *Kontrol'nye tsifry . . . na 1926–1927* (1926), 339–49.
(b) (iv) *Kontrol'nye tsifry . . . na 1927/1928* (1928), 464–7.
(c) (i) *Kontrol'nye tsifry . . . na 1927/1928* (1928), 464–7.
(c) (ii) *Kontrol'nye tsifry . . . na 1928/1929* (1929), 476–7.
(c) (iii) *Sel'skoe khozyaistvo SSSR 1925–1928* (1929), 284–8.
(c) (iv) *Kontrol'nye tsifry . . . na 1929/1930* (1930), 534–5.
(c) (v) *Narodno-khozyaistvennyi plan . . . 1931* (1931), 126–7.
(c) (vi) *Sel'skoe khozyaistvo SSSR* (1929), 281.
(c) (vii) and (c) (viii) Wheatcroft in Stuart (ed.) (1983), 45–7.
(d) (i) *Sel'skoe khozyaistvo SSSR* (1960), 79.
(d) (ii) Johnson and Kahan (1959), 231; 1913 figure is from Johnson in Bergson and Kuznets (eds) (1963), 206.
(d) (iii) As for (c) (vii).

Notes:
[a] Includes hay and fodder.
[b] Included in potatoes and vegetables.
[c] Excluding change in herd.
( ) = Estimated by present author from data provided.

Table 18. Grain–fodder balances

(a) *Uncorrected production data* (million tons)						
	1909–13 (average)	*1912–13*	*1924/25*	*1926*	*1927*	*1928*
Grain production	68	72.8	46.5	67	63	62
Seed	12	11.7	10.0	11	11	11
Food:						
Urban	4	5.1	4.2	4.6	4.9	4.8
Rural	26.4	27.4	24.8	27.2	27.3	27.7
Total food	30.4	32.5	29.0	31.8	32.2	32.5
Livestock fodder						
Urban	1.0	1.1	0.7	1.0	1.0	1.0
Rural	12.6	11.1	6.0	16.0	19.0	21.0
Total fodder	13.6	12.1	6.7	17.0	20.0	22.0
Industry and army	1	1.2	0.7	1.5	1.5	1.5
Exports	11	10.7	0	2.6	0.5	0
All utilised	68	68.2	46.6	63.9	64.7	67.0
Losses, stock changes, etc.	+4.6	−0.1	?	−3.1	+1.7	+5.0
Net balance	63.4	68.3	46.6	67.0	63.0	62.0
Extra-rural	17	18	5.6	9.7	7.5	7.3

(*continued on page 270*)

Table 18. *continued*

(b) Gosplan evaluations with large corrections

	1908–12 (average)	1913	1924/25	1925/26	1926/27	1927/28
Grain production	75.3	93.2	51.7	74.7	78.4	73.6
Seed	13.1	14.3	11.9	11.8	12.2	12.3
Food:						
Urban	5.0	5.4	4.2	4.4	4.6	4.9
Rural	29.8	32.9	27.1	27.4	27.2	27.3
Total food	34.8	38.3	32.3	31.8	31.8	32.2
Fodder:						
Urban	1.2	1.4	0.9	1.6	1.6	1.5
Rural	13.1	17.5	7.9	19.4	22.8	23.3
Total fodder	14.3	18.9	8.8	21.0	24.4	24.8
Army	0.8	0.9	1.6	} 1.0	} 1.1	} 1.2
Industry	0.7	0.8	0.9			
Exports	10.6	13.0	0.2	2.1	2.6	0.5
Other				0.3	0.3	0.4
Total utilised	74.3	86.2	53.7	71.2	75.5	74.4
Stock changes, etc.	+1.0	+7.0	−2.0	+6.6	+9.5	+8.7
Net balance	73.3	79.2	55.7	64.6	66.0	65.7
Extra-rural	18.3	21.5	6.8	9.1	9.9	8.1

Sources: (a) 1909–13 (average), 1912–13, 1924/25: Popov (1925).
1926–28 estimated as follows:
Seed: at same rate as for 1909–13.
Food, fodder, industry, army, etc. : as per Expert Soviet Grain–Fodder Balances.
Losses, stock changes, etc.: calculated as a balancing item.
(b) 1908–12, 1913, 1924/25: *Kontrol'nye tsifry . . . na 1925–1926* (1925), 74–5; 1925/26, 1926/27, 1927/28: *Sel'skoe khozyaistvo SSSR 1925–1928* (1929).

Table 19.   Grain production and transfers, by regions

(a)   Regional grain production (million tons) (USSR minus SCR)

	NCR	SPR	CPR	EPR	USSR	NCR	SPR	CPR	EPR	USSR
(i) *TsSK reorganised*										
1909–13	9.4	28.1	19.6	8.8	67.8					
(average)										
1913	10.1	33.6	22.5	11.3	79.7					
(ii) *TsSU (1924)*										
1909–13	6.9	27.7	17.6	11.0	63.1	100	100	100	100	100
(average)										
1916	6.5	22.8	15.8	11.7	57.0	94	82	90	106	90
1917	5.5	24.1	11.0	14.4	54.9	80	87	63	131	87
1920	3.8	15.9	6.6	7.8	34.1	55	57	38	71	54
1921	4.6	12.3	5.2	5.5	27.7	67	44	30	50	44
1922	5.1	15.6	9.1	6.7	37.8	74	56	52	61	60
(iii) *TsSU (1925)*										
1916	7.0	23.9	19.1	11.5	61.5	(94)	(82)	(90)	(106)	(90)
1923	6.5	20.4	13.7	6.8	47.4	87	70	65	63	69
1924	7.5	15.6	10.7	9.0	42.7	100	54	50	83	62
1925	8.0	27.8	16.6	11.0	63.4	106	95	78	101	93
(iv) *TsSU (1928)*										
1925	11.3	26.1	18.0	13.9	72.7	(106)	(95)	(78)	(101)	(93)
1926	11.5	23.5	21.7	16.5	76.6	108	86	94	120	98
1927	11.4	23.9	19.6	13.7	71.7	107	87	85	100	92
1928	10.8	18.0	21.7	17.4	71.5	101	66	94	126	91

Table 19. *continued*

(b) *Grain production per capita* (USSR minus SCR)

	NCR	SPR	CPR	EPR	USSR
(i) in tons per head					
1909–13 (average)	0.302	0.738	0.596	0.406	0.510
1920	0.181	0.406	0.221	0.235	0.265
1921	0.220	0.310	0.173	0.166	0.214
1922	0.245	0.384	0.304	0.203	0.291
1923	0.275	0.472	0.381	0.207	0.332
1924	0.299	0.362	0.362	0.276	0.291
1925	0.311	0.620	0.453	0.333	0.428
1926	0.305	0.546	0.536	0.386	0.444
1927	0.296	0.546	0.477	0.317	0.408
1928	0.269	0.406	0.512	0.390	0.393
(ii) indices					
1909–13 (average)	100.0	100.0	100.0	100.0	100.0
1913					111.6
1920	60	55	37	58	52
1921	73	42	29	41	42
1922	81	52	51	50	57
1923	91	64	64	51	65
1924	99	49	49	68	57
1925	103	84	76	82	84
1926	101	74	90	95	87
1927	98	74	80	78	80
1928	89	55	86	96	77

(*continued on page 273*)

Table 19. *continued*

(c) *Regional grain transportation balances* (million tons)

	NCR	SCR	SPR	CPR	EPR	USSR
(i)						
1901	−2.9	(+0.2)	+4.6	+2.3	+0.2	+4.5
1913	−4.3	(+1.3)	+8.3	+3.3	+0.8	+9.3
1920	−1.8	(+0.1)	+0.1	+0.3	+0.3	−0.5
1921	−0.9	(+0.1)	0	0	+0.1	−0.7
(ii)						
1913	−3.9	−0.5	+8.7	+4.9	+0.8	+10.0
1922/23	−1.5	−0.2	+1.4	+0.9	+3.2	+ 0.6
1923/24	−2.3	−0.2	+3.8	+1.0	+0.2	+ 2.7
1924/25	−2.5	−0.4	+1.7	+0.2	+1.5	+ 0.6
1925/26	−4.0	−0.8	+4.8	+0.9	+1.1	+ 2.1
1926/27	−3.8	−0.7	+3.3	+2.1	+1.7	+ 2.7
1927/28	−4.3	−0.9	+2.9	+1.7	+1.1	+ 0.6
1928/29	−3.6	−0.8	+0.5	+1.9	+2.2	+ 0.2

Sources: (a) (i) See Wheatcroft (1980), vol. 3, pp. 14–30.
      (a) (ii) *Trudy TsSU*, xviii (1924), 122ff.
      (a) (iii) *Abrégé* (1925), 54–61.
      (a) (iv) *Statisticheskii spravochnik* (1929), 178–203.
      (b) (i)
      and
      (b) (ii) data from (a) applied to population data.
      (c) (i) *Trudy TsSU*, xix, ii (1925), 6–11.
      (c) (ii) *Statischeskoe obozrenie*, no. 8, 1928, 68–72; no. 8, 1929, 83 (G. Vasil'ev).

Table 20.   Gross production of potatoes, vegetables and industrial crops

	Fruit and vegetables				*Industrial crops*				
	Pot-atoes	Vege-tables	Fruit	Total	Fibres	Oil seed	Sugar beet	Other	All indus-trial crops
(a) 50 provinces of European Russia									
(i) Prokopovich (1890–1900 prices)									
1900	154	261		415					196
1909–13	215	311		526					289
(average)									
(ii) Goldsmith (1896–1900 (average) = 100)									
1896–1900	100								100
1908	109.6								134.6
1909	122.9								102.8
1910	144.3								112.0
1911	136.7								119.3
1912	148.7								138.1
1913	140.4								144.6
1914	143.2								123.9
(b) pre-1939 area of the USSR (million rubles, pre-first world war prices)									
(i) Gukhman									
1913	425	699		1124	455	140	116	21	732
1922/23	485	921		1406	83	152	20	2	257
(ii) 1925/26 control figures									
1913	439	836		1275	337	164		140[a]	641
1924/25	509	750		1259	230	165		42[a]	437
(iii) 1926/27 control figures									
1913	437	574		1011	(362)	(187)	(109)	(49)	(707)
1923/24	524	451		975	178	179	28	22	407
1924/25	509	567		1076	243	165	32	22	462
1925/26	657	569		1226	344	250	81	41	716
(c) pre-1939 USSR territory (million rubles at 1926/27 prices)									
(i) 1928/29 control figures									
1925/26	973	789	382	2144	448	270	91	65	874
1926/27	1083	634	395	2122	412	220	66	59	757
1927/28	1038	531	414	1983	476	262	105	59	902
(ii) TsSU (1929)									
1925/26	1037	747	291	2075	441	298	91	61	891
1926/27	1146	736	331	2213	405	239	66	60	770
1927/28	1109	820	270	2199	467	286	105	58	916

(*continued on page 275*)

Table 20. *continued*

	Fruit and vegetables				Industrial crops				
	Pot-atoes	Vege-tables	Fruit	Total	Fibres	Oil seed	Sugar beet	Other	All indus-trial crops
(iii) 1929/30 control figures									
1925	1008	884	289	2181	466	259	105	58	888
1926	1117	874	328	2319	424	210	74	55	763
1927	1059	941	266	2266	488	248	121	54	911
1928	1162	1000	340	2502	550	253	118	43	964
(iv) SIPS (1983)									
1913	798	403	–	1201	248	159	112	–	519
1924	943								
1925	1025	596	–	1621	263	298	94	–	655
1926	1143	478	–	1621	248	221	67	–	536
1927	1135	403	–	1538	285	281	108	–	674
1928	1207	502	–	1709	343	293	105	–	741

Sources: (a) (i) Prokopovich (1918), 33, 44.
(a) (ii) Goldsmith (1961), 448.
(b) (i) Gukhman (1925) 130–4.
(b) (ii) *Kontrol'nye tsifry . . . 1925–1926* (1925), 62–3.
(b) (iii) *Kontrol'nye tsifry . . . 1926–1927* (1926), 339.
(c) (i) *Kontrol'nye tsifry . . . 1928–1929* (1929), 476–7.
(c) (ii) *Sel'skoe khozyaistvo 1925–1928* (1929), 284–8.
(c) (iii) *Kontrol'nye tsifry . . . 1929/30* (1930), 534–5.
(c) (iv) Wheatcroft in Stuart (ed.) (1983), 45.

Notes: [a] Includes sugar beet.

Table 21. Livestock production and numbers

(A) *Livestock produce*						
Meat and Fat	Milk	Skins, wool, etc.	Manure	Growth of herds	Second-ary[c]	Total livestock produce
(a) 50 provinces of European Russia						
(i) Prokopovich (million rubles at 1896–1900 prices)						
1896–1900	160	407	43		(221)[a]		832
1913	176	515	45		(317)[a]		1053
(b) Pre-1939 USSR territory (million rubles at pre-first world war prices)						
(i) Narkomzem						
1916	892	952	315	248	26	224	2717
1917	932	966	283	252	73	179	2687
1918	845	804	252	201	−792	91	1200
1920	475	642	166	172	−351	75	1178
1921	458	486	178	142	−582	44	725
(ii) Gukhman						
1913	970	998	275	–	–	230	2472
1922/23	591	861	184	–	–	122	1759
(iii) 1925/26 control figures						
1913	1021	1134	318	276	–	283	3033
1924/25	869	948	214	185	–	208	2424
(iv) 1926/27 control figures						
1913	(883)	(893)	[b]	(277)	[b]	(283)	(3077)
1923/24	576	893	199	195	402	146	2411
1924/25	746	945	238	185	336	204	2653
1925/26	814	992	260	223	339	246	2874
(c) Pre-1939 USSR territory (million rubles at 1926/27 prices)						
(i) 1989/29 Control Figures						
1925/26	1446	1712	449	223	547	486	4862
1926/27	1605	1836	478	236	466	486	5106
1927/28	1750	1853	513	244	266	543	5169
(ii) TsSU (1929)						
1925/26	1477	1787	463	326	533	471	5057
1926/27	1632	1929	492	340	448	529	5371
1927/28	1734	1928	516	349	294	607	5425
(iii) 1929/30 control figures						
1925	1440	1722	479	326	516	478[d]	4962
1926	1601	1866	519	340	574	478[d]	5377
1927	1738	1933	569	349	403	529[d]	5521
1928	2049	1854	642	350	−79	535[d]	5351

(*continued on page 277*)

Table 21. *continued*

	(A) *Livestock produce*						
	Meat and Fat	*Milk*	*Skins, wool, etc.*	*Manure*	*Growth of herds*	*Second-ary*[c]	*Total livestock produce*
(iv) SIPS (1983)							
1913	1924	1498	284	228	200	352	4486
1924	1592	1582	263	209	284	309	4239
1925	1765	1696	295	221	419	339	4735
1926	1967	1834	314	234	360	370	5079
1927	2083	1840	332	244	310	372	5181
1928	2357	1864	392	246	−59	381	5181

Sources to Table 21 (A): (a) (i) Prokopovich (1918), 41.
                            (b) (i) *Istoricheskie zapiski*, lxxiv (1963), 122.
                            (b) (ii) Gukhman (1925), 132, 134–5.
                            (b) (iii) *Kontrol'nye   tsifry . . .   1925–1926*,   (1925), 62–3[i].
                            (b) (iv) *Kontrol'nye   tsifry . . .   1926–1927* (1926), 340–1, 344–9.
                            (c) (i) *Kontrol'nye tsifry . . . 1928–1929* (1929), 146.
                            (c) (ii) *Sel'skoe khozyaistvo SSSR 1925–1928* (1929), 288.
                            (c) (iii) *Kontrol'nye tsifry . . . 1929–1930* (1930), 535.
                            (c) (iv) Wheatcroft in Stuart (ed.) (1983), 45–7.

Note to Table 21 (A): [a] Total for last three columns (residual).
                       [b] The residual figure for 'skins, wool, etc.' plus 'growth of herds' is 741 million rubles.
                       [c] Normally refers to: poultry products (hens, eggs, feathers) *plus* products of bee-keeping (honey and wax) *plus* products of silk farming. Some minor items like bristles and horse-hair may be included here. The figures for secondary products have been obtained as a residual.
                       [d] Poultry products only.

Table 21. *continued*

(B) *Livestock Numbers* (millions)					
Horses	*Cattle*	*Pigs*	*Horses*	*Cattle*	*Pigs*

(a) Pre-revolutionary estimates
Russian Empire, 1913

	Horses	*Cattle*	*Pigs*	*Horses*	*Cattle*	*Pigs*
(i) TsSK	30.7	45.0	11.6			
(ii) Vainshtein correction	36.8	63.7	22.0			

(b) Post-revolutionary
(i) TsSU (1925) (USSR minus SCR)

1916	31.5	50.0	19.5	100	100	100
1920	25.4	39.1		81	78	
1921	23.3	36.8		74	74	
1922	18.9	33.0		60	66	

(ii) TsSU (1924) (USSR minus SCR)

1916	31.3	50.3	19.3	100	100	100
1922	20.2	35.0	8.6	65	70	45
1923	20.1	38.6	9.1	64	77	47
1924	21.9	45.6	16.8	70	91	87

(iii) TsSU (1925) (USSR minus SCR)

1916	31.5	50.0	19.5	100	100	100
1923	21.4	41.3	9.4	68	83	48
1924	22.9	47.6	17.2	73	95	88
1925	24.2	49.9	16.4	77	100	84

(iv) Gosplan: 1925/26 control figures (USSR minus SCR)

1913	31.3	50.3	19.3	100	100	100
1921	23.7	38.1	13.5	76	76	70
1922	20.2	35.0	8.6	61	70	44
1923	20.1	38.7	9.1	64	77	47
1924	22.3	46.7	16.8	71	93	84

(v) Gosplan: 1926/27 control figures (USSR)

1916	35.5	60.3	20.3	100	100	100
1923	23.3	50.6	10.5	66	84	52
1924	25.3	55.9	18.2	71	93	90
1925	26.8	58.9	17.7	75	98	87
1926	28.2	63.0	20.7	79	104	102

(vi) TsSU (1929) (USSR)

1925	26.0	59.6	20.9			
1926	28.3	63.0	20.9			
1927	30.6	66.0	22.4			
1928	32.0	66.8	25.2			

Sources to Table 21 (B):

(a)	(i)	See Wheatcroft (1980), 123–8.
(a)	(ii)	Vainshtein (1960), 102–4.
(b)	(i)	1916, 1920–2: *Trudy TsSU*, xviii (1925), 136–9.
(b)	(ii)	*Ekonomicheskoe obozrenie*, no. 23–4, 1924, p. lxxii.
(b)	(iii)	*Abrégé* (1925), 73–6.
(b)	(iv)	*Kontrol'nye tsifry . . . 1925–1926* (1925), 76–7.
(b)	(v)	*Kontrol'nye tsifry . . . 1926–1927* (1926), 338.
(b)	(vi)	*Sel'skoe khozyaistvo SSSR 1925–1928* (1929), 188–9.

Table 22.   Gross, net and marketed agricultural production: revised series
(Gosplan evaluations of 1926)

	Grain	Potatoes etc.	Industrial crops	Total arable	Livestock products	Total
(a) Gross production (1909–13 (average) = 100)						
1909–13 (average)	100	100	100	100	100	100
1925	92	133	131	101	123	107
1926	99	149	124	107	129	112
1927	92	148	157	106	128	111
1928	94	157	171	109	120	112
(b) Gross production (1913 = 100)						
1923	60	120	58	68		
1924	56	118	64	66		
1925	78	128	109	87	128	97
1926	84	143	103	92	134	102
1927	78	142	130	91	133	101
1928	80	151	142	94	125	102
(c) Net production (1909–13 (average) = 100)[a]						
1925	82	154	125	94	123	106
1926	83	178	118	98	129	109
1927	72	171	151	94	128	107
1928	79	188	166	104	120	109
(d) Net production (1913 = 100)						
1909–13 (average)	82	96	85	83	104	91
1925	67	148	106	78	128	95
1926	68	171	100	81	134	98
1927	59	164	128	78	133	96
1928	65	180	141	86	125	98
(e) Marketed production (1913 = 100)						
1923	48	71	34	48	43	47
1924	33	75	57	48	59	52
1925	46	82	88	65	63	64
1926	51	93	73	65	68	66
1927	42	90	93	66	77	70
1928	42	109	99	71	86	77
(f) Export production (1913 = 100)[b]						
1923	29		−2	23	12	21
1924	2		+11	4	23	7
1925	22		+15	21	22	21
1926	23		−2	19	31	21
1927	1		+2	2	46	10

Sources: (a)–(d): Calculated from individual product series aggregated using 1913 prices from 1926/27 control figures.

(e): Calculated from 1925/26, 1926/27 and 1929/30 control figures. The 1925/26 control figure calculations for 1913 and 1924/25 marketings have been used as a base for these indices. The comparable 1925/26 and 1923/24 figures have been calculated by applying the 1925/26:1924/25, and 1923/24:1924/25 relationships indicated in the 1926/27 control figures. The 1926/27, 1927/28 and 1928/29 values have been similarly calculated by linking them to the 1925/26 values calculated above.

(f): Calculated from (i) the physical value series in *Vneshnyaya torgovlya . . . 1918–1940* (1960), 45–120 and 204–300 and (ii) the 1913 prices for each product as indicated in the 1926/27 control figures.

Notes: [a] Net production as defined here is gross production less seed and fodder.
[b] The figures given here are as a percentage of 1913. The minus sign for industrial crops in 1923 and 1926 indicates that *imports* took place which were 2 per cent of 1913 *exports*.

Table 23. Capital stock in agricultural sector
(million rubles, pre-1939 USSR territory)

	Inventory[a]		*Livestock*	*Structures*		*Other*	*Total*
	Agri-cultural	*Other*		*Agri-cultural*	*Other*		
(i) Vainshtein (million pre-war rubles)							
Jan. 1, 1914	688	1218	5934/ 6002	7349		1212	16393/ 16461
(ii) Gosplan 1926/27 control figures (million rubles at 1925/26 prices)[b]							
October 1, 1923	1527			5000	8170	1497	16193
October 1, 1924	1506			5090	8317	1503	16415
October 1, 1925	1548			5182	8467	1534	16730
October 1, 1926	1639			5275	8620	1608	17141
(iii) Gosplan 1927/28 control figures (million rubles at 1925/26 prices)[b]							
October 1, 1924	1607			4836	9169	841	16452
October 1, 1925	1636			5029	9535	844	17044
October 1, 1926	1713			5194	9836	850	17593
October 1, 1927	1808			5351	10145	889	18193
(iv) Gosplan 1928/29 control figures (million rubles at 1925/26 prices)							
October 1, 1925	2644		6569	5048	9541	844	24673
October 1, 1926	2889		7155	5277	9973	850	26143
October 1, 1927	3089		7632	5502	10399	869	27491
October 1, 1928	3332		7906	5734	10832	908	28713
(v) TsSU (1929) (million rubles at 1927 prices) (individual sector)							
October 1, 1925	1108	1195	7246	4739	9554	–	24013
October 1, 1926	1206	1225	7771	4939	9955	–	25280
October 1, 1927	1281	1317	8200	5136	10326	–	26468
(vi) Gosplan 1929/30 control figures (million rubles at 1926/27 prices)							
October 1, 1925	900	1479	7462	4550	9940	796	25127
October 1, 1926	973	1510	8011	4850	10407	796	26547
October 1, 1927	1040	1541	8609	5083	10810	816	27899
October 1, 1928	1127	1593	9036	5322	11156	845	29079
October 1, 1929	1285	1635	8978	5620	11571	893	29982

Sources: (i) Vainshtein (1960 (b)), 224–6.
      (ii) *Kontrol'nye tsifry . . . na 1926–1927* (1926), 314–5.
    (iii) *Kontrol'nye tsifry . . . na 1927–1928* (1928), 520–1.
    (iv) *Kontrol'nye tsifry . . . na 1928–1929* (1929), 426–7.
     (v) *Sel'skoe khozyaistvo SSSR, 1925–1928* (1929), 144–5.
    (vi) *Kontrol'nye tsifry . . . na 1929/30* (1930), 448–9.

Notes: [a] 'Mertvyi inventar'' ('dead stock').
      [b] Excludes livestock.

Table 24.   Agro-meteorological deviation from trend in grain yields, 1908–28

	NCR Moscow	SPR	CPR Kiev	CPR Kazan	EPR Saratov	USSR Orenburg
1908	−0.5	−0.8	+1.7	+1.5	+0.5	+0.4
1909	−1.5	−0.5	+2.4	+1.6	+0.9	+0.2
1910	−0.1	+0.3	−0.8	−0.6	−0.3	−0.1
1911	+0.6	+0.3	−1.1	−2.3	−4.8	−0.7
1912	+1.5	0	+1.6	−0.2	+0.6	+0.3
1913	+0.9	+1.5	+2.3	+3.3	+2.7	+1.8
1914	−1.5	+0.9	−0.5	+0.1	+0.6	−0.3
1915	−0.4	−1.1	+0.1	+1.0	+2.6	+0.1
1916	+0.5	+0.3	+1.3	+1.8	+0.9	+0.6
1917	+0.5	−1.5	−0.8	+1.3	+0.6	+0.0
1918	+0.9	+0.7	+2.3	+3.8	+2.1	+1.4
1919	−0.3	0	−0.1	+2.9	+1.1	+1.0
1920	−1.9	−2.4	−1.9	−0.5	−1.3	−0.8
1921	+1.7	−0.6	−3.0	−2.6	−4.2	−1.3
1922	−0.7	−0.4	−1.5	−0.8	−1.0	−0.1
1923	+1.5	+0.4	−0.7	−3.3	−3.0	−0.7
1924	+0.9	−2.2	−0.5	−3.2	−3.0	−1.3
1925	−0.7	−0.2	−2.3	−3.0	−1.8	−1.1
1926	0	−0.8	+2.0	+2.2	+1.2	+0.6
1927	+0.3	−1.6	−1.0	−3.0	−3.3	−1.1
1928	+0.3	+1.0	+1.4	+0.7	+0.7	+0.6

Source: Wheatcroft (1982b).

Note: This table is based on a crop–weather index for 1883–1950 derived from correlating grain yields with various monthly weather variables for 1883–1915 from five locations in the Russian Empire. This was used to predict agro-meteorological deviations from norm (trend) yield levels from the meteorological data.

This table indicates clusters of good and bad years. The commonly held view that any five-year period will cancel out good and bad years is clearly wrong. In the eight years from 1912–19 the weather was apparently above average for seven years and below average for one year. The median weather for these 8 years was +0.6 above the 1883–1915 average. This was followed by six years (1920–5) when the weather was consistently below average (median −0.9).

Table 25.   The Stalin–Nemchinov version of the grain balance, 'pre-war' and 1926/27 (million tons)

| | *Gross output:* | | *Extra-rural sales:* | | |
| | *Million tons* | *Per cent of total yield* | *Million tons* | *Per cent of:* | |
				Total sales	*Farm yield*
Pre-war:					
Landlords	9.8	12	4.6	22	47
Kulaks	31.1	38	10.6	50	34
Middle and poor peasants	41.0	50	6.0	28	15
Total	81.9	100	21.3	100	26
1926/27:					
Sovkhozy and kolkhozy	1.3	2	0.6	6	47
Kulaks	10.1	13	2.1	20	20
Middle and poor peasants	66.4	85	7.6	74	11
Total	77.8	100	10.3	100	13

Source: Stalin, xi (1949), 85 (interview of May 28, 1928) citing the research of V.S. Nemchinov of TsSU; poods in the original have been converted by us into metric tons.

Table 26. Gosplan estimate of the agricultural output share of extra-rural sales,
1913 and 1924/25–1926/27

	1913	*1924/25*	*1925/26*	*1926/27*
Gross agricultural output, mn pre-war rubles	11907	8648	11046	11462
Extra-rural sales, mn pre-war rubles	2639–3021	1394	1817	1932
Extra-rural sales, as per cent of output	22.2–25.4	16.1	16.5	16.9
Extra-rural sales as per cent of output, by commodity:				
Grains	20.3	14.3	14.1	14.7
Industrial crops	73.1	54.4	50.0	53.1
Livestock	30.9	22.4	23.2	25.0

Source: *Byulleten' Kon"yunkturnogo Instituta*, no. 11–12, 1927 (I. Zhirkovich and I.N. Ozerov), 52.

Notes: The researchers of the Narkomfin *Kon"yunktur* Institute used data from Gosplan's 1926/27 control figures to illustrate the decline in extra-rural sales in the 1920s compared to 1913. For total sales in 1913 a range of figures is given. The lower one is that shown in the 1926/27 control figures but the *Kon"yunktur* Institute considered this an underestimate, and also cited the higher figure (from the Gosplan 1925/26 control figures). The *émigré* economist Prokopovich also considered the 1926/27 control figures to understate the decline in extrarural sales compared to 1913; see Davies (1980), 17n. For aggregate sales the source also gives preliminary data for 1927/28, indicating a substantial increase in sales volume (by 13.5 per cent) and improvement in the output share of sales (to 18.4 per cent).

Table 27. Rural and urban food consumption, pre-war and 1926/27
(grams per person per day)

	Rural households:		Urban households:	
	Consumer region	*Producer region*	*Manual workers*	*Non-manual workers*
Wheat and rye flour:				
Pre-war	668–701		621	
Oct. 1926	513	552	462	414
Feb. 1927	492	524	458	411
Potatoes:				
Pre-war	300–404		333	
Oct. 1926	717	453	286	224
Feb. 1927	644	396	247	197
Meat:				
Pre-war	50–61		75	
Oct. 1926	106	97	151	172
Feb. 1927	101	94	152	175

Sources: Pre-war: Wheatcroft (1976), 45. These are ranges representing upper and
lower limits of cited estimates.
1926/27: *Sel'skoe khozyaistvo SSSR, 1925–1928* (1929), 402–5, 408–11.

Table 28. A Soviet commission's estimate of peasant obligations, 1913 and
1924/25–1926/27 (rubles per head of agricultural population)

	Rents	*Taxes*[a]	*Per cent share of net family income*
Gold rubles:			
1913[b]	3.08	7.80	19.0
Chervonets rubles:			
1924/25	–	6.32	7.3
1925/26	–	7.84	6.9
1926/27	–	10.89	9.6

Source: *Tyazhest' oblozheniya* (1929), 62; this is the report of the government
commission (see p. 113 above).

Notes: [a] Direct and indirect taxes paid to government, but not village taxation
(*samooblozhenie*) or insurance payments.
[b] This estimate for 1913 was reportedly based on previous research of I. I.
Popov and M. I. Lifshits. An alternative estimate for 1912 restricted to 50
provinces of European Russia is found in Vainshtein (1924), 116. This
shows land rentals as 3.74 rubles and tax payments (according to the
same definition of taxation) as 6.36 rubles per head.

Table 29.   Gosplan estimate of the price scissors, 1911–14 and 1925/26–1928/29
(1911–14 = 100)

	1925/26	*1926/27*	*1927/28*	*1928/29*
Aggregate producer price indices:				
Grains	161	125	135	190
Oilseeds	108	109	124	137
Technical crops	140	135	140	146
Livestock products	171	179	182	198
All farm products	159	149	156	183
The scissors	139	141	127	111

Source: *Kontrol'nye tsifry . . . na 1929/30* (1930), 579.

Note: The 'scissors' are defined as the ratio of an aggregate index of retail prices
of manufactures to an aggregate index of state collection prices of farm
products; this is the reciprocal of their (incorrect) definition in the original.

Table 30. The finance of socialist and private sector accumulation in 1928
(million current rubles)

	Socialist sector[a]	Private sector
1. Accumulation fund[b]	1574	3563
2. Exogenous losses[c]	−94	−707
3. Net imports[d]	154	–
4. Fiscal and credit effect[e]	1287	−1287
5. Realised accumulation out of national income $(1 + 2 + 3 + 4)$[f]	2921	1569
6. Collectivisation effect[g]	67	−67
7. Total realised accumulation $(5 + 6)$	2988	1502
8. Share of primary socialist accumulation of products in realised accumulation out of national income $(4 : 5)$[h]	0.44	–
9. Share of primary socialist accumulation of products and assets in total realised accumulation $([4 + 6] : 7)$[i]	0.45	–

Source and notes:　[a] The 'socialist' sector combines both the public sector broadly defined (government, public and cooperative enterprise and collective farms) and the total (labour and non-labour) incomes of worker and collective farm households.

[b] This is the financial contribution of each sector to its own accumulation, from *Materials* (1985), 128 (Table 2, row 6).

[c] The most important element here was evidently the destruction of livestock accompanying intensified grain collections and moves towards forced collectivisation (*Materials*, 1985, Table 2, row 10).

[d] All net imports are attributed to the socialist sector accumulation fund in the source (*Materials*, 1985, Table 2, row 11).

[e] Taxes and loans (1,107 mn rubles), excises (812 mn rubles) pensions and allowances (−51 mn rubles) and free medical, social and cultural services (−581 mn rubles) (*Materials*, 1985, Table 2, row 7).

[f] 'Real' accumulation in the original source (*Materials*, 1985, Table 2, row 12 *minus* row 13).

[g] Private sector assets incorporated directly into the socialist sector (*Materials*, 1985, Table 2, row 13).

[h] This ratio seems to me to reflect the magnitudes closest to primary accumulation as conceived by Preobrazhensky: the transfer of products from the private to the socialist sector through direct and indirect taxation.

[i] This ratio is intended to correspond to a broader marxian concept of primary socialist accumulation of resources, including the direct transfer of assets into the socialist sector through a change in ownership.

Table 31.   The balance of visible trade between agriculture and non-agriculture
in 1928 (million current rubles)

	Barsov	*Wheatcroft–Davies corrections*
1. Agriculture sales to non-agriculture[a]	3167	3398
2. Agriculture purchases from non-agriculture[a] of which:	3951	6383
3. Investment goods	601	601
4. Consumer goods of which:	3351	5782
5. Socialised retail market	2990	
6. Non-socialised retail market	360[b]	
7. Net material transfer from non-agriculture (2 − 1)	784	2985

Source: Barsov (1969), Table 10 (facing 112) and 118; *Materials* (1985), 27 (introductory article by Wheatcroft and Davies).

Notes: [a] Material products only, valued at prices facing the rural population.
[b] Calculated as the difference between the sum of retail purchases of
manufactures on the non-socialised market by the rural population and
the sum of the same population's sales of manufactures in the same
market; this measure therefore excludes *both* retraded manufactures
obtained initially from socialised retail outlets *and* manufactures originating in the non-socialised sector, produced by the rural population.

Table 32. Gross production of large-scale (census) industry, 1913, 1926/27 and 1927/28 (USSR pre-1939 territory) (million rubles at 1913 prices, including excises)

	1913	*1926/27*	*1927/28*
Fuel and power[a]	607	890	1072
Iron and steel (inc. ore)	337	370	437
Other metals (inc. ore)[b]	121	69	80
Minerals, glass, building materials[c]	141	145	175
Metalworking	248	240	297
Machine-building	398	476	638
Chemicals Group A[d]	173	99	124
Group B[d]	141	269	356
Woodworking A	124	169	203
B	47	38	61
Food, drink and tobacco[e]	2313	1643	1957
Textiles: cotton	1207[f]	1366	1554
woollen	195	253	299
silk	49	19	28
other	151	174	183
Clothing	17	166	328
Footwear (leather)	30	61	97
Products of animal origin	100	193	249
Paper and Printing	152	174	201
Pottery etc.	13	16	18
Other	22	63	75
Total	6585[g]	6893	8432

Sources: 1913: derived by us from *Trudy TsSU*, xxvi, i (1926), 70–1 (Soviet estimate for pre-1939 Soviet territory, adjusted by further data in Vorob'ev (1961), 122–4 (see notes below)).
  1926/27 and 1927/28: rearranged from data in *St. spr.* (1929), 316–23.

Notes: [a] Power, coal, peat, oil and oil-refining.
  [b] Includes non-ferrous metals, manganese and rare and precious metals; 1926/27 and 1927/28 include 'other mining' which presumably include the gold and platinum industries. We have included 'metalworking with non-ferrous metals' with 'metalworking' in 1926/27 and 1927/28; this was presumably the case in 1913.
  [c] 1913: 'ceramic industry', 'glass industry', 'other' extraction and processing of stones, earth and clay.
  1926/27 and 1927/28: ceramic, glass, cement, extraction and primary processing of minerals, asbestos, and other products from minerals. This is obviously a wider coverage than 1913.
  [d] Classified by groupings used at end of 1920s.
  1913 Group A includes: 'chemical production' and other production of chemical group excluding matches, rubber and soap (except toilet soap, data on which are not available as separate item).
  1926/27 and 1927/28 Group A includes: basic chemicals, paints and dyes, wood-chemicals and other chemicals.

1913 Group B includes: matches, rubber and soap (excluding toilet soap, see above).

1926/27 and 1927/28 Group B includes: matches; rubber; soaps, fats and perfumes; chemical-pharmaceutical. Coverage is obviously much wider than in 1913.

e The data for 1926/27 and 1927/28 include a large residual item which may include vodka production. The items covered by the heading 'food, drink and tobacco' are as follows:

1913: Flour-milling, sugar-beet, groats, wines, yeast, fruit-grape-vodka and cognac production, Treasury alcohol stores (vodka monopoly), tobacco, starch and molasses, vegetable oil, confectionery, sausages etc., and other food, salt, tea-weighing.

1926/27 and 1927/28: flour and groats; sugar beet and refined sugar; confectionery; vegetable oil; wine-yeast; vodka-cognac and grape wine; beer, mead and soda; starch and molasses; other food and drink; tobacco; makhorka; salt; production from bones.

The main shifts in production within the groups were the increase in flour-milling by large-scale industry and the decline in vodka production (million rubles):

	1913	*1926/27*	*1927/28*
Wines	52		
Yeast	9	210	258
Fruit-grape-vodka and cognac	18		
Beer and mead	29	43[+]	44[+]
Treasury alcohol monopoly	599	–	–
Other food and drink	–	256*	367*
Total of above items	707	509	669
Flour-milling and groats	424	617	653

* Includes other items as well as vodka (division not known).

[+] Includes soda.

Following the practice of TsSU, we have included 'tea-weighing' in the 1913 figure, amounting to 166 million rubles, but we do not know how far it is included in the data for the 1920s.

f The figure for cotton textiles includes 141 million rubles for cotton-cleansing.

g The total for 1913 was originally estimated at 5621 million rubles, but to this have been added items not covered by the factory and mine inspectorates, as follows (million rubles):

Treasury alcohol stores	599
Candle factories of church	20
Cotton cleansing	141
Tea weighing	166
Stone breaking	6
Various mining	4
Total	936

This gives a total of 6,557 million rubles, which is frequently cited. It was then necessary to add 28 million rubles in 1913 for the value of iron-ore production, which appears as a separate item in 1926/27 and 1927/28, but was excluded for 1913 (see *Trudy TsSU*, 71); this brings the total to 6,585 million rubles. Some other double-counting may appear in 1926/27 and 1927/28, but not in 1913. A further complication is that various small factories paying excises have been excluded from the 1913 figures (see *Trudy TsSU*, 72); the value of their production amounted to 160.1 million rubles.

Both the 1913 and the 1926/27 and 1927/28 figures include only those power stations controlled by industry.

The official TsSU figure eventually agreed for 1913 was 6,236 million rubles (see Vorob'ev (1961), 122–3); this exceeds the original estimate of 5,621 million rubles by 615 million rubles. According to Vorob'ev, this incorporates both the items amounting to 936 million rubles above and small excisable enterprises producing 160 million rubles, a total of 1,096 million rubles. But he does not explain why the official figure adds in only 615 million rubles; perhaps the 'hidden excise' on vodka (406 million rubles) has been omitted, together with some minor items.

Table 33.   Employment in large-scale industry, 1913 and 1926/27 (USSR
pre-1939 territory) (thousands)

Branch of industry	1913	1926/27	Index	(1913 = 100)
Fuel[a]	287.8	402.9	140	
Ore mining[a]	173.2	81.6	47	
Silicate (glass, brick)	171.5	150.2	88	
Ferrous metallurgy[a]	126.8	204.0	161	
Non-ferrous metallurgy[a]	12.2	5.1	42	
Metal-working and machine-building	352.1	409.4[b]	116	
Woodworking[a]	100.0	96.9	97	
Chemicals	83.5	88.0	105	
Foodstuffs	342.7	283.1	83	
Textiles	687.1	648.7[c]	94	
of which:				
Cotton	479.8	469.5	98	
Woollen	90.7	60.6	67	
Silk	31.5	5.6	18	
Flax, hemp, jute	85.0	113.0	133	
Mixed fabrics (inc. clothing)	25.2	67.7	269	
Paper	41.8	40.4	97	
Total[d]	2,438.8	2,550.3	105	

Source: Mints (1975), 39, 44, 80–101.

Notes: [a] Approximate figure only, derived from percentage shares given in
source, p. 44.
[b] Narkomtrud figures suggest 443.5 (Mints, 1975, p. 87).
[c] Narkomtrud figures suggest 689.4 (Mints, 1975, p. 81).
[d] Excludes printing, reportedly 41.6 in 1913 and 65.9 in 1926/27, and
electric power.

Table 34. Gross production of small-scale (non-census) industry, 1913 and 1926/27 (USSR pre-1939 territory) (million rubles at current prices)

	1913	*1926/27*
Minerals, glass	–	9[a]
Construction materials		
(mostly brick)	33[a]	31
Metal-working	120[b]	204
Machine-building	9[b]	20
Chemicals	9	47[c]
Wood products	147	184
Paper	5	12
Textiles	102[d]	332
cotton	–	67
flax and mixed	17	7
wool	4	74
silk	16	19
hemp, jute	26	17
felt	32	94
knitted goods	7	56
Clothing	249	568
Leather (incl. shoes) and fur	514[d]	765
Food and drink	932[e]	2089
Printing	8	49
Other	39	54
Total[f]	2167	4364

Source: Adapted from data in Kaufman (1962), 79–83.

Notes: Prices probably approximately doubled between 1913 and 1926/27.
  [a] Includes pottery.
  [b] Source gives 129 million for metal products and machine-building combined: 9 million has been assigned to machine building to take account of small-scale production of farm equipment: see Vorob'ev (1925), 645.
  [c] Includes rubber products (1 million) and grease, tallow, soap and perfume (25 million).
  [d] Derived largely from output of large-scale industry in 1913, multiplied by the ratio of small to large-scale output.
  [e] Includes grease, soap, perfume, etc. (see note c).
  [f] Excludes logging and fishing.

Table 35. Numbers employed in small-scale industry, 1913, 1926/27 and 1927/28 (USSR pre-1939 territory) (full-time equivalents, thousands)

	1913	1926/27	1927/28
Building materials	64	19	59
Machine-building and metal-working	211	208	217
Chemicals	16	14	24
Wood products	471	169[a]	251[a]
Food and drink	347	259	282
Textiles and clothing	1075	884	951
Printing and paper	22	12	45
Other	61	24	49
Total	2265	1589	1878

Source: Estimated from Kaufman (1962), 64–74; this was based in turn on estimates by TsSU of number of workers and number of weeks worked per year. Logging and fisheries have been excluded from Kaufman's tables.

Notes: These figures assume that the average number of working weeks declined from 27 in 1913 to less than 18 in 1927/28; this seems implausible. An alternative estimate of the number of full-time equivalents for 1913, using the average number of working weeks for each trade, and the new data for the total number of workers in Rybnikov (1922), 5, 15 amounts to 2,048,000. These figures are further discussed in Chapter 2, Appendix.

[a] These figures for wood products are obviously too low relative to 1913, but we have been unable to nail down the error.

Table 36. Regional distribution of employment and production in large-scale industry, 1913 and 1925–7 (USSR pre-1939 territory) (in percentages of total)

| | 1913 | | 1925/26 | 1927 |
	Gross Output	*Labour*	*Gross Output*	*Labour*
Central Industrial, North-West and Southern Industrial	63.8	64.9	71.8	72.5
Urals, Siberia	8.8	10.5	6.5	9.8
North Caucasus, Crimea	4.4	5.9	5.7	3.7
Transcaucasus	6.3	3.1	4.6	2.5
Central Asia	1.6	2.4	1.9	1.2
Others[a]	15.1	13.2	9.5	10.3
Total	100.0	100.0	100.0	100.0

Sources: 1913: *Trudy TsSU*, xxvi (1926), i, 80–1.
         1925/26: Drobizhev *et al.* (1973), 293.
         1927: Mints (1975), 74–5.
         (1913 and 1927 data reclassified to correspond to Drobizhev classification).

Note: [a] North, Central Black-Earth, Central and Mid-Volga, Belorussia and Far East.

Table 37. Industrial production of selected products in physical terms, 1908–1927/28

	1908 (Russian Empire)	1913 (Russian Empire)	1913 (USSR pre-1939 territory)	1916	1920	1926/27	1927/28
Coal (million tons)[a]	25.91[1]	36.05[1]	29.12[2]	34.48[2]	8.56[3]	31.92[3]	34.51[3]
Crude oil (million tons)	8.74[4]	9.23[1]	9.23[4]	9.97[4]	3.85[3]	10.24[3]	11.51[3]
Pig-iron (million tons)	2.80[1]	4.64[1]	4.22[5]	3.80[5]	0.12[3]	2.97[3]	3.28[3]
Rolled steel (million tons)	2.70[6]	4.04[1b]	3.51[5]	3.38[5]	0.15[5]	2.70[3]	3.23[3]
Copper (thousand tons)	16.4[1]	32.3[1]	31.1[7]	20.8[1]	1.17[c]	27.0[7]	30.0[7]
Cement (thousand tons)	902[6]	2131[6]	1520[8]	–	36[8]	1574[3]	1851[3]
Raw sugar[d] (thousand tons)	–	–	1347[9]	1186[9]	89[9]	985[3]	1259[3]
Cigarettes[e] (milliards)	14.6[6]	25.9[6]	22.1[6]	–	4.9[3]	40.7[3]	49.0[3]
Vodka[f] (million decalitres)	–	–	118.9[10]	0	0	39.6[6]	55.5[10]
Cotton fabrics (million linear metres)	–	–	2582[11]	–	120[3]	2370[3]	2607[3]
Woollen fabrics (million linear metres)	–	–	103[11g]	–	18[3g]	85[3g]	79[3g]

Sources:
[1] (Granat) Entsiklopedicheskii slovar', xxxvi, Prilozhenie (1926), pp. xxvii, xxx–xxxi.
[2] Promyshlennost' (1957), 140.
[3] Statisticheskii spravochnik 1928 (1929), 302–11.
[4] Promyshlennost' (1957), 153.
[5] Promyshlennost' (1957), 106.
[6] See Nutter (1962), 411–95.
[7] Sotsialisticheskoe stroitel'stvo (1935), 190.
[8] Promyshlennost' (1957), 277.
[9] Promyshlennost' (1957), 373.
[10] Nutter (1963), 454.
[11] Promyshlennost' (1964), 364.

Notes: – = not available in sources used.

Data are in metric tonnes.

[a] Includes anthracite and brown coal.

[b] 'Finished iron and steel'.

[c] 1921/22.

[d] *Sakhar-pesok*.

[e] *Papirosy* and *sigarety*.

[f] 40° alcohol equivalent

[g] These figures apparently refer to large-scale industry, and may underestimate the recovery owing to the increase in the proportion of artisan production in the 1920s (see Nutter, 1962, 492, who estimates total production at 105 million metres in 1913, 103 in 1926/27 and 117 in 1927/28; according to *Materials*, 1985, 368, total production in 1928 was 100.5 million metres, including 9.3 millions by non-census industry).

Table 38.   Gross production of metal-working and machine-building by
sub-branch, 1913, 1926/27 and 1927/28 (USSR pre-1939 territory)
(million rubles, 1913 prices)

		1913	*1926/27*	*1927/28*
I.	Metal-working	248[a]	240[b]	296[b]
(a)	non-ferrous	(109)[c]	75	88
(b)	metal goods: mass prodn			
	and pressed	(56)[c]	55	68
(c)	other	(83)[c]	110	140
II.	Machine-building	398[d]	477[b]	638[b]
(a)	transport equipment	90[e]	77	83
(b)	shipbuilding	109[f]	28	46
(c)	industrial equipment	100[g]	170	228
(d)	agricultural machinery and tools	52[h]	116	155
(e)	electro-technical	46[i]	86	126

Sources: 1913 based upon *Dinamika* (1930), iii, 10–11, 18–20, 52–79, 176.
1926/27 and 1927/28: taken from *Statisticheskii spravochnik* (1929), 317–8.

Notes: [a] Includes armaments. Calculated as a residual. *Dinamika* gives 646
million rubles for metal working and machine-building in 1913; we have
deducted 398 million rubles for machine-building, as reported in *Trudy
TsSU*, xxvi (1926), i, 70–1.
[b] Presumably excludes armaments (i.e., small-arms and ammunition
under I and military vessels under II(b)).
[c] No breakdown for metal-working is available for 1913; an estimate is
made on the basis of the percentage shares of individual sub-branches in
1912.
[d] This is the figure given in *Trudy TsSU*, xxvi (1926), i, 70–1. Includes
armaments, mainly military ship-building.
[e] Estimate, based upon evidence of increase in production of physical
units of wagons and locomotives, reported in Rozenfel'd and Klimenko
(1961), 101, and Korelin (1972), 161.
[f] Estimated output, based upon reported output in 1912, inflated in line
with reported increase in employment in private and state shipyards
between 1912 and 1913. Employment data from Shatsillo (1968), 223,
229–30.
[g] Output in 1912 was reportedly 97 million rubles. In 1913, the figure can
hardly have been less than this, given what is known about industrial
investment in that year.
[h] Vorob'ev (1925), 645.
[i] Sarab'yanov (1923), 70.

Table 39.   Internal trade, 1913 and 1926 (USSR pre-1939 territory)

(a) *Organised retail trade turnover* (million rubles)		
1913	*1926* *(current prices)*	*1926* *(1913 prices)*
5,918	12,823	5,780

Source: Dikhtyar (1961), 238, and Dikhtyar (1960), 71–3.

Notes: The 1926 figure (current prices) is taken from contemporary official sources and adjusted by Dikhtyar to take account of changes in retail prices. The 1913 figure derives from Dikhtyar (1960), 73. Here, the author calculates retail trade turnover for 1912 from official tax statistics. Dikhtyar includes trade conducted by large and small permanent outlets (i.e., categories II and III). He reduces the total, in order to exclude non-trading units (insurance firms, etc.) that came into those categories; and inflates the total, in order to take account of retail outlets (including those in Central Asia) that did not contribute to the tax levy (*raskladochnyi sbor*). The 1912 estimates for organised trade are then increased in line with Strumilin's estimate of the increase in turnover between 1912 and 1913. The Empire turnover is finally corrected for territorial losses after 1917, to give organised turnover on USSR territory. The 1913 figures exclude transactions at state vodka stores. The retail price index used by Dikhtyar to obtain 1926 turnover in 1913 prices is 222 (1913 = 100).

Table 39. *continued*

(b) *Number of licensed trading units* (thousands)

Category	1912	1926
I. Wholesale, etc.	8	18
II. Large shops (*magaziny*)	149	62
III. Small shops (*lavki*)	486	259
IV. Stalls, kiosks (*lar'ki*)	289	305
Total (I–IV)	932	644
V. Other (hawkers, pedlars,		
i.e., *razvozki, raznoski*)	310	160
Total (I–V)	1242	804

Source: Strumilin (1958), 677–8, 692.

Note: Official tsarist tax statistics reported only a few thousand trade units in the lowest category (V). But the population census of 1897 suggested that the number of people engaged full-time as hawkers and pedlars was much greater. The total reported in Category V is therefore inflated by Strumilin to take account of under-registration in 1913. Pedlars and others undoubtedly found it easy to evade registration during the 1920s as well, so the total in Category V in 1926 is an underestimate.

Table 40. Net revenue of state budget in comparable classification, 1913 and
1926/27 (million rubles at current prices)

	1913	*1926/27*
Tax on alcoholic drinks	718	585
Other excises	301	625
Customs dues	353	190
Total indirect taxes	1372	1400
Personal income tax	n.a.	114
Industrial tax: private sector	150	109
Agricultural tax	n.a.	358
Other direct taxes (mainly on private property)	122	n.a.
Taxes and deductions from profits, etc.: state sector	75	626
Timber revenue	92	287
Dues (*poshliny*), etc.	231	176
Other revenue	221	134
Net revenue from transport and posts	25	0
State loans: net receipts	–	218
Total revenue	2288	3422

Source: Estimated from data in Davies (1958), 4–5, 83–4, and Carr and Davies
(1969), 975–6. 'Self-balancing' revenue from transport and posts, the
administrative costs of the vodka monopoly, and that part of revenue from
state loans which was expended on repayments and interest, have all been
omitted.

Note: *Price levels*. In 1926/27 the general wholesale price index was 185 and the
retail index 201 (1913 = 100) (*Kontrol'nye tsifry . . . na 1929/30* (1930),
578); the index for transfer prices of Vesenkha-planned industry was 165
(see Davies (1978), 15–6, and pp. 243 above and 336 below).
n.a. = not applicable.

Table 41.   Net expenditure of state budget in comparable classification
(million rubles at current prices)

	1913	*1926/27*
Industry	65[a]	448
Electrification	n.a.	103
Agriculture	139[b]	204
Net expenditure on transport and posts	0	177
Trade	n.a.	91[f]
Municipal economy and housing	n.a.	43
Other	n.a.	134
Total on national economy	204	1199
Social and cultural	143[c]	356
Defence	953[d]	634[g]
Administration	495[e]	369
Transferred to local budgets	n.a.	582
Other, including reserves	74	226
Payments on state loans	424	0
Total expenditure	2293	3366

Source: Estimated from data in Davies (1958), 4–5, 65, 83–4.

Notes: n.a. = not applicable. On price levels, see Note to Table 39(a); and Table 66.

[a] Ministry of Trade and Industry.

[b] Department of Agriculture and Land Settlement, and state horse-breeding.

[c] Ministry of Education.

[d] Includes expenditure by military department for economic and strategic purposes.

[e] Includes 247 million rubles of Ministry of Finance, which includes various expenditures in the economy.

[f] Includes food industry.

[g] For comparability with 1913, should include budget allocations to defence industries (51 million rubles) and probably shipbuilding (18 million rubles) (see *Promyshlennost'* . . . *1926/27* (1928), 72 – 'other' is presumably defence industries). Other defence items lurking elsewhere in the budget may not have been traced.

Table 42.   Output of textiles, 1913–28 (USSR pre-1939 territory)

	Cotton yarn (thousand tons)	Cotton cloth (million metres)	Flax yarn (thousand tons)	Linen cloth (million metres²)	Woollen yarn (thousand tons)	Woollen cloth (million metres)	Silk (million metres)
1913	271.0	2582	53.3	120	46.5	103	42.6
1925	196.9	1677	45.3	125	29.7	56	n.a.
1926	247.3	2273	64.5	163	39.5	72	n.a.
1927	285.6	2609	64.1	180	44.3	86	n.a.
1928	324.0	2670	61.6	174	49.5	87	9.6

Source: Korneev (1957), 78.

Table 43. Number of mills and textile workers, 1913 and 1925/26 (large-scale
industry, pre-1939 USSR territory)

	1913		1925/26	
	No. of working mills	*No. of workers (large-scale industry)*	*No. of working mills*	*No. of workers (large-scale industry)*
Cotton	581	480390	245	472530
Wool	346	92050	148	70155
Linen	254	84423	109	106051
Silk	168	33261	45	7895
Total	1349	720124	547	656631

Source: *Dinamika*, i, iii (1930), 177, 208–9.

Table 44. Railway mileage and traffic, 1908–13

	1908	1909	1910	1911	1912	1913
Route mileage (annual average) (thousand kms)	63.9	64.1	64.6	65.4	66.5	68.0
Freight (milliard ton-km)	53.4	58.2	60.7	65.4	71.6	69.8
Passengers (milliard pass-km)	20.4	21.4	23.2	24.2	26.8	29.3
Conventional milliard ton-km[a]	73.8	79.6	83.9	89.6	98.4	99.1
Traffic density (million ton-km)[b]	1.15	1.24	1.30	1.37	1.48	1.46

Source: Strumilin (1958), 640–1.

Notes: [a] 'Conventional' ton-km is the sum of freight ton-km and revenue passenger-km, and is thus an indicator of a railway's total production, corresponding quite closely to the income-producing work actually performed.

[b] The average intensity of use of the route mileage, expressed in millions of ton-km produced (or endured!) annually by a kilometre of route.

Table 45. Railway productivity indices, 1908–13 (1908 = 100)

	1909	1910	1911	1912	1913
Traffic (conventional ton-km)	108	114	121	133	134
Route mileage	100	101	102	104	106
Railway workers	95	91	96	99	97
Ton-km per worker	114	125	127	135	139

Source: Strumilin (1958), 640–1.

Table 46. Accidents to railway workers, 1904–13

	Casualties per million train-km	Deaths per milliard ton-km
1904	20.6	9.08
1905	23.2	9.95
1906	28.1	11.66
1907	28.1	11.22
1908	29.5	11.01
1909	28.6	8.3
1910	29.4	7.8
1911	29.8	7.5
1912	33.1	8.1
1913	39.6	9.12

Source: Strumilin (1958), 644–5 (rearranged).

Table 47.   The effect on the railways of territorial losses after the Revolution

	1913 (Empire territory)	1913 (pre-1939 USSR territory)
Route mileage (km)	70,500	58,500
Traffic (milliard conventional ton-km)	106.4	90.9
Work-force (thousands) *and hence*	823	691
Line utilisation (thousand ton-km/km)	1510	1554
Labour productivity (thousand ton-km per worker)	129	132

Source: Strumilin (1958), 670–1.

Table 48.   Railway freight commodities and average lengths of haul, 1913–28

	1913 Empire terri-tory	*1913 USSR pre-1939 terri-tory*	*1923/24*	*1924/25*	*1925/26*	*1926/27*	*1928*[a]
Total tons (million)	158	132	67	83	117	136	156
of which hard coal	35	26	12	15	22	27	30
grain/flour	20	18	11	11	14	15	16
timber building materials	15	12	7	10	13	15	17
ferrous metal	5	4	1	3	4	5	6
oil products	6	6	3	5	6	6	9
Av. length of haul (km)							
all freight:	485	496	500	568	590	601	598
hard coal	471[a]	485	526	552	617	660	615
wheat	473		627		890		
grain/flour		544[1]	738	884	851	987	949
timber materials	499[a]	415	469	527	651	621	671
ferrous metals			642	755	756	780	786
oil products	601	601[1]	640	650	797	774	728

Sources: *Materialy po statistike putei soobshcheniya*, lxix (1927), Table 1, and civ (?1928), Table 1, except 1928 and for items marked [1], which are from *Transport i svyaz'* (1957), 35–8.

Note: [a] Excludes railway-service freight not sent beyond the originating railway.

Table 49.　Railway traffic levels, 1913–28

	Freight ton-km (milliards)	Freight tonnage (millions)	Passenger-kms (milliards)	Passenger journeys (millions)
1913 (USSR pre-1939 territory)	65.7	132.4	25.2	184.8
1917	63.0	115.2		
1918	14.2	37.2		
1919	17.5	30.5		
1920	11.4	31.9		
1921	14.0	37.9		83.6
1922	18.2	44.6	9.4	91.1
1923	26.2	60.7	12.8	121.8
1924	36.5	70.7	16.7	170.4
1925	52.6	92.4	20.5	227.3
1926	73.5	122.2	22.8	259.9
1927	82.6	139.6	22.4	258.1
1928	93.4	156.2	24.5	291.1

Source: *Transport i svyaz'* (1957), 17, 32.

Notes:　The earlier Yakobi (1935), a Gosplan publication, makes it clear on p. 20 that 'freight' is defined as that which travels in commercial trains (thus locomotive coal sent by the wagonload would be counted but locomotive coal sent by the trainload would not). Ton-km (and hence length of haul) are calculated according to the tariff distance, which is probably about 5 per cent shorter than the actual average distance.

　　It also seems fairly clear that the 1914–21 figures are not based on inter-war frontiers, but in one way or another on actual frontiers, whose fluidity must have posed some statistical problems; mileage in service, for example, declined from 64,253 km in May 1917 to 22,130 km in October 1918 (see *Materialy po statistike*, i, 1921, 35).

　　Materialy po statistike, iii (1922), Table A, gives series for 1911–20. These are difficult to use, because definitions and coverage are not always self-evident. Moreover, the 'tonnage originated' figures are distorted by double-counting. The ton-km figures, more accurate, are given below. They relate to the actual imperial frontiers:

1911　65.2 milliard ton-km
1912　71.5
1913　75.9
1914　74.7
1915　83.0
1916　–
1917　63.0
1918　14.1
1919　14.8
1920　13.5

　　Later Soviet sources use 76.8 milliard ton-km for the 1913 Empire, and this is presumably the best that could be obtained by the statisticians of the 1920s.

Table 50. Railway accident rates, 1913–1927/28

	1913 Empire	1921	1922	1923/24	1924/25	1925/26	1926/27	1927/28
Accidents per 100,000 train-km	1.45			5.69	4.59	4.84	4.56	3.25
Train collisions		0.54	0.70	0.42	0.35	0.24	0.22	0.24
Derailments (per 100,000 train-km)		1.2	1.66	1.05	0.73	0.43	0.41	0.30
Broken couplings (occurrences)		1181	1246	1408	2917	4066	5209	6258

Sources: *Materialy po statistike*, lxxxv (1927), p. xxi, and civ (?1928), 10.

Note: These figures exclude shunting mishaps and train breakages at stations. Presumably they relate to *train* accidents only. Broken couplings would be expected to increase in line with number of trains operated (or, perhaps, train or locomotive or car mileage), and average size of trains. But a precise correlation is lacking: freight train size rose from 81 axles in 1922/23 to 95 in 1926/27, while total freight locomotive mileage rose from 82 million loco-km in 1922/23 to 195 million in 1926/27. Careless driving, acceptance of overloading, and perhaps higher speeds would presumably have made a substantial contribution.

Table 51.   Locomotive stock, 1913–1927/28 (units)

	1913 Empire pre-terri-tory	1913 USSR pre-1939 terri-tory	1922/23	1923/24	1924/25	1925/26	1926/27	1927/28
Total[a]	19769	16815	18931	19935	20113	19022	18354	17517
% in working order[b]	83	83		45	47	54	61	67
Per cent in use	71	72		30	33	45	49	53
Newly-built in USSR[c]			95	141	101	214	366	455
Condemned				347	344	1531	1013	955
Stored in working order	2350	2020	2369	2843	2857	1072	2132	2536
Dumped ('Reserve Stock')				7267	7055	5632	4474	2575

Source: *Materialy po statistike*, civ (?1928), Table 1.

Notes: [a] 'Total' is the number at the disposal of the railways, and is therefore not quite the complete number (it is usually about 1 per cent less than the grand total; the latter presumably includes units on acceptance trials, etc.).
[b] This includes units undergoing light repairs.
[c] The imports from Germany and Sweden ended in early 1923. This and the next line include narrow-gauge units.
Except where indicated, only broad-gauge units are included.

Table 52. The research effort, pre-war and mid-1920s

		Pre-war	*NEP*
A	*Global data*		
	(i) Budgetary expenditure	1912:6.3[1]	1925/26:40[2]
	on scientific activities	1913:9.6[3]	1926/27:54[2]
	(million rubles)	1914:9.7[4]	1927/28:81[2]
	(ii) Manpower		
	scientific workers[a]	1913:10.2/11.6[5]	1/10/1926:20.0[b6]
	(thousands)		1/10/1927:23.1[b6]
			1/10/1928:24.5[b6]
B	*Research establishments*		
	(i) No. of research	1913:289[7]	1/1/1929:1,263[8]
	establishments		
	(ii) Scientific workers[a]	1913:4.2[7]	1/4/1929:11.6[9]
	(thousands)		
C	*Education sector*		
	(i) Expenditure on science/	1912:1.929[10]	1925/26:9.508[13]
	scientific establishments	1913:2.958[11]	1926/27:11.586[14]
	by ministry/ministries	1914:2.893[12]	1927/28:12.236[15]
	of education (million rubles)		
	(ii) Research establishments	1919:21[16]	1926:84[16]
	under ministry/ministries		1927:86[16]
	of education		
	(iii) Higher educational		
	establishments		
	– no. of *vuzy*	1914/15:91[17]	1927/28:148[17]
	– scientific workers[a]	1913:6.0[7]	1925/26:17.6[18]
	(thousands)		1926/27:18.5[18]
			1927/28:18.4[18]
D	*Agriculture*		
	State budget expenditure	1912:2.535[c19]	1925/26:7.954[d22]
	on agricultural research	1913:3.843[c20]	1926/27:9.513[d23]
	(million rubles)	1914:4.311[c21]	1927/28:12.777[d24]
E	*Industry*		
	(data for Vesenkha SSSR)		
	(i) State budget expenditure	(1912:0.210)[e25]	1925/26:10.7[28]
	on industrial research	(1913:0.467)[e26]	1926/27:18.2[28]
	establishments (million rubles)	(1914:0.431)[e27]	1927/28:21.5[28]

Table 52. *continued*

	Pre-war	NEP
(ii) Industrial research establishments – research institutes (a) numbers		1928:24[29]
(b) total manpower (thousands)		end 1927:3.7[30] 1/10/1928:4.0[30]
of which scientific workers (thousands)		end 1927:1.5[30] 1/10/1928:2.0[30]
F *Academy of Sciences*		
(i) State budget funds (million rubles)	1912:0.924[31] 1913:1.058[32] 1914:1.233[33]	1925/26:2.538[34] 1926/27:2.800[35] 1927/28:2.766[36]
(ii) Scientific establishments – total	1916: 41[37]	1925: 74[37]
of which research institutes research laboratories scientific and experimental stations	_[37] 5[37] 16[37]	7[37] 11[37] 16[37]
(iii) Manpower – total	1913:153[38] 1917:220[39]	1925:1,055[40] 1928:1,045[41]
of which scientific workers (excluding academicians)	1917:109[39]	1925:363[40] 1928:445[41]

Sources: [1] Additions of individual items of expenditure in *Otchet gosudarstvennogo kontrolya . . . na 1912* (1913), 318–697.

[2] Estimates by Lewis (1979), 151–63.

[3] Additions of individual items of expenditure in *Otchet . . . na 1913* (1914), 322–731.

[4] Additions of individual items of expenditure in *Otchet . . . na 1914* (1915), 328–747.

[5] The lower figure is from the early post-Stalin statistical handbooks (e.g., *40 Years of Soviet Power*, 1958, 259) and stated to be for the pre-1939 territory of the USSR; the higher figure is that given in later handbooks (e.g., *Narodnoe obrazovanie*, 1977, 7) and probably refers to post-1945 territory.

[6] Lewis (1975), 378–87.

[7] *40 Years of Soviet Power* (1958), 259, stated to be inter-war boundaries.

[8] *Narodnoe khozyaistvo SSSR v 1958 godu* (1959), 842.

[9] *Nauchnye kadry* (1930), 14–16.

[10] *Otchet . . . na 1912* (1913) 450–67, excluding expenditure on the Imperial Academy of Sciences.

[11] *Otchet . . . na 1913* (1914), 454–73, excluding expenditure on the Imperial Academy of Sciences.

[12] *Otchet . . . na 1914* (1915), 462–81, excluding expenditure on the Imperial Academy of Sciences.

[13] *Ob"yasnitel'naya zapiska . . . na 1925–1926* (1926), 704–7.

[14] *Edinyi gosudarstvennyi byudzhet . . . na 1926–1927* (1927), 184–5.

[15] *Edinyi gosudarstvennyi byudzhet . . . na 1928–1929* (1929), 227–8.

[16] Pinkevich (1935), 99.

[17] *Narodnoe obrazovanie* (1977), 213.

[18] *Nauchnye kadry* (1930), 23.

[19] *Otchet . . . na 1912* (1913), 562–577.

[20] *Otchet . . . na 1913* (1914), 588–91, 602–3.

[21] *Otchet . . . na 1914* (1915), 596–603.

[22] *Edinyi gosudarstvennyi byudzhet . . . na 1925–1926* (1926), 218–19, 234–55.

[23] *Edinyi gosudarstvennyi byudzhet . . . na 1926–1927* (1927), 200–1, 204–5.

[24] *Edinyi gosudarstvennyi byudzhet . . . na 1927–1928* (1928), 244, 251–2.

[25] *Otchet . . . na 1912* (1913), 646–7.

[26] *Otchet . . . na 1913* (1914), 676–7.

[27] *Otchet . . . na 1914* (1915), 744–7.

[28] Lewis (1975), 347–52, 357–358.

[29] Lewis (1975), 399–401.

[30] Lewis (1975), 391–4.

[31] *Otchet . . . na 1912* (1913), 448–9.

[32] *Otchet . . . na 1913* (1916), 454–5.

[33] *Otchet . . . na 1914* (1915), 462–3.

[34] *Edinyi gosudarstvennyi byudzhet . . . na 1926–1927. Proekt* (1927), 69.

[35] *Edinyi gosudarstvennyi byudzhet . . . na 1926–1927. Proekt* (1927), 65.

[36] *Edinyi gosudarstvennyi byudzhet . . . na 1928–1929. Proekt* (1928), 57–8.

[37] *Vestnik statistiki*, no. 4, 1974, 86.

[38] Graham (1967), 164.

[39] Komkov, Karpenko, Levshin and Semenov (1968), 56.

[40] *Kul'turnoe stroitel'stvo* (1940), 240.

[41] *Plan rabot Akademii Nauk*, i (1932), 4.

Notes: [a] Scientific workers (*nauchnye rabotniki*) include specialists in the humanities and social sciences.

[b] Figures for membership of the scientific workers' trade union; they would seem to underestimate the actual number of scientific workers.

[c] Expenditure mostly (90–95 per cent) under the heading 'scientific, experimental and demonstration agricultural establishments and grants for the maintenance of such establishments'.

[d] Expenditure mostly under budgetary division 'Agriculture' on scientific-experimental stations and fields and establishments of special purpose for agriculture (c 75 per cent) and under division 'Education, science and art' on 'learned and scientific establishments' (c 25 per cent).

[e] Funds allocated through the Ministry of War for the organisation of its central scientific and technical laboratory.

Table 53. Russian and Soviet contributions to German scientific journals, 1911–3 and 1926–8

	No. of articles by authors from Russia/USSR (USSR pre-1939 frontiers)		Percentage of total articles in journal	
	1911–13	*1926–8*	*1911–13*	*1926–8*
Annalen der Physik	19	7	3.6	1.6
Berichte der Deutschen				
chemischen Gesellschaft	64	135	4.2	10.0
Matematische Annalen	5	20	2.6	10.9
Zeitschrift für anorg-				
anische und allgemeine	21	89	9.5	10.5
Chemie				
Zeitschrift für				
analytische Chemie	6	23	3.6	14.6
Zeitschrift für Elektro-				
chemie und angewandte	16.5	26	6.7	11.1
physikalische Chemie				
Total	131.5[a]	315	4.6	9.4

Note: [a] Between 1911 and 1913 another 17 articles were published by authors from parts of the Russian Empire which did not become part of the USSR.

Table 54. High technology output in physical terms, 1910–1927/28

(a)	*Means of transport and tractors* (units)				
	Aircraft	*Automobiles*	*Tractors*	*Bicycles*	*Motorcycles*
1910	70[1]	29[4a]		7192 (3192)[4b]	72[4]
1911	120[1]	49[4a]		9149 (4118)[4b]	99[4]
1912	170[1]	106[4a]		11278 (4901)[4b]	133[4]
1913	280[1]		'several 10s'[8]		
1914	535[1]	c 1000 (1896–1915)[5]			
1915	1305[1]				
1916	1870[1]				
1917	1897[1]				
1918	255[2]				
1919	137[2]				
1920	166[2]				
1921	13[3]				
1922	44[3]				
1922/3	146[3]		2[9]	800[12]	0[14]
1923/4	208[3]		10[9]	1500[12]	0[14]
1924/5	326[3]		481[9]		0[14]
1925/6	469[3]	248[6]	823[10]	4263[6]	0[14]
1926/7	575[3]	395[6]	918[10]	7459[6]	0[14]
1927/8	870[3]	671[7]	1273[11]	10847[13]	0[14]

Sources: [1] Shavrov, 2nd edn (1978), 256.
[2] Yakovlev (4th edn, 1982), 350.
[3] Shumikhin (1986), 103.
[4] *Fabrichnozavodskaya promyshlennost'*, vi (1914), 152.
[5] Shugurov and Shirsov, 2nd edn (1983), 18.
[6] *Promyshlennost' SSSR v 1926/27g* (1928), 208.
[7] *Sotsialisticheskoe stroitel'stvo* (1935), 54.
[8] *Ocherki razvitiya tekhniki v SSSR. Stroitel'naya, sel'skokhozyaistvennaya i meditsinskaya teknika* (1971), 201.
[9] *Itogi . . . 1917–1927* (n.d. [?1928]), 244–5.
[10] *Puti industrializatsii*, no. 5–6, 1929, 135.
[11] *Sotsialisticheskoe stroitel'stvo* (1935), 55.
[12] Nutter (1962), 458.
[13] *Sotsialisticheskoe stroitel'stvo* (1935), 65.
[14] *Izobretatel' i ratsionalizator*, no. 8, 1986, 29.

Notes: No figure indicates lack of information.
[a] These data appear to understate the output.
[b] Figure in brackets is for pre-1939 Soviet territory.

Table 54. *continued*

(b) *Machine tools, sewing machines, and timepieces*

	Machine tools		Sewing Machines	Timepieces
	(units)	(million pre-war rubles)	(units)	(units)
1910		1.5[1]	253,461[5]	327,135[10c]
1911		2.4[1]	311,363[5]	365,986[10c]
1912		2.8[1]	460,257[5]	412,531[10c]
1913	1800 (1500)[2a]	3.6[1]	271,800[6]	700,000[11d]
1917		5.2[1]		
1924/5			52,400[7]	
1925/6	1122[3b]	2.6[1]	125,425[8]	500,000[12]
1926/7	1873[4b]	3.0[1]	202,054[8]	
1927/8	1923[4b]	4.8[1]	285,604[9]	950,000[11]

Sources: [1] From, or calculated from, *Sotsialisticheskaya ratsionalizatsiya* (1930), 150.

[2] *Promyshlennost'* (1964), 255.

[3] *Promyshlennost'* (1928), 208.

[4] *Ekonomicheskoe obozrenie*, no. 2, 1929, 158.

[5] *Fabrichnozavodskaya promyshlennost'*, vi (1914), 132.

[6] *Promyshlennost'* (1964), 408.

[7] *Goroda Podmoskovya*, iii (1981), 286.

[8] *Promyshlennost'* (1928), 208.

[9] *Sotsialisticheskoe stroitel'stvo* (1935), 65.

[10] *Fabrichnozavodskaya promyshlennost'*, vi (1914), 148.

[11] *Promyshlennost'* (1964), 406.

[12] Romanov (1985), 14.

Notes: [a] Metal-cutting machine tools only; output on pre-1939 USSR territory in brackets.

[b] Cutting and forming machines.

[c] None produced on pre-1939 USSR territory.

[d] All types, including those assembled from imported parts; present-day USSR boundaries.

Table 55. Foreign trade and balance of payments 1909–13 and 1923/24–1927/28 (millions rubles at current world prices)

	1909	1910	1911	1912	1913	1923/24	1924/25	1925/26	1926/27	1927/28
Exports[a]	1416	1436	1576	1502	1506	523	559	677	779	782
Grain exports (gross)	750	748	740	552	595	192	52	159	208	41
Imports[a]	906	1084	1162	1172	1374	439	723	756	714	946
Balance of trade[b]	522	365	429	347	146	83	−164	−80	66	−164
Balance of payments (current account)							−195	−138	−5	−247
Precious metals and foreign currency exports						−42[c]	+86	+87	+1	+155
Foreign reserves[d] January 1						1,600[e]	360–415	445–540	398–414	408–453	444–455[f]
Foreign debt (September 30)[g]						78	148	209	252	370

Sources: Exports, imports and balance of trade;
1909–1913: Total exports and grain exports from Belen'skii *et al.* (eds), i (1928), 494–7 (N. Vissarionov); imports from Goldstein *et al.*, i (1929), 2 (M. Kaufman), 1.
1913–1927/28: *Vneshnyaya torgovlya* (1960). Figures in current prices for 1923/24 are estimates based on Kutuzov (ed.) (1928), 34.
Balance of payments: *Weltwirtschaftliches Archiv*, no. 36, 1932 (E. M. Shenkman).
Precious metal exports: Dohan (1969), 837–60.
Foreign reserves: Dohan (1969), 861–72.
Foreign debt: *Weltwirtschaftliches Archiv*, no. 36, 1932.

Notes: [a] Excludes platinum and precious metals.
[b] Balance of trade is exports minus imports.
[c] Net import of precious metals for calendar year 1924.
[d] After 1923/24 estimates are for gold and foreign exchange reserves controlled by the State Bank.
[e] On July 1, 1914 the gold reserve in the Russian State Bank was 1,600 million rubles, according to Baikalov (1934), 29. The gold reserve had fallen to 1,292 million rubles by October 1917; between 1917 and 1920 a large portion was lost during the civil war or used for war reparations; it was estimated at 281 million rubles on January 1, 1923 (*Ost-Europa-Markt*, no. 9, 1938, 455–469 (W. v. Golowatscheff).
[f] Foreign reserves on January 1, 1929 had fallen to 313–329 million rubles.
[g] Debt as of end of economic year.

Table 56. Value of exports, 1909–13 and 1923/24–1927/28 (million rubles at current prices)

	1909	1910	1911	1912	1913	1923/24[e]	1924/25	1925/26	1926/27	1927/28
Total exports	1415.5	1435.6	1576.1	1502.7	1505.9	522.6	558.8	676.7	779.4	781.8
Agricultural exports[a]	1109.5	1127.1	1196.2	1099.6	1114.5	364.4	338.1	430.6	476.8	399.7
A. *Crops*[b]	886.2	898.8	907.8	773.4	797.5	[247.0][i]	161.0	248.3	265.4	106.4
grain products[c]	750.1	748.0	739.5	551.9	595.8	192.0	52.3	159.1	208.1	40.5
wheat					225.2		16.4	76.4	126.2	11.5
rye					32.9		5.1	10.8	35.4	10.1
barley					186.2		15.6	50.4	17.6	0.4
oil seed	14.8	24.8	28.8	31.3	21.2	10.7	24.0	13.9	3.8	1.5
oil cake	33.6	31.6	34.4	39.1	38.8	20.8	26.5	24.0	22.7	16.9
flax[d]	67.9	73.9	70.4	116.1	94.2	23.3	52.5	45.5	20.8	26.9
hemp[d]	12.4	11.5	17.6	19.5	23.7	2.0	3.9	2.2	1.9	3.7
B. *Animal products*[f]	169.1	167.1	221.9	250.2	291.3	[45.4][i]	93.9	96.6	109.5	140.3
butter	48.9	51.3	71.1	88.5	71.6	26.5	27.6	30.9	34.2	39.2
eggs	62.2	63.7	80.8	84.7	90.7	13.4	25.7	23.6	29.0	40.5
meat	3.2	5.4	6.1	8.5	16.6		6.2	5.3	12.0	24.3
hides	22.9	16.9	29.1	48.1	47.7		1.6	5.0	5.7	4.5
horsehair	3.7	1.5	2.8	4.3	3.1	1.6	1.9	1.9	2.3	2.4
bristles	4.8	6.0	6.8	9.5	9.9	3.9	15.3	10.3	6.7	6.6
wool	6.8	5.5	8.0	11.2	10.6		5.0	1.4	0.7	0.9
C. *Furs and fish products*	20.1	23.3	24.7	29.8	15.1	[49.7][i]	80.9	82.4	96.3	132.1
fur	12.0	15.1	15.8	22.9	6.5	49.7	67.3	69.3	86.1	118.5
caviar	3.6	3.6	4.3	3.3	4.2		6.7	5.9	3.9	6.2
D. *Other agricultural*[g]	34.1	37.9	41.8	46.2	10.5	[20.4][i]	1.3	2.3	5.6	10.4
Industrial exports[h]	305.9	308.5	379.9	403.1	391.4	158.3	220.7	246.1	302.6	382.1
A. *Timber products*	126.6	138.2	142.4	153.4	166.0	70.4	72.8	58.5	80.4	94.8
unworked					62.8		25.4	20.3	23.2	32.5
sawn					96.4		40.8	32.4	49.7	52.3
B. *Mining products*	58.6	51.8	51.9	61.4	75.2	[51.7][i]	88.8	107.3	126.7	136.6
oil products	34.8	29.7	30.4	38.4	50.4	37.3	66.7	76.0	89.4	107.1

gasoline	7.6	7.7	6.6		8.3		25.9	35.7	40.1	46.5
kerosene					21.8		16.6	14.4	17.5	25.2
diesel and mazut					5.6		13.4	13.3	16.4	18.3
manganese ore	3.2	5.2	5.4	12.0	14.6	14.4	17.9	21.3	24.1	13.8
iron ore				4.1	3.1		1.7	1.4	4.2	4.5
C. Food industry					36.8		21.1	36.7	43.6	52.5
sugar	28.2	25.4	66.2	56.0	27.6	6.6	14.0	19.0	31.2	34.2
alcohol	5.2	5.5	7.5	9.3	5.2		0.1	0.0	0.0	0.5
D. Textile industry					49.9		8.5	19.5	25.3	60.6
cotton cloth	23.4	25.2	32.0	37.8	43.9		5.2	14.7	20.9	50.8
E. Other industries					63.5		29.5	24.1	26.6	37.6

Sources: 1909–12: Belen'skii *et al.* (eds), i (1929), 494–7 (Vissarionov). 1913–1927/28: *Vneshnyaya torgovlya* (1960). Data are reclassified to conform with the export classification during the 1920s as described in Dohan (1969), 736–40. Figures in current prices for 1923/24 are estimates based on Kutuzov (ed.) (1928), 34. Data include exports over all borders at current prices in gold rubles and exclude platinum and other precious metals.

Notes:
a Agricultural exports and industrial exports are classified according to the method used in the 1920s except that vegetables oils, oil cake, and all meat and fish (including canned meat and fish) are classified as agricultural exports.
b Crops include grains, oil seed, oil cake, all other seeds, flax, hemp, tobacco, medicinal herbs and licorice root, fruits, vegetables and potatoes.
c Grains exclude oil seed, oil cake and include beans, legumes and flour.
d Flax and hemp include fibre, tow and combings.
e The data for the 1923/24 exports of specific product categories are based on partial data in current prices available in Kutuzov (ed.) (1928), and are not strictly comparable to the other years.
f Animal products include butter, eggs, meat, raw hides, horsehair, bristles, wool, dead poultry, guts, horns and hooves, down and feathers, silkworm grains, cocoons, and wool.
g Other agricultural products are the residual of total agricultural exports minus crops, animal products, furs and fish, and include live animals and vegetable oil.
h Industrial exports as classified by Vissarionov in Belen'skii, *et al.* (eds), i (1929), 494–7, but excluding platinum exports.
i Sum of products under category.

Table 57. Exports of selected products in physical terms, 1909–13 and 1923/24–1927/28 (thousand metric tonnes)

	1909	1910	1911	1912	1913	1923/24	1924/25	1925/26	1926/27	1927/28
Agricultural exports										
A. Crop exports										
Grain products[a]	12480.0	13899.0	13499.0	9037.0	10331.0	2686.0	606.0	2082.0	2256.0	410.0
wheat	5151.0	6138.0	3940.0	2638.0	3329.4	554.6	167.4	737.2	1198.6	111.3
rye	581.0	664.0	882.0	501.0	646.5	1316.1	72.1	158.3	417.4	114.9
barley	3581.0	4008.0	4302.0	3927.0	3926.5	327.1	199.2	836.1	262.3	5.0
Oil seed	140.0	207.0	252.0	291.0	250.1	79.0	190.9	140.7	30.4	9.8
Oil cake	623.0	576.0	659.0	704.0	736.4	291.6	324.6	405.4	352.4	193.6
Flax[b]	275.1	254.4	225.7	353.2	305.1	35.5	55.6	70.9	43.7	42.5
Hemp[b]	54.6	48.3	67.2	64.5	68.0	4.4	7.6	6.6	8.0	13.6
Tobacco	9.8	9.8	10.8	11.3	12.8	2.6	1.5	1.4	3.9	5.1
B. Animal products										
Butter	57.0	56.4	76.5	72.9	78.0	22.5	24.5	27.3	30.3	32.9
Eggs[c]	202.3	213.2	261.8	241.6	254.0	23.3	49.0	41.4	61.8	94.4
Meat					34.4	0.8	8.3	7.9	16.8	40.5
Rawhides	28.2	22.9	28.0	50.8	52.4	1.0	1.2	2.2	2.7	1.3
Horsehair	3.8	1.6	2.9	3.6	2.3	1.5	1.1	1.0	1.1	1.4
Bristles	2.4	2.4	2.6	2.8	2.6	.8	1.7	1.6	1.2	1.8
Wool					17.5	1.0	7.0	2.2	1.6	1.2
Live animals					71.0	0.0	1.2	.3	1.0	
C. Furs and fish										
Furs	10.5	12.0	12.1	15.5	2.7	1.6	1.8	2.1	2.8	3.4
Caviar	2.6	3.1	2.8	2.5	3.3	1.6	2.7	3.7	2.2	2.3
Industrial exports										
A. Timber products										
Unworked	6945.0	6831.0	6829.0	7012.0	7488.5	2041.3	2126.9	1913.5	2483.6	2979.9
Sawn	3039.0	3207.0	3137.0	3466.0	3799.3	1105.6	1174.4	1030.8	1196.5	1583.7
Plywood					3554.3	403.5	912.1	841.7	1232.6	1329.2
						8.8	8.9	8.7	18.3	30.3

B. *Mineral products*										
Oil products	795.4	858.4	854.4	838.5	925.6	711.7	1372.5	473.5	2086.1	2782.5
gasoline	491.2	512.9			152.2	134.3	277.5	388.0	612.7	760.3
kerosene			448.7	396.2	439.7	335.3	453.9	343.8	474.0	691.3
diesel, mazut					166.8	118.0	555.3	641.6	825.1	1144.3
Manganese ore	620.6	683.9	634.9	1007.8	1193.8	493.8	526.9	628.0	784.7	498.9
Iron ore	517.6	847.1	886.0	663.2	469.7	7.1	189.4	149.8	407.7	428.4
C. *Other industries*										
Sugar	204.9	148.9	453.6	376.5	147.3	15.4	26.2	45.5	122.0	133.1
Cotton cloth	9.8	10.2	12.7	14.9	17.2	0.3	1.1	3.2	5.4	12.5
Alcohol					36.1	1.7	0.5	0.1	0.2	2.9
Machinery					4.5	.4	2.5	2.1	1.3	1.1

Sources: As for Table 56.

Notes: [a] Grains exclude oil seed, oil cake and include beans, legumes and flour.
[b] Flax and hemp include fibre, tow and combings.
[c] 1909–13 data for eggs converted from millions to tons by factor of 14,060 eggs per ton.

Table 58.   Value of imports, 1913 and 1923/24–1927/28
(million rubles at current prices)

		1909–13 (average)	1913	1923/24	1924/25	1925/26	1926/27	1927/28
Total imports		1139.0	1374.0	434.1	723.5	756.3	712.7	944.7
I.	Producer goods	646.0	884.4	362.8	470.6	590.5	626.2	796.1
	A. *machinery for industry and transportation*	127.3[b]	172.4	53.9	71.4	107.6	152.8	255.8
	B. *raw materials*	300.7[c]	343.1	221.2	244.5	274.0	328.1	383.6
	cotton	110.3	114.0	141.8	133.8	117.8	131.5	154.2
	wool	51.5	60.1	43.9	47.5	42.4	51.1	62.1
	leather, unworked	20.7	25.1	7.6	16.7	24.8	38.6	40.1
	rubber[a]	33.2	40.2	8.8	8.4	26.2	23.6	24.1
	non-ferrous metals[a]	39.4[b]	53.1[b]	14.4	18.8	20.7	45.4	57.7
	ferrous metals	8.4	9.0[b]	0.9	3.8	10.4	11.3	16.8
	C. *semi-processed goods*	122.6[d]	212.4	69.9	112.1	145.8	101.9	117.1
	paper and cardboard	25.6	29.5	9.4	22.0	29.3	18.4	14.6
	leather, worked	19.8	21.2	7.8	17.3	21.9	7.5	7.3
	dyes	15.6[b]	15.0	3.5	19.4	17.0	11.1	11.7
	tanning materials	6.7[b]	7.7	13.6	8.8	11.5	12.3	15.7
	D. *fuels*[e]	49.9	91.2	6.3	0.8	3.7	5.6	0.6
	E. *agricultural producers' goods*[f]	45.5[f]	65.3	11.5	41.7	59.4	37.8	39.0
	Agricultural equipment	40.5[b]	49.0	6.2	32.2	48.2	23.8	21.8
II.	Consumer goods	425.3[g]	392.0	67.1	240.8	153.5	80.8	142.3
	A. *foodstuffs*	217.6[h]	261.3	46.1	204.9	70.4	63.5	115.0
	tea	59.9	62.2	10.6	17.3	26.1	27.9	36.8
	herring	22.4	24.3	3.7	9.9	2.1	3.2	2.5
	fruit[a]		38.8	6.9	14.6	13.4	10.1	16.6
	sugar		0.0	4.6	40.4	6.2	0.7	0.6
	grain product[a]		39.5		112.1	11.2	17.3	43.3
	B. *manufactured consumer goods*	207.8[i]	130.7	21.0	35.9	83.1	17.3	28.1
	cloth[a]	30.8	37.1	1.7	12.1	41.1	1.5	0.8
III.	Other	67.7	97.6	4.2	12.2	12.3	5.7	5.6

Sources: 1909–13: All data from Pokrovskii (1947) except as noted. Data for aggregate categories for 1909–13 are estimates and not strictly comparable to the rest of data. 1913, 1923/24–1927/28: All data from *Planovoe khozyaistvo*, no. 4, 1929, 86 (M. Kaufman), except as noted.

Notes: [a] Data for 1913–1927/28 from *Vneshnyaya torgovlya* (1960). Values converted by ratio of 3.4851.

[b] Data from Bakulin and Mishustin (1940). Machinery and equipment is for all equipment minus agricultural equipment. Non-ferrous metals is the sum of copper, nickel, aluminium, lead, zinc and tin. Ferrous metal is the sum of pig iron, ferro-alloys, rolled, and sheet iron. Values converted by ratio of 4.38.

[c] Data for 1909–13 is the sum of cotton, wool, raw hides, rubber, non-ferrous metals, rough ferrous metals, jute, silk and rags and hence understates total imports of raw materials which also includes cork, scrap, ferro-alloys, industrial fats and oils and ores.

[d] Semi-processed materials include leather, chemicals (except fertiliser), dyes and tanning materials, paper and cardboard, wire, timber, building materials, vegetable oils and yarns. Data for 1909–13 is the residual of imports for productive purposes minus machinery, raw materials, agricultural machinery and supplies and fuel.

[e] Fuels include coal and wood and exclude oil products.

[f] Data for 1909–13 includes an estimate of 5 million rubles for fertilisers, seed, binding twine, etc. for agriculture in addition to agricultural equipment and tractors.

[g] Consumer goods for 1909–13 is the residual of total imports minus producers' goods and other.

[h] Foodstuffs are the yearly average of 1909–13 of foodstuffs and livestock in Goldstein *et al.* i (1929), 2 (M. Kaufman).

[i] Manufactured consumer goods for 1909–13 is the residual of all consumer goods minus foodstuffs.

Table 59. Imports of selected products in physical terms, 1909–13 and 1923/24–1927/28 (thousand metric ton)

Producer goods	1909–13 (average)	1913	1923/24	1924/25	1925/26	1926/27	1927/28
I. Producer goods							
A. *equipment*							
lathes – metal[a]	10.3	18.8	1.2	3.0	5.7	18.0	18.6
electrical[a]	8.1	13.5	2.9	5.1	8.3	14.2	27.8
B. *raw materials*							
cotton	192.0[a]	197.2	100.3	107.1	103.2	162.7	145.2
wool	48.5	55.5	14.5	17.8	21.6	29.8	34.7
hides	44.1	59.3	9.5	18.5	36.7	54.4	46.0
rubber	8.7	12.8	2.8	4.9	7.3	11.0	14.7
copper[a]	12.2	13.3	1.4	2.8	12.7	19.5	28.6
lead[a]	49.0	60.0	13.6	14.9	22.7	31.6	50.0
zinc[a]	19.4	28.2	3.8	12.2	15.2	29.8	31.0
ferrous metals, rolled[a]	33.6	43.6	4.2	6.8	46.5	43.1	100.0
C. *semi processed goods*							
paper and cardboard	113.0[a]	144.5	47.8	115.7	146.7	107.8	90.9
leather	6.0[a]	7.4	1.3	2.6	5.0	1.4	1.5
tanning materials[a]	122.0	143.0	29.4	56.7	68.2	72.1	73.7
dyes	48.5	54.7	5.9	7.8	6.5	4.5	6.6
D. *fuel* (coal)		7758.0	318.7	47.6	305.2	471.6	61.4
E. *agric. producer goods*							
equipment and tractors		139.3	12.4	57.7	87.0	45.0	36.0
II. Consumer goods							
A. *foodstuffs*							
tea	71.5[a]	75.8	7.1	11.9	22.1	22.6	28.1
herring[a]	289.9	283.0	45.9	78.0	19.3	36.8	37.3
fruit		277.6	35.1	57.4	42.3	37.1	49.2
sugar		0.2	25.9	227.8	38.1	4.3	3.7
grain products		584.1	56.7	654.7	59.6	60.3	310.0
B. *manufactured consumer goods*							
cloth		6.9	0.5	3.7	11.4	0.4	0.2

Source: *Vneshnyaya torgovlya* (1960).

Note: [a] Data from Goldstein, *et al.*, i (1929).

Table 60. Annual foreign trade plans, 1922/23–1927/28 (million rubles at current prices)

Version (planning agency)	Exports	Imports	Trade balance	Comments
1922/23 Actual	210.6	187.5	+23.1	European borders only
Plan A (unknown)	228.0	162.0	+66.0	European borders only?
% fulfilment	92	116		
1923/24 Actual	523.0	439.0	+84.0	
Plan A (unknown)	500.0	300–350	+150–200	As of January 1924.
% fulfilment	104	88–146		
Plan B (Narkomvneshtorg)	428.7	334.3	+94.4	Final revised plan, June 2, 1924
% fulfilment	122	132		
1924/25 Actual	558.8	723.4	−164.6	
Plan A (Narkomvneshtorg)	507.0	577.0	−70.0	September 1924 or March 1925, may not be first plan.
% fulfilment	110	125		
Plan B (Narkomvneshtorg)	504.0	659.0	−155.0	Final revised plan, June 17, 1925
% fulfilment	111	110		
1925/26 Actual	667.0	756.0	−80.0	
Plan A (Gosplan)	1200.0	[1009.7]	[+190.0]	Gosplan's original projection for export.
% fulfilment	56	75		
Plan B (Narkomvneshtorg)	1105.2	1009.7	+95.5	Cited by Rykov, March 3, 1926 as original plan figures.
% fulfilment	61	75		
Plan C (Narkomvneshtorg)	1000.0	950.0	+50.0	
% fulfilment	68	80		
Plan D (Narkomtorg)	750.0	700.0	+50.0	Preliminary estimate of January revision?
% fulfilment	90	108		
Plan E (Narkomtorg)	720.0	685.0	+35.0	Final revision adopted in January
	93.0	110		
1926/27 Actual	779.4	713.5	+65.9	
Plan A (Gosplan)	829.0	745.0	+75.0	Original control figures (August?)
% fulfilment	95	95		
Plan B (Gosplan)	800.0	704.0	+96.0	Revised control figures (October?)
% fulfilment	97	101		
Plan C (Narkomtorg)	780.0	680.0	+100.0	Control figures by Narkomtorg October 1926
% fulfilment	99	104		
Plan D (Narkomtorg)	762.9	699.0	+63.9	Final revised plan by Narkomtorg
% fulfilment	102	102		
1927/28 Actual	781.8	945.5	−163.7	
Plan A (Narkomtorg?)	754.0	830–860	−76–106	Data are estimates.
% fulfilment	104	110–113		

Sources: *Foreign trade data*
1922/23 and 1923/24: Goldstein *et al.*, i (1929), 7 (M. Kaufman).
1924/25–1927/28: From Tables 56 and 58.

Foreign trade plans
1922/23: Krasin (1928), 141–2: *Vestnik finansov*, no. 5, 1928, p. 119 (T. Engeev).
1923/24 Plan A: Report by Krasin in January, 1924, cited in Krasin (1928), 141–2.
1923/24 Plan B: *Ekonomicheskoe obozrenie*, no. 2, 1926, 66, 72 (N. Sobolev).
1924/25 Plan A: Troyanovskii *et al.* (eds) (1926), 45.
1924/25 Plan B: *Ekonomicheskoe obozrenie*, no. 2, 1926, 72.
1925/26 Plan A: Gosplan estimates cited in Troyanovskii *et al.* (eds) (1926), 57.
1925/26 Plan B: Cited in *Sowjetwirtschaft und Aussenhandel*, vol. 5, no. 6, 1926, 9 (Rykov). These figures are probably orientation figures presented by Narkomvneshtorg and confirmed on July 31, 1925, according to *Ekonomicheskoe obozrenie.*, no. 2, 1926, 72.
1925/26 Plan C: Cited in Troyanovskii *et al.* (eds) (1926), 57. These estimates are significantly lower than the plans cited above and may be an intermediate revision made in the autumn of 1925 before the January revisions.
1925/26 Plan D: *Ekonomicheskoe obozrenie*, no. 2, 1926, 73. This version is probably a preliminary estimate of the final revised plan adopted in January, 1926.
1925/26 Plan E: *Ekonomicheskaya zhizn'*, September 1, 1926.
1926/27 Plan A: *Ekonomicheskoe obozrenie*, no. 11, 1926, 27 (N. Sobolev), citing Gosplan control figures for 1926/27).
1926/27 Plan B: Gosplan's revised control figures for foreign trade from *Ekonomicheskoe obozrenie*, no. 11, 1926, 32.
1926/27 Plan C: Narkomtorg original plan as reported in *Ekonomicheskoe obozrenie*, no. 11, 1926, 32.
1926/27 Plan D: Narkomtorg final revised plan (?) reported by *Sovetskaya torgovlya*, no. 43, 1927, 43 (M. Baksht).
1927/28 Plan: Little is known about the 1927/28 foreign trade plan. These estimates are probably projections of imports and exports made some time after the beginning of the economic year and are based on data in *Sovetskaya torgovlya*, no. 35, 1927 (Kaufman); Goldstein *et al.*, i (1929), 1; and *Planovoe khozyaistvo*, no. 12, 1928, 45 (Geller).

Table 61.   Volume and price indices for foreign trade and output, 1913 and
1923/24–1927/28 (1913 = 100)[a]

	wt year[b]	1913	1923/24	1924/25	1925/26	1926/27	1927/28
Export volume indexes							
Total exports	1927/28	100	24	22	29	33	32
Grain products	1926/27	100	27	6	21	25	5
Other agricultural	1927/28	100	13	19	23	24	29
Non-agricultural	1927/28	100	30	39	45	56	66
Import volume indexes							
Total imports	1927/28	100	17	31	37	38	47
All raw materials	1927/28	100	30	36	44	67	70
Fibres	1927/28	100	31	36	42	58	58
Machinery	1927/28	100	11	23	53	54	75
Food	1927/28	100	13	59	22	22	37
Manufact. consumer goods	1927/28	100	8	11	20	6	8
World trade: quantum index[c]	1929	100	101	111	114	121	127
Trade price indexes							
Export prices	1913	100		170	152	145	158
Export prices	1926/27	100		161	151	144	149
Import prices	1913	100		169	155	139	145
Import prices	1926/27	100		159	151	131	141
Commodity terms of trade	1926/27	100		102	100	110	106
German wholesale price index[d]		100	133	142	134	138	140
Soviet output and price indexes (Soviet data)							
Agricultural output index[e]		100	81	85	103	102	104
Industrial output index[f]		100	48	67	90	104	117
Agricultural wholesale prices[g]		100	[138]	167	169	157	156
Industrial wholesale prices[h]		100	210	177	201	197	172

Sources: Dohan and Hewett (1973) except as noted.

Notes: [a] Not adjusted for territorial change. See text.
[b] Weight year denotes the year used for price or quantity weights for index.
[c] League of Nations, *Review of World Trade* (1939), 60.
[d] *Statistisches Jahrbuch für das Deutsches Reich* (1929).
[e] *Soviet Union Yearbook 1930*, 92–94.
[f] *Soviet Union Yearbook 1930*, 92–94.
[g] *Sovetskaya torgovlya*, various.
[h] *Sovetskaya torgovlya*, various.

Table 62. Official estimates of national income, 1928: 1913 (milliard rubles; per capita income in rubles)

	1913	1928	1928:1913
National income in current prices	14.5	27.2	1.88
National income in 1913 prices	14.5	17.2	1.19
Implicit price deflator			1.58
Per capita income in 1913 prices	10.4	11.3	1.09

Sources and Notes: The 1928 figures are calculated as the averages of 1927/28 and 1928/29. The underlying population figures are 137.2 million for 1913 and 152.2 million for 1928. The official Soviet series is taken from *Kontrol'nye tsifry. . . . na 1928/1929* (1929), 71. We do not cite a nearly contemporaneous calculation by V. Kats in *Planovoe khozyaistvo*, no. 11, 1929 which gives slightly different numbers for national income in 1913 prices: 1913 = 14.0 milliard and 1928 = 16.5 milliard. The growth indexes are nearly identical. Nikitskii's figure for 1913 was 14.8 milliard and Gukhman's estimate was 15.1 milliard according to Vainshtein (1969), 66. The 14.5 milliard figure cited above apparently uses the 1909–13 average harvest.

Table 63. Various estimates of national income, 1913 and 1928, in current prices and constant 1913 prices (using the official national income deflator (milliard rubles)

		1913	*1928*	*1928:1913*
Official estimates[1]	current prices	14.5	27.2	1.88
	1913 prices	14.5	17.2	1.19
Prokopovich (1931)[2a]	current prices	14.5	25.7	1.77
	1913 prices	14.5	16.2	1.12
Falkus (1969)[3]	current prices	15.0	27.2	1.81
	1913 prices	15.0	17.2	1.15
Prokopovich-Falkus[a]	current prices	15.0	25.7	1.71
	1913 prices	15.0	16.2	1.08

Sources: M. E. Falkus (1968), 55.
[1]See sources and notes to Table 62.
[2]*Memorandum*, Birmingham Bureau of Research on Russian Economic Conditions, no. 3 (November 1931), Table 4, p. 12.
[3]Falkus (1968), p. 55.

Note: [a]I have reduced Prokopovich's average 1927/28–1928/29 industry figure by 20 per cent (Prokopovich's suggested quality adjustment)

Table 64.   National income, 1928: 1913, in current prices, various estimates
(milliard rubles)

		1913	1928	1928:1913
A.	Official Soviet estimates	14.5	27.2	1.88
B.	Soviet estimates adjusted to include non-material production (NNP)	15.5	28.9	1.87
C.	Gregory–Bergson, NNP in factor cost	15.55	27.5	1.77
D.	Gregory–Bergson, NNP market prices	16.5	30.2	1.83

Sources: Row A: See Table 62.
Rows B–D: See Gregory (1982), 110, 113.
Notes: The non-material product adjustment in Row B is the ratio of adjusted to official Soviet national income in 1913 prices. The factor cost figures in Row C are the averages of the two factor cost concepts.

Table 65.   Alternative Soviet estimates of national income, 1928:1913
(milliard rubles)

	1913	1928	1928:1913
Official National Income Estimates, Gosplan 1929 (1913 constant prices)[1]	14.5	17.2	1.19
Same in 1913 prices with Vainshtein's implicit deflator (2.0)[2]	14.5	13.6	.94
Control figures 1926/27 estimate (1913 constant prices)[3]	14.5	13.3	.92

Sources and Notes: [1] See Table 62.
[2] Vainshtein's deflator in Vainshtein (1969), 102–7 is applied to the Gosplan 1929 estimate of 1928 national income in current prices.
[3] *Kontrol'nye tsifry narodnogo khoziaistva SSSR na 1926–1927 god* (1927), 215 gives a national income of 11.7 milliard rubles (in 1913 prices) for 1926/27. This figure is updated to the average of 1927/28 and 1928/29 using the official growth indexes of Gosplan cited in the 1928/29 control figures. For 1913, the official Gosplan 1929 estimate of 1913 national income is used.

Table 66. Selected price indices (1913 = 100)

1 Price indices published in the 1920s	
A. Retail Price Indices	
Central Statistical Administration (TsSU)	
general index	214
state	177
cooperative	187
private	272
All-Union index, Kon"yunkturnyi institut	
general index	201
private	234
B. Producer Price Indices	
Producer price index	
general index	162
agriculture	148
industry	171
Producer price index, large-scale industry	
general	155
group A	176
group B	162
All-Union index: state industry transfer prices	
	185
C. Wholesale Price Indices	
Central Statistical Administration (Gosplan)	
general index	174
agriculture	160
industry	186
2 Implicit Price Indices From National Income Studies	
A. National deflator, official	
Soviet series	158
B. Industrial output deflator, official	
Soviet series	165
C. National income deflator, Gregory,	
'best estimate'	195
D. National income deflator, Gregory,	
'lowest estimate'	171

Sources and Notes: Part 1: Vainshtein (1969), 83; *Kontrol'nye tsifry 1928/1929 (1929)*, Table XV–1 and XV–2; *Kontrol'nye tsifry 1927/1928* (1928), 479; *Promyshlennost' SSSR v 1927/28*, ii (1930). The weighing scheme for the TsSU–Gosplan wholesale price index is discussed in Bobrov (1925), 66–8.
Part 2: *Kontrol'nye tsifry 1928/1929*, pp. 68, 71, 435, 436; and see Gregory (1982), 110.

Table 67.   Gregory's estimates of net national product, 1913 and 1928 (milliard rubles at 1913 market prices)

	1913	*1928*	*1928:1913*
Original version			
Net national product	16.5	15.3	.93
personal consumption	13.2	11.2	.85
consumption of farm products in kind	5.4	3.1	.57
retail sales	5.8	5.8	1.00
Maximum upward revision			
Net national product	16.5	17.6	1.07
personal consumption	13.2	13.5	1.02
consumption of farm products in kind[a]	5.4	5.4	1.00
retail sales	5.8	5.8	1.00

Source: See Gregory (1982), Tables 5–3 and 5–4.

Notes: The original figures have been amended according to a suggestion from R. W. Davies to raise the construction price deflator by including an index of construction wages in addition to an index of building material prices. This adjustment lowers 1928 NNP in 1913 prices by 0.3 milliard rubles. The maximum upward adjustment is obtained by assuming that 1928 consumption of farm products in kind equalled 1913. This adjustment raises 1928 NNP by 2.3 milliard rubles.

[a] Consumption of farm products in kind assumed to be equal in 1913 and 1928 to obtain maximum upward adjustment in 1928 NNP.

Glossary of Russian Terms and Abbreviations

chernorabochie	general labourers
chervonets	10-ruble banknote (unit of currency introduced in currency reform of 1922–4)
chiny	ranks (in pre-revolutionary Table of Ranks)
desyatina	1.09 hectares/2.7 acres
dvoryantsvo (*dvoryane*)	nobility (nobles)
eksportnost'	'exportability' (ratio of exports to output)
GAZ	Gosudarstvennyi avtomobil'nyi zavod (State Vehicle Factory)
Glavtekstil'	Glavnoe upravlenie tekstil'noi promyshlennosti (Chief Administration of Textile Industry)
GOI	Gosudarstvennyi opticheskii institut (State Optical Institute)
Gosplan	Gosudarstvennaya Planovaya Komissiya (State Planning Commission)
Group 'A'	producer or capital goods
Group 'B'	consumer goods
guberniya (pl. gubernii)	province (pre-revolutionary unit of local government)
KEPS	Commission for the Study of the Natural Resources of Russia
khozraschet	*khozyaistvennyi raschet* (economic accounting [= profit and loss accounting])

339

kustar' (pl. *kustari*)	artisan(s)
lavka	small shop
makhorka	cheap tobacco
mladshii obsluzhivayushchii personal (MOP)	ancillary personnel
NAMI	Nauchnyi avtomotornyi institut (Vehicle and Engine Research Institute)
Narkomtorg	Narodnyi Komissariat Vnutrennoi i Vneshnei Torgovli (People's Commissariat of Internal and Foreign Trade [1925–30])
Narkomvneshtorg	Narodnyi Komissariat Vneshnei Torgovli (People's Commissariat for Foreign Trade [before November 1925 and after November 1930])
Narkomzem	Narodnyi Komissariat Zemledeliya (People's Commissariat of Agriculture)
NEP	Novaya Ekonomicheskaya Politika (New Economic Policy)
Nepmeny	Nepmen (private traders)
NKPS	Narodnyi Komissariat Putei Soobshcheniya (People's Commissariat of Ways of Communication [= People's Commissariat of Transport])
obshchina	rural commune
pomeshchiki	landowners
Prodameta	Obshchestvo dlya prodazhi izdelii russkikh metallurgicheskikh zavodov (Society for the Sale of the Products of Russian Iron and Steel Works) [a syndicate]

promysly	'industry' (all economic activity of peasants outside own farm)
RSFSR	Rossiiskaya Sovetskaya Federativnaya Sotsialisticheskaya Respublika (Russian Soviet Federative Socialist Republic)
sindikaty	syndicates (= cartels)
sluzhashchie	white-collar employees
sosloviya	estates, 'orders' (legal categories in pre-revolutionary Russian society)
Sovnarkom	Sovet Narodnykh Komissarov (Council of People's Commissars)
SSSR	Soyuz Sovetskikh Sotsialisticheskikh Respublik (Union of Soviet Socialist Republics)
STO	Sovet Truda i Oborony (Council of Labour and Defence [= Economic Cabinet])
stroitel'stvo (chistoe stroitel'stvo)	building work
supryaga	agreement between two or more peasant households on common use of horses and implements
torgovye doma	merchant houses
tovarnost'	'marketability' (ratio of marketings to output)
TsAGI	Tsentral'nyi aero-gidro-dinamicheskii institut (Central Aero-Hydrodynamic Institute)
TsSK	Tsentral'nyi Statisticheskii Komitet ([pre-revolutionary] Central Statistical Committee)
TsSU	Tsentral'noe Statisticheskoe Upravlenie (Central Statistical Administration)

Vesenkha

Vysshii Sovet Narodnogo Khozyaistva (Supreme Council of National Economy [Commissariat responsible for state industry])

VTS

Vsesoyuznyi Tekstil'nyi Sindikat (All-Union Textile Syndicate)

vuz (pl. *vuzy*)

vysshee uchebnoe zavedenie (higher educational establishment)

zemstvo (pl. *zemstva*)

rural local government institution (pre-revolutionary)

Notes and References

1 Introduction: From Tsarism to NEP

1. See Davies (1978).
2. See Davies (1978), 66 (Table 5).
3. Gregory (1982), 56–7.
4. See Wheatcroft (1986), 3.
5. See Wheatcroft (1986), 12.
6. See Wheatcroft (1987).
7. Polyakov (1986), 82–128. Those who died prematurely included 1.3–2 million soldiers who were killed or died of wounds in the tsarist army in 1914–17, 2.4 million soldiers who died during the Civil War (approximately equal numbers on both sides), and over 2 million who died of infectious diseases; in addition some 5 million people died in consequence of the famine of 1921. Lorimer (1946), 39–41, estimated excess deaths at 16 million (including a higher child mortality than that apparently assumed by Polyakov), emigration at 2 million, and the birth deficit at 10 millions. See also Wheatcroft (1988).
8. *Promyshlennost'* (1964), 32, 163.
9. The industrial production statistics are discussed in some detail in Davies (1978).
10. *Vestnik finansov*, no. 8, 1927, pp. 140–1, based on expected fulfilment of 1926/27 state budget. According to this source, the size of the Soviet army in that year was only 43 per cent of 1913 (p. 144).
11. For Gregory's reasons for suggesting a possible 'maximum upward adjustment' to his original estimate, see Chapter 12. Wheatcroft, Davies and Cooper (1986), 268, estimated *gross* agricultural production in 1928 at 110–112 per cent of 1909–13 (average); Wheatcroft now finds that net agricultural production in 1926–8 (average) was only 108 per cent of 1909–13 (average) (see Table 22).
12. *Kontrol'nye tsifry . . . 1928/29* (1929), 71. Other Soviet estimates in the 1920s were lower (see Chapter 12).
13. *Narodnoe khozyaistvo SSSR v 1961 godu* (1962), 597, 292, 169.
14. See, for example, V. Selyunin in *Novy mir*, no. 5, 1988, 171, and O. Latsis in *Kommunist*, no. 18, 1987, 18.
15. See, for example, V. Belkin in *Kommunist*, no. 1, 1988, 102.
16. See Davies (1989a), 82, 277–30.
17. Davies (1980), 10.
18. See Gregory (1982), 155–7.
19. See Gregory (1982), 58–9; these figures refer to the territory of the Russian Empire.
20. *Mirovoe khozyaistvo za 1913–1925gg.: statisticheskii sbornik* (1926), 229–31; comparisons for individual countries may be found in Vainshtein (1972), 88.
21. According to Gregory (1982), 58–9, direct government capital expenditures in 1913 amounted to 126 million rubles; in addition, the bulk of investment in transport (208 million rubles) was financed by the budget (see Strumilin, 1958, 622–3): the total direct state finance of investment was therefore no more than 334 million rubles, as compared with the total net domestic capital formation, which amounted to 2,314 million rubles.
22. See Gindin (1948), 391–404, especially p. 402.

23. Vainshtein (1960b), 436.
24. For data on payments abroad, see Gregory (1982), 97–8.
25. See data in Gregory (1982), 58–9.
26. Crisp (1976), 52.
27. Estimated from *Materials* (1985), 424–5.
28. See McKay (1970).
29. Gregory (1982), 170, 176.
30. Wheatcroft, 'Grain Production and Utilisation in Russia in the USSR before Collectivisation', unpublished Ph.D. thesis, University of Birminghan (1980), vol. 3, pp. 228–69; the jump in livestock numbers in 1909 shown in Gregory (1982), 268, is due to the inclusion of additional regions in the 1909–14 data.
31. Wheatcroft, 'The Agrarian Crisis and Peasant Living Standards in Late Imperial Russia', unpublished working paper (1986).
32. *Slavic Review*, vol. 47 (1988), 514.
33. See Gindin (1948), Bovykin (1984).
34. Von Laue (1966), 36, 223.
35. Geyer (1987), especially 11, 345–6.
36. Lieven (1983), 153–4.
37. Gerschenkron (1965b), 141. See also Sumner (1947), 70.
38. Becker (1985).
39. Seton-Watson (1952), 377–8.
40. *Russian Review*, April 1971, 138 (G. Tokmakoff).
41. Gerschenkron (1965b), 141.
42. Katkov *et al.* (eds) (1971), 45 (L. Schultz).
43. Manning (1982).
44. Rieber (1982) 415–25.
45. Haimson in Black (ed.) (1960), 356, 360.
46. Atkinson (1983), 106.
47. Haimson, in Cherniavsky (ed.) (1970), 357–9; see also the work of Bonnell (1984).
48. Cited in Rogger (1983), 237.
49. Seton-Watson (1952), 377–9.
50. Haimson in Cherniavsky (ed.) (1970), 366.
51. *Slavic Review*, vol. xx (1961), 576 (C. E. Black).
52. Gerschenkron (1965b), 144–60.
53. E. H. Carr in Feinstein (ed.) (1967), 278.
54. This argument is further developed in Wheatcroft, Davies and Cooper (1986), and in Harrison (1984).
55. Schapiro (1985), 219.
56. Tucker (1973), Chapter 12; Medvedev (1972), 362, and Chapter XI generally.
57. See for example Lewin (1985), Chapter 12 ('Grappling with Stalinism'); Davies (1989a), 456–67.
58. Cohen (1974), 328–9.
59. See Davies (1989b), esp. Chapters 3 and 4.

2 The Social Context

1. Lenin (1962), 313.
2. *Statistika zemlevladeniya* (1907), 78; Lenin refers to this source in an article of 1908: Lenin (1961), 200.

3. Each household in the Russian Empire was allocated to an 'estate', the most important of which were hereditary nobles (*dvoryane*), personal nobles, merchants, burghers (*meshchane*) and peasants.
4. *Statistika zemlevladeniya* (1907), 78. The census related to 50 provinces of European Russia.
5. Korelin (1979), 60.
6. Becker (1985), 187–8.
7. Korelin (1979), 62.
8. Robinson (1972), 270. This is compatible with Becker's estimate of an average annual decrease of 1,135,000 desyatinas in 1906–14: Becker (1985), 189.
9. *Statistika zemlevladeniya* (1907), 78.
10. Korelin (1979), 94.
11. Korelin (1979), 98.
12. Zaionchkovskii (1978), 98.
13. Zaionchkovskii (1978), 222.
14. Zaionchkovskii (1978). On the social characteristics of the bureaucracy, see also Pintner and Rowney (1980) and Rowney (1989).
15. Kenez (1973), 131–2; Becker (1985), 110–1.
16. Becker (1985), 112.
17. Manning (1982); Becker (1985).
18. Rieber (1982).
19. Zaionchkovskii (1978), 223.
20. *Obshchii svod*, i (1905), 160.
21. Korelin (1979), 109.
22. Laverychev (1974), 70–71.
23. Gindin (1963), 37–8.
24. *Obshchii svod*, 88 (1905), 256.
25. Zaionchkovskii (1978), 71; this is an estimate based on the reliable data for the number of ranking officials and office clerks in 1857.
26. Erman (1963), 169–70. For more detailed information on the membership and growth of various professional groups, Leikina-Svirskaya (1981), 34–85.
27. *Obshchii svod*, i (1905), 188–9.
28. Leikina-Svirskaya (1971), 65.
29. Leikina-Svirskaya (1971), 67–70.
30. Leikina-Svirskaya (1981), 23. Incomplete data.
31. Leikina-Svirskaya (1971), 18. Data again incomplete.
32. Leikina-Svirskaya (1971), 18–29.
33. *Narodnoe obrazovanie* (1977), 291.
34. *Ezhegodnik Rossii 1905g*, 530.
35. *Ezhegodnik Rossii 1906g.*, 294; *Statisticheskii ezhegodnik Rossii 1914g.*, 100–1. Erman's figures from the same series for 1907 and 1915, 43,189 and 71,921 students respectively, exclude theological academies (Erman, 1963, 172).
36. *Narodnoe khozyaistvo* (1932), 507; *Sotsialisticheskoe stroitel'stvo* (1935), 616.
37. Chutkerashvili (1961), 8; *Narodnoe obrazovanie* (1977), 213.
38. Leikina-Svirskaya (1981), 11.
39. Kenez (1973), 1435–8.
40. According to Wheatcroft (1984), 23: 25, 475 of the 51,400 doctors listed in the 1926 census were aged at least 25 before 1917 and therefore presumably received their training before then; but the total number of doctors in 1917 was only 29,000 (pre-1939 USSR frontiers); on these data, a very high proportion of doctors remained in the USSR.

41. Becker (1985).
42. *Obshchii svod*, i (1905), xviii–xix.
43. *Obshchii svod*, i (1905), xviii–xix.
44. *Tyazhest' oblozheniya* (1929), 74–81; these data are discussed in Lewin (1985), 213–6, and in Wheatcroft (1984).
45. *Byulleten' Ekonomicheskogo . . . Prokopovicha*, lxx (June–July 1929), 25–6.
46. *Tyazhest' oblozheniya* (1929), 74–81.
47. *Tyazhest' oblozheniya* (1929), 74–81. In the 1926 census, the number of personal servants was recorded as 319,000 in the towns; a further 133,000 were employed in the countryside, and 13,000 as a secondary occupation (*Vsesoyuznaya perepis'*, xxxiv, 1930).
48. While the number of domestic servants in Moscow fell from 97,600 to 42,200 between 1912 and 1926, the number of persons in non-industrial employment and the free professions increased from 55,600 to 131,600 (*Byulleten' Ekonomicheskogo . . . Prokopovicha* (Prague), lxx (June–July 1929), 25–6).
49. See *Narodnoe khozyaistvo* (1932), 507.
50. *Izmeneniya* (1979), 166.
51. Sketchy data for individual professions also point to an increase in the number of specialists between the eve of the first world war and the mid-1920s (thousands):

	Eve of first world war	1926 census[c]
Doctors	31.4[a]	51.4
Dentists	5.8[a]	10.0
Teachers in higher education	6.7[b]	13.2

[a] See Leikina-Svirskaya (1981), 50–1; in addition there were 5,400 pharmacists. The number of civilian doctors in 1911 was only 21,700 (see Table 2). According to Wheatcroft (1984), 21, there were only 24,000 civilian plus 4,000 military doctors in 1914, 28,400 in all (Russia Empire).
[b] *Izmeneniya* (1979), 269.
[c] *Vsesoyuznaya perepis'*, xxxiv (1930), 144–80. According to the data in Leikina-Svirskaya (1981), there were in excess of 190,000 secondary and elementary school-teachers in 1914, as compared with 326,000 in 1926 (see note 52). This implies a considerable improvement in the teacher–pupil ratio, which seems unlikely.

52. Estimated from *Vsesoyuznaya perepis'*, xxxiv (1930), 144–80. These figures exclude military officers and specialists, literature, journalism and the arts, libraries and museums, as 'higher' occupations in these fields are not listed separately; on the same grounds we have excluded 326,265 teachers from the total. The total includes 'free professions' as well as those in employment. The principal sub-groups are as follows:

Leading personnel		
Administrators, etc.	197806	
Managers	114048	
Total		311854
Technical and other listed higher posts:		
Engineers and architects	30235	

Higher education	13236
Agronomists	16832
Land surveyors, etc.	12906
Veterinary	5013
Doctors	51430
Dentists	9969
Legal professions	18206
Other	9236
Total	167065

Of the total technical and other higher posts, 10,347 are in 'free professions' working independently, the rest are wage-earners.

53. *Ekonomicheskoe obozrenie*, no. 12, 1929, 102–22 (Kheinman); a further 10.6 per cent only had secondary specialised education.
54. Rowney (1989), 170–1.
55. Bineman and Kheinman (1930), Table 1; see also Rowney (1989), Chapter 5.
56. For this survey see *Statisticheskoe obozrenie*, no. 2, 1930, 82–92 (M. Latsygina).
57. Rowney (1989), 146.
58. *Statisticheskoe obozrenie*, no. 2, 1930, 82–92.
59. *Vsesoyuznaya perepis'*, xxxiv (1930), 144–80. Women played an important part in medicine and education: 40 per cent of doctors, 80 per cent of dentists and 61 per cent of school teachers were women among members of the employed population.
60. *Ekonomicheskoe obozrenie*, no. 12, 1929, 120–1 (Kheinman).
61. *Ekonomicheskoe obozrenie*, no. 1, 1930, 167–8 (Kheinman).
62. Carr and Davies (1969), 580, n. 5.
63. *Ekonomicheskoe obozrenie*, no. 1, 1930, 161–5 (Kheinman).
64. *Obshchii svod*, i (1905), 189.
65. *Ezhegodnik Rossii 1906g.*, 299; *Statisticheskii ezhegodnik 1914 g.*, 124. Erman's figures from the same series, of 129,134 and 195,105 pupils for 1907 and 1914 respectively, omit the figures for theological colleges and professional schools: Erman (1963), 172.
66. *Statisticheskii ezhegodnik 1914 g.*, 126. These figures are not entirely incompatible with the estimates for 1914/15 in Soviet types of education, which use different classifications of types of education, and adjust for 1939 (and present-day) boundaries. See, for example, *Narodnoe khozyaistvo* (1932), 507; *Narodnoe obrazovanie* (1977), 7, 26–7.
67. *Obshchii svod*, i (1905), 188–9.
68. Rashin (1956), 311. The best available comparison with the last figure is 24 per cent literacy for the population aged 9 and over, 1897 (see note 74 below).
69. Rashin (1956), 293, 297, 320.
70. Brooks (1982), 272.
71. *Sotsialisticheskoe stroitel'stvo* (1934) 408–9; *Statisticheskii spravochnik za 1928* (1929), 879; of these the number in *rabfaki* amounted to 49,000; see also Fitzpatrick (1979), 62. An alternative series for all lower trade education (*profobrazovanie*) shows an increase from 267,000 in 1914/15 to 594,000 in 1926/27 (*Narodnoe khozyaistvo*, 1932, 507).
72. *Narodnoe obrazovanie* (1971), 233. We have not established whether the 1913 and 1914/15 figures are accurate.
73. *Ekonomicheskoe obozrenie*, no. 12, 1929, 120–1 (Kheinman).
74. Illiterates were those not recorded as 'able to read' aged nine and over; the

equivalent figure for 1897 is 76.0 (Lorimer, 1946, 198–9), and for 1913 about 62 per cent.

75. *Sotsialisticheskoe stroitel'stvo* (1934), 399.
76. *Trud* (1930) 30–1; this is the report of a survey of 382,000 workers in the metal, textiles and mining industry (20 per cent coverage) carried out by the trade unions in April–May 1929 (*Trud*, 1930, xii).
77. Rashin (1958), 172.
78. Rashin (1958), 172.
79. *Obshchii svod*, ii (1905), 296. For discussion of the problems involved in using the census data to establish the occupational composition of the population, see Kadomtsev (1909).
80. Gukhman (1926). We are grateful to Peter Gatrell for the reference to this article.
81. For January 1, 1914, see *Statisticheskoe obozrenie*, no. 7, 1929, 19 (Vainshtein); for 1927, see Danilov (1977), 211.
82. According to the 1926 census, of the 74.1 million independent persons living in the countryside, 70.1 million were engaged in agriculture as a main occupation; the remainder were engaged in factory industry (0.54), artisan industry (0.87), building (0.16), transport (0.31), trade and credit (0.22), employed in various institutions (0.51) (other occupations unemployed or not known amounted to 1.38 millions) (Danilov, 1977, 48–9).
83. *Ocherki* (1957), 192–3.
84. Rashin (1958), 82. For discussion of war-time growth in employment, see also Gaponenko (1970), 33–87.
85. Barber (1978), 2–5.
86. According to the 1929 survey, 52.2 per cent of workers came from working-class families, 20.6 per cent held land; in the case of the coal industry, where ties with the land were closer, the respective percentages were 34.4 and 24.6 per cent (*Trud*, 1930, 28–9; Barber, 1978, 8–14). Comparable data for the railway workers have not been traced.
87. *Profsoyuznaya perepis', 1932–1933*, i (1934), 94–5; this is a survey of trade-union members who still remained in industry in 1932–3.
88. A 1929 survey of building workers showed the following (in percentages):

	Permanent workers	Otkhodniki
In industry before 1918	37.1	35.9
Working-class parents	37.6	9.2
Own agriculture in countryside	19.9	90.0

(*Trud* (1932), 83, 85; *Izmeneniya* (1961), 152, 180, 194 (Gol'tsman)).

89. The number of party members and candidates on January 1, 1927, was as follows (thousands):

Workers in industry	215.6
Workers in transport	94.3
Other workers	33.2
Non-manual employees	438.8
Peasants	116.2
Other	163.8
Total	1061.9

(*Itogi*, n.d. [?1928], 22–3; these figures exclude the Red Army and Navy). The total number of workers in census industry on January 1, 1927, amounted to 2,365,000 (*Trud*, 1930, 7); the total persons employed in transport in 1926/27 (average) amounted to 1,257,000 (*Trud*, 1930, 7) (this figure includes non-manual employees, so the party membership among workers will be higher than 1 in 13); the total number of peasants working in individual households recorded in the 1926 census was 73,456,000 (*Vzesoyuznaya perepis'*, xxxiv, 1930, 2–3). For party membership among engineers, see p. 37 above).

90. See Carr (1971), 108–9; this was only partly explained by the fact that most of the cotton textile industry, where female labour predominated, was organised into large units.

91. For the regime of economy, see Carr and Davies (1969), 333–8.

92. On the role of the factory engineer, see Carr (1958), 378–9, and Carr and Davies (1969), 578–80; on the foreman, see *Predpriyatie*, 12, 1926, 13–4 (S. Gastev), 22 (Kotel'nikov).

93. See Bergson (1944), 69; the quartile ratio, which is a measurement of equality, increased substantially in seven out of eight industries studied.

94. For the changes in policy see Carr (1958), 376–7, Carr and Davies (1969), 529–37, and Bergson (1944), 69, 108–9. For conflicting evidence on the success of the 1926–8 drive for equalisation, see Carr and Davies (1969), 533, especially note 3, and Bergson (1944), 188.

95. For 12 industries for which data are available for the whole period, covering 76 per cent of industrial workers, the percentages were as follows:

1913	30.7	1922/23	34.7
1915	36.0	1923/24	32.8
1917	39.7	1924/25	34.2
1918	41.2	1925/26	34.3
1921/22	38.0	1926/27	35.0

For all census industry, the percentage increased from 25.2 in 1913 to 29.5 per cent in 1926/27 (*Ocherki* (1957), 244–5, 206).

96. According to Soviet estimates, real wages changed as follows:

	Women as percentage of numbers of workers[a]		Real wages (1913 = 100)[b]
	1913	*1926/27*	*1926/27*
Metalworking	4.8	10.2	85.0
Mining	8.0	14.5	75.0
Woodworking	8.2	16.4	108.2
Printing	9.1	22.1	106.8
Food	21.3	26.8	158.1
Paper	36.7	29.3	126.0
Chemicals	31.3	31.2	127.3
Textiles	56.1	60.2	120.0
All industry	25.2	29.5	99.6

[a] *Ocherki* (1957), 206–67 (Mints).
[b] *Ekonomicheskoe obozrenie*, no. 10, 1927, 144–7 (Kheinman).

97. This did not, however, result in equal earnings for men and women, as female labour was concentrated in the less remunerative jobs. According to surveys

of the central bureau of labour statistics, the average daily earnings of adult women increased from 63.4 per cent of adult male earnings in March 1926 to 67.2 per cent in March 1928; the equivalent percentage for June 1914 was only 51.1 (*Statistika truda*, 9–10, 1928, 2–48 (Rashin)).

98. Bergson (1944), 73–6.
99. A Soviet economist wryly commented: 'We are maintaining a definite policy of eliminating the pre-revolutionary gaps in the payment of male and female labour. But generally the shift in the former relationships of wage payments between the producer goods' and consumer goods' industries is the result of the disruption of the planned control of wages, a disruption due to market conditions' (*Ekonomicheskoe obozrenie*, no. 9, 1929, 147 (Kheinman)).
100. See Carr (1952), 104.
101. *Trud* (1936), 98, 371; according to this source '"the normal length of the working day" refers to the number of hours of work which are fixed for the given worker by existing legislation or the conditions of the labour contract'. These figures are for adult workers. According to *Trud* (1930), 37, the actual average length of the working day amounted to 7.45 hours in 1926/27 and 1927/28, including 0.1 hours overtime, and 7.37 including 0.13 hours overtime, in 1928/29; this figure presumably includes adolescents, who worked a shorter day.
102. See Carr and Davies (1969), 495–500.
103. *Narodnoe khozyaistvo* (1932), 410–1 (total excluding agricultural workers)
104. See Carr and Davies (1969), 454.
105. Estimates from Rashin (1956), 129; we have omitted from the 1881 population 130,000 'lower ranks' and other categories which do not appear in the figures for 1910. Similar figures for Moscow appear in Rashin (1956), 124–5.
106. Gukhman (1926), 248–9.
107. Wheatcroft, Davies and Cooper (1986), 273.
108. *Narodnoe khozyaistvo* (1932), 88–91.
109. *Vsesoyuznaya perepis'*, xxxiv (1930), 118–9.
110. *Vsesoyuznaya perepis'*, xxxiv (1930), 120–73.
111. The 1897 figures used by Gukhman omit day workers and unskilled without a definite specialisation, and this may be roughly equivalent to the *chernorabochie* omitted from the 1926 census.

3   The Socio-economic Differentiation of the Peasantry

1. Lenin, *Polnoe*, iii (1958).
2. Tverdova-Svavitskaya and Svavitskii (1916); Korenevskaya (1954).
3. See, for example, Gaister (1928); Kritsman (1926); Vermenichev, Gaister and Raevich (1927).
4. Chayanov (1925); English translation by Thorner, Kerblay and Smith (eds) (1966).
5. Shanin (1972), 71–7.
6. Shanin (1972), 98–100.
7. See Shanin (1972), 101–9.
8. Shanin (1972), 102–6.
9. See for example Lewin (1968), 41–80; Loewe, in *Jahrbücher für Geschichte Osteuropas*, xxxii (1984), 72–113; Merl (1981), 411–36; Robinson (1932); Volin (1970), 57–116.

10. See for example: Anfimov (1980) and (1984); Danilov (1979), particularly p. 25.
11. Shanin (1972).
12. See for example: Cox in *Journal of Peasant Studies*, vii (1979–80), 70–85; Cox (1986), 220–48; Gatrell (1986), 1–140, particularly pp. 79–83; Harrison in *Journal of Peasant Studies*, iv (1977), 127–61. This controversy does not take into account serious criticisms of the validity of marxist agrarian theory, arising from (1) the survival of the family farm in Western Europe until the present day and (2) the contradictory logical foundations of Marx's theory. Krebs recently pointed out that many elements in Marx's agrarian theory contradict his own basic statements which he derived from his analysis of agricultural production. In fact, Marx saw two different methods of concentration: by 'intensification' where one labourer may cultivate a smaller area, and through machinery reducing the need for labour. See Krebs (1983).
13. Harrison in *Journal of Peasant Studies*, iv (1977), 137–46.
14. The North Caucasus did not form part of European Russia in pre-1914 data.
15. When referring to the general trend in the Black-Earth zone, this region will be excluded.
16. With the exception of Siberia, the Asiatic part of Russia is not considered here, due to lack of pre-1914 data.
17. The data are published for Soviet pre-1939 territory in *Osnovnye elementy* (1930).
18. Svavitskaya and Svavitskii (1926).
19. Lenin, *Polnoe*, iii (1958), 119–33; Anfimov (1980), 98–172.
20. Calculated from data in Anfimov (1962), 204.
21. Calculated from data in Anfimov (1962), 238.
22. Calculated from data in Anfimov (1962), 234–5.
23. Anfimov (1962), 204, 227.
24. Jasny (1949), 148; Lenin, *Polnoe*, iii (1958),70–1; Auhagen in *Berichte über Landwirtschaft, Neue Folge*, x (1929), 383–412.
25. Lenin, *Polnoe*, iii (1958), 70–1; Anfimov (1980), 147–50.
26. Anfimov (1980), 138–45.
27. Calculated from data in Anfimov (1980), 152–3.
28. Loewe (1984), 94–103.
29. Anfimov (1980), 152–4.
30. Anfimov (1980), 147–9.
31. Anfimov (1980), 66; Table 1.
32. Anfimov (1980), 66. In the RSFSR (including Asiatic Russia) in 1927 there were about 8.6 hectares of arable land per household (Danilov, 1979, 28).
33. Data on livestock in Asiatic Russia may be found in *Sel'skoe khozyaistvo* (1923), 216–18.
34. Gregory in *Explorations in Economic History*, ii (March 1979), 135–64.
35. *Osnovnye elementy* (1930), 90–117; Anfimov (1980), 156.
36. Merl (1981), 228–9.
37. Anfimov (1984), 24, gives 3.77 million agricultural workers in 50 provinces of European Russia; Gatrell (1986), 85, cites Rashin with 4.5 million agricultural labourers in the Russian Empire in 1913. Gukhman (see Table 3) gave 3 million for 1913, the increase between 1897 and 1913 was given as 8 per cent, while the number of family members working in agriculture increased by 31 per cent over the same period.
38. Anfimov (1984), 27.
39. Anfimov (1980), 146–7; Loewe (1984), 109–10.
40. Anfimov (1984), 23–9.

41. Anfimov (1984), 27–8; Anfimov (1980), 159–65.
42. Anfimov (1962), 63.
43. Anfimov (1962), 127–35; *Sel'skoe khozyaistvo* (1923), 130–2.
44. Merl (1981), 194–6; Anfimov (1962), 335–9; *Narodnoe i gosudarstvennoe khozyaistvo* (1923), 626.
45. Although there are many older studies on the Stolypin reform, there is still no definite picture of its results. For a recent review of the controversy see Atkinson (1983), 41–113.
46. Atkinson (1983), 71–100.
47. Anfimov (1980), 65–6; Atkinson (1983), 82–4.
48. Male (1971), 18–55; Rostankowski (1982), 106–11.
49. Shanin (1972), 147–61; Timoshenko (1932), 60ff.
50. Danilov in *Leninskii Dekret o zemle* (1979), 261–310, Shanin (1972), 153–6.
51. Estimate cited by Volin (1970), 119; Anfimov (1962), 143.
52. *Sotsialisticheskoe stroitel'stvo* (1934), 202.
53. Kritsman (1926), 18.
54. Meyer (1974), 264–76.
55. Merl (1981), 37.
56. *Osnovnye elementy* (1930), 90–117.
57. Kristman (1926).
58. Merl (1981), 411–36. There is a problem with the uncorrected data on the size of the farms. Taxation was based on natural criteria (area sown, number of livestock), therefore the peasants tended to understate the real size of their farm.
59. Merl (1985), 224; Danilov (1979b), 35.
60. *Statisticheskii spravochnik 1928* (1929), 92–3.
61. *Statisticheskii spravochnik 1928* (1929), 100–3; Danilov (1979b), 104.
62. See Table 7 and Anfimov (1962), 204.
63. *Itogi desyatiletiya* (n.d. [?1928]), 159.
64. *Itogi desyatiletiya* (n.d. [?1928]), 159.
65. *Itogi desyatiletiya* (n.d. [?1928]), 136–41; *Vesennyaya posevnaya kampaniya* (1929), 135; *Statistika i narodnoe khozyaistvo*, no. 7, 1929, 116–29 (Podgorodetskii).
66. On the levelling effect of the coercive measures see Merl (1985), 158–61.
67. *Itogi desyatiletiya* (n.d. [?1928]), 135–41.
68. *Osnovnye elementy* (1930), 90–117; *Statistika i narodnoe khozyaistvo*, no. 7, 1929, 116–29 (Podgorodetskii).
69. *Statisticheskii spravochnik 1928* (1929), 555–6.
70. Danilov (1974), 55–122.
71. *Statisticheskii spravochnik 1928* (1929), 557–8.
72. Danilov (1977), 54–6.
73. Merl (1985), 102–3.
74. Kavraiskii and Nusinov (1929), 85.
75. Merl (1981), 192–284.
76. Merl (1981), 204.
77. *Sdvigi v sel'skom khozyaistve* (1931), 72–3 (data for 1927–9).
78. Merl (1985), 329–30.
79. Merl (1981), 276–7.
80. *Statistika i narodnoe khozyaistvo*, no. 7, 1929, 45–63.
81. *Statisticheskii spravochnik 1928* (1929), 120–1.
82. Merl (1985), 112–37.
83. Merl (1985), 138–212.

84. *Itogi desyatiletiya* (n.d. [?1928]), 124–35.
85. Merl (1981), 431–3.
86. Merl (1981), 219–34.
87. Rosnitskii (1926), 27–8; Merl (1981), 183–92, 219–34; Shanin (1972), 171–2.
88. Merl (1985), 112–27, 138–48.
89. Anfimov (1980), 173–227.
90. Anfimov (1962), 250.
91. Anfimov (1984), 26.
92. Anfimov (1984), 24.
93. Anfimov (1962), 250.
94. *Vestnik statistiki*, no. 9–12, 1920, 5–47 (Khryashcheva).
95. Mints (1929), 466–8.
96. Mints (1929), 466–8.
97. Danilov (1974), 55–122.
98. *Denezhnyi oborot* (1929), 44–5, 50, 57.
99. *Denezhnyi oborot* (1929), 44–5, 50, 57.
100. *Tyazhest' oblozheniya* (1929), 43, 55.
101. *Tyazhest' oblozheniya* (1929), 146–57; (1985), 217–8.
102. Lenin, *Polnoe*, iii (1958), 160–1.
103. Korenevskaya (1954), 116–33; Anfimov (1984), 158–80.
104. *Statisticheskii spravochnik 1928* (1929), 92–9.

4 Unemployment

1. Lenin, iii (1960), 585.
2. Garside (1980), 10–11.
3. Kleinbort (1925), 3, 5.
4. Mints is cited (without reference) as the proposer of this estimate by L. Kritsman, 'Bezrabotitsa v dorevolyutsionnoi Rossii i v SSSR', *Bol'shaya sovetskaya entsiklopediya*, v (1930), col. 214. The article itself, with its tables, is often attributed to Mints (for example in the major contemporary Soviet monograph: Rogachevskaya, 1973, 51–2) but it is the following article in the encyclopedia which is his.
5. See notes to Table 14.
6. 2 per cent of an urban population of 25 million, or 4 per cent of an urban labour force of 12 million would approximate the estimate. To our knowledge Mints never published the basis for this estimate. Of course, even the size of the labour force is debated (see Chapter 2).
7. Gindin, *Regulirovanie rynka truda* (in the 1928, but not the 1926 edition), 6; *Voprosy truda*, no. 10, 1927 (D. Ledayev). Rogachevskaya (1973), 51–2, notes that many researchers cite this estimate; on inspection they were evidently citing each other. The source is often confused. Suvorov (1968), 15, wrongly cites from Ledayev a general 1913 census of major cities.
8. Kruze and Kutsentov (1956), 115, seem to add the workers in the group 'imprecisely specified' to the total of those 'temporarily without occupation'.
9. Bradley (1985), 368–9.
10. Semanov (1966), 398–9, argues that the 1910 census suffered in precision of classification because of conditions of tabulation/publication.
11. Bradley (1985), 189.

12. Bradley (1985), 369 for Moscow; and *Petrograd* [?1915], 37.
13. *Svod otchetov za 1909* (1920), viii; Gregory (1982), 145, shows 1909 as a year of recovery. Yakovlev (1955), 348 ff, considers 1908–9 a crisis period, though his discussion of growing unemployment (on 351, 361) centres on 1908.
14. *Svod otchetov . . . 1910* (1911), xxiii; documents in *Rabochee dvizhenie v Azerbaidzhane*, i (1967).
15. *Svod otchetov . . 1909* (1910), xi, for Sormovo. Finn-Enotaevskii (St Petersburg, 1911), 354, gives more precise figures for Sormovo, but places the cutback in 1908. Other information for Lodz, Tula engineering, in *Svod otchetov . . . 1912*, xxxix. These are repeated by later writers; examples are more abundant for the period before 1910 and the economic expansion.
16. Finn-Enotaevskii (1911), Kleinbort (1925) and Rashin (1958) all make use of the above material, but none systematically. Soviet discussions of the 'condition of the working class' in the pre-revolutionary period have consistently said only a few words on unemployment. See for example Kruze (1976) and (1981), Kir'yanov (1979). Among Western studies Bradley (1985) and the memoirs selected by Bonnell (1983) may be singled out, as well as Bonnell's (1984) monograph.
17. Bonnell (1983).
18. See notes 16 and 19.
19. See Meier (1984), Chapter iii, and Fapohunda (1978), 112–13, for some striking parallels.
20. See Bradley (1985), 190 (references cited there) and Bonnell (1983).
21. *Statisticheskii ezhegodnik* (1910), 186. Other causes were also given: low wages, alcoholism, poor harvests (1909). Local beggars were not usually fit for work, but wanderers were reported to be young and healthy.
22. *Istoriya rabochikh Donbassa*, i (1981), 74–6. Suvorov (1968), 24, cites a study in *Voprosy strakhovaniya*, no. 27, 1914, which estimated that one-third of workers suffered a spell of unemployment during the year, based on sickness fund records. Note that if the mean duration of joblessness was 2 months this would imply a 5 per cent unemployment rate.
23. In Mints's calculation Moscow and St Petersburg unemployment are only about one-seventh of the total, whereas in 1926 they contained one in four of all the recorded jobless.
24. Markus (1939), 75.
25. Morgenstern (1963) is strongly recommended as an antidote to over-enthusiastic faith in many Western economic series.
26. Recent Anglo-American histories of 1917 provoke the reaction that a careful re-examination of magnitudes would be rewarding.
27. In 1917 the problem was dislocation and shortage; following 1905 the major factor was victimisation rather than redundancy.
28. *Statisticheskii sbornik* (Petrograd, 1922), 53.
29. This is to be discussed in a forthcoming paper by Wheatcroft.
30. Davies (1986) and Davies and Wheatcroft (1986). Following up this work was their suggestion; I am exceptionally grateful to Bob Davies for his encouragement. The full bibliography on NEP unemployment in Russian would be immense. The specialist is referred to Rogachevskaya (1973) and V. G. Popov, in *Istoriya SSSR*, no. 5, 1981, 184–8. The scant English sources are listed in the Bibliography. The outstanding qualitative discussion remains the relevant chapters on labour in Carr and Davies (1969) and Carr (1958).
31. These are the data based on the returns from the labour exchanges; differences with other Soviet sources are not significant.
32. Davies and Wheatcroft (1986), 43, 37; Carr and Davies (1969), 456–7, 461–2.

33. Adjustment is also possible for change in the proportion of vacancies filled through the exchanges; see *Voprosy truda v tsifrakh* (1930), 48–9. Further data in monthly tables, in *Voprosy truda*, 1927–8.
34. Davies and Wheatcroft (1986) note the increase in temporary employment, stressed by Filtzer (London, 1986). Redefinition of 'temporary work' at the start of 1927/28 to include jobs of under two – as opposed to one – month's duration must have lent some upward bias to the recorded rate of increase. More sophisticated statistical analysis of existing published data is possible, to allow for possible biases.
35. Davies and Wheatcroft (1986), 39.
36. More detailed statistical argumentation on reconciliation of data is found in my unpublished *Discussion Paper*. Monthly trade union unemployment figures are from *Voprosy Truda* tables. The addition of Soviet trade employees from *Statisticheskoe obozrenie*, no. 9, 1927 (M. Goltsman) and of monthly, as opposed to quarterly, returns for the total registered on the exchanges finds a closer fit.
37. L. Mints and I. Engel', (eds) i (1927), 8–9.
38. *Vsesoyuznaya perepis' naseleniya 1926 goda*, lii (1931), 86–7. This entire volume of the 1926 census returns is devoted to unemployment.
39. Davies (1986), 22; Davies and Wheatcroft (1986), 37. See A. Uspenskii in *Statisticheskoe obozrenie*, 8, 1927, for the earliest embrace of the population census as proof of 'dead souls' on the exchanges.
40. *Vsesoyuznaya perepis' naseleniya 1926 goda*, lii (1931), 86–7 and Mints and Engel' (eds), i (1927).
41. See *Voprosy truda* monthly tables.
42. Lorimer (1946), 42. Lorimer considered that mis-stating of age had occurred, while Anderson and Silver, in *Slavic Review*, vol. xliv (1985), 525, suggest that Soviet censuses undercount 'geographically mobile adolescents'. As Morgenstern (1963) usefully emphasises, this is not uniquely Soviet.
43. Morgenstern (1963), 230–2.
44. *Vsesoyuznaya perepis'*, lii (1931), 86–7; Mints and Engel' (eds) (1927); details on the discrepancies between labour exchange and census data, in the manner of Feinstein for Britain 1931 (see Garside, 1980, 133–5) are available in the Discussion Paper.
45. *Vsesoyuznaya perepis'*, lii (1931), 86–7. Tallies well with trade union census.
46. See Figure 1, and Davies (1986), 23.
47. Davies (1986), 28, underscores this point. A substantial commentary on the special problem of female unemployment is to be found in *Voprosy truda*.
48. For trade employees see Goltsman in *Statisticheskoe obozrenie*, no. 9, 1927, and Shmidt, in *Voprosy truda*, no. 6, 1927.
49. *Vsesoyuznaya perepis'*, kratkie svodki, x (1929), 10–12. Further detail in my Discussion Paper.
50. Also see my Discussion paper and discussion of Gukhman in Chapter 2 above.
51. *Voprosy truda* monthly tables.
52. L. I. Vas'kina's heterodox and emphatic stress on the urban character of the 1926 unemployed suggested this line of investigation (Vas'kina, 1981, 180–2). For more statistical detail see my Discussion Paper.
53. In *Voprosy truda*, no. 6, 1927, 122 for Ukraine. For trade employees see Goltsman, in *Statisticheskoe obozrenie*, no. 9, 1927; Shmidt, in *Voprosy truda*, no. 6, 1927.
54. See *Voprosy truda* monthly labour-exchange tables.
55. D. R. Weiner's conference paper (1986) provides fine coverage of subjective

contemporary perspectives on worker/peasant competition for jobs, though I may have differences of interpretation with him.

56. Danskii (1926), 118–22. By the end of 1925 about one-third of the registered unemployed were receiving benefit. This proportion continued to rise.

57. Sources as given in Table 14: Kritsman (1930); Bradley (1985); *Petrograd po perepisi* [?1915]; *Rabochee dvizhenie v Azerbaidzhane*, i (1967), 97–8, and *Vsesoyuznaya perepis' naseleniya 1926 goda*, lii (1931).

5   Agriculture

1. See *Sel'skoe khozyaistvo SSSR* (1960), 79.

2. While recent Soviet agricultural statistics provided annual agricultural gross production figures (*Sel'skoe khozyaistvo*, 1960, 79), they contained only scattered market production figures for agriculture as a whole for 1913 and 1940 (*Sel'skoe khozyaistvo*, 1960, 83) and for separate products for 1909–13 and 1928 to 1932 (*Sel'skoe khozyaistvo*, 1960, 86).

3. This applies particularly to livestock evaluations. Some of the early Gosplan evaluations failed to include such items as manure and growth of herds. The supply of traction power tends to be under-valued in all calculations.

4. For an account of these rivalries see Wheatcroft, M. Soc. Sc. thesis (1974), 1–8.

5. The failure to cover adequately Stalin's activities as a food supply commissar during the civil war seems to me to be one of the most glaring omissions in the biographical work on Stalin. Most accounts give the impression that Stalin had been sent to Tsaritsyn exclusively to dabble in military activity and annoy Trotsky.

6. Lenin's study of the peasantry in *The Development of Capitalism in Russia* is well known. Tsyurupa had been a *zemstvo* statistician for many years, and together with Popov and Groman carried out detailed investigations of the peasantry. See his obituary in *Statisticheskoe obozrenie*, no. 5, 1928, and the more recent account in *Planovoe khozyaistvo*, no. 1, 1971.

7. Davies (1980), 168–9.

8. See *Literaturnaya gazeta*, August 5, 1987.

9. This is in contrast with the livestock results which quite clearly indicated a large level of under-estimation.

10. Kondratiev and Oganovskii (eds) (1923).

11. Wheatcroft, *Soviet Studies*, xxvi (1974), 157–80.

12. 80 million tons for 1913 (93.7 million hectares and 8.5 tsentners per hectare) and 68 million tons for 1909–13 (average) (90 million hectares and 7.5 tsentners per hectare).

13. See Wheatcroft (1980), 80, 209.

14. V. G. Mikhailovskii in Chayanov (1926), 35; see also Wheatcroft (1980), vol. 3, p. 4.

15. See Wheatcroft (1980), 98–117.

16. The so called biological losses involved in harvesting and transferring grain from the fields to the barns have already been excluded.

17. For estimates of the urban population in 1914, see *Arkheografischeskii ezhegodnik za 1968 god* (1970), 243 (Danilov).

18. See Table 18.

19. See Wheatcroft (1980), 169–76.
20. Paul Gregory, in Stuart (ed.) (1983), 21–6; Gerschenkron in *Cambridge Economic History of Europe*, vii, ii (1965).
21. Since we are dealing with a barn-yield concept of grain harvesting, losses have already been deducted, but it is unlikely that subsequent losses would have been less than 2–5 per cent, and in bumper crop years they could well have been more. On the other hand, since we have been measuring food consumption in grain equivalent, it is necessary to include some of the milling by-products (millfeed) as livestock feed. Consequently a figure of 13.6 million tons, or 20 per cent of the harvest, used as livestock feed is probably as reliable as we can get.
22. Kondrat'ev (1922).
23. Apart from the poor grain supplements, attention will also be paid to the poor pasture supplies.
24. Stalin, xi (1949), 85.
25. *Soviet Studies*, xxi (1969–70), 314–29.
26. See Table 19 for regional grain production.
27. See Wheatcroft (1980), 233–5, based on the work of Kondratiev and Anfimov.
28. Kondrat'ev (1922).
29. In 1913, 92,000 tons of vegetables and fruit were imported, valued at 116 million pre-war rubles (*Vneshnyaya torgovlya*, 1960).
30. See *Kontrol'nye tsifry . . . na 1925–1926* (1925), 66.
31. Gukhman (1925), 130; *Kontrol'nye tsifry . . . na 1925–1926* (1925), 62; *Kontrol'nye tsifry . . . na 1926–1927* (1926), 340.
32. The currently officially accepted figure of 23.3 million tons is derived from 3.1 million hectares sown area and 76 tsentners per hectare yield (*Sel'skoe khozyaistvo*, 1960, 201). Earlier Gosplan figures of 29.9 million tons included 20.4 million tons field crops and 9.5 million tons production from plots. But this had been based on a total sown area of 4 million hectares of which the field sown area had been 3.1 million hectares and the plot sown area 0.9 million hectares. The average yield of 74.8 tsentners per hectare had covered a field crop yield of 65.8 tsentners per hectare and a plot yield of 106 tsentners per hectare. See Gukhman (1925), 130.
33. Calculated from basic TsSK data for the 50 European gubernii (provinces) of Tsarist Russia, given by Goldsmith (1961), 446.
34. *Kontrol'nye tsifry . . . na 1925–1926* (1925), 66.
35. *Vneshnyaya torgovlya* (1960), 54; Gukhman (1925), 131.
36. Computed from TsSK data given in Goldsmith (1955), A13.
37. *Kontrol'nye tsifry . . . na 1925–1926* (1926), 66.
38. *Vneshnyaya torgovlya* (1960), 57; Gukhman (1925), 131.
39. TsSK data indicate that peasant meadow land was being reduced as grain sown area was increasing. In the SPR and CPR the growth in grain sowings was accompanied by a decline in pasture, but this was hidden in the aggregate data by the expansion of pasture in the EPR.
40. Prokopovich (ed.) (1918), 8, 34.
41. R. W. Goldsmith in his 1961 study of pre-revolutionary economic growth estimated the 1860–1914 growth in livestock products at 1 per cent a year. He did cite Prokopovich's figures as indicating that the growth rate after the turn of the century could have been as high as 1.75 per cent a year. Goldsmith also cited, but tended to ignore, the correct criticisms of these estimates which

were made by M. Kubanin in *Problemy ekonomiki* (1940), no. 2, 46, 64 (Goldsmith (1961), 452–3).

42. *Kontrol'nye tsifry . . . na 1925–1926* (1925), 62, 72–3.
43. *Vneshnyaya torgovlya* (1960), 54–5, 224–5.
44. The numbers actually enlisted into the army were of course much larger, reaching 9.9 million by January 1916 and 13.0 million by January 1917, but these figures exclude losses (Volkov, 1930, 104).
45. Volkov (1930), 90.
46. Kondrat'ev (1922), 238–43.
47. See Wheatcroft (1982).
48. Volkov (1930), 186.
49. Wheatcroft (1980), 315, 402.
50. See Polyakov (1963), 213–24.
51. Traditionally much greater emphasis is placed on the political reasons for the change and the large degree of peasant unrest was undoubtedly important. But the economic arguments as given by Popov certainly need greater emphasis. (Popov (1921)).
52. *Itogi* (n.d. [?1928]), 379.
53. *Vneshnyaya torgovlya* (1960), 262.
54. *Vneshnyaya torgovlya* (1960), 262, 294.
55. Calculated from data in Wheatcroft (1980), 92, 301–3.
56. *Kontrol'nye tsifry . . . na 1926–1927* (1926), 342–3.
57. According to *Kontrol'nye tsifry . . . na 1926–1927* (1926), 339, the value of vegetables and fruit fell from 835 million pre-war rubles in 1913 to 750 million rubles in 1925, in comparison with a growth from 439 to 657 million rubles for potatoes over this period. During the same period its commodity share fell from 32.5 per cent to 28.7 per cent (calculated from data in *Kontrol'nye tsifry . . . na 1926–1927*, 339, 342).
58. *Kontrol'nye tsifry . . . na 1926–1927* (1926), 344–9.
59. *Vneshnyaya torgovlya* (1960), 58–9, 84.
60. *Vneshnyaya torgovlya* (1960), 57, 82.
61. Vainshtein (1960), 86–115.
62. See Wheatcroft (1980), 301–3.
63. *Kontrol'nye tsifry . . . na 1926–1927* (1926), 338–9.
64. *Vneshnyaya torgovlya* (1960), 55, 60, 80, 86.
65. *Vneshnyaya torgovlya* (1960), 58, 110, 229, 294.
66. Stalin, xi (1949), 81–97.
67. See *Ezhegodnik po sel'skomu khozyaistvu . . . za 1931* (1933), 246–7.
68. *Sel'skoe khozyaistvo SSSR, 1925–1928* (1929), 266–7.
69. *Sel'skoe khozyaistvo SSSR, 1925–1928* (1929), 288–9.
70. 1913 figures from *Kontrol'nye tsifry . . . na 1925–1926* (1925), 66–7; for 1925–8 see *Sel'skoe khozyaistvo SSSR, 1925–1928* (1929), 290–1.
71. For 1913 see *Kontrol'nye tsifry . . . na 1925–1926* (1925), 62: for 1925–8 see *Sel'skoe khozyaistvo* (1929), 308–19.
72. *Kontrol'nye tsifry . . . na 1925–1926* (1925), 68–9, and *Kontrol'nye tsifry . . . na 1927–1928* (1928), 466–7.
73. *Vneshnyaya torgovlya* (1960), 54, 105, 224, 289.
74. *Kontrol'nye tsifry . . . na 1925–1926* (1925), 68–9, and *Kontrol'nye tsifry . . . na 1927–1928* (1928), 466–7.
75. *Vneshnyaya torgovlya* (1960), 58–9, 111.
76. *Kontrol'nye tsifry . . . na 1925–1926* (1925), 68–9; *Kontrol'nye tsifry . . .*

1927–1928 (1928), 466–7, and *Vneshnyaya torgovlya* (1960).
77. See *Zhivotnovodstvo SSSR v tsifrakh* (1932), 4, 9.
78. V. Drozdov, in *Ekonomicheskoe obozrenie*, no. 2, 1929, 171, stated that the average weight of cattle slaughtered in the Moscow abbatoir had increased from 238 kg in 1913 to 250 kg in 1925/26, 264kg in 1926/27 and 269 kg in 1927/28. V. P. Nifontov, *Produktsiya zhivotnovodstva SSSR* (1937), 27; provides slightly different figures but with the same trend: 227 kg in 1909–13 (average), 247kg in 1927/28.
79. For regional livestock data see Wheatcroft (1980), Appendix, 301–3.

6 The Peasantry and Industrialisation

1. I am grateful to Mark Stewart (University of Warwick) for helpful advice on some econometric issues. I also wish to thank Barbara Pacut for her translation of excerpts from Stephan Merl's valuable *Der Agrarmarkt und die Neue Ökonomische Politik: Die Anfange staatliche Lenkung der Landwirtschaft in der Sowjetunion 1925–1928* (Munich, 1981); where reference is made to this work below, the reader should note that I have not been able to study the full text.
2. Theodore H. von Laue in *Journal of Economic History*, xiii, no. 4, 1953, 425–48; von Laue in Black (ed.) (1960); and von Laue, *Sergei Witte and the Industrialization of Russia* (1963); Alexander Gerschenkron in Black (1960); and Gerschenkron in *Cambridge Economic History of Europe*, vi, ii (1965).
3. Olga Crisp, *Studies in the Russian Economy Before 1914* (1976), especially Chapter 1; Peter Gatrell in *Economic History Review*, 2nd series, xxxv (1982), 99–100; Gatrell, 'Russian Economic Development and the Tsarist State' (unpublished paper to the British National Association for Soviet and East European Studies Annual Conference, 1983); and Gatrell, *The Tsarist Economy, 1859–1917* (1986); Paul R. Gregory in *Review of Income and Wealth*, xxvi (1980), 87–103; Gregory in *Explorations in Economic History*, xvii (1979), 135–64; Gregory, *Russian National Income, 1885–1913* (1982); and Gregory's chapter in Stuart (ed.) (1983); Arcadius C. Kahan in *Journal of Economic History*, xxvii (1967), 460–77; James Y. Simms in *Slavic Review*, xxxvi (1977), 377–98; see also Simms' reply to comments in subsequent issues (xxxvii (1978), 487–90 and xliii (1984), 667–71).
4. See J. T. Sanders in *Slavic Review*, xliii (1984), 657–66. In 1926/27, for example, after recovery from war and revolution, the 24 per cent of the Soviet population defined as 'nonagricultural' generated 55 per cent of indirect tax revenues; see *Tyazhest' oblozheniya* (1929), 43, 45.
5. The foreign sector contributed enterprise and technology, but Russia's net external resource balance was negative over 1885–1913 as a whole, reflecting the excess of debt service over capital inflow; see Gregory (1982), 97–8.
6. See Barsov (1968), 65, 78; this finding is discussed further, in relation to the 1920s, below. As far as 1913 is concerned I should report that Barsov's estimates 'inspire very little confidence, because he does not explicitly demonstrate his procedures and because his sources offer no indication as to his calculations' (private communication from Dr Gatrell). For what Barsov's 1913 estimate is worth, it should be borne in mind that in that year the ratio of agricultural to industrial commodity prices on the domestic market was very

close to the 1907–13 average, and slightly *more* favourable to agriculture than in the decade of the 1890s (*Indeksy*, 1925, 91); therefore, any market discrimination against agricultural produce in 1913 was probably typical of the period since 1890.

7. In 1922, of the 13 main economic regions of the RSFSR, only in the north-western Lake region, Novorossiya in the south, and Western Siberia, did the proportion of cultivable land held in communal tenure fall below 90 per cent, and only in the Lake region was it below 80 per cent; see Danilov (1977), 107.

8. According to Dobb (1966), 117, by 1920 village supplies of manufactures had been reduced to perhaps 12–15 and certainly no more than 20 per cent of their prewar level.

9. See Malle (1985), 323.

10. See Malle (1985), Chapters 7–8.

11. Wheatcroft, Davies and Cooper (1986), 283.

12. See Wheatcroft (1974), 157–80, and his Ph.D. thesis (University of Birmingham, 1980).

13. See Jerzy F. Karcz in *Soviet Studies*, xviii (1966/7), 399–434; R. W. Davies in *Soviet Studies*, xxi (1969/70), 314–29; Karcz in *Soviet Studies*, xxii (1970/71), 262–94. Initially sceptical, Karcz concluded (283) that Stalin's estimate (Table 25) 'could have been made in good faith, but so could others'. Probably included in Stalin's underlying definition of the market surplus of grain was some small but significant element of interregional repurchase by the rural population.

14. Wheatcroft (1980), 264, 637–50.

15. When grain used as seed and livestock fodder is included, the share of grain in gross agricultural production in 1926 rose to 49 per cent. Whether output is measured net or gross, these percentages represented significant declines on prewar ratios (46–56 per cent for 1909–13, and 51–59 per cent for 1913 alone); see Chapter 5.

16. Wheatcroft, Davies and Cooper (1986), 281. According to data reported in *Byulleten' Kon''yunkturnogo Instituta*, 11–12, 1927, 48 (I. Zhirkovich and I. N. Ozerov), the share of non-grain products in sown area had more than doubled in the mid-1920s compared to 1913, rising from 6–7 to 15–16 per cent.

17. One problem of measurement which remains unresolved is how to reconcile this substantial fall in net agricultural marketings with available national income comparisons. Gregory's national-income-based estimates suggest that real farm consumption in kind fell by no less than 57 per cent between 1913 and 1928 – see Gregory (1982), 57 (Table 3.1) and 109 (Table 5.3). Given the roughly completed recovery of agricultural output, Gregory argues that off-farm sales of produce must have correspondingly increased. Two problems seem to be involved. First, Gregory's marketings are based on a broader, 'gross' concept which includes a substantial measure of intra-rural trade in foodstuffs, compared to the concept of 'net' or extra-rural marketings relevant to the present discussions – for reasons for possible distortion of this measure, see Wheatcroft, Davies and Cooper (1986), 268n. Secondly (and this is contrary to Gregory's own view – see Chapter 12), where it proves difficult to draw the line between consumption from retail trade and farm consumption in kind, a given estimate of national income by sector of origin may be consistent with more than one estimate of end-use national income; thus, as long as agricultural output is known with greater certainty than food marketings, direct evidence on the latter should be preferred to the indirect evidence of national income residuals.

18. By 1928 the rural population was nearly 8 million (7 per cent) in excess of the 1914 level within a comparable territory (see Wheatcroft, 1976, 76). However, even in context of the failure of agricultural production to recovery fully, this fact alone cannot explain reduced extra-rural food sales. First, the urban population had simultaneously increased by nearly 3 million (12 per cent). Secondly, access to food supplies must be explained in terms of the distribution of claims and relative entitlements, not just by who has produced it. This means that the ability of the rural population to command an increased share of its own output demands independent analysis – attempted in the following section.
19. Carr and Davies (1974), 123; Bokarev (1981), 246.
20. Consider the grain marketed (M) from a given harvest (Q). From an increase in the harvest, subsistence farms will add to their marketings in the ratio $m_1 = dM_1/dQ_1$, and commercial farms in the ratio $m_2 = dM_2/dQ_2$. The total increment to marketings is given by

$$dM = dM_1 + dM_2 = m_1 \cdot dQ_1 + m_2 \cdot dQ_2$$

Assume a redistribution of agricultural capacity from commercial to subsistence farms such that $dQ_1 = - dQ_2$. The resulting change in total marketings is given by

$$dM = (m_1 - m_2) \cdot dQ_1$$

that is, total marketings will decline *only* if $m_1 < m_2$.
21. Merl (1981), 312, comments that in the 1920s the incidence of direct taxation of rural incomes was insignificant compared to the transfer of resources from country to town by indirect means of the urban–rural price 'scissors'.
22. For 50 provinces of European Russia in 1912 Vainshtein (1924), 116, gives 1.80 rubles of direct taxes and 3.74 rubles of land rentals paid per head of peasant household, to be divided into a net farm income which is not stated but implied as 58.89 rubles per head. For 1926/27 direct tax payments were 51 per cent of the total tax burden on the USSR agricultural population given as 9.6 per cent of per capita incomes (see Table 28).
23. In the years 1923–4 the excess of industrial unit costs above pre-war norms had been attributed partly to reduced work discipline and lower labour productivity in proportion to wages, and partly to deterioration of plant, but the most important factor was reckoned to be inflated overheads – a higher level of administrative staffing and lower plant utilisation (see Dobb, 1966, 173–4, 188). The problem persisted, however, beyond the point of recovery of prewar output and employment of fixed capacity. By 1926, for example, monthly real wages in industry had recovered to prewar levels (see Barber (1980), 3); but with a 15–20 per cent decline in hours worked in 1926/27 compared to 1913, and an increase in hourly labour productivity of only 10 per cent (see Chapter 7), the increase in unit costs attributable to wage costs alone was of the order of 18–25 per cent.
24. Millar (1976), 59.
25. Private communication from Dr Merl to the author. The response of farm sales to a change in food prices is in principle composed of an 'income' effect and a 'substitution' effect. For small farms with low per capita incomes, the income effect of a fall in food prices would tend to dominate – reduced family income would be reflected in reduced consumption of both foodstuffs

(resulting in their increased supply to the market) and manufactures. The larger the farm, and the higher family members' per capita incomes, the less important would be the income effect and the more dominant would be the substitution (incentive) effect of lower food prices; these households would be discouraged by worsened market opportunities, and would tend to reduce sales as food prices fell.

26. Now is the moment to review the result of Harrison (1977), 18. This was an econometric analysis of the influence of the demand price of grain relative to the demand price of non-grain farm produce and the supply price of manufactures, and of other factors such as shortage of manufactures and the application of administrative measures of grain collection. I concluded: 'it is extremely difficult to support or refute any of the major hypotheses at present asserted with confidence by leading scholars concerned with the influence of prices upon grain sales in the USSR in the 1920s'. The main reason for this conclusion was the paucity of data in relation to the number and complexity of hypotheses advanced. More recently I decided not to reopen this investigation for the following reasons, not considered in my original report. First, non-price factors (shortages of manufactures and the application of administrative measures of grain collection) were significantly autocorrelated. Secondly, and more importantly, all our measures of aggregate non-rural utilisation of grain (as distinct from government grain collections) are theoretically tainted in the sense that they are based on estimates of normed utilisations of various types, incorporating the hidden assumption of price inelasticity of demand and supply. The influence of price upon sales can never be estimated from such data. R. W. Davies has suggested to me that a more piecemeal study of contemporary materials such as the *Byulleten' Kon"yunkturnogo Instituta* might give useful results, but I have not had the opportunity to carry it out. There is still room for a substantial project here.

27. This leads me to rule out arguments in favour of a 'Millar effect' based on piecemeal study of year-to-year fluctuations in the grain market, such as those advanced by Merl (1981), 301–3 (also in private correspondence with the author).

28. See Malafeev (1964), 115.

29. Merl (1981), 90–108 and in private correspondence with the author.

30. See Chapter 7, and Wheatcroft, Davies and Cooper (1986), 269.

31. Wheatcroft (1976), 76.

32. Wheatcroft, Davies and Cooper (1986), 269–70.

33. See Harrison in Stuart (ed.) (1983), 76–8. However, evidence from other times and places suggests that under repressed inflation in official markets worker households do not significantly reduce the supply of labour in order to avoid unwanted cash accumulation; their cash needs continue to grow for both speculative purposes (since the supply of goods is uncertain as well as merely short) and for transactions purposes (since there are always some markets in which inflation is not repressed). See Nuti (1985), 20–8.

34. Especially Preobrazhenskii (1926), translated as *The New Economics* (1965).

35. Davies (1958), 65; 1924/25 current rubles are deflated for comparison with 1913 according to a wholesale price index (Davies (1958), 89).

36. *Materials* (1985), 157.

37. See Barsov (1968); Barsov (1969); and his contribution to *Novaya ekonomicheskaya politika: voprosy teorii i istorii* (1974).

38. For a comprehensive bibliography see Harrison (1985), 101–3.

39. *Materials* (1985), 65 (A. Petrov).

40. For a brief survey see Harrison (1985), 96, 101n.
41. Barsov (1968), 65 ascribed this undervaluation to 'the great socio-economic backwardness of the countryside inherited from the pre-revolutionary period'. But in fact the adverse shift in peasant terms of trade in the 1920s compared to the pre-war period was much more to do with urban and industrial developments – higher wage and other costs – than with rural stagnation.
42. Barsov (1968), 65, 78.
43. Carr and Davies (1974), 1004 (Table 12).
44. Davies (1980), 15.
45. See Shiokawa (1982–3), 132 (Table 1).
46. Davies (1980), 14–15.
47. Carr and Davies (1974), 484.
48. See Barber (1978), 4.
49. See Barber (1978), 19.
50. See Barber (1978), 11, 16.
51. For more discussion of these influences see Andrle (1984).

7 The Industrial Economy

1. Gregory (1982), 56–7. A production series for grain is given in Gregory (1982). Appendix D (Table D.1.G) and for livestock in Appendix H (Table H.1.B). Trade turnover is reported in Appendix A (Table A.1, col.1–2b). The industry series derive from Goldsmith (1961), 462–3. Construction remains something of a mystery.
2. In 1913, total net investment amounted to 2,314 million rubles, or 11.4 per cent of NNP. Gregory (1982), 56–7, 90–1.
3. See Gregory (1982), 56–7.
4. The TsSU index of industrial production in 1916 (taking 1913 = 100) was as follows: brick, 105; glass 64; sawn timber and veneer, 61; furnitures, 36. *Trudy TsSU*, xxvi (1926), i, 47.
5. *Trudy TsSU*, xxvi (1926), i, 42; Izmailovskaya (1920), 48–9, 114.
6. *Trudy TsSU*, xxvi (1926), i, 42; *Ekonomicheskoe polozhenie Rossii* (1957), ii, 26; Korelin (1972), 161–4. For the general context, see Sidorov (1973), 565–634.
7. According to a report submitted by industrialists to the Council of Ministers in June 1916, the value of capital equipment in private defence factories increased from 200 million rubles in 1913 to 1000 million in 1916. Allowing for price changes, the real value of equipment probably trebled. The report is cited in Bovykin and Tarnovskii (1957), 21. A price index for machine-building is given in *Trudy TsSU*, xxvi (1926), iii, 6ff.
8. See Strumilin (1958), 569, *Balans* (1926), i, 89–99, ii, 31, and the comments by Erlich (Cambridge, Mass., 1960), 105, and Carstensen (1977), 281.
9. The TsSU index of industrial equipment production stood at 124 in 1916 (1913 = 100) (*Trudy TsSU*, xxvi, 1926, i, 41). This index differs considerably from the index that is employed by Strumilin. Imports of all industrial equipment amounted to 156 million rubles in 1913 and 207 million rubles in 1916 (108 million rubles in 1913 prices, according to Strumilin, 1958, 551). Imports of machine tools were valued at 12 million rubles in 1914 and 46 million rubles in

1916, according to a report in *Promyshlennost' i torgovlya* (1917), 16–17.

10. Gregory (1982), 112–13; this is a reduction of 15–20 per cent per capita.
11. Wheatcroft, Davies and Cooper (1986), 267; Gregory (1982), 112–13. According to Wheatcroft's estimates in Chapter 5 above, net agricultural production amounted to 98 per cent of the good harvest year 1913 in the peak years 1926 and 1928; in 1926–8 (average) it amounted to 98 per cent of 1909–13 (average).
12. *Ekonomicheskoe obozrenie*, no. 9, 1929, 117; *Kontrol'nye tsifry narodnogo khozyaistva SSSR na 1928/1929 god* (1929), 435.
13. See Wheatcroft, Davies and Cooper (1986), 268–9.
14. Wheatcroft, Davies and Cooper (1986), 269.
15. Wheatcroft, Davies and Cooper (1986), 269.
16. It amounted to 162 million rubles in 1913 (in 1913 prices): Vainshtein (1960), 417; and 331 million rubles in 1926/27, measured in 1926/27 prices (*Kontrol'nye tsifry . . . na 1929/30 god* (1930), 446–65). It is certain that the investment costs index more than doubled in this period. Net investment in transport and communications rose, however, to 607 million rubles in 1927/28.
17. The following are the main constituents of net agricultural investment (in million rubles, USSR territory):

	1912[a] at 1913 prices	1913[a]	1926/27 at current prices[b]	1927/28 at 1926/27 prices[b]	1926/27 at 1913 prices[c]	1927/28 at 1913 prices[c]
Dwellings and farm buildings	251	319	636	585	247	237
Equipment	66	60	98	139	57	82
Livestock	126	91	598	427	315	225
Total	443	470	1332	1151	619	544

[a] Derived from Gregory (1982), 56–7. The figures have been roughly adjusted for territory (multiplied by 0.815).
[b] *Kontrol'nye . . . na 1929/30* (1930), 447–8.
[c] Using price index (1913 = 100) of 190 for livestock and 171 for equipment (All-Union wholesale price index) from Gregory (1982), 109–11; building costs index of 257 for dwellings and farm buildings in 1926/27 and 247 in 1927/28, from *Kontrol'nye tsifry . . . na 1929/30* (1930), 578 (the index for building materials used by Gregory is too low for building as a whole).

18. The Kondratiev index implies an average annual increase of 6.3 per cent between 1907 and 1913, compared to 8 per cent in 1890–9. (Gerschenkron, 1947, 152.)
19. *Dinamika rossiiskoi i sovetskoi promyshlennosti v svyazi s razvitiem narodnogo khozyaistva za sorok let (1887–1926gg.)*, Tom 1, parts i–iii (1929–30), ii, 66–77, 106–7; iii, 176–7 (hereafter *Dinamika*). The 1908 estimate derives from the industrial census conducted during that year; the 1913 estimate, which differs slightly from that in Gukhman (1929), was laboriously stitched together from various sources, as described in the preface to part iii of *Dinamika*. To obtain data in 1913 prices we have crudely deflated the current-price data in *Dinamika* with Bobrov's wholesale price index. Bobrov (1925), 91 shows 1908 prices as 91.4 (1913 = 100).

20. By 1909 output in Group A industries had recovered; in 1910, it was already 7 per cent higher than in 1908 and 30 per cent higher than in 1900. Bovykin (1984), 31. See Bovykin (1984), 22–3 for his allocation of sub-branches to Group A and B respectively.
21. Cotton textiles were an exception.
22. Bovykin (1984), 31. The 1913 proportion is tentative; it derives from the highly aggregated data presented in *Trudy TsSU*, xxvi (1926), i, 84–5.
23. Gukhman (1929), 186. This figure is not markedly out of line with the estimate made by Kaufman (1962), 75–81, if we eliminate logging and fishing from Kaufman's total. See Table 34 below.
24. Rybnikov (1922), 5–6; Kaufman (1962), 19.
25. See Gukhman (1927), 82; Kaufman (1962), 25.
26. *Vestnik statistiki*, no. 14 (1923), 152–3 (Vorob'ev). Gukhman (1929), 173, puts the increase at only 17 per cent.
27. *Trudy TsSU*, xxvi (1926), i, 41. Presumably, this includes uniforms, accessories and other material, as well as armaments, and excludes output of rolling-stock and industrial equipment, even if these items were destined for military use. Strumilin (1964), 105–6, arrived at a figure of 50 per cent for the share of defence goods in total output of large-scale industry. However, this estimate derived from figures collected from enterprises that were under the aegis of the Special Council for State Defence. These firms were asked to distinguish between the value of output undertaken on behalf of the procurement authorities and other output. But the total number of firms (3,500) was only half the total recorded in 1916 as given in *Trudy TsSU*, xxvi (1926), 64, and Strumilin took no account of the remainder.
28. Gukhman (1929), 191.
29. *Trudy Pervogo S"ezda Predstavitelei* (1916), 73 (Savin).
30. See *Puti industrializatsii*, no. 14, 1930, 48; *Kontrol'nye tsifry . . . na 1929/30* (1930), 446.
31. *Ekonomicheskoe obozrenie*, no. 9, 1929, 119 (Gukhman).
32. These figures make no allowance for deterioration in the quality of production, which may have been significant.
33. See 1938 industrial census cited in Buzlaeva (1969), 111, 113; the census itself has not been available. The extent of the exaggeration in these figures is discussed in Davies (1978), 25–9.
34. Based upon *Trudy TsSU*, xxvi (1926), i, 80–1; reference is to USSR territory in 1913. Industrial production per capita in 1908 reflects the low level of settlement in Siberia and Central Asia, and the density of settlement in European Russia. Output per head was as follows: European Russia (including Baltic), 30 rubles; Transcaucasus, 34 rubles; Central Asia, 11 rubles; Siberia, 7 rubles; Kazakhstan, 4 rubles. From Drobizhev *et al.* (1973), 293.
35. These rough estimates are based on the data for capital stock in industry on January 1, 1914, in Vainshtein (1960), 368–9, which shows that 21 per cent of capital stock in industry, including equipment valued at 434 million rubles, 24 per cent of all equipment, was located in the lost territories. According to Netesin (1980), 206–7, machinery and equipment evacuated from Riga alone was valued at 108 million rubles; the amount evacuated from Poland is likely to have been much smaller.
36. Drobizhev *et al.* (1973), 293.
37. The value of fuel production is given in *Dinamika*, ii, 106–7, 128, 142–3; iii, 176–7. Volume of output is taken from Khromov (1950), 458, minus reported output at the Polish coalfields (Gukhman, 1929, 174–5; and Kelly and Kano, 1977, 322). Produgol' was unable to prevent a fall in coal prices taking place

between 1909 and 1911. Prices recovered by 1913. Note that the syndicate controlled just 50 per cent of total coal production. See Shelyakin (1930), 45. For coal production see Table 37 below.

38. Shelyakin (1930), 30, 68.
39. *Obshchii obzor glavnykh otraslei gornoi i gornozavodskoi promyshlennosti*, i, (1913), 103–4; *Ocherki istorii tekhniki* (1973), 104–24. For oil production see Table 37 below.
40. Davydova (1966), 63; *Ocherki istorii tekhniki* (1973), 264–73.
41. *Trudy TsSU*, xxvi (1926), i, 62–3. For a general survey, see Sidorov (1973), 524–44.
42. Davydova (1966), 63.
43. See *Promyshlennost' SSR v 1926/27 godu* (1928), 89–10, 153–8. For Kuibyshev's phrase see *SSSR: 4 s"ezd sovetov* (1927), 326–7.
44. *Obshchii obzor*, i (1913), 36; ii (1915), 217; McKay (1970), 124–5.
45. Raffalovich (ed.) (1918), 185–6; *Ocherki istorii tekhniki* (1973), 179; Breiterman, iii (1930), 255.
46. *Ocherki istorii tekhniki* (1973), 181–9; Tarnovskii (1958), 157.
47. *Dinamika*, i, iii (1930), 176–7, 190.
48. See *Kontrol'nye tsifry . . . na 1928/1929* (1928), 410; *Vneshnyaya torgovlya SSSR za 1918–1940 gg.* (1960), 214–5, 278–9.
49. Serebrovskii (1936), 15–6: Stalin reportedly displayed an enthusiastic familiarity with the Californian gold rush and the writings of Bret Harte, as well as of the Russian writer Maimin-Sibiryak.
50. Detailed estimates of machine-building production in 1908, 1912 and 1913 are available from the authors.
51. Trebilcock (1973), 262–7; Gatrell (1982), 104–7. Employment in the Putilov wharves increased from 2,000 to 2,400 between 1912 and 1913; at naval shipyards from 3,200 to 6,700; at Russud, from 1,300 to 2,600. Nevsky alone remained unchanged at 3,400. The workforce at four state works grew from 15,850 to more than 18,000. Shatsillo (1968), 223, 240.
52. Gatrell (1982), 103.
53. Vorob'ev (1925) proposed an additional 9 million rubles for output from small-scale industry.
54. Izmailovskaya (1920), 26–7; Anfimov (1959); Carstensen (1984).
55. For general background, see Rozenfel'd and Klimenko (1916), 97–113.
56. Sarab'yanov (1923), 70; Holzer (1970); Davydova (1966), 158.
57. Shatsillo (1961), 85–6.
58. Eventov (1931), 70; Izmailovskaya (1920), 34: *Ocherki istorii tekhniki* (1973), 332. A contemporary authority put the proportion of machine tools imported at about 66 per cent (*Doklad soveta s"ezdov*, 1915, 171 (Savin)).
59. *Balans* (1926), ii, 34.
60. *Vestnik statistiki*, no. 14 (1923), 127 (Vorob'ev) gives the percentages 26 and 78 without explaining how he arrived at these proportions. *Trudy TsSU*, xxvi, i (1926), 40–1, estimates that in machine-building factories continuously in production between 1913 and 1918 defence production increased from 49.6 out of 189.1 million rubles (26.2 per cent) in 1913 to 327.4 out of 499.7 (65.5 per cent) in 1916.
61. The figure of 300 million rubles is likely to overestimate rather than underestimate civilian engineering in 1913.
62. See the survey in *Industrializatsiya SSSR, 1926–1928 gg.* (1969), 176–86.
63. See Carr and Davies (1969), 406.
64. See *Predpriyatie*, no. 5, 1926, 93; this was previously the 'Novyi Lessner' factory.

65. See Table 38; and Carr and Davies (1969), 951.
66. See Carr and Davies (1969), 448.
67. See Davies (1978), 28–9, 37, and Davies (1989a), 20, n. 83.
68. On the Nikolaevsk shipyards, see *SSSR: 4 s"ezd sovetov* (1927), 387.
69. Mints (1975), 87. For 1930, see *Narodnoe khozyaistvo* (1932), 426.
70. The statistics are difficult to unravel. TsSU estimated an increase of 45 per cent between 1908 and 1913 (to 320 million rubles), but this excludes pharmaceuticals, matches and explosives (*Trudy TsSU*, xxvi, 1926, i, 84–5). The *Dinamika* figure for 1908 output of chemicals, including explosives, is 156 million rubles, rising to 356 million rubles in 1913. This implies an increase of 128 per cent in current prices. Gukhman estimated an increase of 93 per cent, but did not elaborate. *Dinamika* (1930), ii, 66–77, 176–7; Gukhman (1929), 167.
71. Varzar (1918), 145.
72. One cannot be certain about the value of explosives output in 1913. *Dinamika* gives 47 million rubles for 'basic chemicals' in 1912, but this excludes state enterprises and thus excludes most explosives production (private sector output amounted to less than 8 million rubles). Output of basic chemicals in 1913, together with a number of other branches, including explosives, is put at 184 million rubles. Another source testifies to the proposed order of magnitude: TsSU gives a figure of 447 million rubles for total output in 1913 (including state sector) and 320 million rubles for private sector output. The difference of 127 million certainly includes explosives production, but it is unlikely that the value of explosives production exceeded 100 million rubles. *Trudy TsSU*, xxvi (1926), i, 76–7, 84–5. For further information, see Beskrovnyi (1977), 125–8.
73. *Promyshlennost' i torgovlya*, nos. 29 and 31, 1915 (Blokh); *Narodnoe khozyaistvo v 1915g.*, iii (1918) (Pantyukhov); see Haber (1971), 22–6, 169–73 for a general survey.
74. Mints (1975), 87.
75. Ipat'ev (1920), 10–12; Uribes (1961), 53–60.
76. *Trudy TsSU*, xxvi (1926), i, 43.
77. See the circumstantial account in Lel'chuk (1964), 71–87. Employment figures are taken from Mints (1975), 87. For chemical production see Table 32 below. The comments on fertilisers and explosives, by Shlikhter and Voroshilov respectively, will be found in Carr and Davies (1969), 239, 429.
78. *Dinamika*, ii, 198, 202–3, 204–5; iii, 177. Figures exclude state alcohol stores and tea-weighing. Bobrov (1925), 91, shows groceries' prices as 91.1 in 1908 (1913 = 100).
79. Mints (1975), 89–93; the employment data are a more reliable guide in these industries.
80. Lyashchenko (1910), 52; Pelferov (1918), 24–6.
81. Gukhman (1929), 174–5.
82. Mints (1975), 89–93. Further work is required on the food and drink trades during the war.
83. *Dva goda diktatury proletariata* (1920), 118–21. The corollary of this policy was that the rolling equipment tended to wear out more rapidly than hitherto.
84. *Materialy k pyatiletnemu planu* (1927), 464–76; the study did not include grain, where extra-rural marketings declined by almost 50 per cent, or meat and dairy products, where some decline also took place; the estimate for the year 1926/27, made early in 1927, is preliminary.
85. Mints (1975), 89–93.
86. *Trudy TsSU*, xxvi (1926), i, 70, 79, 94. Mints notes that the industry employed

32 per cent of all factory workers in 1908: Mints (1975), 44.
87. *Dinamika*, ii, 248, 256, 264, 268, 276, 280; iii, 176–7. For physical units, see *Dinamika*, ii, 252–3, 260–1 (1908) and, for 1913, Gukhman (1929), 174–5. Bobrov (1925), 91, indicates that textiles, prices in 1908 were 99.3 (1913 = 100).
88. Kaufman (1962), 78–9; Varzar (1918), 135; Laverychev (1963), 28; Khromov (1950), 306. Three-quarters of spindlage in 1912, according to Khromov, was to be found in enterprises that combined spinning and weaving, or spinning, weaving and finishing.
89. Varzar (1918), 113; Zagorsky (1928), 46; Rybnikov (1922), 7–8. According to one estimate, the army consumed less than 5 per cent of leather and fur production in 1913; by 1915 this proportion had increased to about 30 per cent (see *Doklad soveta s"ezdov*, 1915, 53–9, Dembovskii and Novosel'skii).
90. Gukhman (1929), 174–5. His estimate of cloth production is evidently based on the data for yarn production.
91. See Davies (1978), 42–3.
92. Compare the production data for 'clothing and toilet goods' in 1913 and 1915, in *Dinamika*, iii, 176–9. For a description of the pre-war garment industry, see Bonnell (ed.) (1983), 154–83.
93. *Statisticheskii spravochnik* (1929), 347–8.
94. *Na putyakh k obobshchestvleniyu melkoi promyshlennosti SSSR* (1929), 15–6.
95. See data in *Materials* (1985), 365–70. Comparable data for 1913 and 1926/27 have not been available. For general remarks, see Varzar (1918), 132.
96. The increase in production of the leather footwear industry was reported as follows (million rubles at 1913 prices):

	1913	1926/27
Census industry[a]	40	61
Small-scale industry[b]	233	267
Total	273	328

[a] *Trudy TsSU*, xxvi (1926), i, 70; *Statisticheskii spravochnik* (1929), 316–23.
[b] *Na putyakh* (1929), 15.

97. In 1904 the average working day lasted 10.6 hours. The 1905 Revolution reduced this to 10.2 hours. By 1913 the working day fell to 9.85 hours (no figure is available for 1908). Employment data are taken from Mints (1975), 39. Hours of work are given in Kir'yanov (1979), 48. The figures exclude overtime. In 1917, the working day was reduced to 8 hours, a decline of 8 per cent as compared with 1913. (*Trudy TsSU*, xviii, 1924, 170–1.)
98. *Nauchno-tekhnicheskii vestnik*, 1921, no. 4–5 (Vankov). One agricultural engineering firm produced 30 different types of plough before the war. In 1918, the new management reduced the number to three. Even where the government was the main customer (as in transport equipment), no measures were taken before the war to draw up standard specifications.
99. Epstein (1966), 97; Bovykin and Tarnovskii (1957), 25–6; Shatsillo (1959), 49–51.
100. Labour productivity probably increased more markedly in cotton-weaving than it did in cotton-spinning, in contrast to the situation in the 1890s.
101. Hogan (1983), 163–90.
102. *Ocherki istorii tekhniki* (1973), 104–13; Crisp (1978), 402.

103. The higher figure refers to annual gross output in 1913 prices, divided by the average daily workforce in industry. The lower figure is derived from the estimate of output per person, divided by the mean number of days worked. *Trudy TsSU*, xviii (1924), 170–1. The data refer to 2,287 enterprises that operated throughout the period 1913–18. Note that the figure for 1913 in col. 10 of the source is incorrect.
104. *Trudy Pervogo S"ezda Predstavitelei Metalloobrabatyvayushchei Promyshlennosti* (1916), 66 (S. I. Mikhin).
105. Tarnovskii (1981), 18–34; Polner *et al.* (1930), 61–5, 186–7.
106. Kir'yanov (1971), 39. Prisoners-of-war constituted 54 per cent of the labour force in the Krivoi Rog iron ore mines by September 1916. Over one-quarter of the workforce in the coal mines of the Donbass in March 1917 were prisoners.
107. For number of workers, see Mints (1975), 39; for the production index and its defects see Davies (1978), 13–31.
108. For examples of standardisation, see Carr and Davies (1969), 343. For an authoritative account of specialisation and standardisation in the cotton textile industry, see *Predpriyatie*, no. 10, 1927, 10–5 (A. Nol'de). For the introduction of machinery into the oil industry see *Pervye shagi industrializatsii SSSR 1926/27 gg.* (1959), 161–90; in oil mining and extraction, production increased from 390 million rubles in 1913 to 463 millions in 1926/27 (measured in 1913 prices), but the number of workers declined from 49,700 to 43,600 (Mints, 1975, 50, 101; *Trudy TsSU*, xxvi, i, 1926, 69–73; *Statisticheskii spravochnik* (1929), 316–23).
109. Data from Mints (1975), 67 and Grachev (1961), 128–9 (for 1920). The figures were as follows:

Percentage of workers in units of:	*1907*	*1914*	*1920*	*1927*
50 workers	11.7	10.2	5.3	3.4
51–500 workers	35.8	33.3	31.6	24.5
500 workers	52.6	56.5	63.1	72.1

110. *Birzhevye vedomosti*, December 11, 1915.
111. See Carr and Davies (1969), 487–511.
112. Calculated from Strumilin (1958), 680. The corresponding figures for the Empire were 7,813 million rubles in 1908 and 10,855 million rubles in 1913. Transactions at state alcohol outlets were valued at 709 million rubles in 1908 and 899 million rubles in 1913 (794 million, USSR territory). The value of retail trade turnover in constant (1913) prices increased by between 30 and 43 per cent (1908–13), depending on the price index applied. See Gregory (1982), 199–205.
113. Firms registered in Category I had to pay for a licence to trade, but also paid the supplementary industrial tax (*dopolnitel'nyi promyslovyi nalog*). Details of the classification of trading units in the pre-war period will be found in Dikhtyar (1960), 66–8.
114. Details in Bukshpan (1918), 275.
115. Kahan (1985), Chapter 5; Dikhtyar (1960), 141, 143.
116. Nonetheless, turnover at Nizhnii Novgorod attained 195 million rubles in 1912, an increase of one-third over the average turnover in 1897–1906 (Dikhtyar,

1960, 144). It is also worth noting that, after a decade of collapse in dealings (turnover in 1921 was only 10 per cent of the 1912 volume), the fair recovered rapidly in 1922–5, attaining a turnover of 169 million rubles (in current prices) by 1925. (S. Malyshev, *Nizhegorodskaya yarmarka v 1925 g.*, 1925, *cit. Sovetskoe narodnoe khozyaistvo v 1921–1925 gg.*, 1960, 442).

117. Amburger (1974), 184–5; Kitanina (1969), 67–70.
118. Gefter (1969), 88, 114–5; Volobuev (1957), 39–41.
119. Bukshpan (1918), 290–3; Lyashchenko (1952), ii, 294–348; Crisp (1976), 175–7, Gatrell (1986), 177–84.
120. Carstensen (1984), Chapter 12; International Harvester cut back on its inventory investment in Russia in 1914, in the face of an anti-trust suit in the United States.
121. There were five main types of consumer cooperative: factory, railway (both essentially sponsored by employers), worker, city and village. Rural cooperatives provided the bulk of the increase in numbers before 1914. Dikhtyar (1960), 151, 153; Salzman (1977), 2, 5.
122. Dikhtyar (1960), 149–56; Salzman (1977), Chapter 2. Things did not always work out smoothly: Salzman cites cases of a price war between merchants and cooperatives and also alludes to a certain lack of loyalty to consumer cooperatives on the part of members. Some peasants, desperate for cash, would obtain goods from the cooperative store on credit and sell them for cash to unscrupulous merchants, who waited outside for precisely that purpose and who then sold the goods at a knock-down price (117–18).
123. Dikhtyar (1960), 153; Carr (1952), ii, 122.
124. The decision was taken on August 22, 1914; curiously, the government had decreed an increase in the price of vodka only a month earlier (after the war had begun) (Michelson *et al.*, 1928, 80–9).
125. Zak (1927), 89–113. Details of the numbers engaged in trade during the war are unavailable. One may surmise, however, that the ranks of tradesmen and employees were decimated by conscription.
126. Implied in Dikhtyar (1960), 206–7.
127. Shepelev (1973), 311.
128. Kitanina (1969), 100–27. Sidorov (1961), 272, states that there were around 9,000 *torgovye doma* by 1917.
129. Dikhtyar (1960), 230; Salzman (1977), 5, 135.
130. *Narodnoe khozyaistvo v 1915 g.* (1918), 293–5; TsGIA 31/1/5, 50–5. The response of industrial consumers was, as previously, to seek out their own sources of supply. The war thus promoted a fresh round of vertical integration.
131. TsGIA, 31/1/7, 148; Pankin (1952), 42–53; *Ekonomicheskoe polozhenie Rossii* (1957), ii, 94–42. Yugomet was absorbed by Vesenkha in December 1917; Prodamet was formally nationalised in January 1918. (Venediktov, i, 1957, 76.)
132. Zagorsky (1928), 205–34; Dikhtyar (1960), 222–6. These monopolies were confirmed and extended by the Bolshevik government between December 1917 and March 1918. In practice, however, the government disposed of few stocks of basic commodities. The retail trade counterpart of the 'pusher' (who operated in the sphere of wholesale distribution, on behalf of industrial clients) now became the 'bagman'. Carr (1952), 118.
133. See Carr (1958), 245.
134. Dikhtyar (1961), 212, 303.
135. See Carr and Davies (1969), 636–50.

136. In April 1926, for example, 400 traders in the central market were arrested by the OGPU for allegedly purchasing goods for re-sale, in one of a series of raids carried out by the OGPU at the request of the Moscow soviet (*Torgovo-promyshlennaya gazeta*, April 16, 1926).
137. Dikhtyar (1961), 239. These figures all exclude direct sales by peasants and others in bazaar trade.
138. *Vsesoyuznaya perepis'*, xxxiv (1930), 118–9.
139. *Trud v SSSR: spravochnik 1926–1930* (1930), 3.
140. For the numbers employed, see *Trud* (1930), 3; for the number of units, see Strumilin (1958), 694–5.
141. Strumilin estimated the total number of persons engaged in trade in 1913 as 1,185,000 owners plus 487,000 employees, 1,672,000 persons altogether; 1958, 694–5. The equivalent figures for 1926/27 were 628,644 private owners plus 515,200 employed in all sectors of trade, 1,143,844 altogether (*Trud*, 1930, 3; Strumilin, 1958, 694–5); this no doubt underestimated the number of pedlars and persons selling from carts.
142. Gregory (1982), pp. 56–9.
143. See Gatrell, in *Economic History Review*, 2nd series, xxxv (1982), 104–5; an unknown percentage of these totals was met by imports. For a thorough discussion of military expenditure, including the non-weapon components, see *Russian Review*, xi (1984), 231–59 (Pintner).
144. Losses to military shipping and to installations at Port Arthur were officially put at 256 million rubles, equivalent to three or four times the annual capital outlays of the defence budget. See Shatsillo (1969), 124; and Gregory (1982), Appendix Table F2, in which capital expenditures for defence purposes are put at 62 million rubles in 1900 and 80 million in 1903.
145. The main programmes adopted between 1906 and 1914 were valued at 820 million rubles for the navy and 433 million rubles for the army (see Shatsillo, 1968, 62–3, 66, 68, 77, 132–3, 158, 209; Shatsillo, 1974, 36–8, 39, 42–3, 51, 89, 92, 97, 99–100).
146. The 1908 loan from France was the last pre-war foreign loan concluded to stabilise the ruble.
147. Geyer (1987), 255–72.
148. By contrast, direct taxes comprised 13 per cent of budget revenue in 1900: Shebaldin (1959), 168.
149. Michelson (1928), 39–49.
150. Babkov (1912), 78–9 and our Table 32.
151. Thus, the excise on tobacco (3rd grade) was raised in 1909 from 18 to 48 kopeks/funt, and that on cigarettes (2nd grade) from 90k. to 180k. Rates on higher-quality tobacco and cigarettes rose less steeply (Shebaldin, 1959, 169). The excise comprised 51 per cent of the retail price of 3rd grade tobacco after these changes (previously it was 32 per cent) and 45 per cent of the retail price of *papirosy* (cigarettes with long holders) (previously 30 per cent).
152. The impact of the vodka monopoly on the budget should also take account of the minor loss of revenue from the industrial tax (promnalog), hitherto levied on distilleries.
153. Crisp (1976), 29–31; Kahan (1967), 470–4. Customs duties represented 12 per cent of gross ordinary budget receipts in 1903, and 10 per cent in 1913.
154. Note, however, that manufacturing industry faced high input costs because of the impact of syndicates on the price of coal, iron and steel, etc. The tariff was not the sole factor.

155. *Promyshlennost' i torgovlya*, no. 11, 1914 (Ol'shevskii).
156. Gindin (1948), 444–5; Shebaldin (1959), 178–9.
157. Gindin (1948), 256–7.
158. Total bank credits secured by shares and other non-guaranteed paper, on January 1 of each year, were as follows (million rubles):

	Total	*'On call'*	*'Loro'*[a]
1908	251	168	39
1912	806	461	225
1913	1311	720	460
1914	1619	810	642

Source: Gindin (1948), 416–9.

Note:　[a] Accounts extended to corporations, normally secured by the firm's shares.

159. M. I. Bogolepov, cited in Gindin (1948), 254.
160. For government war-time controls, see Gatrell (1979).
161. The 'scissors' was the ratio between the prices received by the peasants for agricultural output and the prices paid by the peasants for industrial goods; when this opened to the disfavour of the peasants the graph resembled the blades of a pair of scissors.
162. For the reintroduction and subsequent history of the vodka monopoly, see Carr (1954), 35, note 2.
163. The official figures (see Table 41 below) also show an enormous reduction in administrative expenditure; this remarkable decline requires sceptical investigation.
164. *Promyshlennost'* . . . *1926/27* (1928), 72; this includes electrification and 'other' (presumably defence) industries.
165. See Carr (1958), 344; Carr and Davies (1969), 829–30.
166. Carr and Davies (1969), 830–1, which also describes the arrangements introduced in other industries in 1926–8.
167. Carr and Davies (1969), 409–11.
168. See *Torgovo-promyshlennaya gazeta*, July 23, 1927.
169. *3 sessiya Tsentral'nogo Ispolnitel'nogo Komiteta Soyuza SSR 4 sozyva* (1928), 167–72.
170. *Ekonomicheskaya zhizn'*, February 23, 1927 (report of Vesenkha plenum).
171. 'The building materials industry', Kuibyshev complained, 'is unfortunately not under an All-Union organisation which could freely plan the industry as it plans metal, coal, or oil' (*Torgovo-promyslennaya gazeta*, March 4, 1928, report of Vesenkha plenum).
172. See Carr and Davies (1969), 357–9, 827–9. This account exaggerates the extent to which the detailed planning of investment was undertaken by the central authorities in 1927–9.
173. According to Soviet figures, the percentage of workers in census industry employed in mining, metals and engineering remained at 37.2 in 1926/27, the same as in 1913, while the equivalent percentage in Germany increased from 41.3 to 46.5 between 1913 and 1925 (*Na novom etape*, ii, 1930, 594–5; the figures for 1913 are from *Dinamika*, iii, 1930, 176–7; and *Mirovoe khozyaistvo*, 1928, 89–91).
174. *Pyatiletnii plan*, ii, i (1930), 98–9.
175. *Materialy* (1927), 29.

176. *Problemy rekonstruktsii narodnogo khozyaistva* (1929), 338 (Eventov); this volume contains the proceedings of the fifth congress of Gosplan in March 1929; L. Y. Eventov's informative report sums up the Soviet view at the time of the comparative economic level of the Soviet economy.
177. The following instructive comparisons, measured in horsepower hours per head of population per year, were presented in *Kontrol'nye tsifry . . . na 1927/1928 god* (1928), 444–5, with a further breakdown for each type of fuel:

	Living energy (human and animal)	*Mechnical energy (coal, peat, oil, firewood and water power)*	*Total*
United States	207.3	1818.9	2026.3
Great Britain	57.4	999.5	1052.9
Germany	93.2	571.2	664.4
Italy	84.8	206.2	291.0
Japan	59.3	190.5	249.8
USSR	181.8	88.4	270.2
India	155.3	17.9	173.2
China	52.7	11.0	63.7

178. *Kontrol'nye tsifry . . . na 1927/1928* (1928), 446.
179. *Torgovo-promyshlennaya gazeta*, May 10, 1928 (E. Konshtadt).
180. See, for example, *Istoriya Moskovskogo instrumental'nogo zavoda* (1934), 114–15.
181. *Fabrichno-zavodskaya promyshlennost' SSSR*, i (1928), 9–22 (V. Veits); the Soviet figure refers to October 1, 1926.
182. *Problemy rekonstruktsii* (1930), 336 (Eventov).
183. The number of engineering and technical workers as a percentage of total personnel was given as follows:

Coal:	USSR 1.45	Germany 4.25	US 25
Chemicals:	USSR 5.7	Germany 31.3	
Electrical Industry	USSR 6.0	US 19	

(*Predpriyatie*, no. 8, 1928, 13; no. 10, 1928, 12).

184. *Na novom etape*, ii (1930), 642–5; the ratio for 1928/29, when Soviet productivity was approximately 28 per cent higher than in 1926/27, was 1: 5.5 in the case of the United States and 1: 1.55 in the case of Britain (the United States figures are for 1927, the British for 1924); all figures are for net output measured in pre-war prices and adjusted for the over-valuation of the ruble. Is the gap much narrower in 1990?
185. *Na novom etape*, ii (1930), 643–4; the percentages for 1926/27 would have been lower, owing to the lower level of Soviet productivity in that year.
186. See the very rough data in *Kontrol'nye tsifry . . . na 1928/1929* (1929), 383.
187. The Soviet percentage share in world production in 1926 was estimated by Vesenkha as follows (with the tsarist share in 1913 in brackets): coal 2.1 (2.4), cotton (consumption) 7.1 (8.7), sugar 4.3 (6.7), iron 3.0 (5.6), oil 5.3 (16.7)

(*Vypolnenie pyatiletnego plana promyshlennosti* (1931), 38).
188. *Kontrol'nye tsifry . . . na 1928/1929* (1929), 378; this passage was written in the summer of 1928.
189. *Predpriyatie*, no. 10, 1927, 72 (Yu. Flakserman).
190. *Kontrol'nye tsifry . . . na 1926–1927* (1926), 166 (approved by the presidium of Gosplan on August 16, 1926).
191. *Kontrol'nye tsifry . . . na 1927/1928* (1928), 442, 449–51 (dated September 30, 1927).

8 The Textile Industries

1. Feoktistov (1924), 6.
2. Khromov (1946), 49; Pazhitnov (1958), 17–18, 132.
3. Laverychev (1960), 137–8; Pazhitnov (1958), 141; Portal (1974), 169; Portal (1965), 854.
4. See Ivanova (1982), 59; Odell (1912), 8–9, 39, 42.
5. Dobb (1966), 56–7; *Trud* (Ivanovo guberniya Trades Council), no. 5, May 1923, 18 (hereafter *Trud I-V*); Korneev (1957), 18; Portal (1965), 855.
6. Kaufman (1962), Tables 1 and 2, 19–20; see also 27–8.
7. Portal (1974), 175.
8. There were just over 84,000 power looms in the Russian Empire in 1890, around 213,000 twenty years later: Khromov (1946), 45, 58.
9. Khromov (1946), 173. See also Statisticheskoe otdelenie Vladimirskoi gubernskoi zemskoi upravy, *Melkaya fabrichnaya sel'sko-tkatskaya promyshlennost'* (1914), iii.
10. Portal (1965), 823.
11. *Byulleten' Ivanovo-voznesenskogo gubernskogo statisticheskogo byuro*, no. 15, 1927, Table 1, 49 (hereafter *BI-VGSB*) gives figures based on *zemstva* data for 1897 and 1900 and adjusted to Ivanovo guberniya in 1926. Further information on artisan textiles can be found in Odell (1912), 17–18.
12. Especially Kaufman (1962).
13. Khromov (1946), 67–8; see also Table 37.
14. *Rabochii krai*, March 10, 1920; *Tekstil'shchik*, no. 1 (24), January 1921.
15. Odell (1912), 9.
16. *Tekstil'shchik, k stanku*, September 10, 1921.
17. *Na novykh putyakh* (1923), 10; Matyugin (1962), 198.
18. Odell (1912), 13, 18; Zaikov (1926/27), 6.
19. Aleshchenko (1959), 109; Yakovlev (1963), 5; *BI-VGSB*, October 1, 1922, 15; Polyakova (1959), 21–2, 27; Shkaratan (1959), 26.
20. *Tekstil'nye novosti*, no. 10–11, 1927, 365.
21. The Textile Syndicate handbook *Tekstil'nye fabriki SSSR* (1927) lists many mills still in mothballs, and many others which existed only in name, all their equipment having been relocated.
22. Anglo-Russian Cotton Factories Ltd, Report of Proceedings of Annual General Meeting of Shareholders at Company Offices, London, 16 June 1926, Guildhall Library L 69.55 MS11-760, 2; Yakovlev (1963), 16.
23. Ward (1985), Chapter IV.
24. *Tekstil'nye novosti*, no. 10–11, 1927, 366.
25. *Vosstanovlenie promyshlennosti Leningrada* (1963), dok. 39, p. 124.

26. *Planovoe khozyaistvo*, no. 4, 1928, 295.
27. Derevnina (1981), Table 5, 60–1.
28. See *BI-VGSB*, no. 1, October 1922, 34–5, 46; 8, 3; 9, 2. Yakovlev (1963), 14.
29. *BI-VGSB*, 8, 1924; *Tri goda raboty* (1925), 10.
30. *BI-VGSB*, no. 20, 1929, Table 1, 36, Table 2, 46, Table 3, 50–7.
31. *Fabrichno-zavodskaya promyshlennost' g. Moskvy* (1928), Table 1, 8.
32. *Rabota moskovskogo gubernskogo soveta* (1926), 77.
33. Vas'kina (1981), 131, 136.
34. *Golos tekstilei, Tekstil'nye novosti*, and *Izvestiya tekstil'noi promyshlennosti i torgovli.*
35. Zhukovskii *et al.* (1931), 19.
36. Ward (1985), 102.
37. *Izvestiya tekstil'noi promyshlennosti i torgovli*, no. 6, February 15, 1926; no. 18, May 15, 1926.
38. *Materials* (1985), 351–70.
39. Pazhitnov (1958), 134–5.
40. Pazhitnov (1958), 135–6.
41. Pazhitnov (1958), 140–3; Pazhitnov (1955), 218–32.
42. Carr (1952), 79–81, 174–5, 178; Dobb (1966), 86–7.
43. Yakobson (1967), 86–7; *Trud I-V*, no. 5, 1923, 19; *Rabochii krai*, November 24, 1920; February 22, 1921; March 17, 1921; March 26, 1922.
44. Ward (1985), Chapters VIII, IX, X.
45. Bandera (1970/71), 111–18; Conyngham (1973), 20.
46. Pikhalo (1971), 22; *Izmeneniya* (1979), 25.
47. Bandera (1970/71), 111–18; Carr (1952), 306–7; Conyngham (1973), 20; Dewar (1956), 90–1; *Tekstil'shchik, k stanku*, September 10, 1921.
48. Bandera (1970/71), 111–15, 118. On the confused relationship between Vesenkha and VTS in the early 1920s see *Rezolyutsii* (1923), 6.
49. Carr and Davies (1969), 375.
50. Dobb (1966), 134–5; Lavrikov *et al.* (1968), 35–6; Pikhalo (1971), 23–4; Sutton (1968), 225, *Vosstanovlenie promyshlennosti Leningrada* (1963), dok. 22, 70–1.
51. *Na novykh putyakh* (1923), 1; Pikhalo (1971), 23–4; *Postoyannaya promyshlennaya* (1923), 282–329.
52. See the listings in *Tekstil'nye fabriki SSSR.*
53. Carr (1952), 306–7; Carr and Davies (1969), 379–80.
54. Carr and Davies (1969), 373–4.
55. Zvezdin (1971), 8, 55.
56. Ward (1985), Chapter VII.
57. Dobb (1966), 159–60; Carr and Davies (1969), 636–7.
58. Carr and Davies (1969), 636–7; Zvezdin (1971), 9.
59. 'During NEP one factory after another was brought back on stream, but the process was hindered by the unplanned, chaotic development of industry; a feature inherited from capitalism' (Glebov and Letukov, 1981, 25).
60. Ward (1985), chapters VIII, IX, XI; Conyngham (1973), 10–12, 14–17, 21.

9 The Railways

1. Vainshtein (1960), 234. These figures comprise virtually all railway assets apart from land and working capital.

2. A. L. Sidorov (1948), 6. These growth rates relate to tonnage, whereas Strumilin's traffic figures, encountered later in this chapter and signalling an absolute decline of freight (but not passenger) traffic in 1913, refer to ton-km.
3. Westwood (1964), 306.
4. Strumilin (1958), 640–1.
5. Sidorov (1948), 4–63.
6. Hunter (1957), 59.
7. *Transport i svyaz'* (1957), 7.
8. Page and Nurminen (1987), unpublished paper. Rakov (1955), 70, gives total (common-carrier plus industrial railways) locomotive production as 654 in 1913, which seems to support Sidorov's figure. Rakov's table is followed by dense footnotes illustrating the difficulty of arriving at indisputably accurate figures; in his figures for the 1920s he is driven to use a treatise on locomotive frames as source.
9. This figure relates to production within the future USSR pre-1939 frontiers, and is from *Promyshlennost' SSSR* (1957), 220. Sidorov's figure of 19,042 for the 1913 Empire is hard to reconcile with this, even though some vehicle-building facilities were lost in the post-war settlement. Other, conflicting, figures are sometimes encountered; it should be remembered that the common-carrier railways received only a proportion of total wagon output (and, for that matter, of all railway-supply production) because the industrial lines took a large share.
10. *Materialy po statistike putei soobshcheniya*, iii(1922), Table A.
11. Sidorov (1948). The 1320km is actually the average length *opened* in those years. The assumption that in 1913, and the 1920s, the figure of rail deliveries includes tonnage delivered for new construction is plausible but as yet unconfirmed.
12. Strumilin (1958), 640–1.
13. Strumilin (1958), 644–5.
14. *Gudok*, February 20, 1922, quoted in *Soviet Studies*, xxxviii (1986), 199.
15. Pogrebinskii (1959), 257.
16. *Materialy po statistike*, iii (1922), Table A, implies that 1915 freight traffic was six per cent higher than 1913, whereas *Materialy po statistike*, ii (1921), 5, suggests that train density per average kilometre was 18 in 1913 and 1914, 20 in 1915, 19 in 1916, 17 in 1917, with the number of axles in the average freight train 40 in 1913, 39 in 1914, 42 in 1915, and 40 in 1917. Vasil'ev (1939), 76, shows a freight ton-km growth of 29 per cent from 1913 to 1916, and implies a doubling of passenger-km from 1913 to 1915. Sidorov (1948), 34, shows a 25 per cent rise in freight tonnage originated and a 48 per cent rise in passenger journeys from 1913 to 1916.
17. *Sotsialisticheskoe stroitel'stvo* (1934), 227.
18. *Transport i svyaz' SSSR* (1957), 116. According to *Sotsialisticheskoe stroitel'stvo* (1934), 228, freight tonnage was 48.3 million in 1913, 19.6 million in 1924, 39.9 million in 1928. The discrepancy *may* be ascribable to the inclusion of traffic carried by craft belonging or chartered to other organisations.
19. *Sovetskii transport 1917–1927* (1927), 177. In this source the actual 1913 figure has been doubled to bring it into line with the depreciated ruble of the 1920s.
20. Blank and Mitaishvili (1972), 78.
21. *Sovetskii transport 1917–1927* (1927), 216–17.
22. *Sovetskii transport 1917–1927* (1927), 223.
23. Westwood (1964), 218.
24. Hunter (1957), 393.

25. *Ekonomist*, no. 1, 1922, 167.
26. Strumilin (1958), 658.
27. Hunter (1957), 411. Rail imports were usually insignificant, being about 1,800 tons in 1913, and less than 1,000 tons each year from 1922/23 onwards. In 1921 (68,651 tons) and 1921/22 (14,808 tons) they appear to have been sizable but not decisive. These figures are from *Vneshnyaya torgovlya* (1960), 213, 246, 278.
28. Strumilin (1958), 655–6.
29. Yakobi (1935), 88.
30. *Promyshlennost'* (1957), 220.
31. The 1928 figure is from Yakobi (1935), 44, which also attempts a 1913 figure for goods wagons within the USSR pre-1939 frontiers (397,200). The 1913 figure is from *Materialy po statistike*, civ (?1928), Table 1.
32. These figures come from Yakobi (1935), 48–56, and from *Transport i svyaz' SSSR* (1957), 46–61. They have to be taken with some caution as their definitions are not always clear, but such imprecision hardly affects the conclusion of this paragraph.
33. Strumilin (1958), 670–1, and Strumilin (1966), 305.
34. *Sovetskii transport* (1927), 92.
35. *Materialy po statistike*, xcvii (1928?), p. vi.
36. *Materialy po statistike*, xxxvi (1925), p. lxxvi.
37. The chapter does not enter into this, but scattered references to the situation can be found in Westwood (1982), especially 23–7.

10 Research and Technology

1. Among Western authors, see Graham (1975), Vucinich (1971) and (1984), 56–122; among Soviet authors see Bastrakova (1968) and (1973), Lebin (ed.) (1980), 99–114. It should be noted that in Russian and Soviet usage 'science' includes the humanities and the social sciences.
2. For this and subsequent data on the research effort of Russia and the USSR see Table 52.
3. *Otchet . . . na 1912* (1913), 516–7, *Otchet . . . na 1913* (1914), 530–1, *Otchet . . . na 1914* (1915), 538–9.
4. Following usual practice, we have excluded geological surveying from our estimates of R&D in both periods. 102,557 rubles were spent on the Committee in 1912 (*Otchet . . . na 1912*, 1913, 552–3), 255,147 rubles in 1913 (*Otchet . . . na 1913*, 1914, 536–7), 246,677 in 1914 (*Otchet . . . na 1914*, 1915, 546–7); 3,005,869 rubles were allocated to its work in 1925/26 (*Edinyi gosudarstvennyi byudzhet . . . na 1926–1927. Proekt* (1927), 103).
5. Bailes (1978), 36.
6. Bailes (1978), 30.
7. *Sovetskaya istoricheskaya entsiklopedia*, vi (1965), 115.
8. Leikina-Svirskaya (1971), 130.
9. Leikina-Svirskaya (1981), 17–18.
10. Bailes (1978), 43.
11. Ahlström (1982), 108.
12. *Historical Statistics of the United States. Colonial Times to 1957* (1960), 75.
13. See Table 53.

14. Shavrov, 2nd edn (1978), 256. The sections on aircraft in this chapter draw heavily on Shavrov's valuable work. Note that the output figures presented by Shavrov are substantially larger than those indicated in the Ministry of Trade and Industry's *Fabrichno-zavodskaya promyshlennost' evropeiskoi Rossii v 1910–1912 gg.*, vi (Petrograd, 1914), 152. According to Shavrov, output in 1910 was 70 units, in 1911 120, and in 1912 170 units, but the prerevolutionary source gives 6, 17 and 59 units respectively.
15. Shavrov (1978).
16. Shavrov (1978), 256.
17. Velizhev (1932), 6.
18. *Ocherki razvitiya tekhniki v SSSR. Energeticheskaya, atomnaya, transportnaya i aviatsionnaya tekhnika. Kosmonavtika* (1969), 330.
19. Shavrov (1978), 256.
20. *Ocherki razvitiya tekhniki v SSSR* (1969), 330.
21. Voronkova, *Istoricheskie zapiski*, lxxv (1975), 147.
22. Shugurov and Shirsov, 2nd edn (1983), 7, 18; our discussion of motor vehicles draws heavily on this informative work.
23. Shugurov and Shirsov (1983), 18.
24. *SSSR i kapitalisticheskie strany: statisticheskii sbornik* (1939), 172.
25. See Voronkova (1975), 147–55.
26. Shugurov and Shirsov (1983), 19.
27. *Ocherki razvitiya tekhniki* (1971), 201.
28. *Sel'skokhozyaistvennaya entsiklopediya*, 3rd edn, v (1956).
29. *Sel'skokhozyaistvennaya entsiklopediya*, 3rd edn, v (1956).
30. See Rosenberg (1976), 24–6.
31. Shugurov and Shirsov (1983), 11–12; *Bol'shaya Sovetskaya Entsiklopedia*, 2nd edn, vii, 348.
32. *Fabrichnozavodskaya promyshlennost'*, vi (1914), 152.
33. *Fabrichnozavodskaya promyshlennost'*, vi (1914), 152.
34. *Zdes' nash dom* (Leningrad, 1982), 46.
35. *Zdes' nash dom* (1982), 47–9; Levitan and Morozov, *Zavod – polveka. Kratkii ocherk istorii ordena Lenina gosudarstvennogo optikomekhanicheskogo zavoda* (1965), 5–6.
36. A. S. Syrov, *Put' fotoapparata* (1954), 69, *Pravda*, December 21, 1932.
37. *Zdes' nash dom* (1982), 56; this was a highly significant development because until the war optical glass making was a monopoly of just three firms in Britain, France and Germany.
38. R. B. Davies (1976), Chapters 10–12.
39. *Industrializatsiya SSSR, 1926–1928gg.* (1969), 186.
40. *Iron Age*, xxxviii, 16 June 1910, 1462.
41. *Goroda Podmoskovya*, iii (1981), 277.
42. *Promyshlennost' SSSR* (1964), 408.
43. *Fabrichno-zavodskaya promyshlennost'*, vi (1914), 132; note that R. B. Davies (1976), 260, drawing on the Singer archives, suggests an output as high as 800,000 units before the war.
44. See Romanov (1985), 9–12, Britsko (1982), xii.
45. *Fabrichnozavodskaya promyshlennost'* (1914), 148.
46. *Promyshlennost' SSSR* (1964), 406.
47. For material on bearings before the revolution and under NEP, see *Pervyi podshipnikovyi. Istoriya pervogo gosudarstvennogo podshipnikogo zavoda, 1932–1972* (1973), 10–13, E. V. Yufereva, *Leninskoe uchenie o goskapitalizme v perekhodnyi period k sotsializmu* (1969), 112–13, V. A. Shishkin,

'*Polosa priznanii' i vneshneekonomicheskaya politika SSSR (1924–1928gg.)* (1983), 259.

48. This section and the section on machine tools under NEP are based on J. M. Cooper's unpublished Ph.D thesis (University of Birmingham, 1975).
49. *Fabrichnozavodskaya promyshlennost'*, vi (1914), 152.
50. Grinevetskii (1922), 42.
51. Rozenfel'd and Klimenko (1961), 12.
52. Bailes (1978), 22.
53. A Narkomtrud survey of 1922–3 identified 38,385 specialists in industry and transport; of the 27,393 who were employed, 12,276, or 44.8 per cent, were graduates (Fedyukin, 1965, 136); we have assumed that non-graduates were five times as likely to be unemployed as graduates, as was the case later in the 1920s (see *Industrializatsiya SSSR. 1926–1928gg.*, 1969, 364).
54. Bailes (1978), 63.
55. *Organizatsiya nauki v pervye gody Sovetskoi vlasti (1917–1925)* (1968), 99.
56. *Organizatsiya nauki* (1968), 300–2.
57. Shavrov (1978), 314–5.
58. Bastrakova (1973), 222.
59. *Organizatsiya nauki* (1968), 142–6.
60. Gregory suggests a best deflator of 2.2 for the government sector in 1928 (1924/25 weights) as compared with 1913 (Gregory, 1982, 107–11); a 1926/27 deflator would be slightly lower.
61. See Bastrakova (1973), 138–52, 177–218; *Organizatsiya nauki* (1968), 232–338.
62. *Organizatsiya nauki* (1968), 301.
63. Almost one-quarter of the funds of research establishments under Vesenkha SSSR in 1925/26 and 1926/27, subsequently even more (Lewis, 1979, 158).
64. Data from Table 52 deflated by Gregory's best deflator for the government sector.
65. Expenditure on it through the budget was 393,000 rubles in 1925/26 (*Prilozhenie k proektu edinogo gosudarstvennogo byudzheta . . . na 1925–1926*, 1926, 222) and 370,000 in 1926/27 (*Edinyi gosudarstvennyi byudzhet . . . na 1926–1927*, 1927, 248–9).
66. See, for example, Vucinich (1984), 91–122.
67. Data from Table 52 deflated by Gregory's deflator; in fact in its consideration of the 1927/28 budget Sovnarkom cut the initially proposed expenditure on the Academy, while increasing that on the other establishments which it controlled and on some of those under the commissariats – particularly Vesenkha (*Edinyi gosudarstvennyi byudzhet . . . na 1927–1928*, 1928, 65–71).
68. The émigré scientist Zhores Medvedev calls this period 'the golden years of Soviet science' in his *Soviet Science* (1978).
69. See Table 53.
70. Almost 20 per cent of the contributions came from the USSR in the 1926 issues of the journal.
71. Yakovlev, 4th edn (1982), 350; *Aviatsiya i kosmonavtika SSSR* (1968), 54; Shumikhin (1986), 103.
72. *Aviatsiya i kosmonavtika* (1968), 55.
73. *Aviatsiya i kosmonavtika* (1968).
74. Shumikhin (1986), 103.
75. The material in this paragraph is drawn from Shavrov (1978).
76. This section is based on *Razvitie aviatsionnoi nauki i tekhniki v SSSR* (1980), 146–58.

77. Shugurov and Shirsov (1983), 31.
78. Alekseev (1983), 24.
79. Shugurov and Shirsov (1983), 32; Epstein, *The Automobile Industry* (1928), 320.
80. *Narodnoe khozyaistvo*, no. 11–12, 1919, 42.
81. Makeenko (1962), 177; this source provides the best available account of the early tractor industry.
82. *Ekonomicheskaya zhizn'*, January 5, 1921.
83. Makeenko (1962), 168.
84. Makeenko (1962), 171–2; *Istoriya SSSR*, no. 1, 1957, 75.
85. Makeenko (1962), 173–4, 186.
86. Makeenko (1962), 176.
87. Makeenko (1962), 179.
88. Wilkins and Hill, *American Business Abroad: Ford on Six Continents* (1964), 212.
89. Wilkins and Hill (1964), 212.
90. *Bol'shaya Sovetskaya entsiklopedia*, 3rd edn, iv, 458.
91. *Promyshlennost' SSSR v 1926/27g.* (1928), 208.
92. *Izobretatel' i ratsionalizator*, no. 8, 1986, 29.
93. *Zdes' nash dom* (1982), 69–70.
94. Levitan and Morozov (1965), 54–5.
95. *Zdes' nash dom* (1982), 74–6.
96. Goryunova and Chernov (1975), 17.
97. *Sotsialisticheskoe stroitel'stvo SSSR* (1935), 65.
98. *Sotsialisticheskoe stroitel'stvo SSSR* (1935), 65.
99. Chernov (1925), 28.
100. *Goroda Podmoskovya*, iii (1981), 286.
101. *Goroda Podmoskovya*, iii (1981), 286.
102. *Sotsialisticheskoe stroitel'stvo* (1935), 65.
103. Romanov (1985), 14.
104. Romanov (1985), 14, and Britsko (1982), 3; note that *Sotsialisticheskoe stroitel'stvo* (1935), 65, gives a 1928/29 output of only 1,859, but this evidently excludes simple wall clocks.
105. *Sotsialisticheskaya ratsionalizatsiya v bor'be s poteryami* (1930), 150.
106. Rozenfel'd and Klimenko (1961), 191.
107. Eudin and Fisher (eds) (1946), 102–6, 167–9; Fedorov (1969), 115–20; Westwood (1982), 1–77.
108. *Berichte der Deutschen chemischen Gesellschaft*, xliv (1911), *Zeitschrift für analytische Chemie*, li (1912), vol. lii (1913).

11 Foreign Trade

1. Soviet foreign trade during NEP is discussed in Baykov (1946); Carr and Davies (1969), 705–18, and Dohan (1969).
2. The debate over the viability of the NEP model continues. See Wheatcroft, Davies and Cooper (1986), which unfortunately ignores the perpetual crisis in foreign trade during NEP and its effect on industrialisation plans.
3. Goldsmith (1961) gives a good overview of tsarist economic growth from 1860 to 1913.

4. See Gerschenkron (1965), 119–51 and Crisp (1976), particularly Chapters 1 and 4. For role of foreign entrepreneurs in Russia, see McKay (1970).
5. Pasvolsky and Moulton (1924), 31–2.
6. Pasvolsky and Moulton (1924), 31–2.
7. Crisp (1976), 98–9 and Gatrell (1986), 222–8.
8. Von Laue (1963).
9. Crisp (1976), 26–31.
10. Wheatcroft, Davies and Cooper (1986), 269.
11. For example, railroad tariffs were set to encourage exports (see von Laue, 1963, 90).
12. The definition of 'agricultural products' varied in usage from period to period and often included furs and fishing which were mostly peasant activities. Sugar, usually treated as an industrial good by Russian and Soviet statistics, is also included. See Dohan (1969), 743–750, for a detailed analysis of trade classification for these periods.
13. This is about average for large industrial economies of the period (*Economic Development and Cultural Change*, xv (1967), 96–120 (Kuznets)).
14. Dohan (1969), 649–52.
15. Dohan (1969), 101–13 and 649–52 and Troyanovskii *et al.* (1926), 145ff.
16. Domestic demand for grain grew along with the growth of industrial urban regions and expansion of livestock and industrial crop production in the grain deficit regions (see Dohan, 1969, 106–13).
17. This paradox is resolved by noting that export/output ratios are averages, exports are incremental, so that as long as absolute output rises more than the absolute increase in domestic demand, exports will continue to rise even though the export/output ratio could fall. A decline in the export/output ratio, however, usually makes exports more sensitive to fluctuations in the harvest. This was the case for grain in the pre-1914 period; the export/harvest ratio for wheat fell from 38 per cent in 1891–95 to 26 per cent in 1906–10 (see Dohan, 1969, 109). Two classic studies of Russian and Soviet grain production are Timoshenko (1932) and Jasny (1949).
18. Dohan (1969), 93.
19. See Lyashchenko (1949), 592, for the role of British capital in butter.
20. McKay (1970). For distribution of total direct foreign investment among various industries in 1916–17, see Lyashchenko (1949), 715, which cited data compiled by P. V. Ol', *Inostrannye kapitaly v Rossii* (1922), 534–8, 686–7, 707–8, 712–7, 737–8. See Pasvolsky and Moulton (1924), 16–22 for growth and distribution of state debt held abroad. Beable (1919) describes the role of foreign managers and capital.
21. The well publicised cases of manganese, asbestos and platinum have created an unrealistic image of the tsarist economy as being an export-enclave, exploited economy – an image often reinforced by Soviet historians.
22. See Lyashchenko (1949), 737–9.
23. The export-enclave model denotes a policy of funnelling a high proportion of investment and resources into sectors producing primarily for export while leaving the rest of the economy relatively undeveloped and backward.
24. Dohan (1969), 120–33.
25. Dohan (1969), 134, Beable (1919), 239, also emphasised this factor in Russian machinery imports. See also Rozenfel'd and Klimenko (1961), 105–9.
26. Dohan (1969), 121–3.
27. The usual pattern was first to import parts for assembly and then gradually to produce domestically an increasing portion of the product, a policy encouraged

by the tariff structure. See Carstensen (1984).
28. Dohan (1969), 137–47.
29. Rozenfel'd and Klimenko (1961) and Lyashchenko (1949).
30. See Carstensen (1984) and McKay (1970).
31. This phenomenon still persists today in the USSR, but for different reasons. See US Congress, Joint Economic Committee, *Soviet Economy in a Time of Change*, ii (Washington, 1979), 342–73 (Dohan).
32. Rozenfel'd and Klimenko (1961), 107 and Troyanovskii *et al.* (1926), 17.
33. Holzman in Bergson and Kuznets (eds) (1963), Chapter 7.
34. Dobb (1928), 82–96.
35. See Day (1973), 21.
36. Dobb (1928), 88.
37. The principal sources of trade data for this period are: *Vneshnyaya torgovlya SSSR za 20 let 1918–1937 gg.: statisticheskii spravochnik* (1938), *Vneshnyaya torgovlya SSSR za 1918–1940 gg.* (1960), and *Vneshnyaya torgovlya SSSR za X let* (1928).
38. Carr and Davies (1969), 707–8.
39. Dohan, unpublished manuscript (1965); Day (1973). The policy of concessions is discussed in Carr (1958), 483–5, and Carr and Davies (1969), 716–18.
40. See Krasin (1928) for collected articles.
41. Smith (1973), 47–74.
42. *Soviet Union Yearbook 1926* (London, 1926), 58–9 and League of Nations, *Memorandum on Currency and Central Banks, vol. 2, 1913–1925* (Geneva, 1926), 694.
43. Dohan (1969), 198–9.
44. The entire policy was subject to fierce debate; initially monetary orthodoxy prevailed. See Sokolnikov *et al.* (1931), Arnold (1937), Dohan (1969), 184–7, and Krasin (1928), 144–55.
45. The five-year foreign trade plan was prepared by Groman. The optimism is reflected in Oganovskii's predictions of grain exports. (*Planovoe khozyaistvo*, no. 2, 1925, 77). This plan, described in Dohan (1969), 203–13, is criticised in Varga and Badmas (eds) (1932) and Baksht, *Voprosy torgovli*, no. 12, 1928, 21–35.
46. *Ekonomicheskoe obozrenie*, no. 2, 1929, 63–73 (Sobolev).
47. Carr (1958), 193.
48. *Sowjetwirtschaft und Aussenhandel*, vol. 5, no. 13, 6 and Krasin (1928), 222.
49. *Ekonomicheskoe obozrenie*, no. 2, 1926, 76 (Sobolev).
50. *Ekonomicheskoe obozrenie*, no. 2, 1926, 73.
51. *Sowjetwirtschaft und Aussenhandel*, no. 4, 1926, 12–17 (Dzerzhinskii) and no. 6, 1926, 10 (Rykov).
52. *Ekonomicheskaya zhizn'*, September 1, 1926 and Sobolev, *Ekonomicheskoe obozrenie*, no. 2, 1926, 35 and *Sovetskaya torgovlya*, no. 11, 1926, 39–43.
53. *Ekonomicheskoe obozrenie*, no. 1, 1928, 110 (M. Kaufman).
54. *Sovetskaya torgovlya*, no. 3, 1927, 1–2 (M. Kaufman).
55. Dohan (1969), 393.
56. *Sovetskaya torgovlya*, no. 38, 1927, 1.
57. *Sovetskaya torgovlya*, no. 34, 1927, 3 (Zalkind).
58. *Sovetskaya torgovlya*, no. 45/46, 1928, 44–50 for shortages of butter and eggs, and *Kontrol'nye tsifry . . . na 1928/1929 god* (1929), 489, for timber shortages. Cotton cloth was exported despite shortages at home.
59. *Sovetskaya torgovlya*, no. 45/46, 1928, 10 (M. Baksht).

60. *Sovetskaya torgovlya*, no. 45/46, 1928, 32–41 (M. Baksht); *Kontrol'nye tsifry . . . na 1928/1929 god* (1929), 201–2.
61. *Kontrol'nye tsifry . . . na 1928/1929 god* (1929), 175 and *Sovetskaya torgovlya*, no. 45/46, 1928, 41.
62. Even allowing for the unrealistic adjustment for loss of territory, Soviet exports reached only 37 per cent and imports 65 per cent of 1913 levels (Dohan and Hewitt, 1973, 72–3).
63. Dohan and Hewitt (1973).
64. Dohan (1969), 651.
65. *Sovetskaya torgovlya* no. 25, 1927, 3 (L. Zalkind).
66. *Sovetskaya torgovlya*, no. 41, 1927, 1 (B. E. Gurevich).
67. *Sovetskaya torgovlya*, no. 11, 1928, 5–12 (Kaufman), and Kaufman (1927), 2.
68. *Sovetskaya torgovlya*, no. 43, 1927, 58.
69. *Sowjetwirtschaft und Aussenhandel*, vol. 7, no. 14, 1929, 21.
70. *Sowjetwirtschaft und Aussenhandel*, vol. 7, no. 14, 1929, 21.
71. Dohan in *Slavic Review*, vol. 35 (1976), 610; *Voprosy torgovli*, no. 12, 1928 (G. Geller and A. Sovalov); *Voprosy torgovli*, no. 1, 1928 (M. Kaufman) and *Pyatiletnii plan*, i (1930), 101.
72. *Sovetskaya torgovlya*, no. 3, 1927, 1–2 (Kaufman).
73. One unexpected consequence of the large German credit for machinery imports in 1926 was that industrial machinery was imported faster than it could be installed at a time when the demand for imported materials and agricultural machinery was not satisfied. See *Planovoe khozyaistvo*, no. 3, 1930, 39 (A. Paskhov).
74. *Economic Review of the Soviet Union*, no. 4, 1928, 61.
75. Dohan (1969), 640.
76. Dohan (1969), 641, 798–800.
77. Dohan (1969), 641. One-half of the 1926 300 million mark credit from Germany had to be repaid by the end of 1928 and the rest by the end of 1930. See *Sowjetwirtschaft und Aussenhandel*, no. 13, 1926, 5–9; no. 12, 1927, 24–5, and no. 8/9, 1928, 18–20.
78. Day (1973) discusses the politics of negotiating long-term loans.
79. *Planovoe khozyaistvo*, no. 10, 1926, 35 (G. Geller).
80. Preobrazhenskii (1926), 180–1, 270 and *Planovoe khozyaistvo*, no. 10, 1926, 34 (G. Geller).
81. *Sovetskaya torgovlya*, no. 43, 1927, 43–5. and *Sovetskaya torgovlya*, no. 11, 1926, 34–6. The extent to which the policy of 'commercial export profitability' actually affected overall policy in setting of 'state prices' is not known, but the preliminary statistical evidence is suggestive.
82. *Sowjetwirtschaft und Aussenhandel*, vol. 5, no. 4, 1926, 15 (Dzerzhinskii).
83. Dohan (1969), 295–303 describes pricing policy for butter, eggs, and flax during 1925/26.
84. *Sowjetwirtschaft und Aussenhandel*, vol. 6, no. 20, 1927, 12 (Vinogradskii). See Dohan (1969), 344 ff and extensive tables of domestic and foreign grain prices.
85. I. Reingold in Sokolnikov *et al.* (1931), 138–273, and *Sovetskaya torgovlya*, no. 9, 1927, 4–9 (A. Potyaev).
86. During that crucial ten-year period, many technological advances made just before the war were introduced on a wide-scale in the West. For example, in the US, tractor output soared from 7000 units in 1913 to 164,000 units in 1919, and autos from 7000 units in 1901 and 181,000 units in 1910 to 3,625,000 in 1923.

87. See Day (1973) and Dohan (1965). Technology transfers to the USSR through concessions and technical agreements from 1917 to 1930 are discussed in Sutton (1968). One difficulty was that the party itself was split over the concessions policy. In addition, foreign firms encountered supply shortages, party zealots, numerous labour and tax laws, and if they managed to earn a profit, difficulty in obtaining permission to remit it (especially after 1926).

12 National Income

1. *Kontrol'nye tsifry . . . na 1928–1929 god* (1929), 68–72.
2. S. N. Prokopovich's 1918 study is: *Opyt ischisleniya narodnogo dokhoda 50 gubernii evropeiskoi Rossii v 1900–1913 gg.* (1918).
3. Vainshtein (1969), 102.
4. Prokopovich (November 1931). Prokopovich's 1918 study of 1913 national income is summarised in Prokopovich (1918).
5. M. E. Falkus, 'Russia's National Income, 1913: A Revaluation', *Economica*, xxxv (1968), 52–73.
6. Actually Falkus compares his results with the original Prokopovich calculation of 1918 and Prokopovich's 1931 calculation.
7. Gregory, *Russian National Income, 1885–1913* (1982).
8. Bergson, *The Real National Income of Soviet Russia Since 1928* (1961).
9. Vainshtein (1969), 102–7.
10. See Vainshtein (1972).
11. *Kontrol'nye tsifry . . . na 1926–1927* (1926), 215.
12. Vainshtein (1972), 14–16.
13. Gregory (1982), 108–15.
14. The Davies–Wheatcroft comment on retained farm products was transmitted via personal correspondence. It is published in Wheatcroft, Davies and Cooper (1986), 267–8.
15. Gregory (1982), Table 3–6.
16. Dikhtyar (1960), 83.
17. Nutter's results are summarised in his chapter in Abshire and Allen (eds) (1963), 165.
18. See Wheatcroft, Davies and Cooper (1986), 267.
19. See Davies (1978).
20. *Kontrol'nye tsifry . . . na 1928/1929* (1929), Tables 6–1 and 6–2.

Bibliography

Place of publication is Moscow or Moscow–Leningrad unless otherwise stated. Major articles in periodicals and books are listed in this bibliography and in the text of the book under the name of the author; less important articles appear under the name of the periodical, or of the editor in the case of a book.

UNPUBLISHED SOURCES

Records of John Hubbard and Co. (1847–1948), Russian merchants, and of its companies: Anglo-Russian Cotton Factories Ltd (St Petersburg); Petroffsky Spinning and Weaving Co. (St Petersburg); Spassky Spinning and Weaving Co. (St Petersburg); Schlusselburg Calico Printing Co. Guildhall Library, London, L69.55 MS11, 759–62.

Andrle, V. 'How Backward Workers Became Soviet: Industrialisation of Labour and the Politics of Efficiency Under the Second Five-Year Plan, 1933–1937', unpublished working paper, Soviet Industrialisation Project (Centre for Russian and East European Studies (CREES), University of Birmingham, 1984).

Barber, J. 'The Composition of the Soviet Working Class, 1928–1941', unpublished *Discussion Papers*, SIPS no. 16 (CREES, University of Birmingham, 1978).

Barber, J. 'The Standard of Living of Soviet Workers, 1928–41', unpublished working paper (CREES, University of Birmingham, 1980).

Cooper, J. M. 'The Development of the Soviet Machine Tool Industry, 1917–1941', Ph.D. thesis (CREES, University of Birmingham, 1975).

Davies, R. W. 'Soviet Industrial Production, 1928–1937: The Rival Estimates', unpublished *Discussion Papers*, SIPS no. 18 (CREES, University of Birmingham, 1978).

Dohan, M. R. 'Soviet Foreign Trade in the NEP Economy and Soviet Industrialization Strategy', Ph.D. dissertation (Massachussetts Institute of Technology, 1969).

Dohan, M. R. 'Soviet Concessions to Foreign Capital: A History, 1917 to 1930', unpublished manuscript (1965).

Gatrell, P. W. 'Russian Economic Development and the Tsarist State' (Paper to the British National Association for Soviet and East European Studies Annual Conference, 1983).

Gatrell, P. W. 'Russian Heavy Industry and State Defence, 1908–18: Pre-War Expansion and Wartime Mobilization', Ph.D. thesis (University of Cambridge, 1979).

Goldsmith, R.W. 'The Economic Growth of Russia, 1860–1913', unpublished conference paper (International Association for Research in Income and Wealth, 1955).

Harrison, M. 'Soviet Peasants and Soviet Price Policy in the 1920s', unpublished *Discussion Papers*, SIPS no. 10 (CREES, University of Birmingham, 1977).

Holzer, G. 'The German Electrical Industry in Russia, 1890–1910', Ph.D. dissertation (Lincoln, Nebraska, 1970).

Lewis, R. A., 'Industrial Research and Development in the USSR 1924–35', Ph.D. thesis (CREES, University of Birmingham, 1975).

Nuti, D. M. 'Hidden and Repressed Inflation in Soviet-type Economies: Definitions, Measurements and Stabilisation', *EUI Working Papers* no. 85/200 (European University Institute, 1985).

Page, F. M. and Nurminen, J. 'Russian Railway Locomotives, 1912 and 1925 – a Statistical Comparison', unpublished working paper to the conference 'From Tsarism to the New Economic Policy' (CREES, University of Birmingham, January 1987).

Pankin, A. V. 'Soobshchenie ob obrazovanii i rabote Yuzhnogo Raiona organizatsii generala Vankova', unpublished manuscript (March 1952).

Salzman, L. 'Consumer Cooperatives in Tsarist Russia', Ph.D. dissertation (Michigan, 1977).

Ward, C. E. 'Russian Cotton Workers and the New Economic Policy', Ph.D. thesis (University of Essex, 1985).

Weiner, D. '"Razmychka?" Urban Unemployment and Peasant In-Migration as Sources of Social Conflict in NEP Russia', unpublished conference paper (Bloomington, 1986).

Wheatcroft, S. G. 'Population Movements 1908–1928', unpublished paper (History Department, University of Melbourne, 1988).

Wheatcroft, S. G. 'The Agrarian Crisis and Peasant Living Standards in Late Imperial Russia: a Reconsideration of Trends and Regional Differentiation', unpublished working paper (History Department, University of Melbourne, 1986).

Wheatcroft, S. G. 'Towards an Analysis of the Class Divisions in the USSR in the 1920s and 1930s, with Special Reference to the Non-Agricultural Non-Labouring Classes', unpublished working paper (CREES, University of Birmingham, 1984).

Wheatcroft, S. G. 'Famine and Factors Affecting Mortality in the USSR: the Demographic Crises of 1914–1922 and 1930–33', unpublished *Discussion Papers*, SIPS no. 28 (CREES, University of Birmingham, 1982a).

Wheatcroft, S. G. 'The Use of Meteorological Data to Supplement and Analyse Data on Grain Yields in Russia and the USSR, 1883–1950', unpublished paper presented to the SSRC Work Group on Quantitative Methods in Economic History (Cambridge, 1982b).

Wheatcroft, S. G. 'Grain Production and Utilisation in Russia and the USSR Before Collectivisation', Ph.D. thesis (CREES, University of Birmingham, 1980).

Wheatcroft, S. G. 'The Population Dynamic and Factors Affecting It in the Soviet Union in the 1920s and 1930s', parts 1 and 2, unpublished *Discussion Papers*, SIPS nos 1–2 (CREES, University of Birmingham, 1976).

Wheatcroft, S. G. 'Views on Grain Output, Agricultural Reality and Planning in the Soviet Union in the 1920s', M. Soc. Sci. thesis (CREES, University of Birmingham, 1974).

PERIODICALS, NEWSPAPERS

Artilleriiskii zhurnal
Berichte der Deutschen chemischen Gesellschaft
Birzhevye vedomosti
Byulleten' Ekonomicheskogo Kabineta Prof. S. N. Prokopovicha (Prague)
Byulleten' Kon"yunkturnogo instituta
Byulleten' Ivanovo-voznesenskogo gubernskogo statisticheskogo byuro

Economic Development and Cultural Change
Economic Review of the Soviet Union
Ekonomicheskaya zhizn'
Ekonomicheskoe obozrenie
Ekonomist
Fabrichozavodskaya promyshlennost'
Golos tekstilei
Goroda Podmoskovya
Gudok
Iron Age
Istoricheskie zapiski
Istoriya SSSR
Izobretatel' i ratsionalizator
Izvestiya tekstil'noi promyshlennosti i torgovli
Journal of Peasant Studies
Literaturnaya gazeta
Matematische Annalen
Narodnoe khozyaistvo
Nauchno-tekhnicheskii vestnik
Ost-Europa Markt
Planovoe khozyaistvo
Pravda
Predpriyatie
Promyshlennost' i torgovlya
Puti industrializatsii
Rabochii krai
Russian Review
Slavic Review
Sotsialisticheskoe khozyaistvo
Sovetskaya torgovlya
Soviet Studies
Sowjetwirtschaft und Aussenhandel
Statisticheskoe obozrenie
Statistika i narodnoe khozyaistvo
Statistika truda
Tekhnika
Tekstil'nye novosti
Tekstil'shchik
Tekstil'shchik, k stanku
Torgovo-promyshlennaya gazeta
Trud
Trudy TsSU
Vestnik finansov
Vestnik statistiki
Vestnik sel'skokhozyaistvennoi kooperatsii
Vneshnyaya torgovlya
Voprosy torgovlyi
Voprosy truda
Weltwirtschaftliches Archiv
Zeitschrift für analytische Chemie
Zeitschrift für anorganische und allgemeine Chemie
Zeitschrift für Elektrochemie und angewandte physikalische Chemie

BOOKS AND ARTICLES IN RUSSIAN

Aizenberg, I. P. *Valyutnaya sistema SSSR* (1962).

Alekseev, Yu. G. *Evgenii Chudakov* (1983).

Aleshchenko, I. M. 'Iz istorii rabochego klassa Moskvy v vosstanovitel'nyi period (1921–1925 gg.)', *Istoriya SSSR*, no. 1, 1959.

Anfimov, A. M. *Ekonomicheskoe polozhenie i klassovaya bor'ba krest'yan Evropeiskoi Rossii, 1881–1904 gg.* (1984).

Anfimov, A. M. *Krest'yanskoe khozaistvo evropeiskoi Rossii, 1881–1904 gg.* (1980).

Anfimov, A. M. *Rossiiskaya derevnya v gody pervoi mirovoi voiny, 1914–1917 g.* (1962).

Anfimov, A. M. 'K voprosu o kharaktere agrarnogo stroya evropeiskoi Rossii v nachale XXv.', *Istoricheskie zapiski*, lxv (1959), 119–62.

Arkheograficheskii ezhegodnik za 1968 god (1970).

Aviatsiya i kosmonavtika SSSR (1968).

Bakulin, S. N., and Mishutin, D. D. *Statistika vneshnei torgovli SSSR* (1940).

Balans narodnogo khozyaistva Soyuza SSR 1923–24 g. (*Trudy TsSU*, vol. xxix, 1926).

Barsov, A. A. 'NEP i vyravnivanie ekonomicheskikh otnoshenii mezhdu gorodom i derevnei', in *Novaya ekonomicheskaya politika: voprosy teorii i istorii* (1974).

Barsov, A. A. *Balans stoimostnykh otnoshenii mezhdu gorodom i derevnei* (1969).

Barsov, A. A. 'Sel'skoe khozyaistvo i istochniki sotsialisticheskogo nakopleniya v gody pervoi pyatiletki (1928–1932)', *Istoriya SSSR*, no. 3, 1968.

Bastrakova, M. S. 'Organizatsionnye tendentsii russkoi nauki v nachale XXv.', in *Organizatsiya nauchnoi deyatel'nosti* (1968), 150–68.

Bastrakova, M. S. *Stanovlenie sovetskoi sistemy organizatsii naukoi (1917–1922)* (1973).

Belen'skii, B. S., Berlin, P. A. *et al.* (eds) *Entsiklopediya sovetskogo eksporta*, i (1929).

Beskrovnyi, L. G. 'Proizvodstvo vooruzheniya i boepripasov dlya armii v Rossii v period imperializma (1898–1917 gg.)', *Istoricheskie zapiski*, xcix (1977), 88–139.

Bineman, Ya. and Kheinman, S. *Kadry gosudarstvennogo i kooperativnogo apparata SSSR* (1930).

Blank, Sh. and Mitaishvili, A. *Ekonomika vnutrennego vodnogo transporta* (1972).

Bobrov, S. *Indeksy Gosplana* (1925).

Bokarev, Yu. P. *Byudzhetnye obsledovaniya krest'yanskikh khozyaistv 20 – kh godov kak istoricheskii istochnik* (1981).

Bol'shaya sovetskaya entsiklopediya, v (1930).

Bovykin, V. I. *Formirovanie finansovogo kapitala v Rossii konets XIXv.–1908 g.* (1984).

Bovykin, V. I. and Tarnovskii, K. N. 'Kontsentratsiya proizvodstva i razvitie monopolii v metalloobrabatyvayushchei promyshlennosti Rossii', *Voprosy istorii*, no. 2, 1957.

Breiterman, A. D. *Mednaya promyshlennost' SSSR i mirovoi rynok*, vol. 3 (Leningrad, 1930).

Britsko K. M. 'Chasovaya promyshlennost' strany sovetov', *Pribory i sistemy upravleniya*, xii, 1982.

Buzlaeva, A. I. *Leninskii plan kooperirovaniya melkoi promyshlennosti SSSR* (1969).

Chayanov, A. V. *Problemy urozhaya* (1926).

Chayanov, A. V. *Organizatsiya krest'yanskogo khozyaistva* (1925).

Chernov, A. S. *Metallopromyshlennost' SSSR* (1925).

Chutkerashvili, E. V. *Razvitie vysshego obrazovaniya v SSSR* (1961).

Danilov, V. P. 'Pereraspredelenie zemel'nogo fonda Rossii v rezul'tate Velikoi Oktyabr'skoi revolyutsii', in *Leninskii Dekret o zemle v deistvii. Sbornik statei* (1979a).

Danilov, V. P. *Sovetskaya dokolkhoznaya derevnya: sotsial'naya struktura, sotsial'nye otnosheniya* (1979b).

Danilov, V. P. *Sovetskaya dokolkhoznaya derevnya: naselenie, zemlepol'zovanie, khozyaistvo* (1977).

Danilov, V. P. 'Krest'yanskii otkhod na promysly v 1920–kh godakh', *Istoricheskie zapiski*, xciv (1974).

Danilov, V. P. *Sozdanie material'no-tekhnicheskikh predposylok kollektivizatsii sel'skogo kkozyaistva v SSSR* (1957).

Danskii, D. G. *Sotsial'noe strakhovanie ran'she i teper'* (1926).

Davydova, L. G. *Ispol'zovanie elektricheskoi energii v promyshlennosti Rossii* (1966).

Derevnina, L. I. *Rabochie Leningrada v period vosstanovleniya narodnogo khozyaistva: chislennost', sostav i material'noe polozhenie* (Leningrad, 1981).

Dikhtyar, G. A. *Sovetskaya torgovlya v period postroeniya sotsializma* (1961).

Dikhtyar, G. A. *Vnutrennyaya torgovlya v dorevolyutsionnoi Rossii* (1960).

Dinamika rossiiskoi i sovetskoi promyshlennosti v svyazi s razvitiem narodnogo khozyaistva za sorok let (1887–1926 gg.), vol. 1, i–iii (1929–30).

Doklad soveta s"ezdov promyshlennosti i torgovli (1915).

Drobizhev, V. Z. *et al. Istoricheskaya geografiya SSSR* (1973).

Dva goda diktatury proletariata (1920).

Edinyi gosudarstvennyi byudzhet Soyuza Sovetskikh Sotsialisticheskikh Respublik na 1925–1926 byudzhetnyi god (1926).

Edinyi gosudarstvennyi byudzhet Soyuza Sovetskikh Sotsialisticheskikh Respublik na 1926–1927 byudzhetnyi god (1927).

Edinyi gosudarstvennyi byudzhet Soyuza Sovetskikh Sotsialisticheskikh Respublik na 1927–1928 byudzhetnyi god (1928).

Edinyi gosudarstvennyi byudzhet Soyuza Sovetskikh Sotsialisticheskikh Respublik na 1928–1929 byudzhetnyi god (1929).

Edinyi gosudarstvennyi byudzhet Soyuza Sovetskikh Sotsialisticheskikh Respublik na 1926–1927 byudzhetnyi god. Proekt (1927).

Edinyi gosudarstvennyi byudzhet Soyuza Sovetskikh Sotsialisticheskikh Respublik na 1928–1929 byudzhetnyi god. Proekt (1928).

Ekonomicheskoe polozhenie Rossii nakanune Velikoi Oktyabr'skoi sotsialisticheskoi revolyutsii, 2 vols (1957).

Epstein, N. P. 'K istorii kontserna "Kolomna-Sormovo"', *Uchenye zapiski Gor'kogo pedagogicheskogo instituta*, lxi (1966), seriya istoriya, sbornik 9, 86–107.

Erman, L. K. 'Sostav intelligentsii v Rossii v kontse XIX i nachale XXv.', *Istoriya SSSR*, no. 1, 1963, 161–77.

Eventov, L. Ya. *Inostrannye kapitaly v russkoi promyshlennosti* (1931).

Ezhegodnik po sel'skomu khozyaistvu Sovetskogo Soyuza za 1931 god (1933).

Ezhegodnik Rossii 1905g. (St Petersburg, 1906).

Ezhegodnik Rossii 1906g. (St Petersburg, 1907).

Fabrichno-zavodskaya promyshlennost' evropeiskoi Rossii v 1910–1912 gg., vi (Petrograd, 1914).

Fabrichno-zavodskaya promyshlennost' g. Moskvy i moskovskoi gubernii, 1917–1927 gg. (1928).

Fabrichno-zavodskaya promyshlennost' SSSR i ego ekonomicheskikh raionov (1928).

Fedorov, A. S. *Tvortsy o metalle* (1969).
Fedyukin, S. A. *Sovetskaya vlast' i burzhuaznye spetsialisty* (1965).
Feoktistov, V. I. *Ekskursiya na bumagopryadil'nuyu fabriku* (Leningrad, 1924).
Finn-Enotaevskii, A. *Sovremennoe khozyaistvo Rossii (1890–1910 gg.)* (St Petersburg, 1911).
Gaister, A. *Rassloenie sovetskoi derevni* (1928).
Gaponenko, L. S. *Rabochii klass Rossii v 1917 godu* (1970).
Gefter, M. Ya. 'Toplivno-neftyanoi golod v Rossii', *Istoricheskie zapiski*, lxxxiii (1969).
Gindin, I. F. 'Russkaya burzhuaziya v period kapitalizma', *Istoriya SSSR*, no. 3, 1963.
Gindin, I. F. *Russkie kommercheskie banki: iz istorii finansovogo kapitala v Rossii* (1948).
Gindin, Ya. I. *Regulirovanie rynka truda i bor'ba s bezrabotitsei* (1926; 2nd edn, 1928).
Glebov, Yu. F. and Letukov, T. N. *Ivanovo* (Yaroslavl', 1981).
Goldstein, J., Folgov, A. *et al.*, *Entsiklopediya sovetskogo importa*, vol. 1 (1929).
Goryunova, G. N. and Chernov, V. G. *Ekonomika kinematografii* (1975).
Grachev, N. G. 'Statisticheskie gruppirovki v itogakh pervykh sovetskikh promyshlennykh perepisei', *Ocherki po istorii statistiki SSSR*, iv (1961).
(Granat) Entsiklopedicheskii slovar', vol. xxxvi.
Grinevetskii, V. I. *Poslevoennye perspektivy russkoi promyshlennosti* (1922).
Gukhman, B. A. 'Na rubezhe', *Planovoe khozyaistvo*, nos. 7 and 8, 1928, no. 5, 1929.
Gukhman, B. A. 'Dinamika promyshlennosti Rossii v svyazi s dinamikoi narodnogo khozyaistva', *Promyshlennost' i narodnoe khozyaistvo: sbornik statei*, (ed.) E. I. Kviring *et al.* (1927).
Gukhman, B. A. 'Dinamika chislennosti i zanyatii naseleniya SSSR', *Planovoe khozyaistvo*, no. 8, 1926.
Gukhman, B. A. *Produktsiya i potrebleniya* (1925).
Industrializatsiya SSSR, 1926–1928 gg.: dokumenty i materialy (1969).
Ipat'ev, V. N. *Rabota khimicheskoi promyshlennosti na oboronu vo vremya voiny* (Petrograd, 1920).
Istoriya Moskovskogo instrumental'nogo zavoda (1934).
Istoriya rabochikh Donbassa, i (Kiev, 1981).
Itogi desyatiletiya sovetskoi vlasti v tsifrakh 1917–1927 (n.d. [? 1928]).
Ivanova, N. A. 'Sotsial'no-ekonomicheskoe razvitie Rossii v 1907–14 gg. Izmeneniya v ryadakh rabochego klassa', in *Istoriya rabochego klassa SSSR. Rabochii klass Rossii, 1907 – fevral' 1917g.* (1982).
Izmailovskaya, E. I. *Russkoe sel'skokhozyaistvennoe mashinostroenie* (1920).
Izmeneniya sotsial'noi struktury sovetskogo obshchestva, 1921 – seredina 30–kh godov (1979).
Izmeneniya v chislennosti i sostave sovetskogo rabochego klassa (1961).
Kadomtsev, B. P. *Professional'nyi i sotsial'nyi sostav naseleniya Evropeiskoi Rossii po dannym perepisi 1897 goda: Kritiko-statisticheskii etyud* (St Petersburg, 1909).
Kaufman, M. *Organizatsiya i regulirovanie torgovli SSSR* (1927).
Kavraiskii, V. and Nusinov, I. *Klassy i klassovye otnosheniya v sovremennoi sovetskoi derevne* (1929).
Khromov, P. A. *Ekonomicheskoe razvitie Rossii v XIX–XX vekakh* (1950).
Khromov, P. A. *Ocherki ekonomiki tekstil'nyi promyshlennosti SSSR* (1946).
Khryashcheva, A. Y. *Gruppy i klassy v krest'yanstve* (1926).

Kir'yanov, Yu. I. *Rabochie Yuga Rossii, 1914 – fevral' 1917g.* (1971).

Kir'yanov, Yu. I. *Zhiznennyi uroven' rabochikh Rossii, konets XIX-nachalo XX v.* (1979).

Kitanina, T. M. *Voenno-inflyatsionnye kontserny v Rossii, 1914–1917 gg.: Kontsern Putilova–Stakheeva–Batolina* (Leningrad, 1969).

Kleinbort, L. M. *Istoriya bezrabotitsy v Rossii, 1857–1919 gg.* (1925).

Komkov, G. D., Karpenko, O. M., Levshin, B. V. and Semenov, L. K. *Akademiya Nauk – shtab sovetskoi nauki* (1968).

Kondrat'ev, N. D. *Rynok khlebov i ego regulirovanie vo vremya voiny i revolyutsii* (1922).

Kondrat'ev, N. D. and Oganovskii, N. P. (eds.), *Sel'skoe khozyaistvo Rossii v XX veke: sbornik statistiko-ekonomicheskikh svedenii za 1901–1922 gg.* (1923).

Kontrol'nye tsifry narodnogo khozyaistva SSSR na 1925–1926 god (1925).

Kontrol'nye tsifry narodnogo khozyaistva SSSR na 1926–1927 god (1926).

Kontrol'nye tsifry narodnogo khozyaistva SSSR na 1927/1928 god (1928).

Kontrol'nye tsifry narodnogo khozyaistva SSSR na 1928/1929 god (1929).

Kontrol'nye tsifry narodnogo khozyaistva SSSR na 1929/30 god, odobrennye Sovetom Narodnykh Komissarov SSSR (1930).

Korelin, A. P. *Dvoryanstvo v poreformennoi Rossii, 1861–1904 gg.* (1979).

Korelin, A. P. 'Monopolii v parovozo i vagonostroitel'noi promyshlennosti Rossii', *Voprosy istorii kapitalisticheskoi Rossii: problema mnogoukladnosti* (Sverdlovsk, 1972).

Korenevskaya, N. N. *Byudzhetnye obsledovaniya krest'yanskikh khozyaistv v dorevolyutsionnoi Rossii* (1954).

Korneev, A. M. *Tekstil'naya promyshlennost' SSSR i puti ee razvitiya* (1957).

Krasin, L. *Voprosy vneshnei torgovli* (1928).

Kritsman, L. 'Bezrabotitsa v dorevolyutsionnoi Rossii i v SSSR', *Bol'shaya sovetskaya entsiklopediya*, v (1930).

Kritsman, L. *Klassovoe rassloenie v sovetskoi derevne. Po dannym volostnykh obsledovanii* (1926).

Kruze, E. E. *Polozhenie rabochego klassa Rossii v 1900–1914 gg.* (Leningrad, 1976).

Kruze, E. E. *Usloviya truda i byta rabochego klassa Rossii v 1900–1914 godakh* (Leningrad, 1981).

Kruze, E. E. and Kutsentov, D. G. 'Naselenie Peterburga', *Ocherki istorii Leningrada*, iii (1956).

Kul'turnoe stroitel'stvo SSSR. Statisticheskii sbornik (1940).

Kutuzov, A. I. (ed.) *Vneshnyaya torgovlya Soyuza SSR za X let* (1928).

Laverychev, V. Ya. *Krupnaya burzhuaziya v poreformennoi Rossii (1861–1900 gg.)* (1974).

Laverychev, V. Ya. *Monopolisticheskii kapital v tekstil'noi promyshlennosti Rossii, 1900–1917 gg.* (1963).

Laverychev, V. Ya. 'Protsess monopolizatsii khlopchatobumazhnoi promyshlennosti Rossii (1900–1914 gg.)', *Voprosy istorii*, no. 2, 1960.

Lavrikov, Yu. A. *et al. Ocherk ekonomicheskogo razvitiya Leningradskoi industrii za 1917–1967 gg.* (Leningrad, 1968).

Lebin, B. D. (ed.) *Ocherki istorii organizatsii nauki v Leningrade 1703–1977* (Leningrad, 1980).

Leikina-Svirskaya, V. R. *Intelligentsiya v Rossii vo vtoroi polovine XIX veka* (1971).

Leikina-Svirskaya, V. R. *Russkaya intelligentsiya v 1900–1917 godakh* (1981).

Lel'chuk, V. S. *Sozdanie khimicheskoi promyshlennosti SSSR* (1964).

Lenin, V. I. *Polnoe sobranie sochinenii*, 5th edn, iii (1958), xvi (1961), xxxiv (1962).

Levitan, I. I. and Morozov, G. M. *Zavod – polveka. Kratkii ocherk istorii ordena Lenina gosudarstvennogo optikomekhanicheskogo zavoda* (Leningrad, 1965).

Lyashchenko, P. I. *Istoriya narodnogo khozyaistva SSSR*, vol. 2, *Kapitalizm* (1952).

Lyashchenko, P. I. *Mukomol'naya promyshlennost' Rossii* (St Petersburg, 1910).

Malafeev, A. N. *Istoriya tsenoobrazovaniya v SSSR (1917–1963)* (1964).

Makeenko, M. M. *Ocherk razvitiya mashinostroeniya SSSR v 1921–1928 gg.* (Kishinev, 1962).

Markus, B. *Trud v sotsialisticheskom obshchestve* (1939).

Materialy k pyatiletnemu planu razvitiya promyshlennosti SSSR (1927/28–1931/32 gg.) (1927).

Materialy po balansu narodnogo khozyaistva za 1928, 1929 i 1930 gg. (1932). (See also Wheatcroft, S. G. and Davies, R. W. (eds.), p. 403 below.)

Materialy po statistike putei soobshcheniya (published sporadically by the NKPS Central Statistical Dept from 1922 to, probably, 1929).

Matyugin, A. A. *Rabochii klass SSSR v gody vosstanovleniya narodnogo khozyaistva (1921–1925 gg).* (1962).

Melkaya fabrichnaya sel'sko-tkatskaya promyshlennost' vladimirskoi gubernii (Vladimir' na Klyaz'me, 1914).

Mints, L. E. *Agrarnoe perenaselenie i rynok truda v SSSR* (1929).

Mints, L. E. *Trudovye resursy SSSR* (1975).

Mints, L. E. 'Ocherki razvitiya statistiki chislennosti i sostava promyshlennogo proletariata v Rossii', *Ocherki po istorii statistiki SSSR* (1957).

Mints, L. E. and Engel', I. (eds) *Statisticheskie materialy po trudu i sotsial'nomu strakhovaniyu za 1926/7 god*, i (1927).

Mironov, B. N. *Khlebnye tseny v Rossii za dva stoletiya (XVIII–XIX vv.)* (Leningrad, 1985).

Mirovoe khozyaistvo: sbornik statisticheskikh materialov za 1913–1927 gg. (1928).

Mirovoe khozyaistvo za 1913–1925 gg.: statisticheskii sbornik (1926).

Moshkov, Yu. A. *Zernovaya problema v gody sploshnoi kollektivizatsii sel'skogo khozyaistva SSSR* (1966).

Na novom etape (1930), ii.

Na novykh putyakh: itogi novoi ekonomicheskoi politiki, 1921–1922 gg, iii (1923).

Na putyakh k obobshchestvleniyu melkoi promyshlennosti SSSR (1929).

Narodno-khozyaistvennyi plan SSSR na 1931 god (1931).

Narodnoe i gosudarstvennoe khozyaistvo SSSR k seredine 1922/23g. (1923).

Narodnoe khozyaistvo v 1915g. (Petrograd, 1918).

Narodnoe khozyaistvo v 1916g., 7 vols (Petrograd, 1921).

Narodnoe khozyaistvo (1923).

Narodnoe khozyaistvo SSSR: statisticheskii spravochnik (1932).

Narodnoe khozyaistvo SSSR v 1958 godu (1959).

Narodnoe khozyaistvo SSSR v 1961 godu (1962).

Narodnoe obrazovanie, nauka i kul'tura v SSSR: statisticheskii sbornik (1977).

Narodnoe obrazovanie, nauka i kul'tura v SSSR: statisticheskii spravochnik (1971).

Nauchnye kadry i nauchno-issledovatel'skie uchrezhdeniya (1930).

Netesin, Yu. I. *Promyshlennyi kapital Latvii, 1860–1917 gg.* (1980).

Nifontov, V. P. *Produktsiya zhivotnovodstva SSSR* (1937).

Obshchii obzor glavnykh otraslei gornoi i gornozavodskoi promyshlennosti, 2 vols (Gornyi Otdel., St Petersburg / Petrograd, 1913–15).

Obshchii svod po Imperii rezul'tatov razrabotki dannykh pervoi vseobshchei perepisi naseleniya, proizvedennoi 28 yanvarya 1897 goda, 2 vols (St Petersburg, 1905).

Ob"yasnitel'naya zapiska k proektu edinogo gosudarstvennogo byudzheta Soyuza Sovetskikh Sotsialisticheskikh Respublik na 1925–1926 byudzhetnyi god (1926).

Ocherki istorii tekhniki v Rossii: gornoe delo, metallurgiya, energetika, elektrotekhnika, mashinostroenie, 1861–1917 (1973).

Ocherki po istorii statistiki SSSR (1957).

Ocherki razvitiya tekhniki v SSSR. Energeticheskaya, atomnaya, transportnaya i aviatsionnaya tekhnika. Kosmonavtika (1969).

Ocherki razvitiya tekhniki v SSSR. Stroitel'naya, sel'skokhozyaistvennaya i meditsinskaya tekhnika (1971).

Ol', P. O. *Inostrannye kapitaly v Rossii* (1922).

Organizatsiya nauki v pervye gody Sovetskoi vlasti (1917–1925): sbornik dokumentov (Leningrad, 1968).

Osnovnye elementy sel'skokhozyaistvennogo proizvodstva SSSR 1916 i 1923–1927 gg. Itogi sel'skokhozyaistvennoi perepisi 1916g. i vesennikh vyborochnykh 10%-ykh obsledovanii po edinolichnym krest'yanskim khozyaistvam za 1923–1927 gg. (1930).

Otchet gosudarstvennogo kontrolya po ispolneniyu gosudarstvennoi rospisi i finansovykh smet na 1912 god (St Petersburg, 1913).

Otchet gosudarstvennogo kontrolya po ispolneniyu gosudarstvennoi rospisi i finansovykh smet na 1913 god (Petrograd, 1914).

Otchet gosudarstvennogo kontrolya po ispolneniyu gosudarstvennoi rospisi i finansovykh smet na 1914 god (Petrograd, 1915).

Pazhitnov, K. A. *Ocherki istorii tekstil'noi promyshlennosti dorevolyutsionnoi Rossii: khlopchatobumazhnaya, l'no-penkovaya i shelkovaya promyshlennost'* (1958).

Pazhitnov, K. A. *Ocherki istorii tekstil'noi promyshlennosti dorevolyutsionnoi Rossii: sherstyanaya promyshlennost'* (1955).

Pervye shagi industrializatsii SSSR 1926/27 gg. (1959).

Pervyi podshipnikovyi. Istoriya pervogo gosudarstvennogo podshipnikogo zavoda, 1932–1972 (1973).

Petrograd po perepisi naseleniya 15 dekabrya 1910g. (Petrograd, [?1915]).

Pikhalo, V. T. 'Trestovanie promyshlennosti SSSR v 20-e gody', *Istoriya SSSR*, no. 4, 1971.

Plan rabot Akademii Nauk SSSR na vtoroe pyatiletie (1933–1937). Chast' 1: Obshchie osnovy plana (Leningrad, 1932).

Pogrebinskii, A. *Gosudarstvenno-monopolisticheskii kapitalizm v Rossii* (1959).

Pokrovskii, S. A. *Vneshnyaya torgovlya i vneshnyaya torgovaya politika Rossii* (1947).

Polyakov, Yu. A. *Sovetskaya strana posle okonchaniya grazhdanskoi voiny: territoriya i naselenie* (1986).

Polyakov, Yu. A. *Perekhod k NEPu i sovetskoe krestyanstvo* (1967).

Polyakov, Yu. A. 'Selskoe khozyaistvo nakanune perekhoda k NEPu', *Istoricheskie zapiski*, lxxiv (1963).

Polyakova, N. V. 'Bor'ba rabochikh-tekstil'shchikov za povyshenie proizvoditel'nosti truda v 1921–1925 gg. (po materialam Moskvy i moskovskoi gubernii)', *Voprosy istorii*, no. 6, 1959.

Popov, P. I. 'Khlebofurazhny balans', in Kritsman, L., Popov, P. I. and Yakovlev, Ya. (eds) *Sel'skoe khozyaistvo na putyakh vosstanovleniya* (1925).

Popov, P. I. *Proizvodstvo khleba v RSFSR i federiruyushikhsya s neyu respublikakh* (1921).

Popov, V. G. 'Sovetskaya istoriografiya likvidatsii bezrabotitisy v SSSR', *Istoriya SSSR*, no. 5, 1981.

Postoyannaya promyshlennaya pokazatel'naya vystavka VSNKh. Vystavka tekstil'nykh trestov. 16 oktyabrya 1922g. (1923).

Preobrazhenskii, E. *Novaya ekonomika* (1926) (translated by Brian Pearce as *The New Economics*, Oxford, 1965).

Prilozhenie k proektu edinogo gosudarstvennogo byudzheta Soyuza Sovetskikh Sotsialisticheskikh Respublik na 1925–1926 byudzhetnyi god (1926).

Problemy rekonstruktsii narodnogo khozyaistva SSSR na pyatiletie (1929).

Profsoyuznaya perepis', 1932–1933 gg., i (1934).

Prokopovich, S. N. (ed.) *Opyt ischisleniya narodnogo dokhoda 50 gubernii evropei-skoi Rossii v 1900–1913 gg.* (1918).

Promyshlennost' SSSR: statisticheskii sbornik (1957).

Promyshlennost' SSSR: statisticheskii sbornik (1964).

Promyshlennost' SSSR v 1926/27 godu: ezhegodnik VSNKh (1928).

Promyshlennost' SSSR v 1927/28 godu: ezhegodnik VSNKh, i [?1930], ii (1930).

Pyatiletnii plan narodno-khozyaistvennogo stroitel'stva SSSR, 2nd edn, 3 vols (1930).

Rabochee dvizhenie v Azerbaidzhane v gody novogo revolyutsionnogo pod''ema, i (1967).

Rabota moskovskogo gubernskogo soveta profsoyuzov s oktyabrya 1924g. po yanvar' 1926g. (1926).

Rakov, V. A. *Lokomotivy zheleznykh dorog Sovetskogo Soyuza* (1955).

Rashin, A. G. *Formirovanie rabochego klassa Rossii: istoriko-ekonomicheskie ocherki* (1958).

Rashin, A. G. *Naselenie Rossii za 100 let (1811–1913 gg.): statisticheskie ocherki* (1956).

Razvitie aviatsionnoi nauki i tekhniki v SSSR (1980).

Rezolyutsii 3-go plenuma TsK soyuza tekstil'shchikov (12–15 aprelya 1923g.) (1923).

Rogachevskaya, L. S. *Likvidatsiya bezrabotitsy v SSSR, 1917–1930 gg.* (1973).

Romanov, P. M. *Detishche pervoi pyatiletki* (1985).

Rosnitskii, N. *Litso derevni. Po materialam obsledovaniya 28 volostei i 32 730 krest'yanskikh khozyaistv Penzenskoi gubernii* (1926).

Rozenfel'd, S. Ya. and Klimenko, K. I. *Istoriya mashinostroeniya SSSR* (1961).

Rybnikov, A. A. *Melkaya promyshlennost' i ee rol' v vosstanovlenii narodnogo khozyaistva* (1922).

Sarab'yanov, V. 'Elektrotekhnicheskaya promyshlennost'', *Narodnoe khozyaistvo* (1923).

Sbornik statisticheskikh svedenii po Soyuzu SSR, 1918–1923 gg. (*Trudy TsSU*, xviii, 1924).

Sdvigi v sel'skom khozyaistve SSSR mezhdu XV i XVI partiinymi s''ezdami. Statisticheskie svedeniya po sel'skomu khozyaistvu za 1927–1930 gg. (1931).

Sel'skoe khozyaistvo Rossii v XX veke. Sbornik statistiko-ekonomicheskikh svedenii za 1901–1922 gg. (1923).

Sel'skoe khozyaistvo SSSR 1925–1928 gg.: sbornik statisticheskikh svedenii k XVI Vsesoyuznoi partkonferentsii (1929).

Sel'skoe khozyaistvo SSSR (1939).

Sel'skoe khozyaistvo SSSR: statisticheskii sbornik (1960).

Sel'skokhozyaistvennaya entsiklopediya, 3rd edn, v (1956).

Semanov, S. N. 'Sostav i polozhenie rabochikh Peterburga po dannym gorodskikh perepisei', in *Rabochii klass i rabochee dvizhenie v Rossii (1861–1917 gg.)* (1966).

Serebrovskii, A. I. *Na zolotom fronte* (1936).

Shatsillo, K. F. *Rossiya pered pervoi mirovoi voinoi: vooruzhennye sily tsarizma v 1905–1914 gg.* (1974).
Shatsillo, K. F. 'O disproportsii v razvitii vooruzhennykh sil Rossii nakanune pervoi mirovoi voiny (1906–1914 gg.)', *Istoricheskie zapiski*, lxxxiii (1969).
Shatsillo, K. F. *Russkii imperializm i razvitie flota nakanune pervoi mirovoi voiny, 1906–1944 gg.* (1968).
Shatsillo, K. F. 'Inostrannyi kapital i voenno-morskie programmy Rossii nakanune pervoi mirovoi voiny', *Istoricheskie zapiski*, lxix (1961).
Shatsillo, K. F. 'Formirovanie finansovogo kapitala v sudostroitel'noi promyshlennosti Yuga Rossii', *Iz istorii imperializma v Rossii* (1959).
Shavrov, V. B. *Istoriya konstruktsii samoletov v SSSR v 1938g.*, 2nd edn (1978).
Shebaldin, Yu. N. 'Gosudarstvennyi byudzhet tsarskoi Rossii v nachale XXv.', *Istoricheskie zapiski*, lxv (1959).
Shelyakin, P. 'Voina i ugol'naya promyshlennost' ', *Voina i toplivo 1914–1917 gg.* (1930).
Shepelev, L. E. *Tsarism i burzhuaziya vo vtoroi polovine XIXv.* (Leningrad, 1981).
Shepelev, L. E. *Aktsionernye kompanii v Rossii* (Leningrad, 1973).
Shishkin, V. A. *'Polosa priznanii' i vneshneekonomicheskaya politika SSSR (1924–1928 gg.)* (Leningrad, 1983).
Shkaratan, O. I. 'Izmeneniya v sotsial'nom sostave fabrichno-zavodskikh rabochikh Leningrada 1917–1928 gg.', *Istoriya SSSR*, no. 5, 1959.
Shugurov, L. M. and Shirsov, V. P. *Avtomobili strany sovetov*, 2nd edn (1983).
Shumikhin, V. S. *Sovetskaya voennaya aviatsiya 1917–1941* (1986).
Sidorov, A. L. *Ekonomicheskoe polozhenie Rossii v gody pervoi mirovoi voiny* (1973).
Sidorov, A. L. 'O strukture promyshlennosti Rossii v kontse XIXv.', *Istoricheskie zapiski*, lxix (1961).
Sidorov, A. L. *Finansovoe polozhenie Rossii v gody pervoi mirovoi voiny* (1960).
Sidorov, A. L. 'Zheleznodorozhnyi transport Rossii v pervoi mirovoi voine', *Istorichiskie zapiski*, xxvi (1948).
Sidorov, V. A. *Klassovaya bor'ba v dokolkhoznoi derevne* (1978).
Smirnov, A. P. *Sel'skoe khozyaistvo za desyat' let* (1927).
Sotsialisticheskaya ratsionalizatsiya v bor'be s poteryami (1930).
Sotsialisticheskoe stroitel'stvo SSSR: statisticheskii ezhegodnik (1934).
Sotsialisticheskoe stroitel'stvo SSSR: statisticheskii ezhegodnik (1935).
Sovetskaya istoricheskaya entsiklopediya.
Sovetskii transport 1917–1927 (1927).
Sovetskoe narodnoe khozyaistvo v 1921–1925 gg. (1960).
SSSR: 4 S"ezd Sovetov (1927).
SSSR i kapitalisticheskie strany: statisticheskii sbornik (1939).
Stalin, I. V. *Sochineniya*, xi (1949).
Statisticheskii ezhegodnik Moskovskoi gubernii za 1909 god (1910).
Statisticheskii ezhegodnik Rossii 1914g. (Petrograd, 1915).
Statisticheskii sbornik po Petrogradskoi gubernii, 1922 g. (Petrograd, 1922).
Statisticheskii spravochnik SSSR za 1928 (1929).
Statistika zemlevladeniya 1905g. (St Petersburg, 1907).
Strumilin, S. G. *Ocherki ekonomicheskoi istorii Rossii i SSSR* (1966).
Strumilin, S. G. *Ocherki sotsialisticheskoi ekonomiki SSSR* (1964).
Strumilin, S. G. *Statistiko-ekonomicheskie ocherki* (1958).
Suvorov, K. I. *Istoricheskii opyt KPSS po likvidatsii bezrabotitsy* (1968).
Svavitskaya, Z. M. and Svavitskii, N. A. (eds) *Zemskie podvornie perepisi, 1880–1913* (1916).
Svod otchetov fabrichnykh inspekterov za 1909g. (St Petersburg, 1910).

Svod otchetov fabrichnykh inspekterov za 1910g. (St Petersburg, 1910).

Syrov, A. S. *Put' fotoapparata* (1954).

Tarnovskii, K. N. 'Organizatsiya melkoi promyshlennosti v Rossii v gody pervoi mirovoi voiny', *Voprosy istorii*, no. 8, 1981.

Tarnovskii, K. N. *Formirovanie gosudarstvenno-monopolisticheskogo kapitalizma v Rossii v gody pervoi mirovoi voiny* (1958).

Tekstil'nye fabriki SSSR (1927).

Transport i svyaz' SSSR: statisticheskii sbornik (1957).

Tret'ya sessiya Tsentral'nogo Ispolnitel'nogo Komiteta Soyuza SSR, 4 sozyva (1928).

Tri goda raboty vladimirsko-aleksandrovskogo tresta khlopchatobumazhnykh fabrik, 1922–1924 gg. (1925).

Troyanovskii, A., Yurovskii, L. and Kaufman, M. (eds) *Eksport, import i kontsessii Soyuza SSR* (1926).

Trud v SSSR: materialy k otchetu Narkomtruda SSSR na IX vsesoyuznom s"ezde professional'nykh soyuzov (1932).

Trud v SSSR: spravochnik 1926–1930 (1930).

Trud v SSSR: statisticheskii spravochnik (1936).

Trudy Pervogo S"ezda Predstavitelei Metalloobrabatyvayushchei Promyshlennosti, 29 fevralya po 1 marta 1916g. (Petrograd, 1916).

Trudy TsSU, see under *Balans narodnogo khozyaistva; Vserossiiskaya promyshlennaya perepis'; Sbornik statisticheskikh svedenii.*

Trudy TsSU, tom XVIII, tom XIX.

Tyazhest' oblozheniya v SSSR (sotsial'nyi sostav, dokhody i nalogovye platezhi naseleniya Soyuza SSR v 1924/25, 1925/26 i 1926/27 godakh): doklad komissii Soveta Narodnykh Komissarov SSSR po izucheniyu tyazhesti oblozheniya Soyuza (1929).

Uribes, E. 'Koksobenzol'naya promyshlennost' Rossii v gody pervoi mirovoi voiny', *Istoricheskie zapiski*, lxix (1961).

Vainshtein, A. L. *Tseny i tsenoobrazovanie v SSSR v vostannovitel'nyi period, 1921–1928 gg.* (1972).

Vainshtein, A. L. *Narodnyi dokhod Rossii i SSSR* (1969).

Vainshtein, A. L. 'Iz istorii predrevolyutsionnoi statistiki zhivotnovodstva', *Ocherki po istorii statistiki SSSR*, iii (1960a).

Vainshtein, A. L. *Narodnoe bogatstvo i narodnokhozyaistvennoe nakoplenie predrevolyutsionnoi Rossii* (1960b).

Vainshtein, A. L. *Oblozhenie i platezhi krest'yanstva v dovoennoe i revolyutsionnoe vremya* (1924).

Varga, E. and Badmas, S. (eds) *XV let bor'by za monopoliyu vneshnei torgovli* (1932).

Vasil'ev, N. *Transport Rossii v voine 1914–1918 gg* (1939).

Vas'kina, L. I. *Rabochii klass SSSR nakanune sotsialisticheskoi industrializatsii (chislennost', sostav, razmeshchenie)* (1981).

Velizhev, A. A. *Dostizhenie Sovetskoi aviapromyshlennosti za pyatnadtsat' let* (1932).

Venediktov, A. V. *Organizatsiya gosudarstvennoi promyshlennosti v SSSR*, i (Leningrad, 1957).

Vermenichev, I., Gaister, A. and Raevich, G. *710 khozyaistv Samarskoi derevni* (1927).

Vesennyaya posevnaya kampaniya 1929g. Predvaritel'nye itogi po materialam upolnomochennogo STO (1929).

Vneshnyaya torgovlya SSSR za X let (1928).

Vneshnyaya torgovlya SSSR za 1918–1940 gg. Statisticheskii obzor (1960).

Vneshnyaya torgovlya SSSR za 20 let 1918–1937 gg. Statisticheskii spravochnik (1938).

Volkov, E. Z. *Dinamika narodonaseleniya SSSR za vosemdesyat' let* (1930).

Volobuev, P. V. 'Toplivnyi krizis i monopolii v Rossii nakanune pervoi mirovoi voiny', *Voprosy istorii*, no. 1, 1957.

Voprosy truda v tsifrakh (1930).

Vorob'ev, N. Ya. *Ocherki po istorii promyshlennoi statistiki v dorevolyutsionnoi Rossii i v SSSR (metody nablyudeniya i razrabotki)* (1961).

Vorob'ev, N. Ya. 'Promyshlennost'' kak postavshchik sredstv proizvodstva dlya sel'skogo khozyaistva v usloviyakh dovoennogo vremeni', *Sel'skoe khozyaistvo na putyakh k vosstanovleniyu*, iii (1925).

Vorob'ev, N. Ya. 'Izmeneniya v russkoi promyshlennosti v period voiny i revolyutsii (po dannym perepisi 1918g.)', *Vestnik statistiki*, xiv (1923).

Vosstanovlenie promyshlennosti Leningrada (1921–1924 gg.) (Leningrad), i (1963).

Vserossiiskaya promyshlennaya i professional'naya perepis' 1918g: Fabrichnozavodskaya promyshlennost' v period 1913–1918 gg., 3 parts (*Trudy TsSU*, xxvi, 1926).

Vsesoyuznaya perepis' naseleniya 1926g., kratkie svodki, x (1929).

Vsesoyuznaya perepis' naseleniya 1926g., xxxiv (1930), lii (1931).

Vypolnenie pyatiletnogo plana promyshlennosti (1931).

Yakobi, D. *Zheleznye dorogi SSSR v tsifrakh* (1935).

Yakobson, Yu. A. 'Uchastie Ivanovo-voznesenskikh rabochikh v formirovanii komandnykh kadrov tekstil'noi promyshlennosti (1921–1925 gg.)', *Iz istorii rabochego klassa SSSR* (Ivanovo, 1967).

Yakovlev, A. F. *Ekonomicheskie krisisy v Rossii* (1955).

Yakovlev, A. S. *Tsel' zhizni* (4th edn, 1982).

Yakovlev, Yu. F. *Vladimirskie rabochie v bor'be za ukreplenie soyuza s krest'yanstvom v 1917–1925 godakh* (Vladimir, 1963).

Yufereva, E. V. *Leninskoe uchenie o goskapitalizme v perekhodnyi period k sotsializmu* (1969).

Zaikov, A. M. *Na khlopchatobumazhnoi fabrike* (1926/27).

Zaionchkovskii, P. A. *Pravitel'stvennyi apparat samoderzhavnoi Rossii v XIXv.* (1978).

Zak, S. S. 'Tovarooborot i torgovaya set' v Rossiiskoi imperii i v SSSR', *Planovoe khozyaistvo*, no. 11, 1927.

Zdes' nash dom. Istoriya Leningradskogo optiko-mekhanicheskogo ob''edineniya imeni V.I. Lenina (Leningrad, 1982).

Zhivotovodstvo SSSR v tsifrakh (1932).

Zhukovskii, S. *et al. Pervaya udarnaya* (1931).

Zvezdin, Z. K. 'Vsesoyuznyi tekstil'nyi sindikat v 1922–1929 gg.', *Istoricheskie zapiski*, lxxxviii (1971).

BOOKS AND ARTICLES IN NON-RUSSIAN LANGUAGES

Abrégé des données statistiques de l'URSS (Moscow, 1925).

Abshire, D. and Allen, R. V. (eds) *National Security: Political, Military and Economic Strategies in the Decade Ahead* (New York, 1963).

Ahlström, G. *Engineers and Industrial Growth* (London, 1982).

Altrichter, H. *Vom Leben auf dem russischen Dorfe zwischen Revolution und Kollektivierung* (Munich, 1984).

Amburger, E. 'Das Haus Wogau & Co. 1840–1917', *Kieler Historische Studien*, Band 22 (Stuttgart, 1974).

Anderson, B. A. and Silver, B. D. 'Demographic Analysis and Population Catastrophes in the USSR', *Slavic Review*, xliv (1985).

Arnold, A. Z. *Banks, Credit and Money in Soviet Russia* (New York, 1937).

Atkinson, D. *The End of the Russian Land Commune, 1905–1930* (Stanford, California, 1983).

Auhagen, O. 'Agrarverfassung und Landwirtschaft im Bezirk Odessa', *Berichte über Landwirtschaft, Neue Folge*, x (1929).

Babkov, A. 'National Finances and the Economic Evolution of Russia', *Russian Review*, 3 (1912).

Bailes, K. E. *Technology and Society Under Lenin and Stalin* (Princeton, 1978).

Baksht, M. 'The Gold Industry and the Gold Reserves of the Soviet Union', *Money, Prices and Gold in the Soviet Union*, Monograph No. 3 (London, 1934).

Bandera, V. N. 'Market Orientation of State Enterprises during NEP', *Soviet Studies*, xxii (1970/71).

Baykov, A. *Soviet Foreign Trade* (Princeton, 1946).

Beable, W. H. *Commercial Russia* (New York, 1919).

Becker, S. *Nobility and Privilege in Late Imperial Russia* (Dekalb, Illinois, 1985).

Bergson, A. *The Real National Income of Soviet Russia since 1928* (Cambridge, 1961).

Bergson, A. *The Structure of Soviet Wages: a Study in Socialist Economics* (Cambridge, Mass., 1944).

Bergson, A. and Kuznets, S. (eds) *Economic Trends in the Soviet Union* (Massachussetts, 1963).

Black, C. E. (ed.) *The Transformation of Russian Society* (Cambridge, Mass., 1960).

Bonnell, V. *Roots of Rebellion: Workers' Politics and Organizations in St. Petersburg and Moscow, 1900–1914* (Berkeley, 1984).

Bonnell, V. E. (ed.) *The Russian Worker: Life and Labor Under the Tsarist Regime* (Berkeley, 1983).

Bradley, J. *Muzhik and Muscovite* (Berkeley, 1985).

Brooks, J. 'The Zemstvo and the Education of the People', in T. Emmons and W. S. Vucinich (eds), *The Zemstvo in Russia* (Cambridge, 1982).

Bukshpan, Ya. M. 'Internal Trade in Russia', in Raffalovich (ed.) (1918), 268–97.

Carr, E. H. *Foundations of a Planned Economy, 1926–1929*, vol. 2 (London, 1971).

Carr, E. H. 'Some Random Reflexions on Soviet Industrialisation', in Feinstein (ed.) (1967).

Carr, E. H. *Socialism in One Country, 1924–1926*, vol. 1 (London, 1958), vol. 2 (London, 1959).

Carr, E. H. *The Interregnum, 1923–1924* (London, 1954).

Carr, E. H. *The Bolshevik Revolution, 1917–1923*, vol. 2 (London, 1952).

Carr, E. H. and Davies, R. W. *Foundations of a Planned Economy 1926–1929*, vol. 1 (London, 1969, 1974).

Carstensen, F. V. *American Enterprise in Foreign Markets: Singer and International Harvester in Imperial Russia* (North Carolina, 1984).

Carstensen, F. V. 'Number and Reality: A Critique of Foreign Investment Estimates in Tsarist Russia', in Levy-Leboyer, M., (ed.) *La Position Internationale de la France* (Paris, 1977).

Cherniavsky, M. (ed.) *The Structure of Russian History: Interpretative Essays* (New York, 1970) (originally published 1964–5).

Cohen, S. F. *Bukharin and the Bolshevik Revolution: a Political Biography, 1888–1938* (London, 1974).

Conyngham, W. J. *Industrial Management in the Soviet Union: the Role of the CPSU in Industrial Decision-making, 1917–1970* (Stanford, 1973).

Cox, T. *Peasant, Class and Capitalism. The Rural Research of L. N. Kritsman and his School* (Oxford, 1986).

Cox, T. 'Awkward Class or Awkward Classes? Class Relations in the Russian Peasantry before Collectivisation', *Journal of Peasant Studies*, vii (1979–80).

Crisp, O. 'Labour and Industrialization in Russia', *Cambridge Economic History of Europe*, vii, ii (Cambridge, 1978).

Crisp, O. *Studies in the Russian Economy Before 1914* (London, 1976).

Davies, R. B. *Peacefully Working to Conquer the World. Singer Sewing Machines in Foreign Markets, 1854–1920* (New York, 1976).

Davies, R. W. *The Soviet Economy in Turmoil, 1929–1930* (London and Cambridge, Mass., 1989a).

Davies, R. W. *Soviet History in the Gorbachev Revolution* (London and Indiana, 1989b).

Davies, R. W. 'The Ending of Mass Unemployment in the USSR', in Lane, D. (ed.) (1986).

Davies, R. W. *The Socialist Offensive: the Collectivisation of Soviet Agriculture, 1929–1930* (London and Cambridge, Mass., 1980).

Davies, R. W. 'A Note on Grain Statistics', *Soviet Studies*, xxi (1969/70).

Davies, R. W. *The Development of the Soviet Budgetary System* (Cambridge, 1958).

Davies, R. W. and Wheatcroft, S. G. 'A Note on the Sources of Unemployment Statistics', in Lane, D. (ed.) (1986).

Day, R. B. *Leon Trotsky and the Politics of Economic Isolation* (Cambridge, 1973).

Dewar, M. *Labour Policy in the USSR, 1917–28* (London, 1956).

Dobb, M. H. *Soviet Economic Development since 1917*, 6th edn (London, 1966).

Dobb, M. H. *Russian Economic Development since the Revolution* (London, 1928).

Dohan, M. R. and Hewett, E. *Two Studies in Soviet Terms of Trade, 1918–1970* (Bloomington, Indiana, 1973).

Epstein, R. C. *The Automobile Industry* (New York, 1928).

Erlich, A. *The Soviet Industrialization Debate, 1924–1928* (Cambridge, Mass., 1960).

Eudin, X. J. and Fisher, H. F. *The Life of a Chemist: Memoirs of Vladimir N. Ipatieff* (Stanford, 1946).

Falkus, M. E. 'Russia's National Income, 1913: A Revaluation', *Economica*, xxxv (1968).

Fapohunda, E. R., in Olakoku, F. A. (ed.) *Structure of the Nigerian Economy* (London, 1978).

Feinstein, C. H. (ed.) *Socialism, Capitalism and Economic Growth: Essays Presented to Maurice Dobb* (Cambridge, 1967).

Filtzer, D. A. *Soviet Workers and Stalinist Industrialization: the Formation of Modern Soviet Production Relations, 1928–1941* (London, 1986).

Fitzpatrick, S. *Education and Social Mobility in the Soviet Union, 1921–1934* (Cambridge, 1979).

40 [Forty] Years of Soviet Power (1958).

Garside, W. R. *The Measurement of Unemployment* (Oxford, 1980).

Gatrell, P. W. *The Tsarist Economy, 1850–1917* (London, 1986).

Gatrell, P. W. 'Industrial Expansion in Tsarist Russia, 1908–1914', *Economic History Review*, 2nd series, xxxv (1982).

Gerschenkron, A. 'Agrarian Policies and Industrialization, Russia 1861–1917', *Cambridge Economic History of Europe*, vi, ii (Cambridge, 1965a).

Gerschenkron, A. *Economic Backwardness in Historical Perspective* (New York, 1965b).

Gerschenkron, A. 'Problems and Patterns of Russian Economic Development', in Black (ed.) (1960).

Gerschenkron, A. 'The Rate of Industrial Growth in Russia since 1885', *Journal of Economic History*, 1947 (Supplement 7).

Geyer, D. *Russian Imperialism: the Interaction of Domestic and Foreign Policy, 1860–1914* (London, 1987).

Goldsmith, R. W. 'The Economic Growth of Tsarist Russia, 1860–1913', *Economic Development and Cultural Change*, ix (1961).

Gorlin, R. H. 'Problem of Tax Reform in Imperial Russia', *Journal of Modern History*, xlix (1977).

Graham, L. R. 'The Formation of Soviet Research Institutes: a Combination of Revolutionary Innovation and International Borrowing', *Social Studies of Science*, v (1975).

Graham, L. R. *The Soviet Academy of Sciences and the Communist Party, 1927–1932* (Princeton, 1967).

Gregory, P. R. 'The Russian Agrarian Crisis Revisited', in Stuart (ed.) (1983).

Gregory, P. R. *Russian National Income, 1885–1913* (Cambridge, 1982).

Gregory, P. R. 'Grain Marketing and Peasant Consumption, Russia, 1885–1913', *Explorations in Economic History*, ii (1979).

Haber, L. F. *The Chemical Industry, 1900–1930* (Oxford, 1971).

Haimson, L. 'The Problem of Social Stability in Urban Russia, 1905–1917', in Cherniavsky (ed.) (1970).

Harrison, M. 'Primary Accumulation in the Soviet Transition', *Journal of Development Studies* (1985).

Harrison, M. 'Why was NEP Abandoned?', in Stuart (ed.) (1983).

Harrison, M. 'The Problem of Social Mobility among Russian Peasant Households, 1880–1930', *Journal of Peasant Studies*, iv (1977).

Harrison, M. 'Chayanov and the Economics of the Russian Peasantry', *Journal of Peasant Studies*, ii (1974/75).

Historical Statistics of the United States. Colonial Times to 1957 (Washington, 1960).

Hogan, H. 'The Reorganisation of Work Processes in the St. Petersburg Metal-Working Industry, 1901–1914', *Russian Review*, xlii (1983).

Holzman, F. *Foreign Trade Under Central Planning* (Cambridge, Massachussetts, 1974).

Holzman, F. 'Foreign Trade', in Bergson and Kuznets (eds) (1963).

Hunter, H. *Soviet Transportation Policy* (Cambridge, Mass., 1957).

Jasny, N. *The Socialized Agriculture of the USSR: Plans and Performance* (Stanford, 1949).

Johnson, D. G. 'Agricultural Production', in Bergson and Kuznets (eds) (1963).

Johnson, D. G. and Kahan, A. 'Soviet Agriculture: Structure and Growth', in *Comparisons of the United States and Soviet Economies*, i (Washington: US Government Printing Office, 1959).

Kahan, A. *The Plow, The Hammer and the Knout: An Economic History of Eighteenth-Century Russia* (Chicago, 1985).

Kahan, A. 'Capital Formation During the Period of Early Industrialization in Russia, 1890–1913', *Cambridge Economic History of Europe*, vii, ii (Cambridge, 1978).

Kahan, A. 'Government Policies and the Industrialization of Russia', *Journal of Economic History*, xxvii (1967).

Karcz, J. F. 'Back on the Grain Front', *Soviet Studies*, xxii (1970/71).

Karcz, J. F. 'Thoughts on the Grain Problem', *Soviet Studies*, xviii (1966/67).

Katkov, G., Oberlander, E., Poppe, N. and von Rauch G. (eds) *Russian Enters the*

Twentieth Century (London, 1971).

Kaufman, A. *Small-Scale Industry in the Soviet Union*, National Bureau of Economic Research, Occasional Paper 80 (New York, 1962).

Kelly, W. J. and Kano, T. 'Crude Oil Production in the Russian Empire, 1818–1919', *Journal of European Economic History*, vi (1977).

Kenez, P. 'A Profile of the Prerevolutionary Officer Corps', *California Slavic Studies*, vii (1973).

Kingsbury, S. M. and Fairchild, M. *Report on Employment and Unemployment in Pre-War and Soviet Russia* (World Social Economic Congress, 1931).

Krebs, Chr. *Die weltanschaulichen und wirtschaftstheoretischen Grundlagen der Agrartheorie im Marxismus–Leninismus* (Berlin, 1983).

Lane, D. (ed.) *Labour and Employment in the USSR* (Brighton, 1986).

League of Nations *Memorandum on Currency and Central Banks*, vol. 2, *1913–1925* (Geneva, 1926).

League of Nations *Memorandum on International Trade and Balance of Payments 1912–1926*, ii (Geneva, 1926).

League of Nations *Review of World Trade, 1938* (Geneva, 1939).

Lewin, M. *The Making of the Soviet System: Essays in the Social History of Interwar Russia* (London, 1985).

Lewin, M. *Russian Peasants and Soviet Power: a Study of Collectivisation* (London, 1968).

Lewin, M. 'Who was the Soviet Kulak?', *Soviet Studies*, xviii (1966/67).

Lewis, R. A. *Science and Industrialisation in the USSR* (London, 1979).

Lieven, D. C. B. *Russia and the Origins of the First World War* (London, 1983).

Loewe, H.-D. 'Lenins Thesen über Kapitalismus und soziale Differenzierung in der vorrevolutionaren Bauerngesellschaft', *Jahrbücher für Geschichte Osteuropas*, xxxii (1984).

Lorimer, F. *The Population of the Soviet Union: History and Prospects* (Geneva, 1946).

Lyashchenko, P. I. *History of the National Economy of Russia to the 1917 Revolution* (New York, 1949).

McKay, J. P. *Pioneers for Profit: Foreign Entrepreneurship and Russian Industrialization, 1885–1913* (Chicago, 1970).

Male, D. J. *Russian Peasant Organisation before Collectivisation: a Study of Commune and Gathering, 1925–1930* (Cambridge, 1971).

Malle, S. *The Economic Organization of War Communism, 1918–1921* (Cambridge, 1985).

Manning, R. T. *The Crisis of the Old Order in Russia: Gentry and Government, 1861–1914* (Guildford, 1982).

Medvedev, R. *Let History Judge: the Origins and Consequences of Stalinism* (London, 1972).

Medvedev, Z. A. *Soviet Science* (New York, 1978).

Meier, G. M. *Leading Issues in Economic Development* (Oxford, 1984).

Merl, S. *Die Anfange der Kollektivierung in der Sowjetunion: Der Übergang zur staatlichen Reglementierung der Produktions-und Markt-beziehungen im Dorf, 1928–1930* (Wiesbaden, 1985).

Merl, S. *Der Agrarmarkt und die Neue Ökonomische Politik. Die Anfange staatlicher Lenkung der Landwirtschaft in der Sowjetunion, 1925–1928* (Munich, Vienna, 1981).

Meyer, G. *Studien zur sozialoekonomischen Entwicklung Sowjetrusslands 1921–1923. Die Beziehung zwischen Stadt und Land zu Beginn der Neuen Oekonomischen Politik* (Cologne, 1974).

Michelson, A. M. *et al. Russian Public Finance During the War* (New Haven, 1928).

Millar, J. R. 'What's Wrong with the "Standard Story"?', *Problems of Communism*, July–August, 1976.

Morgenstern, O. *On the Accuracy of Economic Observations* (Princeton, 1963).

Moritsch, A. *Landwirtschaft und Agrarpolitik in Russland vor der Revolution* (Vienna, 1986).

Nutter, G. W. 'The Soviet Economy: Retrospect and Prospect', in Abshire, D. and Allen, R. V. (eds) (1963).

Odell, R. M. *Cotton Goods in Russia*, Department of Commerce and Labor, Special Agents Series 51 (Washington, 1912).

Pasvolsky, M. and Moulton, H. *Russian Debts and Russian Reconstruction* (New York, 1924).

Pelferov, J. J. 'Agriculture', in Raffalovich (ed.) (1918).

Pinkevich, A. P. *Science and Education in the USSR* (London, 1935).

Pintner, W. M. and Rowney, D. K. (eds) *Russian Officialdom: the Bureaucratization of Russian Society from the Seventeenth to the Twentieth Century* (Chapel Hill, 1980).

Polner, T. I. *et al. Russian Local Government During the War* (New Haven, 1930).

Portal, R. 'Muscovite Industrialists: the Cotton Sector (1861–1914)', in Blackwell, W. L. (ed.) *Russian Economic Development from Peter the Great to Stalin* (New York, 1974).

Portal, R. 'The Industrialization of Russia', *Cambridge Economic History of Europe*, vi, ii (Cambridge, 1965).

[Prokopovich, S. N.] 'The National Income of the USSR', Birmingham Bureau of Research on Russian Economic Conditions, *Memorandum*, no. 3 (November 1931).

Raffalovich, A. (ed.) *Russia: its Trade and Commerce* (London, 1918).

Reingold, I. 'The New Economic Policy', in Segal, L. and Santalov, A. (eds) *Commercial Yearbook of the Soviet Union, 1925* (London, 1925).

Rieber, A. J. *Merchants and Entrepreneurs in Imperial Russia* (Chapel Hill, 1982).

Robinson, G. T. *Rural Russia Under the Old Regime* (Berkeley, 1972, first published 1932).

Rogger, H. *Russia in the Age of Modernisation and Revolution, 1881–1917* (London and New York, 1983).

Rosenberg, N. *Perspectives on Technology* (Cambridge, 1976).

Rostankowski, P. *Die Entwicklung osteuropaeischer ländlicher Siedlungen und speziell der Chutor-Siedlungen* (Berlin, 1982).

Rowney, D. K. *Transition to Technology: The Structural Origins of the Soviet Administrative State* (Ithaca and London, 1989).

Sanders, J. T. 'Once More Into the Breach, Dear Friends: A Closer Look at Indirect Tax Receipts and the Condition of the Russian Peasantry, 1881–1899', *Slavic Review*, xliii (1984).

Schapiro, L. *1917: the Russian Revolutions and the Origins of Present Day Communism* (Harmondsworth, 1985).

Segal, L. and Santalov, A. (eds) *Soviet Union Yearbook 1926* (London, 1926).

Segal, L. and Santalov, A. (eds) *Commercial Yearbook of the Soviet Union 1925* (London, 1925).

Seton-Watson, H. *The Decline of Imperial Russia* (London, 1952).

Shanin, T. *The Awkward Class: Political Sociology of Peasantry in a Developing Society: Russia, 1910–1925* (Oxford, 1972).

Shiokawa, N. 'The Collectivization of Agriculture and *Otkhodnichestvo* in the USSR, 1930', *Annals of the Institute of Social Science*, no. 24 (1982–3) (Tokyo).

Simms, J. Y. 'The Crisis in Russian Agriculture at the End of the Nineteenth

Century: A Different View', *Slavic Review*, xxxvi (1977).

Smith, G. A. *Soviet Foreign Trade: Organization, Operations and Policy, 1918–1971* (New York, 1973).

Sokolnikov, G. Y. *et al. Soviet Policy in Public Finance 1917–1928* (Stanford, 1931).

Solomon, S. G. *The Soviet Agrarian Debate: A Controversy in Social Science, 1923–1929* (Boulder, 1977).

Stalin, J. *Leninism* (London, 1940).

Stuart, R. C. (ed.) *The Soviet Rural Economy* (New Jersey, 1983).

Sumner, B. H. *Survey of Russian History* (London, 1947).

Sutton, A. C. *Western Technology and Soviet Economic Development, 1917–1930*, i (Stanford, 1968).

Thorner, D., Kerblay B. and Smith, R. E. F. (eds) *Chayanov: The Theory of Peasant Economy* (Homewood, Illinois, 1966).

Timoshenko, V. P. *Agricultural Russia and the Wheat Problem* (Stanford, 1932).

Trebilcock, R. C. 'British Armaments and European Industrialization, 1890–1914', *Economic History Review*, 2nd series, xxii (1973).

Tucker, R. C. *Stalin as Revolutionary, 1879–1929: a Study in History and Personality* (New York, 1973).

Varzar, V. E. 'Factories and Workshops', in Raffalovich (ed.) (1918).

Volin, L. *A Century of Russian Agriculture* (Cambridge, Mass., 1970).

Von Laue, T. H. *Why Lenin? Why Stalin? A Reappraisal of the Russian Revolution, 1900–30* (London, 1966).

Von Laue, T. H. *Sergei Witte and the Industrialization of Russia* (New York, 1963).

Von Laue, T. H. 'The State and the Economy', in Black (ed.) (1960).

Von Laue, T. H. 'The High Cost and Gamble of the Witte System: A Chapter in the Industrialization of Russia', *Journal of Economic History*, Autumn 1953.

Vucinich, A. *Empire of Knowledge. The Academy of Sciences of the USSR (1917–1970)* (Berkeley and Los Angeles, 1984).

Vucinich, A. *Science and Russian Culture, 1861–1917* (Stanford, 1971).

Westwood, J. N. *Soviet Locomotive Technology during Industrialization, 1928–1952* (London, 1982).

Westwood, J. N. *A History of Russian Railways* (London, 1964).

Wheatcroft, S. G. 'Doctors and the Revolution in Russia', *Bulletin of the Society of the Social History of Medicine*, no. 34 (1984).

Wheatcroft, S. G. 'A Reevaluation of Soviet Agricultural Production in the 1920s and 1930s', in Stuart (ed.) (1983).

Wheatcroft, S. G. 'The Reliability of Russian Prewar Grain Output Statistics' *Soviet Studies*, xxvi (1974).

Wheatcroft, S. G. and Davies, R. W. (eds), *Materials for a Balance of the Soviet National Economy, 1928–1930* (Cambridge, 1985).

Wheatcroft, S. G., Davies, R. W. and Cooper, J. M. 'Soviet Industrialisation Reconsidered: Some Preliminary Conclusions About Economic Development Between 1926 and 1941', *Economic History Review*, 2nd series, xxxix (1986).

Wilkins, M. and Hill, F. E. *American Business Abroad: Ford on Six Continents* (Detroit, 1964).

Zagorsky, S. O. *State Control of Industry in Russia during the War* (New Haven, 1928).

Name Index

Subject Index